Oct 92

Best Wishes,

James R. Cooper

Michael

Thanks for your help
in starting my new life.

TWILIGHT'S LAST GLEAMING

TWILIGHT'S LAST GLEAMING

THE PRICE OF HAPPINESS IN AMERICA

JAMES R. COOPER

PROMETHEUS BOOKS
Buffalo, New York

Published 1992 by Prometheus Books

96 95 94 93 92   5 4 3 2 1

Library of Congress Cataloging-in-Publication Data

Cooper, James R.
    Twilight's last gleaming : the price of happiness in America / by James R. Cooper.
        p.   cm.
    Includes bibliographical references and index.
    ISBN 0-87975-719-1
    1. United States—Social conditions—1980-   . 2. United States—Moral conditions. 3. Social change. 4. Social ethics. 5. Social problems. 6. National characteristics, American. I. Title.
HN65.C623   1992
306'.0973—dc20   92-16854
                                                                                         CIP

Printed in the United States of America on acid-free paper.

Contents

6   *Contents*

Preface

For years Americans have hoped for more interdisciplinary work, research, and reporting to enable us to solve common problems. Instead, intellectuals continue to provide us with finely worked pieces to the puzzles of history and social organization that the rest of us must fit together on our own. I grew tired of waiting for American colleges and universities to nurture the growth of interdisciplinary work, so I wrote this book. In it I attempt to cut across scholarly disciplines to crosslink the cultural effects of segregated knowledge.

I am a business-school professor of real estate investment and legal studies. This book began in countless dialogues with former pupils seeking ways to be productive, socially responsible, ethical, and successful people in the murky milieu that is today's United States. The arrogant intellectualism of professors who wish to keep their effete hands clean and stay above the "smell of the crowd" has caused many of my former pupils to turn to a cynical, pessimistic nihilism. Too many students of recent generations believe the investment banker's motto, "The winner is the one who dies owning the most toys!" Such a world view does not empower one to take an enlightened pursuit of happiness. The main theme of this book is that we can have a less stressful pursuit of happiness. The book also has several *leitmotifs;* this is the complexity of life and the human condition.

The pursuit of happiness is an important mythological, categorical imperative of healthy Americans. This book seeks to reconcile the workaday demands of our market-oriented political economy—democratic capitalism—with the high ethical ideals of the modern enlightenment that produced our constitutional culture. I have seen many of the best and the brightest of our young people cynically discard the noble values of our constitutional culture. Instead, they are opting for amassing more toys. This book investigates why they did not choose personal growth to leave a more enduring legacy of good ideals in the minds of their children. Today, this nation proceeds on the brash assumption that rigorous, narrow training at the graduate level is the better way. This is because information and knowledge have exploded beyond the ability of humans, as individuals, to grasp, even within their chosen vocation or calling. We are turning out cultural nudniks who believe themselves to be experts in dealing with life.

As a real estate professor, for example, the faculty reward system has forced me to teach a system of analysis that focuses on the valuation of net income derived from real estate projects over a future period. To carry out a rigorous analysis I must teach my students that they can accurately estimate the future rent schedules; the mortgage terms (variable though they probably will be); future tax policies; the price they will sell the property for, say, six, or fifteen years hence; and so on. This may seem astonishing. Still, that is the paradigmatic world of real estate analysis. Meanwhile, blithe spirits that we are, we give little if any attention to many critical factors. Examples are the architecture, the rise and fall of underlying urban economies, the balance of trade with foreign nations, race relations, crime in the streets, highway construction, water, and sewage—all will affect the rent schedules, the mortgages, and the rise and fall of value of the property at a particular location. Of course, this narrow-minded approach is thought to be proper because we are narrow specialists—real estate analysts. We ignore the other factors by using the naive assumption that the "other things being constants," they are outside our analysis. I am told that it enables us to be more rigorous in our analysis. I have never been convinced.

By way of this book I hope to spur interdisciplinary research, reporting, and networking. It is rare to find interdisciplinary work in the American culture. Minnesota leads the way with the Humphrey Institute under Harlan Cleveland and Dean Szuch. The institute was set up, in memory of Hubert Humphrey, to encourage work in interdisciplinary research. Its goal is to "combat specialized achievement, the chief bottleneck in our society." This institute has been preparing a program for politicians, administrators, and journalists that is to be an inquiry into the nature, techniques, ethics, and purposes of leadership in the late twentieth-century city, state, nation, and international order.

A Spiral Way of Reading and Knowing

This book presents its interdisciplinary ideas in a spiral form. It is a literary device of Jean Shinoda Bolen,[1] a psychiatrist. Like a musical composition the theme that runs through each movement is that humans need an environment in which their rights shall be taken seriously by those in power. This will nurture healthy growth of human personalities and diminish stress in the pursuit of happiness. The spiral form introduces ideas and then reintroduces them in differing contexts. Each time, with each repetition, the main theme becomes more fleshed out, showing it in all its multifaceted dimensions. The spiral form of writing invites both halves of the brain to be involved in reading. Understanding comes through our linear mind, the left brain, which absorbs information and logic. The right brain is in touch with images, sensations, memories, and feelings that are personal and collective in time and timeless. It imposes no logical order. An "Aha!" of recognition comes whenever there is a crossover between the understanding of different ways of thinking from right to left and from left to right. This treatise seeks to have a holistic body of interdisciplinary knowledge fall into place.

A troubling issue has been the level of scholarly detail and documentation appropriate to this book. I cover a very wide range of material. I have no desire to pose as an author of ideas of which I am only an interpreter and synthesizer. Yet modern editorial practice does not encourage quotation unless it is verbatim. I have sought, by endnotes, to show when (and it is often) I am taking from some main source or another. Occasionally I cite specific quotations, but I have avoided as much as possible long notes and a discursive parade of well-known sources. This book is a synthesis of many sources with my own ideas and changes. Any errors or omissions are my own.

I have no delusions that my lofty aims have been achieved in this book. I hope it to be one voice of an ordinary man who cared enough to cry out for help. It is a pebble that I hope makes a ripple in a too quiet pond. Perhaps, ultimately, there will be enough commotion by others that we will see the pond's waves dancing in the light of a new day.

Acknowledgments

I wish I could give proper thanks to the many who encouraged me to complete this work. It has been an ordeal. I pay homage in particular to the readers of the earlier draft notes. Without their expert guidance and moral support this book would not have been finished. All are experts in their vocations or professions. My special thanks to Dean Michael Mescon of the College of Business Administration at Georgia State University in Atlanta. My heartfelt thanks to Robert Basil for acquiring the book for Prometheus, and to Reg Gilbert for editing it with vigor. All have been very patient. I thank the staff of Wordperfect in Orem, Utah. They were more than helpful. I want to thank my word processors: Marjorie Hudson, Anna Shaw, and Caroline Collins. One usually closes with a "thank you" to the spouse. My wives have taught me much about life and given me more of some things than I wanted. I owe a special debt to Nyda Williams Brown, M.D., who taught me about the evil of sociopathic behavior. From her I gained a more balanced sense about the kinds of animals human beings really are.

Cary Bynum, director of GSU's publishing division, is a special case. He is a gentleman, a scholar, and a playwright. Without his guidance and encouragement I know I would not have persevered. I have a special debt of gratitude to Frederick Lee Ring of the Future Vision Press for his invaluable editorial work. Without his loving attention to earlier versions of this treatise this new version could not have been produced. I also give a note of appreciation to Richard Grant and Diane Calhoun at GSU for their special help. My children have been very patient and supportive. Most important to this old man, by their example, are Rachel, Julia, Evan, and Jennifer and their loved ones, who have convinced me that the United States has a fine generation coming along. We can count on them.

Atlanta, May 1992

Part I: A New Creed

1. The American Creed

I believe in the United States of America as a Government of the people, by the people, for the people; whose just powers are derived from the consent of the governed; a democracy in a republic; a sovereign Nation of many sovereign States; a perfect union, one and inseparable; established upon those principles of freedom, equality, justice and humanity for which American patriots sacrificed their lives and fortunes. I therefore believe it is my duty to my country to love it; to support its Constitution; to obey its laws; to respect its flag; and to defend it against all enemies.

This official creed, written in 1917 by William Tyler Page, was accepted for the American people by the House of Representatives on April 23, 1918.

In contrast, the subjects of medieval kings of Spanish Aragon once pledged a marvelously qualified pledge of allegiance:

We who are as good as you swear to you who are no better than we, to accept you as our king and sovereign lord, provided you observe all liberties and laws; but if not, not.

Americans need to reexamine carefully their so-called American Creed. Is it a tattered cloth of worn out ideals? I believe it more a victim of neglect. We need to bring it out into the open. We need a national colloquy on what rights we "all" have as American citizens. We especially need a national dialogue to discover some of these universal "other" rights that shall not be disparaged or denied because they are not enumerated in the Ninth Amendment to our U.S. Constitution. We sorely need a clearer, holistic world view to deal with the uncertain future as the United States is forced to join the global economy. We are drifting toward a future where a too-powerful American elite will permit only those variations that have official sanction. Such approval will come only after that same power elite has determined that it will be "good" for the majority of docile consumerists. These so-called citizens will be acting as the poseurs of a democratic citizenry. They will in daily life be in a conformist happy state of fascism.

Let us look to our past, for our origins are different than what we have been and are now being taught. During the bicentennial of the U.S. Constitution, 1987–1991, we celebrated the memory of James Madison as the father of our Constitution. Little was said about Madison's opposition to attaching the Bill of Rights (the first ten amendments) to the Constitution. Madison felt they were unnecessary. George Mason, a wealthy planter, refused to sign the Constitution without these rights. I believe Madison, the plantation manager of a large tract of real property, responded to the riotous unrest of the "rabble in the streets" of New York, Boston, and Philadelphia. The "common sort" made clear they opposed ratification. They wanted no part of this "brilliant document," known as the Constitution, unless it had a Bill of Rights for the common man. Like the common sort of Los Angeles who rioted in 1992, they wanted justice for every man. The landed gentry, the professionals, the merchants, who were the founding-father "Federalists," opposed the idea that a federal citizen should have the rights of due process, trial by jury, equal protection before the law, the privileges and immunities of citizenship as federal citizens superior to their rights as state citizens. To the founding fathers, providing ordinary men with federal rights would carry our system of dual sovereignty too far. If it were not for heros such as George Mason, Thomas Paine, Patrick Henry, and others, we would have failed to create the unique environment wherein our constitutional culture slowly evolved a dual citizenship. The current Rehnquist Supreme Court intends to reverse this trend. We must either do a paradigm shift in how we perceive reality and how we solve problems, or our unique and highly successful way of life will not survive.

That extraordinarily adaptable creature known as the human has, in the United States, one of the world's best opportunities to approach the maximum spiritual potential. The milieu for that opportunity is the American metropolitan areas. I call these areas *metroareas* to show their unitary nature, despite the fact that they are fragmented by adjacent or overlapping political jurisdictions known variously as counties, cities, towns, townships, or villages. American metroareas have many things wrong with them. There are many obstacles and barriers to human development within them. Nonetheless, these same metroareas have developed a social, political, and economic system so pluralistic that it is much more likely that the "good" will rise, that worthwhile ideas will come to the fore. The status quo can be forced to give way to healthy change. This system still works.

There is no American Ideology found in the libraries. There is no single definition of the many governments in our metroareas. There is no typical person known as the American City Dweller. This citizen, fortunately, cannot be defined. The Boston Irish would fight at the drop of a hat if someone tried to define them. We are not a homogeneous Japan. This has been our strength. Today, happy fascism threatens. A pervasive corporate socialism seeks to turn us all into consumers behaving according to the stereotyped images of advertising and cable television. These manipulative techniques have been adapted to the political process by using psychosocial profiles of the centrist majority. Concentrate on the central, say 68 percent, of voters (ignoring either of the tails of the standard distribution curve), as any good statistician would suggest you can do—and you can win: an election, market share, whatever you want! Still, it is our diversity that has been the wellspring of the innovations that have made our metroareas fountains of ideas and inventions that have produced a favorable environment. America's belief system, carried out primarily in our metroareas, is one of the best in human history. America the Beautiful!—does it feel that way about itself? Many question the way the leaders elected and appointed by the polity are running our national economy. Our trust in the media and those in high office is low. The cynical leveraged buyouts that are pillaging some of our large corporations discourage confidence in some of our self-perpetuating corporate management. The military-industrial complex is a strange pax-machina. Its powers of self-aggrandizement seem limitless as it gains greater energy by feeding on the vitals of our limited resources. Bureaucracy, American corporations, the press, communication media, all are beyond effective constructive criticism. Yet, these same social institutions sorely need ennobling goals to fulfill their lofty aims. Our metroareas are the places where there is a major battle for the minds of men and women. Many powerful leaders would have our citizens become nothing except professional consumers for the mass markets. This may soon result in a new corporate state of happy fascism.

A major thesis of this book is that our metroareas are too stressful an environment for the new knowledge worker. A heavy cost is imposed on our national economy through losses in American productivity. High medical and health costs result from treating stress as an individual problem. This book will argue that external stressors of our metroareas are public health problems. They can be ameliorated by empowering individual and group action. A new, healthier environment can be created in which American human personalities can grow and prosper in the pursuit of happiness, in this service-economy information age.

Robert Ornstein and David Sobel, in *The Healing Brain,* say that medicine has made a contribution to health, but its effort has in large part been misdirected, misspent, and its successes misattributed. Providing more medical care does not produce a healthier population. There is more to be gained by a study of how humans *avoid* illness. The biological survival of humans is much more closely linked to emotions and the system of automatic safeguards than with conscious thought and reason. In commenting on the "placebo effect," Ornstein and Sobel said, "The long history of medical treatment is . . . a history of how strong beliefs heal. How positive emotions . . . hope, and wishful thinking, promote healing maintain health in the face of disease?"[1]

One primary goal of the next decade or two could be to develop and implement policies that diminish adverse external stress in our metroareas. In emergencies the body prepares for battle or for flight, the heart beats faster, thus supplying the muscles with more blood. The capillaries contract, making eating less likely. If such stress were induced over a long period, one can see how it might lead to high blood pressure. Diseases of the skin often have an emotional origin. Skin rashes are on the increase in our metroareas. Although the incidence of skin rashes has also correlated with the increased pollution of our atmosphere, still, manic depressives suffer from psoriasis and the condition often gets worse when they are depressed and clears up when they are manic. It is significant that powerful emotions can generate inhibitions or accelerations of basic sensory and motor pathways. Though psychiatrists know this, the neurologists have been slow to fit the clinical material into their concepts.

Gordon Taylor adds that the term "stress" does not necessarily mean extreme pressure. Any demand for readjustment seems to create a significant measure of stress. Thomas Holmes devised a scale for measuring a number of significant changes in a peoples's lives. Have they moved? Have they changed jobs or been promoted? Have they recently experienced divorce, death, or other family crises? Holmes and physicist Richard Rahe found that people who had experienced marked changes in the preceding year were much more likely to fall ill. In fact, the 10 percent who had experienced the most change were almost twice as likely to fall ill as the 10 percent who had experienced the least change. There are many instances in the medical literature of what we might term "mind over body." It is physical evidence that physical illness arises out of mental or brain-driven processes.

Earth's Metroarea Cities Can Save Humankind

A human society in a metroarea is an agglomeration of brains. It is childishly optimistic to suppose there are simple systematic mechanisms easily discoverable and readily comprehensible to define and comprehend large metroareas. To do so would be to alter the inhabitants to fit the procrustean bed of twentieth-century society's past knowledge. This is especially so because our current society's cities are plainly obsolete. Fortunately, in the United States, our constitutional culture provides freedom of creative action.

What do Americans mean when they say—This, I believe? Is there an ideal American? Was it John Wayne, who only acted the part of the hero? Consider Audie Murphy, our most decorated hero. Think again: was it a Martin Luther King, Jr.? He died for his country. Do none of these fine men fit the beau ideal we are seeking? Clearly, they tried and did serve their country well. This young nation needs to pause and consider what it believes. What do we demand of our heroes, who are only human? We have a blurred vision because we avoid confronting ourselves. Our leaders in politics, economics, religion, education, our intellectuals of the arts, do not see the tides that are washing away our sand-castle myths—the deeply held set of beliefs that inspire people to social or political actions. We know there are myths we cherish. Yet, the fast-rising level of our knowledge of reality is eroding the credibility of these highly valued myths. Let us find the myths that bind us together. Some myths are operational, such as how our courts rule America. Others are mere fantasy, such as the belief that in these terrifying days our military can provide us with real security.

The need is to reawaken and reform the spirit of the Enlightenment. The days of the American and French Revolution were times that tried mens' souls. Thomas Hobbes and Edmund Burke sought to lead us to peace and tranquility through subservience to a wise and benign sovereign who would rule for the common weal. These men were dominated by fear of the rabble. On the other hand, John Locke, Thomas Paine, and Adam Smith sought to promote freedom of humanity to exercise its natural rights. They had a serene confidence in the ability of autonomous humans to exercise individual power and liberty. This major confrontation was never resolved. The blurred vision of the American Creed arises out of the irreconcilable conflict between the fear-dominated Hobbesian view and the freedom-dominated Lockeian world view.

Our blurred vision promotes conflict in America. The conflict arises, on the one hand, from those who feel that the state as an institution should force men to virtue!—in effect, that the law of the state and the task of education is to train men to desire internally what they are forced by law to obey. On the other hand, there is the opposing idea of freedom and autonomy that forms the basis of the Lockeian social contract. To follow nature may well be to follow human nature, in effect, the organic and primordial feelings of natural man. The problem is how to do this. What are the best methods to develop the conscience that will cause someone to autonomously choose virtuous conduct over evil? The modern understanding of the human brain ought to put to rest this age-old debate. The hormonal "wetland" of the human brain discourages the blissful assumption that humans are essentially virtuous and good, or, for that matter, that they are evil. It is wishful thinking to believe that humans can properly design a society or charter metroareas whose institutions or laws are in accordance with the true nature of man. Such thinking assumes that man is essentially virtuous and good. For those who accept society as the chief source of man's misery, the path to utopia could lead to such diverse solutions as controlled social freedom through rigid Skinnerian structured society. But, our current understanding of the hormonal human brain suggests otherwise. Man's inhumanity is as much an expression of his human nature as is his humanity. Translated into moral terms this means that man has as much of the possibility of evil within him as that of virtue.

Human Are Not Essentially Loving and Cooperative

One of the great virtues of our constitutional culture in America is that in a tentative way we have acknowledged this ambivalent nature of humans. The reality is that crime pays very well for those who have no fear of the consequences of being caught. It is irrational to entrust such persons with all the powers of citizenship. Such sociopaths are dangerous to our constitutional culture. Some humans are evil. What if man's capacity for evil is an essential rather than an accidental or acquired part of his nature? What if his very capacity to love and create depends upon how he "lives through" and assimilates his primordial urge to hate, to murder, to destroy? What if good and evil, rather than being opposites, are in fact dialectical partners in the normal human personality? The main point is that we as humans need neither to accommodate evil nor to ignore it, but to find a way to transcend it. Only when man learns how to celebrate in and ritualize his primordial nature can his evil be transcended. The reptilian brain is still within us all. Is that why we love dinosaurs?

Society sorely needs the individual goals of hard work and dedication. They can eventually result in a real experience of accomplishment. Nothing is more potentially explosive, or, alternatively, disintegrating, than individuals who have lost their sense of autonomy and self-worth. I urge, therefore, that we restructure the function of our metroareas along the lines of a constitutional culture, which takes rights seriously, and a vibrant democratic capitalism, which is centered on a holistic view of the human personality. The human personality needs to be more than that of a mere worker and consumer. The work ethic should be only part of the virtuous circle of good conduct we seek from every citizen. In effect, the work ethic should be a virtue we encourage, but it should not be forgotten that there are others things that are just as important. The mature adult needs the sense of competence that comes from the work ethic. Yet he also needs the exercise of will and the sense of hope that comes from a purpose in life. He also needs the fulfillment of love through fidelity and loyalty.

The alienated youths of the 1960s, who have become the "yuppie" generation of today, have lost faith in their effectiveness. They no longer believe in social change. Instead, they choose nihilism, narcissism, hedonism, and consumerism as substitutes for involvement in their cities, their states, and their country. Our political economy has stifled the imagination and let economic utility replace social utility. The result is that apathy rides high on the indifference curve. The gist of the complaint is that the society we live in is no longer adequate to the needs of man. We need to recognize that humans "need" to seek the fulfillment of their spiritual potential.

Thomas Hobbes and John Locke were trailblazers, given the mental perceptions of humans in their day. Neither had the global impact of Jesus Christ, Adolf Hitler, Mahatma Gandhi, Mohammed the prophet, Suliman the Great, or many others. Yet, for Americans in particular, they had great impact. The average American believes that, "We hold these truths to be self-evident, that all men are created equal," is the core of our American creed. The reality is that throughout our history the power elite has operated with a Hobbesian world view, which is a direct contradiction to the widely held populist creed of equality of opportunity. The Hobbesian—fear-dominated—world view cannot be reconciled with the Lockeian freedom-dominated concept of human interplay. Although the Declaration of Independence is founded on the natural rights of man developed by John Locke, most of the founding fathers, who were the writers of the Federalist papers, personally subscribed to the fear-dominated psychology of Thomas Hobbes.

Thomas Hobbes and the Need for Security

Hobbes held that the fear of death and the need for security are the psychological foundations of worldly prudence and of civilization. To Hobbes, peace was something that humans desired because they feared death. Furthermore, because of other things that they desired to do, a state of war was made impossible. Morality, to Hobbes, was not the pursuit of a personal sense of good; it was accepting rules that limited the pursuit of personal good. These rules were laid down by the sovereign. Hobbes argued that man shuns death by a certain impulsion of nature, no less than that whereby a stone moves downward if dropped. This fear of death is what saves man from anarchy and civilizes him, for if man was driven merely by his sexual desire to reproduce there would be no society, and the life of man would be solitary, poor, nasty, brutish and short. To Hobbes, all men are equal enough in body and mind to render negligible any claims to superior benefits—even the weakest, under certain circumstances, is able to kill the strongest. Man's fear of death brings him up short in his pursuit of power. It leads him to reflect upon the predicament of a state of nature. To Hobbes, given that there is a state of nature, given man's prudence, and given his overwhelming aversion to death, he must accept the conditions necessary for avoiding death. Thus, the uses of power by the sovereign (state) to control the passions of man were a necessity.

The sovereign's use of praise, blame, reward, and punishment do, by example, make the will of ordinary humans conform to good instead of evil. To the charge of injustice, Hobbes argued that the exercise of the sovereign "will" was the law. As Oliver North, said, "If the President says go over and stand on your head in the corner, this man will do so." Therefore, precedents and principles were not needed to cause action by the common sort who were to follow the orders of the sovereign. To his credit Hobbes saw clearly that retribution is part of the meaning of punishment by the state. To Hobbes, when retributive justice is connected with the state's authority, that distinguishes it from other sorts of retributive acts by ordinary humans.

For many centuries tradition and custom had been the main force of social control. These customs and traditions stretched back into the distant past. They assigned to individual men their relatively fixed places in society. Unfortunately, Hobbes pictured life as a competitive race in which we must suppose that to all individuals there is no other good, no other garland, but being foremost. This was a gruesome caricature of an age of awakening individualism, restless competition, and social mobility. To Hobbes, the way out of this vicious competition was found by increasing the executive power of the sovereign or the state, and by the development of internal individual conscience subservient to that external authority. Hobbes distrusted what he perceived as the anarchic tendencies of the individual conscience as much as he loathed the extraterrestrial authority asserted by the pope. He cleverly adapted the theorem of the social contract, arising out of the natural rights of many, to provide for the absolutist claims of the monarchial sovereign. (In modern times we should replace the word "sovereign" with "the imperial presidency.") Hobbes prided himself on grounding the authority of sovereigns, as well as the liberty and duty of subjects, upon axioms of human nature rather than on tradition and super-natural authority. Still, one must keep in mind that he perceived this human per-sonality—man—as dominated by the fear of death and economic insecurity.

When Americans speak of a "right," we are saying there is a universally held rule that protects, or should protect, a person from interference by others in doing something that he might want to do. Hobbes used rights to talk about what a person has a right to do for survival and self-preservation only. In a peculiar twist of logic, Hobbes argued that the natural right of self-preservation empowered or entitled the individual to renounce individual exercise of rights. Hobbes felt it was psychologically impossible for humans to do otherwise.

"Natural" rights have a very different meaning for Locke. To Locke humans' natural rights are interests protected by the natural law against the interference of others. In modern times, in the following chapters, I adapt this philosophical argument to current scientific ideas. I argue that our knowledge of the human brain and body urges that healthy humans need independence and liberty of decision making (some say autonomy) to be productive humans seeking to fulfill their spiritual potential. The outmoded ideas of Thomas Hobbes arose when we had almost no understanding of the relationship of the human brain to a man's body, mind, and soul. I cannot fault Hobbes in view of the universal ignorance that prevailed. In fantasy, it appeared that to Hobbes the average man had a reptilian brain coupled to a limbic system that concentrated on survival tactics. The convolutions of the human cerebral cortex had not yet occurred in our fantasy of Hobbesian perception.

There are two obvious flaws in the Hobbesian argument. The first is the hidden assumption that the desire for security derived from the fear of death as the sole reason for the institution of a commonwealth. Obviously, there are other human motivations that would cause people to agree to a representative form of government. Furthermore, as in the United States, the people may choose to divide the sovereignty by a separation of powers.

John Locke pointed out the second flaw. Even if one were to argue that security was the sole reason for the institution of a commonwealth, absolute authority is a dangerous expedient for the individuals who are making the contract. The twentieth-century experience makes that clear enough. In Communist states, for many decades, the people were subjected to a monolithic universal authority without any checks and balances. It has been a bitter example of the abuse of undivided power. Also, the fascistic dictatorships such as those of Hitler, Peron, and Idi Amin, point to the great difficulty in reversing the contract with a monolithic authority, especially given the terrible firepower of the modern state. Pitchforks just won't do anymore. Romania in 1989 has shown the terrible carnage when dictators must be driven from office.

John Locke and Natural Rights

Locke's world view is more human, less rational. It is more holistic. Thomas Hobbes was much more consistent, logical, and, one might say, defensible in debate, because of his rationalist style of philosophy. Locke had a tendency toward inconsistency. Still, he was sure that common sense and the facts justified his convictions. Today, we agree. Whatever faults there were in Locke's position lay in the difficulty of stating a coherent theory about human conduct in earlier times. Therefore, Locke has been easy prey to skillful dialecticians. Still, his work is closer to the modern perception of the way the human brain works. We have discovered that the human brain is a gland instead of something more like a computer. Much that happens in the mind occurs by way of hormonal transfers. The logical inconsistency of Locke is more appropriate to the image-making power of the human mind.

Locke argued that there are no principles to which all give assent. Principles such as, "Whatever is, is" and "It is impossible for the same thing to be and not to be" are not known to children, idiots, and a great part of mankind. To some extent Locke's targets were Descartes and Spinoza, who argued that all men know and assent to certain truths when they come to the use of reason.

Locke argued that the senses first furnish us with particular ideas, which the mind by degrees becomes familiar with, remembers, and names. The human's mind later extracts from these particular ideas, coming up with and naming general ideas. Thus, general ideas, general words, and the use of reason grow together. Assent to the truth of propositions depends on people having clear and distinct ideas on the meanings of terms.

The Law of Nature

Locke began his treatise on the law of nature through the proposition that all men are originally in a state of nature. It was a state of perfect freedom. This was a philosophical fiction. Nonetheless, it fits well with the utopian state of the fetus in the womb. Locke was vague about the law of nature. He held that the law of nature rests ultimately on God's will. Reason discovers it. It is not innate. On the other hand, Locke spoke as though it was written in the hearts of all mankind, suggesting some sort of innateness. This conforms well with our modern view of man's human condition, confused about his divine intellect and his animal desires.

In Locke's state of nature men are bound to preserve peace, preserve mankind, and refrain from hurting one another. Carrying out the law of nature is the responsibility of each. If any man (or woman) violates this law, he thereby puts himself or herself in a state of war with his or her fellow man, who may then mete out punishment.

The power that one man may hold over another is neither absolute or arbitrary, and is restrained by contract. Thus, to Locke the state of nature was a society of men distinct from a state of government or political society. But Locke saw there were certain inconveniences in this state of nature in that some men will violate the rights of others. The remedy for this is a civil government by which men (and women) by mutual consent make a social contract and create a single body politic. Here, we see a major difference between the fear-dominated Hobbesian personalities and those who would support a freedom-oriented, Lockeian way of life. Locke held that this contract is not between ruler and ruled, but between equally free men. Unlike Hobbes, Locke was convinced that men are capable of judging whether they are cruelly subjected and unjustly treated.

One reason for men entering into the social contract is to avoid a state of war. Therefore, the contract is broken when the sovereign puts himself or herself into a state of war by becoming a tyrant, as did the Ceaucaescii of Romania. No matter how we perceive the modern-day skills of those who control, the leaders of the state use media manipulation, misinformation, and disinformation to promote their self-aggrandizing goals and thus break the Lockeian social compact. In such a situation the state prevails by imposing Hobbesian techniques that violate the rights of those with a Lockeian world view.

Locke used the idea of property in both a broad and narrow sense. To Locke it was a primary end of the state to preserve the rights of property. Another function of the state is to make laws governing the use, distribution, and transference of property. To Locke, men and women, by binding themselves to the social contract, were seeking protection of property and themselves. Therefore, by such agreements, they gave up rights, doing so solely to champion their own causes. Thus, the right to self-help is subsumed under the contract with the state. Men have a right to self-preservation and therefore to possess things they need for their subsistence. Locke saw that man by the labor of his body and mind and the work of his hands removes things from the state of nature and makes them his property. Without labor, the earth and things in general have little value. Though the right to property arises out of nature, it is not made secure there.

Not all important activities in U.S. society are done within the simplistic relationship between the state, on the one hand, and the individual on the other. In reality, the state is at one level, the federal government and its myriad agencies with their conflicting mandates and goals at another. Also, we have the innumerable agent-instrumentalities of the fifty states—the counties, cities, library districts, sanitary sewage districts, etc. In addition, the individual operates through proprietorships, partnerships, corporations, trusts, blind trusts, and other ways of owning and controlling property. Thus the social contract that controls our property and our relationships to property are very complex, even bewildering, today.

In John Locke, we find the first full-blown account of the need for the separation of executive and legislative powers, only later the judiciary. In another major departure from the Hobbesian world view, Locke saw the monarch or the sovereign as merely another man or woman. Thus, if the king, or today a president or governor, was disputing about a claim of right or property, it followed that since no man could judge his own case, the judiciary must be independent of the executive. This is a central tenet of political liberalism. Unfortunately, part of our blurred vision is that Americans erroneously view liberals and conservatives in the United States as extremes of the political spectrum. This is probably because of the general lack of power in the hands of those who are anarchists and absolute totalitarians in our midst. In the United States, conservatives and liberals alike should be viewed as liberals in the universal political spectrum. Both oppose the anarchy of individual self-governance and self-help on the one hand, and the autocratic imperialism of a Hobbesian absolute sovereign on the other.

A serious flaw in the Lockeian view is that it fails to recognize that there may be large wellsprings of power that arise neither from the state nor from individuals. Instead, for example, they may arise from the agglomeration or concentration of wealth into the hands of a few, or the power over the communication media in the hands of a power elite. In effect, the perception of rights, as political and civil rights, ignores that power may arise out of controls over the flow of knowledge and the concentration of economic control over the distribution of goods, instead of control of the state.

The Hypocrisy of U.S. "Happy Fascism"

Today, we fail to acknowledge the presence among us of sycophants of power. We have avoided the confrontation by giving in to the happy fascism of a consumerist state. We have tarnished the dignity of the utilitarian approach to the pursuit of happiness by a debasing mass-media circus that encourages pursuing happiness by way of a mere pursuit of economic goods and services. In effect, we have accepted the economist's limited view of man as primarily an acquisitive creature. We appear to be on the road to a happy fascism that is hedonistic and narcissistic. It encourages the concentration of power in the hands of powerful private interests who will "make their deal" with the leaders of the state. Fascism—not communism—is the real danger in the United States.

Gwin Owens of the *Baltimore Sun,* a newspaper recently sold to a telecommunications conglomerate, provides us with some ideas about fascism in the United States. Owens feels the term "fascist" was overused in the 1930s and 1940s because in those days the political left wing favored it as a rejoinder for its opponents on the right, to whom they cried out "fascist!" with sometimes devastating effect. Today, the numbskulls on the right have used "Communist" in the same way. In the 1930s, when the capitalistic system broke down, bringing misery to the innocent, a businessman was called a fascist just for belonging to the Chamber of Commerce. Today a citizen can favor anything from public tennis courts to food stamps and be called a Communist.

Until 1989, the Communist states were not made up of the workers, as their promoters falsely claimed, but instead of tyrannical, oligarchic, central authority that promoted the interests of a privileged class—itself. It had no reason to fear the people, because all power had been centralized in the oligarchy.

It is clear that Communism is in fact just another variant of fascism. Understanding fascism as an ideology is far more difficult, because it is a condition that evolved in response to certain stresses after World War I. We will take up this discussion in later chapters.

The danger of fascism is real because it is alluring to the human mind. The best protection from fascism in the United States is to strengthen our constitutional culture. We need a reaffirmation of our universal commitment to profound, though simple ideas such as the fiduciary values of: fidelity, loyalty, competence, full and fair disclosure to our principals, good faith in bargaining, trust, commitment, reasoned dialogue, the adversarial system of searching for the truth, and conflict resolution without violence.

Though we have not led the world in any constructive way since the days of the Marshall Plan, we could raise our aims, again, to ennobling goals. As a result we could join others in lifting the hopes of mankind and give greater meaning to our own existence. This book expands on the idea of international peace projects in a later chapter. Meanwhile, we must first cure ourselves. In the Taoist sense, to cure society, its individuals must first cure themselves. On the other hand, to cure the individual, society must first cure itself. Today, we have a sick society. Perhaps if we celebrate the bicentennial of our constitutional culture with a national dialogue we will be on the way to curing our society. I believe we will. First, we should focus on improving our understanding of the human brain.

> In the sixth century B.C., Alcemaeon dissected the human brain. He found that it is connected to our ears and eyes, and insisted that it is where we do our reasoning. He even dared to connect the mind to the soul; since both are located in the same place, he speculated, perhaps they are one and the same thing.[2]

Today, we must take an expanded view of the human brain. Ted Turner's Cable News Network is received and viewed by millions in the rooms of major hotels throughout the world. Fascistic China in 1989 ordered its hotels to shut off the satellite dishes that were bringing in CNN. Americans are an English-speaking people who may have a special opportunity to be a beacon to lead others to the discovery of the pursuit of happiness, not as fascist subjects but as autonomous persons. It is an ennobling thought. Today, English is used by about 750 million people, though barely half speak it as a first language. English is more widely spoken and written than any other language. English has become the language of the planet, the first truly global language. Perhaps thi is because it has the richest vocabulary. Three-quarters of the world's mail, telexes, faxes, and cables are in English. More than half the earth's technical and scientific periodicals are in the tongue spoken by Americans. Therefore, much global communication will be in English for the near-term. Later, it will probably break down into dialects, unless a concerted effort is made to preserve its universality.

Americans need to improve their linguistic capacities and ability to reason. In the eighteenth century it was easier to believe that laws were proclaimed as sanctioned by morality and the divine will of God. A twentieth-century tragedy is that logic urges that virtue is merely an expedient. Through the arrogance of rational insight virtue has become a mere convention which men tolerate simply as a defense against the possibility of mutually assured destruction. Thomas Hobbes argued,

The natural passions of men [are such that] there is no visible power to keep them in awe, to tie them by fear of punishment to the performance of their covenants, and observation of the laws of nature . . . justice, equity, modesty, mercy . . . of themselves without the terror of some power, to cause them to be observed, are contrary to our natural passions, they carry us to partiality, pride, revenge, and the like. Covenants without the sword are but words, and of no strength to secure a man at all.

I urge that Hobbes wrote the preamble for the constitution of the modern fascist state. He believed our fear of death, insecurity, would cause us all to turn over our powers as individuals to the sovereign absolutists who would rule for the "good of all." Why should we adapt these ideas to the late twentieth century? On the one hand, certainly, our updated understanding of the "brain" commands no logic. It states that because man is basically irrational he ought therefore to live a life of irrationality, or, on the other hand, that he ought to submit to the terms of some contract. Humans are free either to resign themselves to what they are, and passively submit to their irrational nature, or else revolt against this nature by coming to terms with it and thereby transcending it.

The American Myth of Progress

Until recently the myth of progress has been a central theme of America's past. At the time of the founding fathers, the myth of progress was a powerful and revolutionary idea. Seen in the perspective of traditional, Old World Christianity, Catholic or Protestant (and in the perspective of traditional Judaism), the modern myth of progress is a heresy. Christianity has always been pessimistic, both about man and about his ability to construct his own history. The literally godless optimism of the myth of progress clashed directly with the rule of the proclamations of Christian traditions. When the myth of progress was first propounded by men such as Voltaire and Jefferson it was perceived as dangerous by the official guardians of the Christian tradition. Modern Americans seem generally to be unaware that the story of the creation of the King James Bible is a story of a monarch resolving life and death issues, invoking repression with resulting martyrdom.

John Wyclif freed the common man from the tyranny of ignorance. It was Wyclif who translated the scriptures from Latin to English to make it readable by the common man. In 1380 this hero of populism was denounced as a heretic for doing what a scandalized contemporary wrote, "This Master John Wyclif translated from the Latin into English—the Angle—not the angel speech—and so the pearl of the Gospel is scattered abroad and trodden underfoot by swine." In 1525, William Tyndale published a translation of the New Testament from Greek to vernacular English for which he was burned at the stake! In the seventeenth century, Thomas Hobbes sourly observed, "After the Bible was translated into English every man, nay every boy and wench who could read English thought they spoke with God Almighty and understood what He said."

By order of James I, the leading Protestant monarch of his day, the Church of England's clerics produced a common man's bible, the King James Bible. This was in the last year of Shakespeare's imaginative, word-strewn playwriting. By contrast, this new Bible used a bare eight thousand words—God's teaching in homely English.[3] The Anglo-Saxon world was hardly a hotbed of progressivism. The aristocracy and landed gentry, taught by tutors such as Edmund Burke and Thomas Hobbes, disdained as contemptible the rights of every man. Indeed, they deeply feared the idea of such rights. The American Revolution differed from the French. The United States's founding fathers were men of practical affairs. The predominant style of the men who made the American Revolution was that of accomplished persons of practical affairs who were, without flights of poetic oratory or theatrics, calmly confident of a whole series of radical propositions:

- That the new nation should be governed by public elections;
- That press and speech should be open to all (when the capitalization cost of a new press was such that newspapers could sprout like dandelions);
- That every man could worship as he would;
- That men were innocent until proven guilty;
- That men may be indicted and judged only by their peers;
- That men should be protected from government intrusion in their homes and their papers.

The ideas of the Enlightenment were the underpinning of the widespread acceptance of these tenets. No one had ever tried to run a country on these principles. This nation was born under God. At the time of the Slaveholders' Rebellion (the Civil War) the progressive spirit of the Enlightenment reasserted itself in the spirit of the Union boys whose blood was spilled by the sharpshooting rebels. Still, the Declaration of Independence and the U.S. Constitution were also based on secular myths. A myth such as progress locates its promises in this life, in this world, and thus is under pressure to produce results. From the beginning, the myth of progress promised a better life, if not for the individual, then for his children. The ideas of progress have produced results and kept promises. The application of rational scientific methods to nature (the physical and cultural environment) has transformed the world. To many people, the transformation continues to seem benign in spite of toxic wastes. During the period of dominance of the ideology of progress, we have seen the prolongation of individual life spans through a long series of victories over disease and hunger, the astronomical increase in the capacity to satisfy material needs, the increase in the safety and comfort of everyday living, the extension of educational and cultural participation to most Americans. These achievements are a wide and deep river of promises made and kept. Still, average Americans are disquieted by the failure of leaders.

Defenders of Capital?

According to Henry Kaufman, once with Salomon Brothers, it is believed (i.e., it is an operative myth) that business and the investor are defenders of capital. But, Kaufman says, in fact this is not so. The institutional portfolio practices of today, taught by finance professors, emphasize modern portfolio theory and equity risk diversification, not stockholder-management involvement and fiduciary responsibility. The worldwide tragedy of Bank of Commerce and Credit International, a bank holding company that defrauded its depositors, is excused by many Americans as an aberration conjured by foreign cultural mystics. No such obfuscation will work to cover our embarrassment over the Salomon Brothers' flagrant breach of the nation's trust. We are fortunate that the company's management has been replaced. Here is perhaps the heart of the corrosion of trust. Lending and investing institutions are holders of huge amounts of our savings. They have awesome fiduciary responsibilities that ought to temper their entrepreneurial drive—their liabilities are large and their capital is relatively small. We need the restoration of the primacy of the fiduciary ethic.

In the spring of 1990 Michael Milken, finance graduate of the Wharton School, agreed to a $200-million fine and to set aside $400 million as a restitution fund for those he bilked as he violated his fiduciary responsibilities. The six felony counts Milken faced included conspiracy, securities fraud, mail fraud, tax evasion and aiding and abetting others in the commission of criminal breaches of trust. Milken was sentenced by Judge Kimba Wood in October 1990 for rigging the junk bond markets he had created. The worst wrong Milken did was the appalling example he set for the youth of America. Michael Milken was the leading role model of Wall Street during the 1980s. Thousands of young men and women emulated him.

The duties of being an American are similar to that of being a fiduciary to this constitutional culture. This is because we use democratic capitalism as the chosen political economy to be the driving force of the system. The duties we owe each other are:

1) To be loyal to each other, our employers, our networks, our organizations, our United States of America and its Constitution;
2) To protect privacy—confidentiality and confidential information;
3) To obey fair, honorable, reasonable instructions of our current superiors, e.g., the child to the parent, the employee to the employer, the members of a team, the police, we could go on;
4) To inform our principals (higher levels in our hierarchical relationships) of material facts that affect that relationship. Would we better off as a nation if Admiral Poindexter had observed this simple rule of conduct?
5) To be competent in our work—to refrain from negligence—to have the skills we tell other we have—to use our best judgment for others as well as ourselves;
6) To hold in trust the property or funds received for the benefit of others—not to treat them as our own.

At the foundation of this mutual stewardship is the avoidance of unfair and deceptive practices, and the continuous effort to build the confidence and loyalty of those persons with whom we deal in the marketplace of ideas as well as the marketplace of goods and services. Some may sneer, saying this sounds like the Boy Scout (or Girl Scout) oath. There are too many benighted souls out there in America who feel that the "bottom line" is—who ends up with the most toys! If their spirit prevails, this nation will not survive as a constitutional culture.

2. Exploring Ourselves: What Do We Believe?

American thought about political ideology has been pluralistic through the years. No single generality could describe it. The United States Constitution was designed by our founding fathers as a working, dynamic compact among the people of America, the federal government, and the states. All these units of the state were created by the people and for the people. Today, the modern American has a personality whose psyche is different from that of our founding fathers. We should derive American political ideology from today and not from the distant past of the Federalist papers. Nor should we look to the irrelevant character of the colonial American who founded this good country. We can be certain that men and women such as Abigail Adams, Thomas Jefferson, Betsy Ross, James Madison, Molly Pitcher, Benjamin Franklin, and Thomas Paine would have perceived their world, and the basic needs of men and women, differently if they had the human experiences of the Americans of the last decade and a half, the time of the bicentennial celebration of our founding.

Today, we derive our heritage from George Gershwin, Martha Graham, Scott Joplin, Diane Barrymore, and the Julliard String Quartet. We see America by way of virtuoso artists such as Arlo Guthrie, Kate Smith, Stephen Foster, Aaron Copeland, Rogers and Hammerstein, and Louis Armstrong. Our life was revolutionized by Cyrus McCormick, Henry Ford, Pierre DuPont, Steven Jobs, and the Mayo Brothers. The profound ideas of Albert Einstein, Linus Pauling, and Niels Bohr have reshaped our minds. We are aware of the social impact of Jane Adams, Sara Barton, Margaret Mead, Irving Fisher, Arthur Burns, Oliver Wendell Holmes, Jr., John Marshall, and Thurgood Marshall, to name a few more. We will never be the same as we were because of Malcolm X, Ella Fitzgerald, George Washington Carver, Muhammed Ali, and Martin Luther King, Jr. Each are among many worthy to be named.

The Enlightenment that gave us the guiding principles of progress may have been wrong. That Enlightenment said that education was the major way for reason to do its work of reforming humans to enable man to achieve his potential. Education today has serious shortcomings because it perceives Western man as rational, logical with a great emphasis on such analysis. But while "American" brains are being trained in logic, they are experiencing life. In the 1980s, did the modern American perceive reality more clearly than realized by the intellectuals and the leaders of the country? Perhaps this explains the extraordinarily heavy use of alcohol, drugs, hallucinogens, and other pharmacological wonders, all designed to suppress human perceptions, or to provide symptomatic relief from distorted perceptions of reality. There was a pervasive escapist mentality.

The Edge of History?

William Irwin Thompson speculated on this possible transformation of culture in his brilliant commentary *At the Edge of History.*[1] He made a pungent reply to the hippies' declamation of the 1960s. Thompson said, "Within a few years, Americans will undergo a complete transformation of its consciousness, as every thirteen-year-old turns on (to LSD or crack) and walks out of his father's cracked home." The industrial-chemical mysticism of Timothy Leary was no more satisfying than the industrial sexuality of Hugh Hefner. Thompson went on,

> We were all caught in a shoddily built house in which the lights had gone out. . . . The hippies wanted the penny jammed behind the fuse; the radicals wanted to burn the house down and make for the exits by the light of the flames; and the moderates wanted to call in the "experts" who had built the house in the first place. . . . As for me, I simply depended on some personal insights to help me see my way out of the social dark.

Thompson then looked into the eyes of all who were listening and said that he realized they were all insane.

> There are only two choices open to those who have discovered that society is a mad house. First, in the tradition of Plato's cave, they can withdraw and seek light elsewhere and thus discover the larger landscape on which the mad house is located. Alternatively, if that platonic tradition of the good seems merely an infantile fantasy, they can deny self-determination to the insane majority and burn the mad house to the ground before people go out into the open.

Looking at the Platonic and Marxist choices, Thompson knew he would withdraw. So much for subjective determinism.

It is a reduction to an absurdity of life in any city to believe that one can withdraw his or her mind. The Chinese opium smokers, fed by the commercialism of the barbaric British, proved that this does not work. It destroys the human personality. Thompson saw American conservatives and liberals as affirming the value of a technological culture. Soon we will electronically retrieve information from computer systems and video phones available to everyone. Perhaps we will all become a new kind of idiot savant. Will we become present-oriented, self-gratifying individuals who have intelligence only by way of knowledge transfers retrieved from the computer banks by way of our loving personal terminals?

Marshall McLuhan has remarked that the effect of the electronic informational explosion is to make possible a new, nonverbal cosmic conscience. Thompson, however, feels it is more likely to be a new cosmic unconsciousness. We have gained much insight from Thompson's mordant view of the future. He will be right if we do not make the right choices that are still available. As Thompson sees it, we have reached the edge of history. "History itself can no longer help us, and only myth remains equal to reality. The future is beyond knowing, but the present is beyond belief. . . . And now we sleep in the brief interval between the lightning and the thunder."

The American set of beliefs or ideology arises out of not only the United States Constitution but also the Declaration of Independence. The Constitution has provided a psychic atmosphere that enabled Americans to achieve an extraordinary growth in the productivity of the nation, through high technological achievement and the nurturing of a creative civilization with a mass culture. We acknowledge that some scholars have argued we owe our powerful position to an abundance of natural resources and to favorable climatic conditions. Nevertheless, their analysis is incomplete. Other continents have also, simultaneously, been provided similar geographical opportunities (see the discussion about Latin America in the chapters on democratic capitalism). For its first two hundred years the United States experienced one of those moments in history when a vision of future progress was a driving force that propelled a whole society. It is the sharing of such an energizing vision that propels the people forward to a better quality life.

Vision of a Transcendent Power

Other people who have held such a vision have performed prodigious feats, uncommon in ordinary human history. Malachi Martin, in *The New Castle,* speaks of occasions when mankind's ancient vision of an existence perfected by a spirit, invested human beings and their material condition with a liberating and transcendent power. Martin belongs to a small but growing group bent on restoring the balance that the West began to lose seven centuries ago when Roger Bacon failed to persuade the Roman Catholic Church to embrace experimental science. From that terrible rejection came the real schism that has divided the Western world ever since. With the developing triumph of science, the realm of the spirit shrank, slowly, almost imperceptibly at first, and then at an ever-quickening pace from the Renaissance to the depths of the twentieth century. Today our American visionary spirit has lost its momentum. It can be resuscitated. We are clambering out from the hard, cramped spaces where men's theories and ambitions imprison us.

The American Vision

At its beginning, and for over a century, America had its vision. Those who came to its land to become Americans molded, and still mold, its cities. They came because of a vision of an ideal state. They had seen it in their restless minds while leaving the villages and cities in England, Germany, Ireland, Poland, Russia, Spain, Hungary, Tunis, Italy, Lebanon, Armenia, Turkey, and elsewhere. They would seek to carry out that vision on the landscape of the North American continent. The relation of Americans, not only to the land, but to one another, and to their past and future, was new in human history. So was their effort to create a new cultural environment. The American vision of loveliness is that of a human being as no man's serf but every man's fellow, a person not controllable by any dimensions of human power— and all such power destructible by sedition. This vision is one of the individual's humanist, active participation in the American covenant. It is by an almost perfect analogy reproduced in the changing face Americans have thrown over the landscape of the United States's very different metroareas.

American cities differ considerably. The variations express a variety of cultural and architectural heritages. These cities have been happy in carrying out the desire to surpass what they have seen achieved elsewhere. Each achievement was a step onward and inevitably upward. The United States population has grown five times in the last 115 years, from 44 million in 1876 to 245 million in 1990. In an extraordinary burst of human productivity, the gross national product of the United States rose from $41.5 billion in 1876 to $6 trillion in 1984, an increase of thirty-four times. And this does not include do-it-yourself activities such as housework, home gardening, and hobbies and crafts, nor does it measure things like the quality of our environment.

There is an inner dimension to America's spirit. It is independent of the charisma of individual leaders and of whatever sociopolitical structures and institutions have evolved over the nearly two hundred years since independence. Individual leaders within groups and organizations come and go but they do not appropriate to themselves this flowing vision. The American people are the living proof of a truth yet to be learned by the wide world. Americans themselves are only now awakening to it—that the "castle vision high on the hill" cannot be static. Americans are locked into a course of action that may produce what has never been witnessed: a social and political organization of millions of men, women, and children whose commonality is not homogenized, but instead, intentionally diverse.

Finding Our Creed

The U.S. Constitution is a source document for peaceful resolution of the conflicts that exist in a society as diverse as ours. We certainly have some beliefs that are not enunciated in the Constitution. They are generally held as myths and thus should be standards of conduct. Using the Constitution as our source document is instructive, for if we find the Constitution wanting in some significant way then we should change it.

It is urged that all Americans are agreed in thinking that the Constitution of the United States is one of the greatest living documents of man. There is a real difficulty imbedded in this mystical perception of the Constitution. It is passive in nature. Law-abiding citizens prefer to obey the law, as it is.

The judicial process on the other hand is mythically passive. True, it "awaits" the actual case in controversy. Nonetheless, the legislative and executive branches of the federal and state governments can pass laws that are unconstitutional and enforce them as legal enactments. We are required to await some courageous citizen, for whatever reason, to violate that law or refuse to abide by it, then endure the confrontation of the court case, pay the cost of litigation, and ultimately obtain a declaration by the court, on judicial review, that the enactment or official action was unconstitutional in the first place! In this case one person serves us all at great personal expense. As Oliver Wendell Holmes, Jr., once said, "He who confuses the law with morals is a fool."

The Right to Trust

The right to trust in others, to be confident of the integrity of our fellow citizens and of those in authority, especially the judicial branch and the life-tenured federal judiciary is a critically important premise that underlies the individualistic ideology of America. It is an unspoken foundation principle that buttresses and supports the court and the other rights we hold precious. Despite this, however, very few public schools and few colleges and universities spend much time on the bedrock concept of trust. I have found that my students have little understanding of it. Few relate it to the fiduciary duties of loyalty, integrity, competence, fidelity, and commitment to the goals of those who are trusting. Yet trust is essential to our personal relationships, our constitutional culture, and to the successful workings of democratic capitalism.

Judgments of the courts and laws of our legislatures would not be enforceable without trust. Any market economy would be a failure but for the existence of trust. It is the merchants' confidence in the integrity of the citizen that enables him to bear the risk of extending credit on charge card, credit cards, and open accounts. Plastic money has a 97 percent record of collection without delinquency, showing that in the United States, trust in the integrity of the consumer is well-placed. Businessmen make market decisions about the production, sale, and development of their products that are based on the honesty and integrity of data generated by the federal and state governments, as well as private concerns. When the press, radio, television, and cinema transmit allegedly documented reports, it is not the force of law that causes us to believe in their accuracy, but simply our trust. Today, trust has been eroded.

Crises of Morals, Not Laws

Through the diligence of investigators and the effectiveness of our telecommunication media and press, every American knew that our White House was occupied in the Nixon years by many men who had blind ambition for power and believed that as long as they followed their own peculiar perceptions of the law they were compelled to meet no other meaningful standard. Yet, in 1971, in *Bivens* v. *Six Unknown Named Agents of the Bureau of Narcotics,*[2] the U.S. Supreme Court clearly affirmed that when a federal or state official knowingly abridges the rights of a citizen and damages that citizen, then the elected or appointed official may be held personally liable. The standard is conscious and willful use of a public office to attack the constitutional rights of an ordinary citizen. If we could ignore the barrier of the economics of litigation, this would be a great change in the law to protect our individual rights.

The crisis of our so-called democratic system is evident. Recently, the weekly *Washington Watch* observed that some constitutional lawyers are literally aghast at how the social contract between the government and the people has been torn, mostly by the "party of the first part," the government. One lawyer said, "If the party of the second part [the people] had as arrogantly torn up the contract, we would call it a violent revolution." *Washington Watch* cites a few instances of contractual violations within the body of the Constitution itself, without going into the Bill of Rights and the later amendments about the rights of ordinary citizens. The dolorous list is long:

1) The decades-old projects of the FBI and CIA to open mail to and from American citizens;
2) Surveillance of international communications (letters and phone calls) of American citizens by the National Security Agency;
3) The taking of taxes of citizens to pay bribes for arms contracts at home and abroad and to join in waging illegal wars;
4) The taking of taxes of citizens to make illegal campaign contributions;
5) Consorting with criminals to assassinate "undesirable" foreign (and possibly domestic) leaders;
6) The campaign by the FBI to discredit Martin Luther King, Jr., and the civil rights movement;
7) The 1969 operation by the Internal Revenue Service to gain political intelligence on Americans that continued for some years;
8) The domestic surveillance project of the CIA, "Operation Chaos" begun in 1967;
9) The 1966–71 FBI "Cointelpro" counterintelligence project against so-called radical groups;
10) The lies and perjury by government officials and the military to the citizen's Congress at committee hearings under oath and to the court that we have all witnessed in the Iran-Nicaragua arms-for-hostages scandals.[3]

Those who support the continuance of the secret surveillance and "dirty tricks" activities of the CIA and FBI as the necessary price of liberty are not in touch with the mood of the average American citizen. Americans do not want to live in a society where "the walls have ears." The restoration of a sense of trust and confidence in the integrity of public officials and others is essential.

In the 1980s an Israeli spy was convicted for espionage activities within the United States. The case raised a crucial question: Have any of the U.S. intelligence agencies developed informational agreements with foreign intelligence agencies that would permit them to operate in the United States in return for allowing U.S. agencies to operate abroad? The dangers of such cooperation are apparent. The next step could well be that U.S. intelligence agencies carry out illegal investigations of American citizens and resident aliens by making contract with foreign intelligence agents to do the dirty work for them.

Other Basic Rights

There is a restrictive scope and reach of those constitutional provisions designed to protect the privileges and immunities of our citizens, their equal protection before the law, and their right to the due process of law in their diverse pursuit of happiness. The solemn reality is that the real existence of those rights is dependent upon the honor and integrity of other men and women, as judges, to acknowledge the right whenever the occasion arises. These all-important rights are merely an innate penumbra, a part of our natural law. This is especially the case for the federal government and the spirit of the common law of the states in their action on private citizens.

Freedom of Worship

At the founding of our republic, any ordinary student of history was aware of the great danger to domestic tranquility resulting from religious conflict. As Hans Küng, the Christian theologian has said, "The most fanatical, the cruelest political struggles are those that have been colored, inspired, and legitimized by religion. . . . [We] take seriously the fact that religions share the responsibility for bringing peace to our torn and warring world."[4] Today, the terrible wars between Iran and Iraq, Israel and Syria, Pakistan and India, and among the Irish of Northern Ireland tell us that religion does not bring peace to the world. Our founding fathers provided that no religious test should ever be a qualification for any office or public trust. Under the U.S. Constitution, religious minorities can promote the election of one of their faith to public office. They are protected in their faith to feel free to practice their religion openly with a free conscience.[5]

Our founding fathers have been misinterpreted. A purpose of the First Amendment was to build a wall of separation between the church and state. However, the fact that there was to be no state church did not mean that the founding fathers were lacking a profound respect for spiritual belief. Although not all founders acknowledged a formal faith, clearly their view of man had a deeply religious foundation. In the Declaration of Independence rights were "God given." Man was "endowed by his Creator." There were "natural laws" and "natural rights." Freedom was related to the "sacredness of man." The development of a free person was not separated from the idea of a moral person, any more than a religious man was separated from a moral man. Against this background, the founding fathers were determined that a man's religious beliefs were to be his private concern and his personal protected right. Some history texts have set forth the erroneous belief that our founding fathers were agnostics or atheists. Some historians have set forth that erroneous belief about Jefferson. Yet, Jefferson, for one example, wrote to a friend in 1822, "I rejoice that in this blessed country of free inquiry and belief, which has surrendered its creed and conscience to neither king nor priest, the genuine doctrine of only one god is reviving."

The separation of the church and state and the guarantee of religious freedom caused some confusion on where American ideology stands concerning religion. Yet, there is no question about the predominance in our society of Judeo-Christian ethics. Indeed, some form of Christianity, in its many sects, is the pervasive religion of America. The Jews are accepted by the majority as coequals. By doing so, it is clear we deny that Christianity is the preferred religious way in the nation. However, when it is a sect of Christianity that deviates from the mainstream, such as Jehovah's Witnesses or the Quaker friends, we have been much less tolerant. We have a tragic record of intolerance and bigotry. Our persecutions of the Mormons, the black Muslims, and the Hari Krishnas are a clear sign that Americans encourage religious freedom that is not Judeo-Christian only while it is conducted in private.

Religion in America is shaped by the need for social order, particularly by the effects on personal self-identity of increasing social fragmentation. Closed religions or cults have been in the ascendancy. They are the result of the hunger for meaning and belonging that issues from a search for identity and for community. All too often this expresses itself along authoritarian lines.

The Myth of Equal Opportunity

Throughout its first few hundred years, the dream of equal opportunity and its treasured counterpart, vertical social mobility, have been a basic cause for high worker productivity in this nation. Lee Iacocca is a folk hero primarily because he fulfills that myth. Americans want someone to have a chance to come from the fabled bottom and get to the top, to advance to become wealthy, to rise from being an unknown to the status of being a nationwide entertainer, sports hero, etc. The average person shares nothing else with those who "make it." Nonetheless, it is of great psychic value that they share the dream.

The Right to an Education

We have followed a tortured path searching for a universal right to an education for all who merit it. The nation has slowly sought ways to find equality of opportunity by way of the common school for all, for blacks especially, through education. Recently, the Supreme Court observed that the affirmative duty to desegregate arose only when school attendance patterns were attributable to past or present official discriminatory action.

The court has found no constitutional violation when the separation of the races in public school systems has resulted from racial concentrations in residential areas due to market forces (private action), rather than as the result of official state action.[6] The court has stated, "The objective today remains to eliminate from the public schools all vestiges of [only] state imposed segregation." We must remember that the federal judicial powers may be exercised in such cases only on the basis of a federal constitutional violation.

There is a real question whether the American citizen has any "right" to be educated. At this time, the federal citizen does not. The real issue in these school segregation cases concerns the use of state action to officially and affirmatively provide for a segregated and unequal public school facility. In the California case *Serrano* v. *Priest*,[7] the plaintiff sued the state on the ground that its financing plan for all public schools resulted in some local school districts being enriched while others were impoverished. This was due to the way school budget financing was administered by the state.

The higher courts followed the *Serrano* doctrine. Those particular states ordered a redesign of their financial aid to local school districts. Thus, the state aid plus the local revenues would result in equality of per student revenue and expenditures throughout the state.

There was strong opposition to this approach nationwide. The problem reached the Supreme Court by *Rodriguez* v. *San Antonio School District*.[8] Here, the Court found that the American "federal" citizen has no right to a public school education. It found that education was not a right that was "justiciable" under the Fourteenth Amendment. In effect, the Supreme Court determined that education was a matter left up to the various states.

As the Supreme Court "abstains," it is now possible for us to have extremely different educational quality from one state to another. It even appears possible that a state could withdraw from education (so long as it was not for discriminatory objectives), leaving it to the private sector to educate or not educate our children, depending on their family's ability to pay for it. Fortunately, in 1989, the state of Kentucky decided that equal opportunity in public school education was a Kentucky constitutional right. As we seek to compete in a global economy this uneven quality in education from state to state could be a disaster. This is because United States's changing mores have disintegrated the family and its power to instill good ethical values and the ideal of the work ethic in our young. We have become highly dependent on the public schools, or some working alternative (not yet on the horizon) to instill the values that cause a person to want to be a good, productive citizen.

The public schools are doing a very poor job of it, but they are the best available alternative. Chester Finn has been chronicling the ineptitude of the motley aggregation know as the U.S. educational system. Actually, there is no system because the Supreme Court ran away from the opportunity in *Rodriguez*. As director of the Educational Excellence Network Finn continues to battle for responsible teaching in America's schools.

Although the deplorable state of our schools along with the embarrassing performance of American students is a fundamental defect of our society it is outside the focus of this treatise. Finn states we must take charge of our schools and our future.[9] I agree with his call for accountability, the end of grade inflation, nationwide testing, merit pay, and a national core curriculum. American students are not only ignorant but also arrogant. Finn argues that the Judeo-Christian tradition is the tradition on which mass American democracy rests. "Multiculturalism" is attacking the Anglo-American cultural tradition that generated many of the ideas of democracy and our constitutional culture.

It clearly appears that the Ninth Amendment affirms rights that are not enumerated in the Constitution. Nonetheless, there is no reason for anyone to think that the right to be educated is among them. Many had thought we settled this issue in a series of common school cases that arose at the time we pressed for compulsory education in the 1890s. However, *Rodriguez* makes it clear that the battle has just begun. Fortunately, Justice Thurgood Marshall wrote a passionate dissent on which to base a fight for reversal of this ruling.

A Job at a Fair Wage

In the United States there is no right to be gainfully employed. Absent union or other contract constraints, employers have the right to discharge employees at will and without cause in most states. The idea is growing that employers should have just cause for discharge, arising out of federal legislation against job discrimination. Some would require that the government should be the employer of last resort when the economy provides no job for a person ready, willing, and able to work. Some believe we have reached the point in our development where there is a need for a leveling of income distribution. This emanates from the drive for egalitarianism that must be clearly distinguished from equalitarianism, that is, equality of access to political and civil rights. Our Congress has moved in the direction of egalitarianism with public alms such as aid to dependent mothers, food stamps, and other grant programs designed to ameliorate poverty. True, egalitarianism is a moving spirit in the United States of America, today. Nevertheless, until we find very low-cost energy and stabilize planetary population, egalitarianism is an unrealistic goal.

This treatise does not support egalitarianism. However, the myths about equalitarianism must promptly become a reality or both the constitutional culture and its workhorse, democratic capitalism, are doomed. Instead, our chosen political economy will be replaced by a fascistic state within about a hundred years.

The Supreme Court has rejected the idea of the poor, as a class, having rights as such to equal protection before the law. Yet, from the cases about the right to vote, the right of interstate travel, the right to be free of wealth distinctions in the criminal process, the right of procreation, it can be said that there are rights that have been denominated as basic, rights that require the courts to make active review of the controversies arising from the states' action in such areas.

There are other inalienable rights that are not explored in this treatise such as: the right of trial by jury, the guarantee against cruel and unusual punishment, and the guarantee against being forced to make witness against oneself. Theoretical and philosophical considerations aside, the question is whether the Bill of Rights are incorporated into the Fourteenth Amendment, and therefore, are a limitation on the states. Also, do the same standards restrict the federal government? The courts have, over time, consistently held that the standards are identical whether the federal government or a state is involved. The Court has rejected the notion that the Fourteenth Amendment applies to the state only a "watered down subjective version of an individual's guarantees of the Bill of Rights."[10]

One should not gather from this that the fundamental right to privacy of the mind, the person, and the right to safety and security of our person and property, is fully protected by this statement. We have yet to resolve the problems of invasion of privacy arising out of the congressional statutes conferring immunity. This is used in both federal and state courts to compel testimony that may incriminate others.[11] Also, the heavy economic costs imposed on an ordinary citizen whenever the state forces the citizen to assert his constitutional right, by way of attorney's fees and court costs, is not a trivial form of economic coercion upon ordinary citizens.

The Right to Privacy: A Myth?

Significant sections of the Bill of Rights indicate that there may be some fundamental right to privacy and security of the person and property in the Constitution. The Third Amendment prohibits the government from forcing upon a homeowner a soldier as an occupant of his home in peacetime. It requires the consent of the owner in a manner prescribed by law even in wartime. The Fifth Amendment provides that no U.S. citizen can be deprived of life, liberty, or property without due process of the law. Thus, we have security against invasions by states or the U.S. government of our right to security of property and person.

However, as any student of labor history can verify, there is little if any protection recited in the Constitution against activities such as were carried out by the Colorado Coal & Iron police, and other company police, in steel and coal company towns yesterday and by ITT and Bechtel in modern times. We could recognize that the principal objective of the Fourth Amendment is the protection of privacy rather than property. In this way we could be on the way to discarding the fictional and procedural barriers rested on property concepts. Of course, such an inference remains only if the personnel on the Court agree with the reasoning in the precedents cited. Apparently, Judge Robert Bork did not or does not agree. Bork said he could not find the right to privacy in the Constitution, as such.[12] In our search for the idea of privacy and security of the person and property within the Constitution and the laws and statutes, the Fourth Amendment is the most important amendment to the Constitution.

For the Fourth Amendment to be applicable there must be a "search" and a "seizure." Typically, this occurs in a criminal case, with a later attempt by the state to use in the judicial process whatever was seized. What does the amendment protect? Under the common law there was no doubt. But, the broader rights of both property and person that were protected in English law did not find quick acceptance in the United States of America. In 1886, the Supreme Court did find protection of property interests based on the Fourth Amendment.[13] Standing to contest unlawful searches and seizures was based on property interests. Thus the court ruled that mere evidence could not be seized but rather only the fruits of crime, its instrumentalities, and contraband.[14]

In an example too recent for comfort, one of the two premises underlying the holding that wiretapping is not covered by the Fourth Amendment was that there had been no actual physical invasion of the defendant's premises.[15] On the other hand, in a case where entry to the premises was necessary in order to push a spike mike through a party wall until it hit a heating duct, the invasion constituted a technical trespass and the electronic surveillance was deemed subject to the Fourth Amendment restrictions.[16]

We face improved technology and the knowledge of the use of sophisticated, long-range electronic surveillance devices in private industry and foreign police states. The premise that some property interests (at the "wall" or "perimeter" of the property) effectively control and limit the abuse of the power of the government to search and seize has been discredited. The new tests under the Fourth Amendment turn on whether there was a reasonable expectation of privacy on which the person may "justifiably" have relied.[17] The newer, two-pronged test is, first, whether the person exhibits an actual (subjective) expectation of privacy, and second, whether the expectation is one that society is prepared to recognize as reasonable.[18]

Of course, such a person is still protected by a rule that there be probable cause for entry and that a warrant be issued. The Supreme Court tries to stress the importance of warrants. It has repeatedly referred to searches without warrants as exceptional. In practice, the greater number of searches as well as many arrests do take place without warrants. Thus our discussion of privacy and other rights not enumerated in the Constitution trails off into the vague penumbra of our Constitution, and of the "other" rights not yet identified or defined in our Ninth Amendment.

Nevertheless, Americans believe they have a right to privacy and to the safety and security of their persons and the property they own, both physical and personal. "Every man's house is his castle," was a maxim much celebrated in England and was demonstrated in a case decided in 1603.[19] A most forceful expression of the maxim was one made by William Pitt in Parliament in 1763. Pitt stated, "The poorest man may in his cottage bid defiance to all the force of the crown. It may be frail, its roof may shake, the wind may blow through it, the storm may enter, the rain may enter, but the king of England cannot enter. All his force dares not cross the threshold of the ruined tenement."

We look in vain for a basis of the right to privacy and security of our persons and property in the privileges and immunities clause of the Fourteenth Amendment. In modern times, the Court has assigned a minor role to this clause. In *Oyama* v. *California*,[20] a 1948 case, the Supreme Court declared "outrageous" the wrong done to Japanese-American citizens in the hysterical, concentration-camp internments and property seizures during World War II. Nonetheless, it was not until 1988 that the United States decided to make reparations to the Nisei-Americans to right the wrongs they had experienced. Few other nations would have admitted the wrong. Certainly, the arrest and internment of the Japanese-Americans was a warning of how important the rights to privacy are, if they exist.

Though many valuable rights and privileges of natural citizenship are protected by the Constitution, only a few concern the myth of the right of privacy and the right to be secure in person and property. These are the right to demand protection of the federal government on the high seas or abroad; the right to be protected against violence while in the lawful custody of a U.S. marshall; and the right to inform U.S. authorities of violations of federal law without protection by the government.[21]

The case of Oyama, son of Japanese parents, is important. The Court agreed with the native-born youth that a state law used to cause a forfeiture of property purchased in his name, with funds advanced to him by his Japanese alien parents, had acted to deprive him of his privilege as an American citizen. The case appears to protect the right to acquire and retain property against a state taking without just compensation. Property before this had not been set forth in any of the enumerations as one of the privileges protected against state abridgement.

Although a federal statute enacted in 1866 did confer on all citizens (especially blacks) the same rights to purchase and hold real property as white citizens enjoyed, only in 1987 did the Supreme Court acknowledge that the 1866 statute applied to all citizens.[22] In other respects, the claims based on this clause seeking to prohibit states from infringing upon U.S. citizens' rights have been rejected.

Police Power

Fortunately, the federal government has no police power. The police power of each of our modern fifty states, today, embraces regulations designed to promote the general welfare, the public convenience, for the general prosperity. It also promotes public safety, health, and morals. The state police power is not confined to the suppression of what is offensive, disorderly, or unsanitary, but the power extends to what is for the greater welfare of the state. If a police power regulation concerning real estate goes too far, it may be recognized as a taking of property for which compensation must be paid.[23] On the other hand, mere cost and inconvenience would have to be very great before such an element would conflict with the right of the state to exert its reserve power or its police power. It is elementary that enforcement of uncompensated obedience by a person to a regulation in exercise of the police power is not a taking without due process of law.[24]

A proper taking for public purpose is construed very broadly by the Supreme Court. So long as the legislature adequately safeguards the condemnees' rights to just compensation, there is little question whether public purpose is a justiciable issue. Therefore, it appears that the Fourteenth Amendment does provide the right of ownership (one form of a private right) as a privilege and an immunity of a citizen and limits the power of the government to take private property in that it requires just compensation be paid.

Griswold v. *Connecticut* and the Ninth Amendment

Most of the justices, in 1965, rejected reliance on substantive due process, but did decide that a Connecticut statute "invaded privacy" and therefore was unreasonable. The Connecticut statute at issue, strongly supported by Catholic Church and others who are opposed to family planning, banned the use of contraceptives even by married couples under any circumstances. It also banned a physician from prescribing them and their sale in stores. The Court voided the statute as an infringement of the right to marital privacy. Justice William Douglas, who wrote the opinion of the court, asserted that the specific guarantees in the Bill of Rights have "penumbras formed by emanations" that help give them life and substance. While privacy is not mentioned, it is one of the values served and protected by the First Amendment. It also gives protection through its associated rights, by the Third, Fourth, and Fifth Amendments. Justice Douglas referred also to the text of the Ninth Amendment to support the thought that these "penumbrous" rights are protected by both one and a complex of amendments despite the absence of a specific reference. Justice Tom Clark joined this opinion without comment. Justice Louis Goldberg, concurring, devoted several pages to the Ninth Amendment.

> The language and history of the Ninth Amendment revealed that the framers of the Constitution believed that there are additional fundamental rights, protected from governmental infringement. They exist alongside those fundamental rights specifically mentioned in the first eight constitutional amendments. . . . To hold that a right so basic and fundamental and so deep-rooted in our society as the right of privacy in marriage may be infringed because that right is not guaranteed in so many words by the first eight amendments to the Constitution is to ignore the Ninth Amendment and to give it no effect.
>
> Moreover, a judicial construction that this fundamental right is not protected by the Constitution because it is not mentioned in explicit terms by one of the first eight amendments or elsewhere in the Constitution would violate the Ninth Amendment. . . . Nor do I mean to state the Ninth Amendment constitutes an independent source of rights protected from infringement by either the state or the federal government. Rather, the Ninth Amendment shows an intent of the Constitution authors that fundamental rights exist that are not expressly enumerated in the first eight Amendments.

Therefore, neither Douglas or Goldberg sought to make of the Ninth Amendment a substantive source of constitutional guarantee. Both did read it as indicating that it is a function of the Court to interpose a veto with regard to legislative and executive efforts that abridged other fundamental rights. So I raise the question: If there is a claim of a fundamental right that cannot reasonably be derived from one of the provisions of the other amendments in the Bill of Rights, even with the Ninth Amendment, how is the Court to determine first, that it is a fundamental right, and second, that it must be protected from abridgement?[25]

Privacy As a Natural Right

The right to privacy and the safety and security of our persons and property are among the fundamental liberties and rights that are a part of the social contract of man with a free government. With due respect for Judge Bradley's dissent in the *Slaughterhouse* cases, the "fundamental right" theory has its more recent origins in a 1942 case in which the Court subjected to strict scrutiny a state statute providing for compulsory sterilization of habitual criminals, such scrutiny being necessary because it affected "one of the basic civil rights."[26] When certain fundamental liberties and rights are involved, government or state classifications affecting them must be justified by a compelling interest. Further, the distinctive classification or action is necessary to further a proper purpose.

This is a stricter test that no state has succeeded in passing in any case in which it has been applied. Thus, in *Shapiro* v. *Thompson*,[27] involving the right of a person to welfare payments when he had just arrived in a state to take up residency, the traditional criteria for reviewing equal protection did not apply. This is because the classification touched the fundamental rights of interstate movement (the right to travel). The constitutionality of residency requirements for eligibility to receive welfare assistance was judged by the much stricter standard of whether it promoted a compelling state interest. This supports the reasons for which the Ninth Amendment was adopted. Today, the fundamental unenumerated rights are the rights of the people in accordance with the Ninth Amendment.

But what are the criteria by which a right is included or excluded? For example, is education a basic right? The answer appears to be no. Is there a right to a minimum level of income to prevent malnutrition, or other problems of health, to provide a sufficiency of food, clothing, and shelter according to society's concept of minimalist levels of adequacy? The answer is no. Is there a right to a safe quality of environment for all Americans? The answer is no. The only course of action soon available for those who feel that such rights should exist is the right to vote. The Supreme Court showed a sorry lack of vision in holding there was no right to education in *Rodriguez*. We need to increase the productivity of human intelligence wherever it is found. On the other hand, the unwillingness of the Court to recognize a right to a minimum income seems reasonable. We have a critical need to defend the work ethic in a culture based on democratic capitalism, especially given the current state of technology.

An unconscious bias is implicit in the U.S. Constitution of the founding fathers. When an actual case or controversy arises and a branch of government is charged by a citizen with infringement of fundamental unenumerated rights, it is, first, a function of the allegedly wrongdoing branch of government to interpret whether such an infringement actually occurred. The personal values of those so charged will affect this judgment.

In the early nineteenth century, when high school and college education was a rare experience for the average American citizen, judicial determination of vague, penumbrous fundamental rights was carried out by the educated classes. However, such a value bias is quite inappropriate today. It is now necessary to hold a constitutional convention to carry out a national dialogue to enumerate certain additional rights, and thus to avoid the heavy-handed enforcement of these value biases.

The Fourteenth Amendment has a limited scope. It nullifies and makes void all state legislation and state action of every kind that sponsors or indirectly supports private action that impairs or denies equal protection of the laws. Although the Fourteenth Amendment provides that Congress shall have the power to enforce, by its appropriate legislation, what has actually happened is that unless they arise from fundamental rights, such laws are treated as suspect by the Supreme Court. Thus Congress cannot act to protect the rights of a resident of a state from the restrictive actions of that state toward its own citizens unless the right is a "fundamental" right. Without any enumeration under the Ninth Amendment, we are running into serious problems as to application and interpretation of the Fourteenth Amendment by the courts.

Given the narrowing effect of these restrictive interpretations on the concept of equal opportunity (implicit in the privileges and immunities clause), it is not surprising that Congress sought to pass the Fourteenth Amendment after the Slaveholders' Rebellion. The rights of a federal citizen, killed by the early Court, appeared to be reborn. There is an absence of any directive within the Fourteenth Amendment to protect ordinary citizens against "private" actions that deprive private people of their fundamental rights. The Supreme Court has held that the Fourteenth Amendment did not increase the power of the federal government to come to the aid of a person *vis a vis* private individuals such as large corporations, but only with regard to the states themselves.[28]

However, the *Cruickshank* case did recognize a small category of federal rights that Congress could protect against private deprivation—rights to petition Congress for redress of grievances and to vote free of interference on racial ground in a federal election.[29]

The right to privacy, safety, and security of our person and property is one of the vague rights that a U.S. citizen has because of his social contract as a free citizen with the United States government. On the other hand, dual federalism explicitly recognizes the dual citizenship of all Americans and the equal supremacy of the states and their people in areas outside of the enumerated and reserved powers of our federal government. The result is that penumbrous, vague rights are not well-protected by our Constitution from interference by the states, powerful private parties, or arrogant federal or state officials who willfully risk violating the protection provided by the *Bivens* and *Westfall* cases. Furthermore, the Anglo-American legal system imposes very heavy economic costs of litigating constitutional questions. This severely limits the practical usefulness of fundamental rights that are not recited in the U.S. Constitution. It is a thesis of this text that access to justice has great economic value. If ordinary citizens believed they lived in a society that made our constitutional myths a practical reality, then real increases in the productivity of the individual members of society would occur.

3. Rights We Take Seriously

"Due process of law" is an unmistakable reference to Anglo-Saxon common law. The idea that the landed gentry and other aristocratic Englishmen had a right to due process that the king could not abridge was not, at first, meant for the common sort. Still, the right to be accused and have a speedy trial (the writ of *habeas corpus*), along with the right to hear and be heard, to confront witnesses, a trial by a jury of peers, to cross examine witnesses, and other procedural rights were all attributes of that unique Anglo-Saxon common law system.

The idea of due process also empowered courts to review state actions and to reverse arbitrary, capricious, and discriminatory actions. Our common law courts only consider actual cases and controversies. This requires an aggrieved party who believes he or she was wronged to seek redress in the courts. Usually an essential ingredient is missing for this system to achieve fair play—plaintiffs are forced to bear the burdensome costs of the litigation. Attorneys' fees, witness fees, and the expenses of documentation, producing exhibits such as graphics, printing, and the like can be very large, even unduly burdensome. Furthermore, a plaintiff is struggling against the deeper pockets of the public treasury not only in the original case but through all appeals.

It is arrogant indifference to argue that the United States has been protecting the rights and powers of ordinary citizens who cannot afford the costs of constitutional litigation. Only the well-to-do, or a *pro bono publico* plaintiff such as the American Civil Liberties Union, acting for the public good, would even consider paying the costs of such litigation. Fighting for rights usually does not provide any economic reward. This has been true for centuries.

It is largely for that reason that the ACLU, the National Association for the Advancement of Colored People, the Southern Poverty Law Center, and others came into being. Americans of all political persuasions should not accept this practical limitation on our rights. The level of development of the human personalities known as Americans has reached the point where they probably need more rights enumerated. They no longer want them to be solely under the control of the power of the brains of judges who may or may not discern these rights as existing in a particular case.

Long ago, Justice Bushrod Washington, nephew of George Washington, tried to make these mythical rights operational for everyone. In an early case, Washington argued that the privileges and immunities clause was a guarantee of a basic right to the citizens of every state. To Washington, the federal clause provided a natural and fundamental right inherent in the citizenship of persons in a free society. In effect, there were privileges and immunities of free citizens that no state could deny to citizens of other states, regardless of how it treated its own citizens.[1]

Washington's perception of a federalized sense of values was rejected by the majority of the Supreme Court. If the Court had accepted this concept of the privilege and immunities clause it would have endowed itself with a reviewing power over restrictive state legislation. Many such cases later arose over fifty years later from the due process and equal protection clause of the Fourteenth Amendment.[2]

Arizona v. *Fulminante*[3] demonstrates that the present Supreme Court is willing to jettison even the oldest and most established constitutional protections afforded criminal defendants. The police are to be given much greater leeway as the Court authorized lower courts to affirm otherwise tainted convictions. Search of bus passengers and automobiles will be less likely to require a warrant. During 1991, the court authorized police to chase down citizens who they have no reason to believe have committed a crime. They have permitted random interrogations, as well as requests to search people who have only one alternative to consenting, which is to disembark from the public transportation they are using. The new standard invites broad search actions by police. As Justice John Paul Stevens points out, "If carried to its logical conclusion, unlawful displays of force will frighten countless innocent citizens into surrendering whatever privacy rights they may still have." The dissent further notes that a police officer may now fire his weapon at an innocent citizen and not implicate the Fourth Amendment so long as he misses his target.[4] These cases suggest how the Court is willing to proceed as it carries out its political agenda.

Edwin Meese III, recently our attorney general, and others such as Chief Justice William Rehnquist, want to return to the days of that early Court that rejected Justice Washington's dissent. Though discouraging, it is instructive to continue. In early cases, a determination was made that the privileges and immunities clause was "self-executory." The clause did not impose an affirmative duty on the executive branch to enforce legislation by Congress or opinions of the Court pursuant to the clause. This means its enforcement was dependent upon an actual case and controversy in the judicial process. Note, again, the disabling effect such rules have on political, civil, and human rights where there are no monetary compensatory damages.

The early courts also struck down federal statutes seeking to limit local conspiracies to deprive a person of rights or privileges. In the early years it also declared unconstitutional congressional statutes punishing private individuals who sought to limit the rights of U.S. citizens to reside peaceably in the several states.[5] It may be fortunate that most U.S. citizens were illiterate in the nation's first century. Otherwise we may have experienced rebellion over these issues. Certainly, many educated men knew that the Supreme Court had severely restricted the ideas of equal opportunity set forth in our Constitution. From 1783 to 1787 the propertied elite were aware of riots in the street. In a rebellion led by the unruly rabble under Capt. Shay of Massachusetts, thousands took up arms against the confederacy of states brought into being by the short-lived Continental Congress. These responses could have shortened the life of our young republic.

Several states' elected officials exerted totalitarian command over their local jurisdiction. For all practical purposes, they used and brutally abused their unfettered powers. For example, an early Georgia governor violated federal treaties and killed dissident prisoners with arrogant caprice while he seized land for his cronies. In those early days, a prudent man could still make his way and accumulate an estate. However, this could be done only if he was careful to avoid using the judicial process to declare that some act favoring the local citizenry was capricious and, thus, discriminatory against the newcomer. These states did not take "rights'" of the ordinary citizens seriously; such "rights" were for the gentry. The Civil War was, in part, a result of such uneven justice among our states. After the defeat of the Confederacy, the nation saw the adoption of the Thirteenth, Fourteenth, and Fifteenth Amendments. Intelligent post–Civil War citizens might have felt that one could now appeal to the judicial power of the Supreme Court and the inferior federal courts when a state denied him equal protection before the law and the privileges and immunities of federal citizenship. A federal judge's independence was, and is, protected by the right to hold his office for life without threat of loss in pay or political pressures.

However, in implementing the Constitution, by enacting the Judiciary Act of 1789, Congress chose not to vest "federal questions" jurisdiction solely in the federal courts. It empowered the state courts to review these questions as well.[6] Very early, the federal judicial branch saw fit to place strict limitations on their power to exercise judicial review. This was done by freely carrying over to the federal jurisdiction most common-law maxims of judicial restraint. These were the doctrines of abstention, strict necessity, clear mistake, presumption of constitutionality of a state law, paramountcy of state appellate decisions within their jurisdictions, and a few others. The common denominator of these maxims of judicial prudence is the idea that the Anglo-American common-law judicial system restrains a judge's behavior. This may seem strange to laymen but it is of critical importance in considering the expanding application of these ideas by the Rehnquist court.[7] All judges, of course, claim adherence to proper restraint. The degree of a restraint, the degree to which legislative enactments are subjected to judicial scrutiny, the readiness or unwillingness of the Court to take on a political question, is affected by the shifting personal values of the individuals who serve on the Court.

Naturally, the Supreme Court is the least restrained of all courts, feeling that these maxims are more appropriate to the prudence of lower courts. When the Supreme Court overturns one of its own decisions, it will raise critically important questions for the next decade or two. It was the central issue in an important case of the 1988–89 term, *Wards Cove*.[8] In this case the Rehnquist majority severely undermined eighteen years of employment discrimination law based on an earlier unanimous decision, *Griggs v. Duke Power Co.*[9] Justice Stevens called the decision the Court's "Latest sojourn into judicial activism." Precious little of the law of employment discrimination was left standing. *Wards Cove* made a startling change. Without the intervening remedy of Congress's 1991 Civil Rights Act, employers would have had much lighter burdens of evidence to demonstrate "business justification" for discrimination.

Access to the Supreme Court

The Supreme Court does not consider itself a tribunal whose purpose is to correct the mistaken judgments of the lower courts. It will not take an appeal simply because the lower court's decision may have been erroneous. To a disappointed litigant, it is shocking when he is told by his lawyer, the law is clearly on his side and the appellate court made an egregious error of law in deciding against him, nevertheless, he or she must produce large sums for additional legal fees if he is to win the award won at the lower court, but not paid because of a technical reversal. The case must be retried simply because the Supreme Court does not consider the case important enough to right an obvious miscarriage of justice.

Where a criminal case is involved, the sense of shock obviously will be even greater. As Felix Frankfurter stated in a book written before his rise to the Supreme Court, "To remain effective, the Supreme Court must continue to decide only those cases that present questions whose resolution will have immediate importance far beyond the particular facts and parties involved."[10]

The Eleventh Amendment to the Constitution, adopted in 1794, after the Bill of Rights, was to restrict the judicial power of the United States from being extended to cases where a citizen of one state was to bring suit against one of the several states. Also barred were suits where the citizen of some foreign nation was to bring suit against one of the several states. In addition, Congress passed in 1793 a statute prohibiting federal court injunctions against state court proceedings.

The historical record is replete with examples of various state courts and states disobeying the federal authority of U.S. courts. A spectacular disobedience of federal authority arose out of the conflict between the Creeks, the Cherokees, and Georgia. The state sought to remove the Cherokees and seize their land in defiance of a federal treaty with the Cherokees. The treaty was the supreme law of the land. The Georgians had the active support of President Andrew Jackson. This and other actions by Georgia were often resurrected by latter-day defiant officials when they knew they were supported by any president who had the power to refuse to call out the troops to enforce the Court's edicts.

1868's "Morning in America"

There must have been high hopes among ordinary folk when the U.S. Congress, in 1868, passed what the Supreme Court then sullied by referring to as the "War Amendments," which we now call the cherished Thirteenth, Fourteenth, and Fifteenth Amendments. Some may have felt that a new day was dawning, that equal protection before the law, due process of law, and the privileges and immunities of citizens would now be available to everyone.

Then came the morning after. American citizens were deprived of power by the federal courts. The potentially powerful so-called War Amendments were sharply cut back and narrowly restricted by the Supreme Court. The privileges and immunities clause of the Fourteenth Amendment was made a "practical nullity" by the *Slaughterhouse* cases of 1873.[11]

The Fourteenth Amendment is directed primarily at state action:

No state shall make or enforce any law which shall abridge the privileges or immunities of the citizens of the United States nor shall any state deprive any person of life, liberty, or property without due process of laws; nor deny to any person within its jurisdiction the equal protection of the law.

The Fourteenth Amendment was necessary to make the enforcement of the Emancipation Proclamation an unequivocal duty of all federal and state officers. This was because in the *Dred Scott* case[12] the Supreme Court had ruled that U.S. citizenship was enjoyed by only two classes of individuals: white persons born in the United States as descendants of persons who were at the time of the adoption of the U.S. Constitution recognized as citizens in the several states, and those who, having been born outside the dominions of the United States, had migrated thereto and been naturalized therein. The Negro, according to the court, was ineligible to obtain United States citizenship, either from a state or by virtue of birth in the United States. This rule extended even to a free man descended from a Negro residing as a free man in one of the states at the date of the ratification of the Constitution.

The case clearly established a national rule concerning national citizenship and thus seemed to settle a controversy of long standing. The case also stirred deep, angry responses from abolitionists who believed in the natural rights of all men who were, to their mind, created equal. The Slaveholders' Rebellion and the fight to preserve the union put that idea to a test. The Fourteenth Amendment did not obliterate the distinction between national and state citizenship, but rather sought to reinforce and preserve it.[13]

In the *Slaughterhouse* cases, a New Orleans butcher sought to set aside a Louisiana statute that conferred upon a single local corporation a monopoly on the business of slaughtering cattle. Congressional sponsors of the privileges and immunities clause had sought to expand the federal system by converting the rights of the citizens of each state into privileges and immunities of United States citizenship. After the amendment, it was believed that this newly defined status quo was to be perpetuated through judicial condemnation of any state law challenged as "abridging any one of the federalized privileges." In any case, that was not to be. The Supreme Court refused to foster the growth of such "federal rights" to all citizens in the *Slaughterhouse* cases. The judges then sitting on the Court declared that such an interpretation would have transferred the security and protection of all the civil rights to the federal government and to bring within the power of Congress the entire domain of civil rights, "hereto belonging exclusively to each state." Many had thought it was reserved also to the people, as declared in the Ninth and Tenth Amendments.

The Court concluded by stating, despite much legislative history to the contrary, that no such results were intended by the Congress, nor by the state legislatures that ratified the Fourteenth Amendment. The Court contended that the sole, pervading purpose of the Fourteenth Amendment and the other War Amendments was merely the "freedom of the slave race." It appeared to the post–Civil War court that the only privileges that the Fourteenth Amendment expressly protected against state encroachment were declared to be those that "owed their existence to the federal government, its national character, its Constitution, or its laws." By this sophisticated action, a conservative *Slaughterhouse* Court, which feared a federal government and basic rights in the hands of the common man, took the noble clauses of a plainly empowering Fourteenth Amendment and reduced it to a superfluous reiteration of prohibitions which may or may not be operative in various states, according to their will. The current Court is doing a very similar rhetorical trick with the Fourth Amendment and the common law writs such as *habeas corpus*.

Other Barriers to Access

The "actual case and controversy" requirement already barred the low-cost "declaratory judgment" and "advisory opinion," whose procedures might have broadened the privileges and immunities of citizens and their equal protection before the law and due process. The conservative American courts moved aggressively to use important procedural rules of judicial restraint, which to laymen appeared to be mere lawyer's jargon. These powerful tools controlling access to the courts are: standing, jurisdiction, exhaustion of remedies, *stare decisis,* choice of law to be applied in diversity litigation, ripeness, mootness, presumption of constitutionality, political question, and others. They are currently being used by many judges to bar access to the federal courts.

The Rehnquist Court is likely to act aggressively in using these tools of abstention to force cases into the state jurisdiction. Class bias, for many judges, tends, today, to prefer the status quo and constitutes a heavy cultural lag on social change. It slows the broadening or even clarifying of the rights of ordinary citizens, especially those rights that have been left undefined but guaranteed to exist under the Ninth Amendment. The Rehnquist Court intends to use these rules of judicial restraint to skillfully pick and choose among the cases appealed to it, giving access or denying access to the Court as the members' brains so choose. For example, the astonishingly huge superstate power of the Central Intelligence Agency arises, in part, from the reality that the Court will not act to compel disclosure of the size or nature of the CIA's colossal budget. Nevertheless, as a "secret appropriation" the CIA's budget is not in keeping with the republican form of government. The court eschews review on the ground that this is a "political" question.

The Supreme Court has a long history of jealously guarding the powers of the states to make their own body of the common law, as set forth in the Tenth Amendment. This is insufficient protection for our basic rights. There are many instances where officious intermeddling into the conduct of private parties by political organizations, corporation, churches, and also the private action of state and local officials has been inadequately protected by our federal constitutional rights. This is because the local state citizen's power to intermeddle is conduct that is deemed not an infringement of the federal person's rights as a U.S. citizen—because these rights are penumbrous and vague. There is a very real possibility that the vague fundamental Ninth and Tenth Amendment rights may be sharply diminished.

Democratic Capitalism and Constitutional Culture

The right of the federal government to know facts about the people is more and more derived from the commerce clause. We are making attempts to pursue economic stability, in part, by improving the accuracy of the knowledge base about Americans as consumers. However, knowledge is a major source of power. Congress has the power to gather information on us by way of the article providing the government the right to census or enumeration.[14] Most Americans now suspect that the details of our personal affairs are recoverable in some computer network's memory banks. Some of these computer banks are in the hands of private corporations and thus beyond the protection of constitutional rights as now construed.

The thought is disquieting. Americans have begun to demand that the meaning of privacy be more precisely defined. They want their privacy enforced by the law. Only aggressive citizen actions under the Freedom of Information Act would reveal approved taps and electronic surveillance. Such suits may not survive putative assertions of "national security" and "executive immunity." Most would agree there is a serious problem of invasion of privacy when the U.S. counterintelligence agencies wish to tap the phones of Americans because they fear that the citizens may be spying. Six requests by the FBI and the CIA to do so were turned down by Attorney General Edward Levy in 1976.[15] Levy held that they had failed to show probable cause. Did Attorney General Meese do the same? The Iranagua mess indicates that some government officials practice little restraint in carrying out the orders of their "commander-in-chief." Either they do not understand the constitutional culture they have pledged to defend or it is of very low value to them.

If the separate but related ideas of our constitutional culture and democratic capitalism are to survive, we must consider where we have been and what we have done in the past two hundred years, and, more important, where we are trying to go in our third century. By looking back we see that America's greatness is based not only on the power of its physical resources, its military might, its technological prowess, its material productivity, but also on the vision and beautiful ideals of individual citizens with fire in their minds and a desire to bring them to reality.

We are at the edge of a time when the average citizen will be so well educated that he will know the past has been a sham. He is alienated from the state. He already fails to vote and has little confidence that due process is either available in the practical sense or that it would work if he tried it. There are effective alternatives for adjusting the system to restore confidence in its workability. We need to renovate the elaborate maze of particular laws and customs designed to operate as barriers to using the courts for social justice for particular individuals. The nature of due process in the face of the increasing complexity of the legislative, judicial, and executive branches of government requires the acceptance of the idea of public interest litigation.

Part II: Myth Versus Reality: Pulling the Curtain on the Wizard of Oz

4. The Supreme Court and the Federal Judiciary

> There has grown up a feeling of worship and a sentiment of idolatry for the Supreme Court that claims for its members an almost entire exemption from the fallibilities of our nature.
>
> —Martin Van Buren, 1826

The United States of America is a nation dedicated to the proposition that all men and women are created equal. Nonetheless, some are more equal than others, at least, for the rest of their natural lives. They sit on the Supreme Court. Though there has been much controversy over the nature and scope of the idea of equality, our founding fathers made it clear there was to be no hereditary aristocracy. They imbedded a prohibition against the creation of an aristocracy in the Constitution. Yet Americans are no less human than Roman citizens, who sought an emperor. And what can we say about the French, who fawned over the Bourbon monarchy, then followed their revolution by making a Corsican corporal an emperor? We Americans have found our mortals to venerate. They are the black-robed men, and, at long last, a woman, who occupy the seats of the highest court of the judicial branch of our federal government.

In the fall of 1987, we experienced a bruising, hard-fought battle over whether Ronald Reagan's offer of a nomination for the Supreme Court, Robert Bork, would be approved by our hundred U.S. senators. After their independent review of a life record and interviews with the nominee, the Senate rejected him. There is no doubt that Robert Bork is well-qualified to serve on the Supreme Court. In fact, unlike most attorneys, he appears to have spent his life preparing in the hope that he would serve there. There is also no doubt that a hundred U.S. senators were elected by their constituencies to decide whether Bork should be appointed. Our Constitution imposes the heavy duty of making that decision on the Senate, not on the president. Despite qualifications, there is and ought to be a real political battle over whether anyone who seeks to serve up opinions of their own will be affirmed.

This is constitutional culture at work during one of its finest moments, so long as the Supreme Court holds the power that it does. In the summer and fall of 1991 the nation witnessed an insidious attack on that process. An ambitious, qualified nominee, Clarence Thomas, made every effort to avoid answering sincere questions about his values and attitudes put to him by the Senate. Weary of the avoidance tactics the Judiciary Committee reported a split vote to the Senate. Then, Anita Hill, a former employee of Thomas's, stepped forward with serious charges of sexually harassing conduct by nominee Thomas. The nation witnessed a banquet of perjury by eloquent witnesses as the incredible testimony unfolded. Only Thomas and Hill know the truth.

Justice Clarence Thomas, age forty-three years, now serves, confirmed by the U.S. Senate. He is able and competent, but we know very little about him. Our representative republic was struck a serious blow by those who managed the too-ambitious nominee. The marketplace of ideas was turned into a media circus. The nominee's managers' arrogant lack of respect for the senatorial duty of inquiry was designed to gather even more power to the imperial presidency. It was probably successful. The Senate is likely to be more timid and less inquisitive next time.

Justice Bernard Cardozo explained the reasons for the contest in his treatise *The Judicial Process*. The rationale of a decision by a judge is ostensibly based on traditions, customs, history, philosophy, logic, deduction, reasoning by analogy, and the changing mores and social attitudes of the people. Therefore, we would be greatly disappointed if the U.S. senators did not try to look into the mind of a nominee for the Supreme Court. The fundamental issue before the U.S. Senate is always: can the nominee be trusted to uphold our constitutional culture, as the Senate sees that culture? For some nominees the answer has been no. Others have sailed through the process easily. Justice Thomas is an enigma who wrapped himself in the cloak of racism to avoid the inquiry.

Our representative republic is now threatened by a highly organized majoritarianism that lacks the ethical values of the past. The fascist soul of Hannah Arendt's "captive public" may well prevail over our constitutional system designed to conserve and protect the rights of our minorities. In *Abrams* v. *U.S.* Justice Oliver Wendell Holmes, Jr., warned of the dangers of majoritarianism: "Persecution for the expression of opinions seems to me perfectly logical. If you have no doubt of your premises or your power and want a certain result with all your heart, you naturally express your wishes in law and sweep away all opposition."[1]

This is the silent threat of the majority who believe, first, in the righteousness of themselves and only second in our constitutional culture. "The best truth," Holmes said, "is the power of the thought to get itself accepted in the competition of the market. . . . That at any rate is the theory of our Constitution."

If a brilliant intellect such as Judge Bork cannot find the right to privacy in the Constitution, we ought to set it forth as one of the Ninth Amendment rights that are not to be disparaged or denied. The Ninth Amendment to the U.S. Constitution has been discussed by the Supreme Court in only about three cases. The amendment reads:

> The enumeration in the Constitution, of certain rights, shall not be construed
> to deny or disparage others retained by the people.

Our nation prides itself as a representative democracy. Yet it is strange that nine persons, appointed not elected, hold their office for life and have traditional power, not explicitly stated, to reverse the actions and judgments of the executive and legislative branches of our government, which are elected by the people. Although the Court functions as a court of appeals, it is the Court's constitutional law decisions that give it such an exalted position in our society. The sense of awe in which the average American holds the Supreme Court is with reason. It is a sensible recognition of the reality of power held and used.

In the 1970s Americans witnessed a spectacular controversy between the legislative branch and the presidency of the United States over President Richard Nixon's firing of his special prosecutor, Archibald Cox. As before in our history, a tense nation witnessed a confrontation between the titans of Congress and the executive branch. This was because the special prosecutor's status and duties had been the subject of negotiation between the Nixon administration and the Senate Judiciary Committee. The nation saw the forced resignation of an attorney general and then a deputy attorney general. Nixon was seeking someone who would accept his order to dismiss the special prosecutor. This devious man finally found Robert Bork to do his bidding.

The United States waited peacefully for the processes of the law to take effect. In a twentieth century of global dictatorship, riots, terrorism, secret police, and governmental upheaval, such a tense domestic tranquility was an extraordinary event. Knowing what a violent people we are, the rest of the world sat in wonder as Americans calmly waited for nine men of good conscience to interpret the oracle, the U.S. Constitution. The Supreme Court was the final arbiter of the propriety of President Nixon's assertion of executive immunity and other arguments. In *United States* v. *Nixon,* the Court upheld the authority of the new special prosecutor to take Nixon to court to obtain evidence in his possession.[2] Nixon did not prevail over the judiciary's opinion (9–0) about the primacy of the criminal process. Nixon was ordered to turn over tapes he had made. History recorded his compliant behavior.

The routine work of the Supreme court is very broad in scope. Most of the Supreme Court's decisions are not what are called constitutional law cases. Instead, they are decisions in which the Court interprets the many statutes enacted by Congress. Still, the court's constitutional law decisions are the most dramatic of its actions. These are the cases in which the Court's justices invoke their superior authority derived by inference from the Constitution to check action by Congress, the president, or the states. The uniqueness of the Supreme Court as a judicial tribunal is found in these decisions. In other countries (except the few whose governments are modeled after that of the United States) decisions such as these are not made by the judiciary but by the political powers of the government. In many other countries it is the cabinet and the parliament, or fascist oligarchies such as the former Politburo or juntas that have the final say, not the courts.

When the Supreme Court decides constitutional questions, it is not really a court of law, at least, not in the usually accepted sense. It uses all the forms and ritual of a court of law, and on its surface, its decisions appear like those handed down by a conventional court. However, brushing aside the black robes and marble columns, taking a square look into the reality of a particular constitutional case, the conclusion is inescapable: in such cases the Court acts as a political rather than judicial organ of government. Its decisions read like political essays, not legal documents. They are used as a part of a book of readings in courses in political science, urban planning, sociology, and real estate, classes populated by nonlawyers.

Though often eloquent and persuasive, the decisions are accepted as law because of our general acceptance of the operational myth established by John Marshall in the early case of *Marbury* v. *Madison*. That myth is the undiluted power of judicial review and constitutional interpretation by the Supreme Court. In a real sense, the Supreme Court is legislating or at least participating in the legislative process.

Justice Samuel F. Miller who served from 1862 to the late nineteenth century was to complain after a conference of the justices in which his liberalism again found itself in a minority, "It is vain to contend with judges who have been, at the bar, the advocates of railroad companies, and all the forms of associated capital, when they are called upon to decide cases where such interests are in contest. All their training, all their feelings are from the start in favor of those who need no such influence."

Supreme Court Abuse in Labor-Management Relations

The history of labor-management relations provides us with important insight into the central problems raised by the Supreme Court's legislative character. In 1990, statistics show a total of about sixteen million workers as union members in the United States. These are relatively good times, but the road to power and success for craft and industrial unionism and the workers in the United States was long and bloody. The average worker who now owns his home, his car, and sends his sons and daughters to college, did not achieve this high economic status through the largess of a benevolent employer. Union-management relations were once a jungle of violent conflict. The American laborers' battle to improve his working conditions and the quality of life for his family is a story of victory within the law and within the democratic process. Those, today, who say you can't beat the establishment have not studied the history of American labor. The battle carried on in the courts by the American labor movement during the late nineteenth century and the first half of the twentieth century virtually constructed the political and civil rights of everyone. Our current rights to free speech, free press, peaceful assembly, marching and picketing, and other forms of lawful dissent were actually expanded and hammered out by the ordinary working man using labor unions and other means over the past one hundred years.

Throughout the nineteenth century and into the twentieth the idea of "liberty of contract" prevailed. So long as both parties were of full age and competent to contract, it was believed that the state should not interfere with anyone's right to bargain. Each individual worker had the right to bargain with his boss. On the other hand, the employer had a right to refuse to pay the price demanded by the worker and discharge him if he so desired. In this enlightened time of the 1990s, the fallacy of the assumption that these parties bargained based on parity or equality is clear to anyone who has ever held a job. Nonetheless, for much of the nineteenth century, it was a crime for workers to join to achieve parity through the collective bargaining with their employer.

The first recorded labor relations case in this country involved journeymen shoemakers in Philadelphia, Pennsylvania. In 1806 they were indicted and convicted when, according to the indictment, they combined, conspired, confederated, and unlawfully agreed together that they would not work except at a certain wage rate. This case, the *Philadelphia Cordwainers* case of 1806, began a pattern of characterizing the common activity of an employee group as a "criminal conspiracy." It is instructive to hear some of the charge that Judge Moses Levy made to the jury.

> It is an unnatural, artificial means of raising the price of work beyond its standard and taking undue advantage of the public to fix a positive and arbitrary price governed by no standards, controlled by no impartial person, but dependent on a few that are interested in raising the price on the goods for work done.

Does this measure tend to make good workmen? "No," answered Levy. "Such a combination is a conspiracy against others. Criminal intent and purpose and therefore a crime." For the first fifty years of the 1800s a combination of workers who united to improve wages or working conditions was, at law, acting criminally.

The court's application of criminal conspiracy doctrine to early employee activities eventually aroused a storm of public protest. The Supreme Judicial Court of Massachusetts in 1842 finally acted to set aside the conviction of the Boston Bootmakers Society for criminal conspiracy. The court deemed it a lawful purpose of concerted action to join a group and refuse to work with wage-cutters. However, this was not a breakthrough. The law grinds slow and exceedingly fine. It is a curiosity that in the same year the Massachusetts court adopted the "fellow servant rule," which prevented an employee from recovering damages from his employer for any injuries caused by the negligence of another employee on the job site. It took over seventy years to replace the fellow-servant rule and the hardships that it imposed upon employees. Eventually the workmen's compensation and employer liability laws were passed. This was many years after Chancellor Otto von Bismarck's Germany had led the way in this respect.

Though laborers by 1850 were generally relieved of the charge of criminal conspiracy so long as their united efforts had a lawful purpose, laborers' adversaries soon persuaded the Court to adopt a novel principle. They decided that organized labors' pressures on the supply of labor and the terms of employment sought by union membership constituted an actionable tort available to the employer to bring against the members of unions who refused to work. The theory was that there was an intentional infliction of harm on the employer or on the nonunion employees. The threat of this new tort and court action by the employer, who had the deep pockets to pay for litigation costs, certainly was a major deterrent to gaining new members for the trade societies.

Another phase of judicial activism in the evolution of the employment relationship was initiated toward the end of the nineteenth century. Labor activity, first considered the subject of criminal proceedings, became identified as an appropriate activity to be enjoinable by injunctions issued by the courts of equity in various states. The common-law courts in our states suddenly "stumbled upon" a major departure from what had always been the English rule against the issuance of an injunction in labor disputes.

The most alarming feature of the anti-labor injunction in the United States was that its use increasingly tempted judges to dispense with any well-founded theory of illegality of purpose in the use of picketing. The courts came to look on much of organized labor's economic course of activity as enjoinable in itself, *per se,* without a hearing on the facts. The injunction would issue without statement of opinion and without determination that it was based on some unlawful economic activity or purpose. As a result, labor union activity was severely constrained because labor unionists did not know what could be a lawful activity. It was a flagrant lack of due process according to the English common law. But American propertied classes were not yet affected by our twentieth-century due process attitudes.

Working men turned to the Odd Fellows Halls, Free Masons, Woodmen of the World, and other secret fraternal societies as a way to meet lawfully. It was illegal for men to gather for the purposes of discussing their job and working conditions. This was a time when workers averaged twelve hours per day, six to seven days per week. Working conditions were typically hazardous, to say the least, and often resulted in disabling occupational diseases.

With No Justice, Violence

Under these wretched conditions, it is no surprise that the labor movement then turned to dynamite in the notorious 1893 Homestead strike against the steel and coke manufacturers of the Pittsburgh area. In a pitched battle, three thousand Pinkerton men hired by management as strike breakers waged virtual war against thousands of laborers. The 1886 Pullman strike in Chicago was another violent expression of the laboring man's frustration over his plight. A long, drawn-out strike in the McCormick Harvester Company had culminated in a riot in which the city police killed or wounded a half dozen labor demonstrators. On the following day, the police were breaking up a mass meeting that was being held in Hay Market Square to protest this massacre. Someone threw a bomb into the crowd. Seven persons were killed and over sixty injured. The actual perpetrators of the crime were never known or apprehended. Nevertheless, a criminal court judge in Chicago held that the speakers at the Hay Market meeting were "anarchists" who had incited the violence. He urged that they were equally guilty with those who threw the bomb. Accordingly, eight known anarchists were arrested, tried, and convicted of murder. One was sentenced to imprisonment and the other seven to death.

The convicted anarchists appealed to the Supreme Court. Gov. John P. Altgeld of Illinois reviewed the record of the trial and said that the judge had conducted the trial with "malicious ferocity." The record showed that the judge permitted some men to serve on the jury despite the fact that they had candidly admitted that their minds were made up against the defendants before hearing a word of testimony. One argument presented by the defendants to the Supreme Court was that trial by an impartial judge and jury was one of the privileges and immunities of the Fourteenth Amendment. But, the *Slaughterhouse* decision had already adversely disposed of such an assertion of individual rights. The Fuller Court spurned the request for review. Convinced there had been a miscarriage of justice, Gov. Altgeld in 1894 pardoned the three defendants who were still alive and so committed political suicide.

In 1895, regarding the case of *in re Debs*,[3] the Fuller Court was again to show that neither logic nor consistency with previous decisions would seriously interfere with the judicial posture that property interests were superior to individual rights. The *Debs* case grew out of another Pullman strike. Under the leadership of Eugene V. Debs, the American Railway Union voted a boycott against all Pullman cars. The newly organized General Managers Association of Railroads promptly championed Pullman's cause and paralyzed transportation throughout the North. U.S. Attorney general Richard Olney, a former railroad lawyer, whose loyalties to his erstwhile client had not abated, urged President Grover Cleveland to take action. Although Gov. Altgeld had protested that the state militia was adequate to preserve order and protect property, Cleveland sent a regiment of soldiers into Chicago. Olney obtained an federal injunction against the strikers' interference with the delivery of mail and the obstruction of interstate commerce.

Debs deliberately defied the injunction by urging the workers to stay out on strike. He was the Lech Walesa of his day. Debs was held in contempt of court and sentenced to six months imprisonment. He appealed to the Supreme Court but the conviction was affirmed.

Debs was later jailed again for rallying against the dangerous working conditions and dismal lives of his fellow workers. Debs promised a social revolution by which his Socialist Party would bring a government to power that would require equity in the distribution of wealth and fairness in the treatment of men both on and off the job. Debs spoke in the tradition of laborers and leaders who had turned to political action in Western Europe. Debs's ideology was not to carry the day. Clearly, democratic capitalism had not yet been born; laissez-faire capitalism was not "trickling much of anything down." Nonetheless, the workers' faith in the resiliency of the constitutional culture prevailed.

American workers chose to follow labor leaders who sought more immediate goals. Samuel Gompers, during the late nineteenth century and early twentieth century, was painstakingly building the American Federation of Labor, a confederation of craft and artisan unions working in the skilled trades. When asked to state the goals of the American trade movement, Gompers supposedly replied, "Jobs and more." The American newspapers intentionally misled the American public by truncating this quotation to make it appear greedy. What Samuel Gompers really said, was, in paraphrase, "Jobs and more schools, more hospitals, jobs with better working conditions, and more churches and better homes for our families." In sum, the American labor movement concentrated on improving working conditions and raising the level of wages, while driving hard for collective bargaining contracts and the right to membership in the union.

In 1898, Congress adopted the Erdman Act to regulate the labor relations of railroad employees. It appeared the nation had entered a new era in the use of the commerce clause to protect individual workers' rights. The Erdman Act came before the Supreme Court in 1908 in the famous *Adair* v. *Coppage* case.[4] Unfortunately, the conservative Court held that this statute, which limited the employer's right to demand a nonunion shop, was a violation of the due process clause of the Constitution. The language of the Court was truly disheartening. The Court stated that it was a legal right of the defendant, Adair, to discharge Coppage because of his being a member of a labor organization, just as it was the legal right of Coppage, if he saw fit to do so, to quit his job if the defendant employed non-union members. In the words of the Court, "The employer and the employee have equality of right and any legislation that disturbs that equality where there is an arbitrary interference with the liberty of contract no government can legally justify in a free land."

Fine libertarian rhetoric though this was, it was also completely out of keeping with the reality of the great disparity of power between boss and the worker. In 1915, the Supreme Court invalidated a Kansas statute that sought to use state power to prohibit employers from requiring employees to sign and then enforce "yellow dog" employment contracts that precluded union membership while the employee worked for the employer. The Supreme Court of Kansas, had found the new act constitutional. It was said in defense of the "anti-yellow dog" act that it was a matter of common knowledge that employees, as a rule, are not financially able to be as independent in making contracts for the sale of their labor as the employers are for the making of labor contracts for the purchase of the same. The Supreme Court's property-class bias was apparent in its reversal. It struck down the Kansas statute. The Court replied, "Where the state steps in on one side of an employment contract to deny equal protection before the law to the other party, it is an improper use of the police power to so aid one side of the contract."

Danbury Hatters

The skills of the educated managerial class persuaded a sympathetic court that the famous Sherman Antitrust Act of 1890 was designed, in part, to restrain trade-union action. Everyone knew the Sherman Act was a response to a popular demand to prevent the seizure of control by monopolistic trusts of the manufacturing and marketing of goods. It was not intended to apply to the banding together of labor to get better wages, hours, and working conditions.

In 1908 the AFL sought to unionize the shop of a Connecticut hat manufacturer by inducing a strike at his factory and by boycotting his products. The entire AFL had cooperated, causing an alleged $80,000 in damages. The Supreme Court held that the activities were an illegal boycott and that the prohibitions of the Sherman Act covered a combination of labor as well as capital. Under the Sherman Act the damages were tripled to $240,000, about $7 million in today's dollars. The rule of reason was not applied. Questions of motive or the reasonableness of the restraint received no consideration. The judgment was enforced mercilessly against poor individual workers and their families. It made them destitute simply because of their membership in the offending unions.

Ordinary Americans were outraged. Congress responded to *Danbury Hatters* with the Clayton Act of 1914, which provided that labor unions were to be exempt from the impact of the antitrust laws and placed drastic limitations on the granting of injunctions in labor disputes unless necessary to prevent harm or grievous harm to property or person. In 1921 the Supreme Court virtually disemboweled the Clayton Act in the now-notorious *Duplex Printing Co.* case. After a strike failed at the Duplex Printing Company, the only nonunion establishment of its type in the United States, the AFL's International Association of Machinists decided to boycott the company's printing. With the help of affiliated AFL unions, the IAM threatened sympathetic strikes against trucking companies, repair shops, and other shops of the printing industry. The court decided that such sympathetic strikes were a violation of the Clayton Act.

At last, the general labor movement gained an outstanding legislative victory with the passage of the Norris-LaGuardia Act of 1932. The act regulated the issuance of injunctions in labor disputes by the federal courts, generally barring them. The act also barred yellow-dog contracts and declared it a matter of national policy to favor collective bargaining of labor disputes over wages, hours, and working conditions.

In 1933, Congress adopted the National Industrial Recovery Act, with its famous section 7a. This section made it a duty for employers to bargain with duly elected representatives of labor who did have the right to organize. In May 1935, the Supreme Court declared the NIRA unconstitutional in the *Shechter Poultry* case. Section 7a was not deemed to be severable so it, too, was voided. It is fortunate for democratic capitalism that the Court so acted. NIRA was a move in the direction of a command economy. Each industry would have had a board, responsible to the president of the United States, that would have controlled production and prices. It was a clearly unconstitutional delegation of law making by Congress to the executive branch, and it contained the seeds of fascism.

After *Shechter,* Congress revised the NIRA to apply specifically to the coal industry. This act was sponsored jointly by elements of the coal employers and the United Mine Workers. The act was declared unconstitutional on many grounds in *Carter* v. *Carter Coal.*[5]

Congress responded with the National Labor Relations Act of 1935, often called the Wagner Act, which prohibited unfair labor practices by employers. Beforehand, Congress had stopped at the mere pronouncement of a national policy principle. In the Wagner Act it required employers to bargain in good faith. Democratic capitalism was born! The National Labor Relations Act was to prove to be a real bill of rights for the American labor movement. Until then, only about 10 percent of the American labor force was organized, mostly the skilled trades. In 1936, John L. Lewis of the United Mine Workers decided to finance the organization of semi-skilled and unskilled industrial workers, and not along craft lines, but on an industry and companywide basis. The Steel Workers Organizing Committee under Phil Murray moved in the coal and steel fields of Pennsylvania and West Virginia. This was the beginning of the Congress of Industrial Organizations, known as the CIO.

Because the NIRA had been recently ruled unconstitutional, management's resistance to organizing was firm and resolute. Management sincerely believed the act to be unconstitutional. On the other hand, the desperate plight of the average worker during the Great Depression was very real. Many wage earners could not meet the payments on their families' mortgages. Foreclosures were common. The bread lines, soup lines, and church rummage sales of the day are part of the historical record.

Union organizers found a ready and willing audience among the workers. The labor movement became the darling of liberal college students, who offered to do volunteer work at union headquarters. Organizational picketing became militant. Mass and violent picketing was used in violation of the law. Sit-down strikes occupied factories in a militant and wrongful way to demand management recognition. Words such as *scab* and *fink* were not tossed around loosely. To be so labeled could put a man's life in danger. The battle was ongoing. There was serious violence in Alliquippa, Pennsylvania, in Gary, Indiana, and in South Chicago.

Fortunately, a now beleaguered Court saw the right course and the Wagner Act won out. In 1937 the court found it constitutional in *National Labor Relations Board* v. *Jones and Laughlin.*[6] Said Justice Charles Evan Hughes, "We are dealing with the power of Congress and not with the extent to which it goes." The decision was five to four! It had taken thirty-one years, dating from the Erdman Act 1908, for the court to see the merits of the working man's need for equitable bargaining power. This could facilitate capitalism as our chosen political economy. Corporate and monied resistance nearly destroyed our representative republic by creating a fertile field for fascism and Communism, ideologies incompatible with our constitutional system of government.

Our experiences of the 1970s and 1980s make clear we should enact similar legislation to force socially responsible conduct on the officers and directors of our large corporations. Bribery, sweetheart loans, "golden parachute contracts," and corporate officials using company prerogatives for private gain are regularly reported by the media. If the myth of social justice and equal opportunity are to continue to be among major beliefs of American citizens, access to the Supreme Court continues to be critically important.

Some are proposing that we interpose a "National Appeals Court" between the Supreme Court and the circuit courts of appeal. There are other ways that Congress could help the Supreme Court handle its growing docket before it becomes too burdensome. One way would be to enlarge the Court to, say, fifteen justices. The objective would be to enable them to exercise independent, individual choice to sit in groups of three, five, seven, nine, eleven, thirteen and fifteen (the Court *en banc*). Most cases would be handled by groups of three. All co-equal, these subsidiary courts would be formed by voluntary informal collegiality by the justices themselves. All justices who absented themselves from hearing the case would be bound by the ruling. An exception could be for the power and authority to seek other justices who might authorize, say, reargument by a larger group up to the Court *en banc*. Such innovative docketing and handling of cases would result in many cases being handled within the procedure described by the smaller coequal subgroups of three justices sitting as the Supreme Court. It would also permit and encourage justices to develop expertise while in no way diminishing their authority to gadfly about and be involved in a case in which they felt a contribution could be made by their individual presence. This seems a most workable plan for maintaining access to the Court without unduly burdening our Supreme Court justices.[7]

This review of labor management relations and the law has made it clear that our rights and powers do, in fact, change over time. This is because the Supreme Court has the implicit power to expand or contract them as it sees fit. My purpose in this text is to encourage a national colloquy on the preservation and revision of the U.S. Constitution. By relating the basic beliefs held by all Americans to the Constitution, we should discover the reasons why we hallow it. Such close analysis should also reveal the need for greater participation of the citizenry. This enterprise could discover the meaning of the Ninth Amendment.

America waited over a hundred years for the Supreme Court to confirm that the Bill of Rights in any way limited the action of the several states.[8] Finally, in 1908, the court did allow the possibility that some personal rights safeguarded by the first Amendment are safeguarded against state action.[9]

Obviously, the average American needs to know how our judges perceive due process. Worse, we need to know if they have understandings that are divergent from most ordinary citizens. Gaining lawful assurance of our rights is a very slow process. But our current understanding of what is human indicates a fundamental need for ennobling, spiritual, goals for life to be satisfying.

Part III: The Human Brain

Preface

Roger Sperry, Nobel laureate in physiology and medicine for his study of the human brain stated in 1981,

> Current concepts of the mind-brain relation involve a direct break with long established materialist and behaviorist doctrine. . . . Instead of renouncing or ignoring consciousness, the new interpretation gives full recognition to the primacy of inner consciousness as a causal reality. . . . Beliefs concerning ultimate purpose and meanings in life and the accompanying world view perspectives that mold beliefs of right and wrong are critically dependent, directly or by implication, on concepts regarding the conscious self and the mind-brain relation and the kinds of life goals which we allow. Directly and indirectly social values depend . . . on whether consciousness is believed to be mortal, or immortal, reincarnate, or cosmic . . . localized and brain-bound or essentially universal. . . . Developments in mind-brain science rejecting mechanistic and reductionist perceptions along with dualism are clearing the way to a rational approach theory and prescription of values and to a natural fusion of science and religion.[1]

Lewis Mumford said that we stand on the brink of a new age, an open world with a self capable of playing its part in a larger sphere. The Institute of Noetic Sciences, under Willis Harman's leadership, argues that humans are going through a profound change. Global mind change is challenging the prevailing knowledge authority system. In the United States, however, Americans are avoiding personal responsibility. They live for the pursuit of consumer goods, encouraged to do so by the failed leadership of many large corporations that lack social responsibility. Today, the pursuit of happiness has been redefined to focus attention on materialism when the human brain sorely needs a metaphysical perception.

The narrowly trained specialists who dominate the intellectual life of the United States see the basic stuff of the universe as matter-energy. To them we learn about reality from studying the measurable world. Many of them grudgingly concede to a dualistic, metaphysical view separating matter-energy from the mind-spirit. They leave the latter out of their "real" world of measurable things. Yet there is a change going on. The new metaphysics urges that the ultimate stuff of the universe is consciousness. In effect, the ultimate reality behind the phenomenological world is contacted through a deep intuition that guides the physical senses. This holistic world view arises from developing perceptions generated by quantum physics and crosscultural transfers from Eastern mysticism.

Because of the ongoing battle for our minds, this section of the book explores the present state of mind in the United States. Some urge major changes in the social contract of the American people, a Lockeian, holistic world view of ecological awareness, a feminine perspective, social responsibility, nonviolent change, human-scale technologies, and empowerment of the people. On the other hand are the adherents of a Hobbesian system, a patriarchal corporate socialism for the loyal, further specialization and bureaucratization for economic security, masculine competitiveness, aggressive defense and exploitation of nature.

Many Americans are in a crisis of the mind because they are being offered happy fascism as a way to end the pilgrimage. Americans find wanting the view of European intellectuals so brilliantly set forth by Colin Wilson in *The Outsider*. Wilson identifies those who can see the truth and face the reality of the human condition as outsiders. To Wilson the outsider's basic problem is his instinctive rejection of the everyday world. To the outsider there is a feeling that life is somehow boring and unsatisfying. America listens to the sound of the pragmatic realism of a William James and the distant drum of a Henry Thoreau. They stayed home and founded psychology and the American philosophy of utilitarianism. Americans follow "insiders" those who stay within society to work in nonviolent ways to confront their fellow humans with the reality that they can do something to better the human condition. Americans such as Thomas Jefferson, Upton Sinclair, John Lewis, Walter Reuther, Martin Luther King, Jr., Reinhold Niehbur, Robert Taft, Louis Armstrong, Martha Graham, Jane Addams, and Georgia O'Keefe were not outsiders.

In this section I detail the United States as a developing culture in search of role models. We need a national dialogue about the nature of a mature human personality. This search for an acceptable definition of the human personality, given our new understanding of the human brain, could yield the benefit of identifying the kind of human who can successfully pursue happiness. American civilization is bursting at the seams with crime and neuroses because of the dominance of the marketplace of goods and services over the marketplace of ideas. Humans must learn to express their dominance in new ways—in the realm of the mind.

5. The American Mind

America and its political leadership does not understand American minds, nor do we relate effectively to the post-McLuhan generation. There is a myth that all humans have some minimum necessary quantity and quality of knowledge. However, creeping into awareness is the stark reality that our myths are mere convenient paradigms that have served us all well in the past. The commercial substitute for reality is not satisfying. It is a technicolor, multimedia, mythic sitcom. Alcohol and pharmacological hallucinogens provide "escape" from personal reality. Technology has become a dangerous cornucopia with recombinant DNA offering alluring and tantalizing promise of genetic engineering. Algeny's guru, Jeremy Rifkin, warns us that scientists are loose in the china shop. Yet nihilism, or, alternatively, evangelists, fearfully inveigh against the demonic unknown, which is an even worse way to deal with the effects of scientific change on our future. We do not know our own minds.

The human brain is the true battle ground of geopolitics. Humans as brains, minds, and souls prefer to live in cities. If we are to make a breakthrough, we need an in-depth discussion about the many kinds of uniquely different humans. We must break away from the political ideologies that treat humans as easily classified masses, such as classes, castes, ethnic groups, and power elites. We must seek to integrate the neurobiological and psychiatric paradigms of human personality with the working political and economic definitions of humans. Progress cannot be made until political and economic definitions of man change. This is because humans are not rational. In truth, they are quite irrational.

In America's metroareas there are major disparate crosscultural mindsets. Multiculturalism in its most intense and divisive forms is a major problem for educators. It is a developing political problem. Although the educational establishment will not admit it, multiculturalism is a strategy for dealing with the educational deficiencies of some ethnic groups. It promotes a contemptuous, even hostile attitude toward Judeo-Christian ethics and the West's Greaco-Roman heritage.

Multiculturalism is befuddling tens of thousands of our black students. They seek to find their roots in the Sudan, or other exotic places, rather than embracing the unique constitutional culture of America that has at long last been made accessible to them. They seek their home in ancient Egypt rather than striving to make the United States a better place. In contrast, most Hispanics and Orientals are preoccupied with the process of "Americanization." The "roots" these groups seek are here in the United States, not among the Aztecs or in Angor Wat. We need to establish open pathways to conflict resolution. Although ethnic differences often lead to misunderstanding, in the long term such differences might be a basis for our coming together in a more synergistic way. The conflict between diverse groups is good when it is a reasoned dialogue with fair play.

Though our educational system fails to teach the idea, our constitutional culture actually promotes tension, even conflict, between our different races, sexes, and generations. It is a tension that arises out of different perceptions of the appropriate ways to pursue happiness. We are in a period of profound disorientation for the average American. How we come to know reality depends on our socialization. Somehow we need to grasp the understanding that what we say and think about the future is going to influence the nature and quality of the future. According to Linda Groff, a professor of political science and coordinator of future studies at California State University, Dominguez Hills, how we come to "know" reality depends on our socialization. Once we understand the sources of our perceptions of reality, we can see how others have arrived at different mind sets that may cause conflict.

Physics and Objective Reality

We are discovering through quantum physics that "What is real?" is a profoundly significant question, the answer to which deeply affects the way we think. Physics supposedly deals with objective realities, but developments in quantum physics have shattered that view. It is now a question whether anything can be called real.

Niels Bohr, Werner Heisenberg, and others may have changed forever the way humans perceive reality. If the Bohrean view prevails across the board, and the other view—whose titular genius was Albert Einstein—is revised, then there will be a very serious philosophical revolution for humankind. Quantum theory in physics, of which Bohr was a main progenitor, is anything but concrete. It comes with built-in existential difficulties. Einstein could not put up with any of this. He insisted that objects must have physical attributes that are always actual and real, quite independent of any observer or act of measurement. Thus Einstein made his famous remark that, "God does not throw dice." As Spinoza was once called the "God-drunken philosopher," perhaps the great Einstein will be known as the "God-drunken physicist."

Although Einstein believed quantum mechanics to be the best theory available under the circumstances, he thought it incomplete. According to him, there are aspects of the life situation we do not see, so called "hidden variables." If we could know the hidden variables, these problems of reality, duality, and uncertainty would fall away. Bohr insisted to the contrary that quantum mechanics is all there is in theory, and physicists had better adjust their expectations and their attitudes toward reality.

Bohr's Uncertainty Principle

Contrary states of being seem somehow united in the same object. A thing is both a particle and a wave. Bohr built on the work of Heisenberg. A particle is something with a well-defined and relatively small extent in space. It is localizable. A wave cannot be localized, in principle, and it can extend from infinity to infinity. Classical physics can easily answer the question: Where is the planet Jupiter now? Quantum mechanics has no answer to the similar question: Where is the electron now? From this conjunction of opposites follows the so-called uncertainty principle. The physical characteristics of objects come in pairs indissolubly linked together. Position and momentum, and energy and time are good examples. The better one knows one member of these pairs, the worse one knows the other. Under this constraint, what can measurement mean?

The scholarly dispute between Einstein and Bohr concerning the meaning of reality continued until their deaths. It is important for our pentecostal friends to know that they remained personal friends. Quantum theory is incomplete. Physicists wondered whether experiments could really say anything about it. John Bell of the Swiss CERN laboratory solved that problem for now. In 1964 he developed a theorem about the reality that nature is paradoxical. He found that despite one's philosophical presumptions, the mathematics of quantum mechanics allowed the calculation of numbers, even the correlation of rates that can distinguish between the reality of quantum mechanical correlations and the nonreality of them, making it a simple case of one number or the other. Over the last few years Elaine Aspect, Phillippe Grangier, and Jacques Vigue have done experiments considered compatible with the reality of Bell's quantum correlations. Nature is paradoxical, inconsistent, and lacks the symmetry that an orderly mind like Einstein's would have preferred.

Bohr's Principle of Complementarity

This led Bohr to propose the principle of correspondence as one of the main tenets of the Copenhagen interpretation: our way into the quantum world is through the classical physics of Newton. This point implies that somewhere there is a boundary between the quantum and the classical regimes, but it is an elusive one: wherever anyone searches for it, it refuses to be found; the act of measurement somehow affects the reality of its existence.

Bohr perceived the meaning of change, a profound human accomplishment for a classically trained Western mind. He fixed his attention no longer on transitory individual things but on the immutable eternal law at work in energy that is change. Eventually all humans must have understanding of the immutable laws of change. The two foundations of twentieth-century physics, quantum (Bohrean) theory and relativity (Einsteinian) theory, both force us to see the world very much like a Hindu, a Buddhist, or a Taoist. The parallels between modern physics and Eastern mysticism are striking. The basic elements of the Eastern world view are also those of the world view that has emerged from Bell's theorem.

The New Reality and Constitutional Culture

Our nation provides a process of conflict resolution that may be the salvation of American democracy by way of the U.S. Constitution. In this new sense of reality there is a unified world view of one force or energy field. The classical, Western perception is that each individual is split into mind, body, and soul. We are further divided into talents, beliefs, and feelings. All of these are engaged in an endless stressful conflict, generating frustration, anxiety, creativity, and much else. It is a fundamental Western belief that these fragments in ourselves, our environment, and our society are well and truly separate. But now we can see this perception as an essential cause for the present series of social, ecological, and cultural crises. Americans need to accept the Bohrean principle of complementarity.

In *The Tao of Physics,* Fritjof Capra explores parallels between modern physics and Eastern mysticism. In the Eastern (and Bohrean) view, the division of nature into separate objects is not fundamental and any such objects have a fluid and everchanging character. The Eastern world view is therefore intrinsically dynamic and contains time and change as essential features. There is an essential harmony between the spirit of Eastern wisdom and religions and Western science. Perhaps Western physics is the path of science with a heart that will lead us to spiritual knowledge and self-realization.

Consider the role of Allah, Christ, and all other changing energy forms. Since prehistory, many gifted men and woman have perceived that the world they knew in all its many forms consisted of a single primal force. This fact is now becoming clearer to everyone. However, the contemplative power of many humans has not yet advanced enough for most to know the source or the goal of this one primal force, or energy, or mass. Nor are most of us ready to comprehend the nature of the life force that drives through or in it.

These constantly changing concentrations of energy would not evolve without the Force. Thus we discover that all concentrations of energy, human beings, even the gods of the minds of this earth, Christ, Mohammed the Prophet, Ghatama Siddhartha Buddha, Lao Tze, and other transitory forms of the evolving Force who have learned to love, are transitional objects in this cyclical evolution. That was Christ's meaning when he said, "I am the light." The sun of our solar system is a mere stage in this development toward other forms. It follows as the night does the day that the purpose of these changing energy forms, and, therefore, the purpose of men and women, is to serve well and properly as transitory forms of energy, energizing the ascending and descending progression and regression of the primal force that is in constant cycle.

Hans Küng, the great Christian theologian, said in *Christiantity and the World Religions,*

> Man's eternal questions about the meaning of life, suffering, and death, about the highest values and ultimate norms for the individual and society, about where humanity and the cosmos have come from and where they are going are not simply still with us, but have grown far more urgent in the face of political catastrophes and disenchantment with blind faith in progress. . . .
>   The only reality proper to man and the world is conditioned in every way. . . . Modern atomic physics does not claim to know the inner most essence of matter . . . experimental psychology does not pretend that it knows the inner most essence of the person. . . . We have no recourse but to grope our way to reality with interpretive concepts with the proviso that they do not take us to the bottom of phenomena.

Küng credits Capra's 1975 *Tao of Physics* and his 1982 *The Turning Points* with leading to the convergence of Western physics and Eastern wisdom. Küng points out that the Buddhist concept of reality has consequences for the understanding of person that will pose serious problems for Christian thinkers. Küng asked, "Can we take human dignity seriously if we deny man a self?" Christian thinkers who have long understood "person" in an individualistic sense are trying nowadays to work out a deeper relational understanding of the person. It appears the true self is a selfless self, constantly losing itself in its relation to others. Historically, Christianity was unable to prevent dehumanizing uses of power in its own sphere of influence (state and church) and totalitarian systems triumphed under the banner of de-Christianization. In the ecumenical sense, are Americans also ready to accept the obvious affinities of Eastern thought and Western physics? Can they be capable of taking seriously the unity of humanity with the cosmos without religious assumptions that lie beyond the scrutiny of reason?

The United States, as a so-called advanced country, has a profound problem of meaning and purpose. We never take the time to contemplate what it is we are defending. This is especially true of the military. Technology is going to be humanized not through the managerial sciences but through history, mystery, religion and philosophy. American citizens have the capacity to lead all the world's people toward ecological citizenship by recognizing that market economies produce some market failures. The ozone hole over the Antarctic grows larger as we await the confrontation of our dualistic blurred vision. To survive we will sorely need deeper roots of personal identity than consumerism. We will need major paradigm shifts, a revolution of consciousness.

We must be highly dependent on individual action and self-selected groups of people, not institutions, if we are to succeed in reorienting the American mind. First, we must attack the confusion of scholarship with culture. Technical specialization is destroying our cultural values. Jacques Barzun calls for all to acknowledge the essential conflict between scholarship and culture. Barzun uses the word culture in a traditional sense—things of the mind and spirit, interest, and abilities acquired by training thought and by the effort that is used to cultivate one's self. The "cultivated" person in this sense has read books of many kinds, attended concerts and exhibits, takes time to ponder the mysteries of religion, the puzzles of philosophy, the perplexities of moral conduct, and the tentative definitions of the good life. Barzun holds that in the qualitative sense culture is declining.

The mistake Americans are making may be that we think we find the best evidence of high culture at colleges and universities. Instead, what is really there is "scholarship." One obvious result of this specialization of scholarship is that experts become specialists in a small subject area within their discipline, yet remain crass provincials throughout their lives. Indeed, this specialism in art, theater, prints and engraving, music, and other area has resulted in delegating culture to the experts. The truth is that art and culture are not at home in a university because culture proper and scholarship proper are diametrically opposed.

America is a young culture. In its haste to pursue the benefits of scientific technology and analysis America has failed to keep in the forefront of its mind the possibility of another entirely different way to think. Pascal called this way of thinking *esprit de finesse*. Barzun calls it intuitive understanding. This way of thinking does not analyze or break things down into parts but seizes upon the character of the whole. The understanding derived from the experiences is direct. It lacks definitions, principles, or numbers. Such an understanding is not readily conveyed to somebody else. When one spends a half hour studying a Salvador Dali one has a visual, spiritual experience. To put it into words is to reduce it to something else.

This book was written because of the feeling that mistaking scholarship for culture may bring down America's constitutional culture—scholarship fails to have a holistic world view. We sorely need individuals who speak for a return to the function of scholarship that provides readable texts, explaining obscurities and clearing up confusions in thinking. This cannot be done by teaching students to watch situation comedies or to buy product after product to assuage acquisitiveness.

Early man believed that the universe was ruled by gods and animals of supernatural power. According to the Egyptians, the sky god Nut ate the sun in the west, causing nightfall, and excreted it again in the east to start the following day. The human bicameral mind of early times probably heard voices and saw what we call hallucinations as a part of everyday life. Gods were everywhere. Aristotle taught that the sun, stars, and planets circled the earth—a view that held sway in Western culture for two thousand years. Today, scientists are searching for evidence to support a new theory or theories that the universe did—or did not—originate in a "big bang." Tomorrow, who knows which of today's scientific principles will be considered mythical errors? Ideas are the things that shape conduct. For humans the most significant real things are actually ideas of the mind that shape every person's conduct. Mankind's most epochal changes occurred when man's perception of the world in which we live was changed by some major event. Some great turning points include the rediscovery of classical civilization in the Middle Ages, the discovery of perspective painting, the invention of the printing press, the Copernican vision of the universe, the Industrial Revolution, the revolution of modern medicine, the development of the theory of evolution, and the rise of modern physics.

Another turning point is occurring now—the extension of the human capacity to use intelligence by the development of microcomputers and multistation networks. If we learn to use peaceful forms of conflict resolution, to reduce cross-cultural conflicts, it will radiate through telecommunications over the next few decades. We can strengthen the peculiar American invention that our unique constitutional culture derived from the U.S. Constitution and its workhorse, the political economy of democratic capitalism.

Conflict of the Sexes

The open constitutional culture of our American metroareas permits us to have healthy conflict as we seek to modulate the differences between man and woman. It is an external and internal complementarity. This willingness to have the conflict would be unthinkable in other cultures. In parts of Africa, for example, beautiful Kenya, female circumcision—the brutal act of a clitorectomy—is still practiced on pubescent females. When we see the battle of the sexes in America it ought to be perceived as more peaceful than elsewhere. After sexism is stripped away there will still be some real differences between men and women grounded in biology. Unfortunately, from Freud to Piaget the psychologists have judged women's moral development by standards derived from observations of male lives. The result has been a definition of women's moral judgments as illogical, irrational, and under-developed. Carol Gilligan's *In a Different Voice* presents a psychological theory of women's development. She celebrates a distinctly feminine moral voice, with its own inner logic. Women know much about women. This fact is ignored in a male-dominated world, yet the United States may lead in diffusing this knowledge. There are many distinguished women scientists who have devoted their lives to the study of brain, hormones, and behavior, human and animal. Each has suffered personally and professionally from the discrimination against women common throughout the world.

There is no society in the ethnographic or historical record in which men do nearly as much baby and child care as women. This is not to say anything, yet, about capacity. It is merely a statement of fact. Men are more violent than women. Women are more nurturant, at least toward infants and children, than to men. Elenor Maccoby and Carol Jacklin, in *The Psychology of Sex Differences,* review studies of sex differences in scores of dimensions, including tactile sensitivity, vision, discrim-ination, learning, social memory, general intellectual abilities, achievement-striving, self-esteem, crying, fear and timidity, helping, competition, conformity and imitation, to name only a few. For most of these dimensions it is emphatically stated that there is no consistent pattern of gender difference.

The main thrust of their book is to demolish cliche after cliche about the differences between boys and girls, men and women. Still, there is a difference in aggressive behavior. The strongest case for gender difference is made in the realm of aggressive behavior. Fifty-two of fifty-seven studies showed boys more aggressive than girls. On the other hand, in another category, called "nurturance and affiliation," in forty-five of fifty-two studies the girls and women showed more nurturance than boys and men.

Consider the evidence that comes from studies of hormones, behavior and the brain. The principal male gonadal hormone in mammals is testosterone. It belongs to a chemical class known as steroids. The steroid class also includes the two principal reproductive hormones, estradiol, the key estrogen in humans, and progesterone, the gestation-promoting substance secreted in massive quantities by the placenta and in lesser quantities in nonpregnant women by the ovaries. There is much in common between the testosterone's mode of action and that of the two female sex steroids. Sex steroid hormones affect behavior. We know they get around quite well in the brain. Using radioactive labeling, it has been easy to show not only that they pass from blood to the brain but also that they concentrate selectively in certain brain regions. That is, concentrations occur in brain regions that play an important role in courtship, sex, maternal behavior, and violence. Thus the behaviors in which the sexes most differ are the ones most subject to influence by testosterone, estradiol, and progesterone.

Alice Rossey has accepted this idea. A family sociologist who became dissatisfied with sociologist Emile Durkheim's dictum that only social facts can explain social facts, Rossey began to take seriously the notion that at least some social facts might be explained by biological facts. She finds that some observed gender differences in social behavior, for example, in parenting, are clearly attributable to endocrino-logical factors. From a hormonal perspective, nurturance has not been as well-studied as aggressiveness, which is in some ways the antithesis of nurturance. No one with any experience in this field thinks there is a simple relationship between testosterone and aggression. But most people now accept that some such relationship does exist.

The focus of discussion in this text is the leaps in knowledge about the relationship of hormonal flows to humans and what they are. In 1973, for the first time, it was shown that male and female brains differed structurally. The most forward portion of the hypothalamus in male and female rats differs in the density of synaptic connections among local neurons. The difference was in a region concerned with the brain's regulation of the very gonadal hormones we have been looking at. Taken with the increasing evidence from animal experiments, it appears that humans may experience psychosexual differentiation affecting both behavior and the brain as a result of hormones acting near or before birth. Scientists have discovered that gender differences result from male-female differences in the biology of the brain as well as from the way we are raised. Women have superior language skills. The corpus callosum, a thick bundle of nerves connecting the left and right hemispheres of the brain, is wider among women and probably facilitates more rapid crosstalk and intuitive flows through more rapid hormonal transfers.

Anthropologist Ashley Montagu, author of *The Natural Superiority of Women,* is convinced that women are the superior sex. Montagu sees women as having a superior immune system. That seems to be supported by their much lower ratio in the spread of the incidence of AIDS in the heterosexual population. Montagu feels women also have superior verbal skills. Furthermore, Montagu feels, as I do, that men suffer from a biological inferiority complex. Since they cannot conceive children, only ideas, it prompts their drive to work. A male proud of something, says "It's my baby," or he "conceives" or "gives birth" to something.

Montagu sees the women who are overachieving in our present culture as taking on masculine values. He feels that women have to remember that feminine qualities are human qualities. They are the kind of qualities that women should be teaching men when they are children. Women should not be tempted away from their true loving capabilities by the false idols created by men—the acquisition of things and riches.

In *The Aquarian Conspiracy* Marilyn Ferguson encourages the growing idea of "networking," the promotion of affiliations of kindred spirits throughout a metroarea, a nation, and the world by telephone or mail. Women have a strength and talent at networking that men need to learn to emulate. Most men have found that their women friends are much more adept at using the telephone for friendly conversation than men. The telephone is the backyard fence of people throughout a metroarea and women are better at using it.

Plato believed that the rational soul of man, "the divinest part of us," must be in the brain. For 2,400 years man followed this male-dominated, wrong-headed notion. Plato attributed a superior function to the male brain. Plato then made the wrong assumption that genetic material must be formed in that place. He postulated that the brain was the organ that produced semen. This notion had such longevity that it can be seen in a sketch by Leonardo da Vinci drawn 1,900 years later. This paradigm gave the female brain no role at all and regarded women only as flower pots for male seeds. The general acceptance of this paradigm led to the exclusion of women from the governance of academic, religious, and governmental institutions for millennia. This is the best example that Richard Bergland gives, in his brilliant treatise *The Fabric of the Mind,* that the form of human culture and our civilizations can be shaped, in this case misshaped, by the scientific views concerning the human brain.[1]

In the past century, the United States has moved rapidly from an extractive mineral and agricultural economy based on manufacturing toward a service-dominated society with emphasis on the accumulation and use of knowledge. As the function of human settlements is changing toward a service orientation, much more attention must be given to reducing urban stress. We need to improve the external environment that is the milieu in which humans work and play. Stress reduction results not only in happier people but also in more productive people, people more capable of using their imagination and creativity. I do not seek to idealize the environment that we have created in our modern metroareas. I seek instead to emphasize the need to develop and implement public health plans. Their function would be to improve the external environment of the cities and therefore the quality of its inhabitants' mental health.

As Desmond Morris says in *The Human Zoo,* "Under normal conditions, in their natural habitats, wild animals do not mutilate themselves, masturbate, attack their offspring, develop stomach ulcers, become fetishists, suffer from obesity, form homosexual pair bonds, or commit murder. . . . The zoo animal in a cage exhibits all these abnormalities that we know so well from our human companions. Clearly then the city is not a concrete jungle, it is a human zoo."

"Leisure"

In his classic *The Harried Leisure Class,* Staffan B. Linder makes a penetrating analysis of the relationship between increasing availability of goods and services and decreasing discretionary time to use them. We once expected that as general welfare increased people would become successively less interested in further rises in income and would show more interest in other kinds of pursuits. It was thought that one result of economic affluence would be a more tranquil and harmonious manner of life. The exact opposite has happened. The pace is quickening and our lives are becoming steadily more hectic. Almost everyone in our modern American metroareas feels the growing pressure on the available hours of the day. Linder observed that we have responded, for example, by changing our attitudes toward eating. Cooking is a time-consuming process, but it can give one pleasure. However, most people have abandoned cooking for thawing. Linder makes similar observations about lovemaking. Historically, love took time. To court and to love someone satisfactorily was a game. There were many and time-consuming phases to lovemaking. Modern love affairs, however, are more efficient. Those who complain that women in these days are "easy" fail to understand that in a hectic age, women must accelerate to save time for themselves and for their male friends.

There has been a sorry neglect of research into how the average city worker's so-called "leisure time" is actually used. Considerable frustration, even anxiety and stress, is experienced by city dwellers in carrying out tasks imposed upon them to be an effective, cost-efficient consumer. Voice mail that imposes touch-tone duties on the caller is a classic example of the economist's view that "large-scale organizations have the right to use and abuse the time of the caller." We ignore the social cost of consuming to our detriment.

Metroareas and Leisurely Social Intercourse

Americans have misused our affluence by destroying the extended family in the reach for maximum individual privacy. We have more single-person households than at any other time or place in history. At the same time, the central nodes of activity in America's metroareas are crowded with the hurried traffic of people and cars by day but empty late at night. People return to their homes, as turtles withdrawn into their shells. This is not so in Chinese cities. There everyone takes to the streets in early evening for conversation, a low-cost, healthy form of human entertainment. In the United States, at home, Americans enjoy the warmth of family life and, on occasion, the company of carefully chosen friends. Nonetheless, there is often little conversation: the television usually dominates.

Unfortunately, domestic conflict and the domestic crises that result are over-burdening more of the poor and disadvantaged households in this nation. This is because poor families live in dwelling units that tend to be of much higher density than that of most Americans. Yet activities in the streets and meeting places such as cafes or game arcades are discouraged by public authorities because of our fear of street gangs and crime. Thus, we have increased stress on the urban poor. We force them to look to their family for surcease and amelioration of stress. At the same time, we deny them the outlets of street activities and meeting places such as cafes and taverns, which worked so well in the nineteenth-century industrial city. We should spend public funds to set up free or subsidized "penny" electronic arcades, well-supervised, to encourage playful activities among the poor teenagers in our poverty enclaves. The overstimulated responses to the boredom of unemployment and the lack of sanctuary in the home could be diminished by making the streets and meeting places more attractive and enjoyable.

Stress

Individual vulnerability interacts with organizational structure and practices to produce stress. The foci of stress include superego conflict, arousal of intense feelings, developmental issues of childhood and adulthood, rivalry, aging and obsolescence, life-cycle changes and unintended losses, violations of contract, neurotic conflict, character, and sex role issues. People experience stress and guilt when they must circumvent policies and channels to accomplish their tasks, are required to implement policies they feel are unfair, must lower product or service quality due to economic pressure, or must treat consumers or colleagues in ways that they find unconscionable. This guilt may be diminished by finding a rationale or pretext upon which to base angry and sometimes hostile behavior. The result of events that widen the gap between self-image and the ego ideal is a lowering of self-esteem.

Prolonged stress endangers health. Those who are burdened by long-standing and excessive feelings of anger may show behavior characterized by scapegoating, overcontrolling others, sadistic attack, accidents, absenteeism, resistance to supervision, or, given sufficient self-suppression, chronic high blood pressure and its attendant ills.

Thomas Holmes and Richard Rahe compiled a scale of life events and stress. In case after case, the year in which a major stressful life event occurred was followed by the onset of a serious illness.[2] Hans Selye, a preeminent figure in modern stress research, helped to give stress some of its modern meaning. He calls stress a nonspecific response of the body to any demand upon it. The response is independent of the specific activity that caused the rise in requirements. Those urban humans involved in traffic congestion understand that particular activity. They are aware of their rising aggression and the need to control it. This specific demand for adaptation is the essence of urban stress. The brain recognizes the attack of the stressor, which may be anything from the approach of a lion to the appearance of a threatening office memorandum. In contrast, Brugh Joy has hypothesized that a sense of well-being might even stimulate the efficacy of the immunological mechanism. It, along with other factors yet undiscovered, works to help the body cope with and end any disease process. I urge that it would be cost-effective for American society to reduce external stressors such as crime, ill-housing, traffic congestion, and water and sewage problems.

Thomas Mann, the celebrated German author, once said that the human animal likes sex, food, and drink much more than work, but it is work alone that he can do continuously for eight hours a day. Perhaps that is how humans avoid boredom. What can we do to improve the environment of our cities in order to raise the chances that men and women would seek to achieve the spiritual potential within them? Jean Houston and her husband Robert Masters have been exploring ways to extend and refine our sensory and perceptual capacities and the self-modulation of pleasure and pain.[3] They have discovered what many psychiatrists, psychologists, and other mental health workers apparently do not perceive—the vital balance. One cannot have a successful and permanent extension of mental, psychological, and spiritual capacity without working toward an enhancement of physiological capacity. One reason that talking therapies do not work as well as they might is because they do not usually fully involve the body in the therapeutic process.

How can we bring on the change? The change can come by acceptance that all humans are alike. Mahatma Gandhi said that we are all brothers (and sisters). In *The Fabric of the Mind,* Richard Bergland gives this idea new meaning.

> I am not certain what force came into my life that led me to go deeper into the relationships between the brain and the pituitary, but eventually I came to the point where I knew as much about this minuscule part of the body as anybody on earth. I say that without conceit, and would tell any young person that with enough dedication, focus, gumption and time anybody can reach and shape a frontier.

Houston calls people like Bergland "people of the breakthrough"—men and women who find in the present period of epochal change an extraordinary opportunity for seeding and nurturing both personal and social transformation. She finds these people everywhere, in citizens' volunteer associations, in storefront self-help agencies, in teachers who stay after school to help the child society forgets, in physicians trying to treat the whole person. Young and old and in between, from all walks of life these people demonstrate remarkable similarities in both commitment and belief. They have little interest in protecting their own turf. They work freely in networks to exchange ideas, information, and resources. They daily rid themselves of unneeded rancor and deliberately pursue ways, both mental and physical, of penetrating deeply into the depths of which they are a part. Nor are they afraid of the bouts of despair that occasionally attend any quest for the pattern that connects. They know that this suffering is integral to the coming of wisdom.

I proceed from the presumption that life is a psychosomatic process. Since the dawn of culture our human ancestors have each used their unique brains to overcome their physical limitations and to improve their environment. Humans are brains, minds, and souls, and they prefer to live in cities, artificial environments we have formed to overcome human biological shortcomings. These cities do not work well today, but they can. The appalling complexity of today's metropolitan life engenders psychosomatic diseases in metroarea inhabitants. Let us then consider the human brain and how it reacts to its environment. This will enable us to turn to some tentative ideas about improving the quality of America's metroareas.

6. The Architecture of the Brain

Steven Hawking's body is wasted by the Lou Gehrig nerve disease. He weighs under a hundred pounds and lives in a motorized wheelchair. He personifies what is best about humans. Stephen Hawking uses his amazing brain! A Cambridge don, Hawking is a loving family man with compassion for his fellow humans. He has done what no cheetah, dolphin, elephant, or gorilla could do. Steven Hawking has an amazing brain that has gone on tour through time, space, and knowledge to encompass the universe. He has provided the human race with a better understanding of the creation and human existence. Millions have enjoyed his explanation of the creation of the universe in his bestselling book. Hawking's life is a triumphant march up heights only his brain could scale. The way he has lived has been a blessing to us.

The brain is about the size of a grapefruit. It is one organ, related to others in our body. It regulates all bodily functions. It controls our most primitive behavior— eating, sleeping, and keeping warm. It is also responsible, of course, for our most sophisticated activities—the creation of civilization, with its music, art, science, and language. Our hopes, thoughts, emotions, and personality are all lodged somewhere inside the brain.

There are about one hundred billion nerve cells in the brain. In a single brain the number of possible interconnections between these cells is greater than the number of atoms in the universe. The brain was evolved, over time, into three somewhat generalized divisions. The first, the hind brain, is the oldest part of the brain. It includes most of the brain's stem. The second is the midbrain, which is the uppermost portion of the brain stem. The third is the forebrain. It contains some older structures, but it is primarily made up of the most recently evolved areas of the brain, including the cerebrum and its covering, the cerebral cortex. Humans evolved the brain to keep themselves alive.

The highest level of the brain is the cerebral cortex. The surface of the cerebrum, made up of more neurons than any other brain structure, is called the cortex. The cortex is only about an eighth of an inch thick. It is intricately folded. Some call it the rind of the brain, which may be appropriate because the brain is about the size of a grapefruit. The cortex performs the functions that greatly increase adaptability. It is where decisions are made, perceptions of the world organized, individual experiences stored in memory, speech produced and understood, paintings seen, and music heard. We know little about how the cortex works.

The cerebrum makes up a large part of the brain by volume. It is divided into two hemispheres; each is ordinarily responsible for the opposite half of the body, but not always. In the lay sense, the left-hand side of the brain controls movements of and receives information from the right-hand side of the body and vice-versa. It has been recently discovered that this is not true for some left-handed people. The two hemispheres are connected by a group of nerve fibers called the corpus callosum, the largest fiber pathway in the brain. It is a "bridge" of some three hundred million nerve fibers.

Each hemisphere of the cerebrum is similarly divided into four areas called lobes. At the rear of each hemisphere is the occipital lobe. Visual information is sent from the eyes to the occipital lobes, where it is analyzed for indentation, position and movement. The temporal (near the temples) lobes of each hemisphere, about the size of poker chips, are responsible for hearing. They are often called the auditory cortex. Other temporal lobe functions appear to involve perception and memory. When the temporal lobes are electrically stimulated, some people report the feeling of being in two places at once; memory of an event and the present coexist in the person's consciousness. The frontal lobe, just behind the forehead, is the largest of the four lobes. It oversees much of the rest of the brain's activity. It has an especially rich connection with the limbic system. The frontal lobe is primarily involved with planning, decision making, and purposeful behavior. The parietal lobes, located toward the rear of each hemisphere, seems to be where we assemble our world. It is probably here that letters come together as words and words get put together into thoughts.

Although there seems to be a division of labor between the hemispheres of the brain, this division is not absolute. The left hemisphere of the brain is currently perceived as much more involved and more proficient in language, sequential thought, logic and deductive reasoning than the right. The right hemisphere is much more involved in spatial abilities and "gestalt" thinking—imagination, innovation, and creation—than the left.

What the brain chiefly regulates is the body. Our brain is the largest, relative to body size of all land mammals. Yet, it is not just the size of the brain that matters. It is especially important in what respects the brain is large. Our cerebral cortex, the uppermost part of the brain, the rind, is much larger and more intricate than in any other animal. It is the most distinctive part of the human. It enables us to carry ourselves beyond our past and create our own environment as we participate in changing it.

The biggest change that has come over brain research in recent years is a realization that the brain is also a complex chemical system. Some of the chemical substances that exist in the brain are neurotransmitters, which facilitate the transmission of nerve impulses. Other chemicals inhibit this transmission. Some brain chemicals are neuroregulators, which modulate the sensitivity of target cells to such substances. Other chemicals control the rate at which key substances are produced or reabsorbed. Chemical substances usually move slowly compared with electrical impulses. They mediate changes over hours rather than seconds, sometimes much longer. Their action is probably not indiscriminate, but targeted to particular cells. A reassessment of our whole conception of how the brain functions is in train because of these discoveries.[1]

Today, most brain scientists know that the brain is a gland. The outmoded paradigm that the brain is an electrically driven computer is too narrowly focused. It was a mere starting premise to all brain doctors. Increasingly it is clear the electrical signals that are involved in pain are akin to the sparks that are produced by a fire. Hormones in the brain govern the fires and produce these sparks. This new paradigm for pain modulation was named "gate control," because one of these systems "closes" gates after the first news of pain reaches the brain. Another "opens" gates after the first pain message is sent to the brain. The power within humans to control these neural gateways is not yet understood.

We know that the Indian fakir lying on a bed of nails has developed control over his pain. He can modulate gates. He can close them at will and limit the number of pain signals that reach his brain. In the United States some facilitators are conducting workshops during which Americans walk on hot coals without harm or pain. Yet, in the United States in the 1990s, the harried housewife who is insecure, lonely, and depressed, cannot muster the brain energy to put any pressure on the brain side of the gates that control pain. Her gates stay open. Any sensation can pass through the gates and on to the brain. Backache, neckache, and headache are the natural consequences of this situation. These pains are not imagined. They are real. They are the result, often, of urban stress. The palliatives of drugs are a poor and expensive substitute for greater insight into gate controls. Stress relief can be learned. Public-school educators could use "quiet times" to teach Eastern yoga meditation techniques. They could use biofeedback machines to enable urban Americans to modulate effects of external stress.

In *The Anatomy of an Illness* Norman Cousins describes his experiences with the healing power of what he calls "joy-laughter." Diagnosed terminally ill, Cousins used a variety of techniques, including watching Marx brothers films, to stimulate himself to laughter. His severe bone-and-joint problems were driven from his body. We are on the edge of an important breakthrough to understanding the hormonal back-and-forth flow between the brain, the body, the mind, and the soul.

Today brain-scientists could do more for us in the way of important breakthroughs than space scientists. In 1984, Richard Bergland predicted that physicians and scientists will measure hormones in brain ventricular fluid (with catheters). They will then be able to link detected hormones to specific diseases and devise modern techniques to restock the mind's hormonal pantries.

It is conceivable that if we would treat urban stress as external disruptions and distortions in normal brain functioning, we could seek public action to create an expanded public health service. Much progress could be made in the pursuit of happiness. Why not develop public policies to diminish urban stress? We could produce a happier human being able to function more effectively. The study of hormones may someday produce pharmaceuticals for hormonal therapy to minimize the impact of external urban stress on our internal beings.

We cannot afford to wait, however. We should take action on the external stressors. The first step would be to end the separation of psychiatry from neurobiology. As Richard Restak has said in *The Brain,*

There is no separate and overseeing "medium" as I write these words. Instead there is the me—now—writing—the—word. This me corresponds to my brain, which is engaged in a constant and ever-changing activity. The "I" or the mind is a fiction, it gives the illusion of permanence to my ever-changing perceptions. The use of "my" and "mind" in the previous sentences is part of this fiction. There is simply nothing to prove that anything exists other than the brain interacting with some aspect of external or internal reality. So, it should not be surprising that brain scientists haven't yet discovered the "seed of the mind." It is not likely that they will.[2]

To Restak "mind" is nothing more than a term employed to describe some functions of the brain. Brain research isn't going to define "mind" any more accurately than turning over all the turf in Ireland is likely turn up a colony of leprechauns. However, as brain researcher Sir John Eccles points out,

> Neuroscience, rightly understood as an aspect of the biological and not the social sciences, doesn't make any promises about such things as the mind. The term "mind" is used in the same way as terms such as "inflation," "peace," and "progress" are useful ideas about processes in life. One cannot locate "inflation" within a department of economics. One cannot travel to the United Nations to interview "peace." Put slightly differently, to deny that a mind exists separately from a brain doesn't imply any position at all on the existence of a soul, God, or a hereafter—those are within the bailiwick of theologians and the religiously committed. Neuroscience cannot and should not bolster or undermine these beliefs.

Increasing knowledge ought not diminish our capacity for awe and wonder. As we close the twentieth century, those who keep truth at the center of their island of knowledge must now contemplate the wealth of new information about the mind coming from the "truth finders" at Bergland's shoreline of wonder. Berglund asks, "How will those who keep the 'truth' deal with the evidence that the thought emerging from the minds spring from hormonal harmonies—from molecules of many kinds coming together in many places? Will they recognize the cosmic entity that orchestrates the anatomical trysts of the hormones that steer the mind?"

What force moves these molecules? Out of a question can grow a new beginning. The miracle of hormonal activity, like the miracle of gravity and memory, demands a new "force" of some kind—a unifying force. It is not explained by any of the four forces known to physicists: the "strong" force that holds together the major pieces of the atomic nucleus; the "weak" force, which influences the little atomic pieces; "gravity," the attraction between large amounts of mass; and "electromagnetic" force, which permeates all matter. Many scientists are convinced there is a fifth force that unites and drives the other four. Nonetheless, Einstein went to his grave trying to prove a "unified field theory" that would bring the other four forces together. It remains inexplicable.[3]

If we accept that the human animal's actions are affected by the good health of the human brains that live in their bodies, if we conclude that our bodies and brains and minds are one, it follows that the pursuit of happiness requires a good environment to pursue a high-quality life. In this way we can begin a new approach for governing metroareas throughout the world. The American constitutional culture provides a unique atmosphere in which to work on the resolution of this age-old conflict.

Consider the American welfare system, which depends on a large number of supervisory staff who act like policemen. One of their major functions is to see that welfare recipients have no other funds outside the welfare handout. We actively discourage the presence of a male adult in the household. Our policies encourage some welfare mothers to repeat pregnancies for emotional security and the self-esteem of being a mother. If we could find a less intrusive way to provide a minimum level of income while strengthening the work ethic and the dignity of work by providing day care centers, we could minimize the invasion of privacy and the degrading nature of the supervised public handout. By providing welfare mothers and their children with a minimal standard of food, shelter, clothing, and medical care, we could improve their chances of becoming healthy human beings. We cannot measure what such changes would do to improve the mental health of urban dwellers. If urban services and facilities were required to be responsive to their users, or customers, or clients, would we see a healthier response by the users? The human brains on welfare are a high percentage of our future perception of reality. It will yield healthy dividends for our society to learn to respect and provide dignity for all American brains.

Celebrating the Human Brain

In 1972 Joseph Bogen proposed the creation of a giant walk-through brain. Ornstein and Thomas joined with David Macaulay in illustrating such a brain large enough to wander through its spaces, systems, and structures. Organizations such as Walt Disney Productions, creators of theme parks such as Disney World, can create a dramatic and enjoyable way of gaining an understanding of man's common heritage and the complex organization of the brain's interior parts. Bogen and others proposed a replica of the human brain that would be almost fifty stories tall and about one and a half times the length of a football field. Such a dramatic tourist attraction would be an exciting way to convince all human beings of their unifying identity, regardless of race, color, creed, national origin, sex, or age. The pharmaceutical companies could join in creating such a structure at an attractive metropolitan location. It would be a fitting contrast to space-center blastoff sites. It would evoke Alexander Pope's aphorism that, "The proper study of mankind is man." As Charles De Gaulle once said in response to the question of whether he felt the United States would reach the moon, "I have little interest in that . . . I feel man has a greater distance to travel within himself." An act of even greater wisdom would be to combine this proposed "Brain Park" with an adjoining park containing Buckminster Fuller's World Peace Game, an experiential place for resolving global conflicts without war. What a wonderful way to celebrate the year 2000! It could be a real money maker and profits could be devoted to relieving world hunger and malnutrition among younger brains.

If the human balance of reason and emotion were not pretty good, we could not have prospered as we have. Most humans are successful, most of the time, at sustaining the right emotional tone for everyday life. Often they do it without lapsing into apathy or unreasoning, fanatic idolatry. The record is impressive. Being inherently more emotional, humans have achieved civilized conduct by enforcing prolonged learning. Our unusual reasoning ability, skills of hand, and powers of language modulate our emotional behavior. Animals know nothing of either romantic love or the legalized murder of warfare, except possibly baboons. Any reading of history or observation of our present follies and wickedness shows that man is not biologically perfect. Obviously human aggressiveness is deadly dangerous to us all in our present world. Nevertheless, who would dare to promise that excision of our capacity for anger, righteousness, or unrighteousness, would not be as potentially dehumanizing as the loss of love?

Body-Driven Stress

So far I have emphasized the effect of the brain on the body. Can the circulation or process flow the other way? Can the body influence the mind? There is evidence that the body's muscles issue referent discharges to the brain. Even facial muscles do it. It is not out of the question that posture influences mental attitude. Look friendly and you become friendly. Leaders of men and women operate on the assumption that the external world influences the internal one. Army leaders assume that a unit that is smartly turned out and drills well will have high morale. A unit that is slack in attitude will be slack in discipline. Residential units in New York hospitals have discovered that windows, walls, bedding, and furniture must be carefully maintained and scratches, tears, and breakages promptly removed or disorder will follow.

I urge that metroareas should be a place for people to pursue happiness. Philip Zimbardo states that, to be more responsive to the needs of people, psychology does not have to give up its efforts to understand basic human phenomena.[4] I add that to be more responsive to the needs of people, public policymakers for our metroareas should make greater efforts to understand basic human phenomena. Zimbardo provides some thoughts on emerging areas of concern for the remainder of the century:

1) The electronics revolution will transform our work and our schools, our patterns of leisure and home life, and our sense of self-identity more than any technological innovations in history. It is happening now. For example, video games are proving so addictive to young people that they may not only be socially isolating but may actually encourage violence. On the other hand, as stress-alleviators the games could be reprogrammed to promote cooperative action among several players, e.g., by focusing on mountain-climbing rescue operations, or saving people during a hurricane, earthquake, or flood instead of performing Nintendo destruction. Such electronic toys should be made available "free" to lower-class children. It would diminish the educational gap between the children of affluent parents and those of lower-class parents. Perhaps our American computer wizards, Steve Jobs, Steve Wozniak, Bill Gates, and others, could join in producing electronic games to promote competitive/cooperative behavior.

2) We should permit the work of cognitive psychology to influence major changes to our educational curricula. Children can be taught strategies for more effective studying, for improving memory, for avoiding pitfalls in problem solving, and for making less-biased inferences and more accurate predictions. School texts could be much better designed to improve story comprehension and the ability to generalize across domains of knowledge in different settings. This could reduce crosscultural

conflict and provide skills in conflict resolution.

3) Cable television could be put to better use. People could gain access to expert therapists, social skills trainers, and other professionals who are willing to undertake the responsibility of "therapy for the masses." Sex therapy by Dr. Ruth is an excellent example. This would be a revolutionary change from the limited, wasteful, extravagant, one-on-one model of traditional psychotherapy. Many clinicians and health psychologists have been advocating community mental health programs that emphasize preventive treatment and health maintenance.

4) Developmental psychologists have made most of us aware of the importance of early attachments for infants and young children. On the other hand, scant attention has been paid to how we might encourage meaningful attachments among adults.

America has been a nation that loves institutional answers to questions about social change. But institutions seldom generate paradigm shifts. New paradigms are usually made by adventurous individuals, risk-takers willing to try new paths toward intellectual good sense. Such humans are usually driven by the pattern-dependent mental qualities of searching, probing, balancing, and questioning. The twentieth century taught us by way of Hitler, Stalin, Castro, Idi Amin, Somoza, Marcos, Brezhnev, and Beria, among others, that the right of self-help must remain viable. It is a tragic necessity. There is a threat to humans of governance by modern fascism that poses under many guises. It has evolved in response to certain worldwide stresses after World War I, as monarchy died, and, sadly, with it the ennobling human spirit of *noblesse oblige*.

Fascism

Fascism has no religious ethos equivalent to the Marxist *Das Kapital*. However, as Hannah Arendt has pointed out in *Origins of Totalitarianism*, fascism finds its roots in man's fear of death, his need for security, and his common willingness to turn his power over to others. To Gwin Owens, editor of the *Baltimore Sun*, fascism is essentially a totalitarian state created by an amalgam of powerful private interests for their self-aggrandizement. One definition he provides is that under Communism the state controls production while under fascism producers control the state. In the life of the ordinary citizen in the old Soviet Union and any other fascist state, the effect has been much the same.

I focus on fascism's psychological allure. Fascism is based on super-patriotism, to which many citizens respond with fervor. The principle psychological weapon most modern fascist states have used has been fear of Godless Communism and other socialist states. In the same way the Soviet *nomenklatura* used fear of American "capitalistic imperialism."

Assume for a moment that America's most powerful corporations and media barons acquire enough wealth and influence to dominate both unions and Congress. Eventually they achieve such power that they can control the outcome of presidential elections and thwart any other force that challenges their leadership, including whatever independent press remains. Over time, the country becomes ruled by an oligarchy that, under the worst possible scenario, is as repressive as Communism could be. The United States of 1992 is far removed from the hysteria that engulfed Germany in 1933. Nonetheless, America has the potential for becoming a fascist state. A synchronicity of bad events could bring it on: the collapse of stock values on Wall Street brought on by panic selling among program traders, more failures in the farm economy, collapse of the fragile federally insured financial services system, followed by either deflation or hyperinflation. Our constitutional culture empowers the elected representatives to make any change in our choice of a political economy. This could result in rapid amendatory changes in the constitutional culture.

We have large corporations becoming more centralized and getting closer to the center of power in the White House. Unions have been greatly weakened. Our patriotism is called upon, with regularity, to whip up support for military actions in Lebanon, Grenada, and Nicaragua, the Persian Gulf, and elsewhere around the globe. Our Congress is under severe attack for its opposition to the imperious foreign policy of a president who views himself first as a commander-in-chief and second as the head of a constitutional culture. If we weigh the latent elements in the United States, fascism remains by far a greater threat than Communism. We have been alerted against Communism; it is cryptofascists who could take over without our realizing it.

Arendt provides us with an important insight into the powerful grasp that totalitarianism can have on the minds of a nation's citizens. A totalitarian government's open criminality notwithstanding, its central power rests on mass support. A recent publication of secret reports on German public opinion during World War II edited by Heinz Boberac is very revealing. Boberac shows that the population, including Konrad Adenauer, the first president of democratic Germany after the war, was remarkably well-informed about all of the country's so-called "secrets." They knew of the massacres of Jews in Poland, the preparation for the attack on Russia, and much more. Further, Boberac's analysis concludes, the average German "remained able to form independent opinions." But this did not in the least weaken the general support of the Hitler regime. Mass support for totalitarianism comes neither from ignorance nor from brainwashing.

Arendt notes that in modern states, with representative government and popular voting among the masses, it is often possible to have an alliance between capital and the hedonistic mob. Fascist leadership engages in completely unprincipled power politics in their electioneering techniques. A mass of people available to those who are free of political principles may grow so large that it can surpass the ability of humane and compassionate people (the responsible masses) to encourage tolerance and oppose bigotry. The mob would serve up its votes in docile subservience to the power elite that delivers consumer delights.

People who prefer to be blind followers may also be lacking in cultural depth and breadth of education. They attribute to the would-be leaders a supernatural capacity. It is a search for the perfect mother or father figure, and an unwillingness to face themselves and their frailties as humans. Tragically, most of those who are handed such power by the fascistic masses do not understand the crucial concept of *noblesse oblige.*

Time is running out. Unlike less powerful nations, the United States still has a choice. We may be leading the world into oligarchic, fascistic capitalism posing under the guise of a happy fascism, or we may be the leading edge of an epochal cultural change in which society will focus on the growth and development of autonomous individuals. In 1988 a bemused, somewhat nonchalant press reported

SHOWING SUPPORT: As Donna Mason (right) of Stone Mountain folds her hands, her husband, Bob, holds a bumper sticker backing the contras, and son, Matthew, holds a toy gun while the three listen to pro-contra speeches in a rally for Oliver North at the State Farmers Market in Forest Park on Saturday.

that Oliver North and his profiteering friends had flaunted the Constitution and violated the laws of Congress with their covert operations. The "mob" hurrahed! Olliemania prevailed. We know the mob can be organized to the end of subverting the democratic process. Photographer John Spink caught the mood of such a fervent crowd "showing support" for their noble leader, the video hero, Ollie North.

In *Friendly Fascism: The New Face of Power in America,* Bertrum Gross offers a provocative view of the growth of a new type of totalitarian process in America, and, possibly, in the world at large. Gross argues there is a process in which the interest of big business and big government are aligning closely to form a new network of power. Gross calls it "friendly fascism." Unlike the fascist movements of Italy, Germany, and Japan of a half century ago, friendly fascism requires no dictator, no glorification of the state, no repression. Friendly fascism operates much more subtly—by operating a powerful oligarchy outside of the democratic process that manipulates that process and permeates the government. Democratic participation in the decisionmaking process is subverted through the control of information flows designed to misinform the lower and middle class and thus gain their support for plans that are not in their interest.

Gross argues that the masses (read Arendt's mob) support the concentration of power in the hands of the business government oligarchy. The American masses resent the rise of third-world demands, recession uncertainties, inflation, and numerous subsurface social conflicts. Gross invokes no naive conspiracy theories to explain his analyses, nor does he suggest that friendly fascism is already here. He simply urges that steps can be taken to stem this powerful political undertow. Sadly, most Americans who favor the democratic processes fail to perceive there are millions in America who already prefer friendly fascism.

The Civil War, also known as the Slaveholders Rebellion of 1861-65, did not bring an end to the plantation management model of governance. Its management methods still dominate the South, the largest region of the United States in terms of population. The governing myths perceived in Georgia, North Carolina, Alabama, and the like by those born and raised in the South are different from those believed in other parts of our American representative republic. Fortunately, the millions of Yankee migrants who have "invaded" the South since World War II are insisting on major cultural changes. The natives are finding it unsettling. The South is becoming more democratic.

Nonetheless, the power of the has-been southern aristocracy is not yet eliminated. For more than a century it has placed an oppressing hand on the attempts of lower- and middle-class whites and blacks that has hindered them from achieving status through merit. For more than 150 years this southern aristocracy has sent its children, men and a few women, to Harvard, Princeton, Virginia, and Yale. Simultaneously it used its power to prevent the improvement of public education in the South that trains poorer whites and blacks. For many decades the only way for a lower- or middle-class white to achieve any kind of status or success in the South was either to go North or to become a sycophant of this inbred aristocracy. But the post–*Brown* v. *Board of Education* South, the "New South," has made extraordinary strides to create high-quality colleges and universities. There has been a surging forward of a new middle class seeking to create a major educational base for the future generations of the region.

American politics is now dominated by a new politics of affluence. The major political parties are narrowing their bases. They are ignoring both "tails" of that "bell-shaped curve" that is the normal statistical distribution of the voting population. First, the parties ignore active opinion makers at the extreme right of the normal statistical distribution and, second, they ignore the powerless lower strata that is the left of that same normal distribution of the statistical universe of eligible voters.

Modern-day political consultants are appealing to the younger, upwardly mobile professionals who are not frustrated, alienated, or unhappy. Instead they live with a sense of security and self-satisfaction and a desire to be a part of the upper middle class. Both the New Right and New Left of American politics have roots in yuppie protest-discontent born in the 1960s. The focus of the new American politics, both left and right, is a politics of values rather than interests that thrives by playing to a sense of resentment.

The New Right resents that the country is being run by relativists and subversives, not by moral and patriotic people "like us." The nouveau-riche ("yuppie") culture of Orange County, a vast suburb of metropolitan Los Angeles, first made viable the candidacies of Barry Goldwater (1964) and Ronald Reagan (1966). The New Left's political ethos is to resent the fact that the country is being run by bigots and warmongers, not by tolerant, peace-loving people "like us." Witness, at the other extreme, Marin County, north of San Francisco, the home of the laid-back and fashionable liberal upper middle class. Marin County regularly votes about 20 percentage points more Democratic than conservative Orange County.

The difference is one of acculturation, not class. The prevailing culture of Orange County is that of business and patriotism. Marin County attracts high-income professionals, often educated at elite universities. Their family origins tend to be in the Northeast. Orange County, near Los Angeles, and Marin County, near San Francisco, illustrate a pattern that can be found all over the nation in various metroareas. These are the two distinct political subcultures of the American upper middle class. Both the New Right and the New Left are seeking a realignment of the lower middle class, the working class. It is a quiet battle for the minds of Americans. The new American conservative coalition is an attempt to ally "country-club businessmen" with "rednecks" and fundamentalists. Lower-status people are not being left out by the new politics. They are being divided by it. The new-style American liberals are appealing to economic populism and an expansion of political rights while the New Right is using racial fear and "law-and-order" sentiment to reap a happy fascism based on fear.

Paid political professionals are giving political candidates greater access to Arendt's mob. They are clearly affecting the quality of political campaigning for the worse. They come in four basic types—strategists, pollsters, media consultants, and direct mail experts. Some see the consultants as new political bosses. However, the old bosses such as Richard Daley, the elder, had real power, derived from the individual precinct and voter. Consultants, however, are comparatively interchangeable. Most have no ethical or political commitment. They are more like guns for hire or high-priced lawyers, than political bosses.

Stanford's "VALS" Analysis

Paid political professionals operate in a world of target audiences. They speak of, say, an "achiever" target audience, and when they do, they are "talking VALS"— talking of one of the consumer types identified by the values and lifestyles program of Stanford Research Institute, located in Menlo Park, California. The Stanford VALS typology divides Americans into nine lifestyles or types that are grouped into four categories based on their self-images, their aspirations, and to some extent the products they use. VALS is a systematic attempt to analyze the values and lives of Americans to discover why people believe and act as they do. In late 1987 the Los Angeles *Times* announced a refined, eleven-lifestyles typology. It is not significantly different from the original nine-lifestyle system detailed here:

1) Survivors and sustainers account for about twenty-five million people, or about 11 percent of the population. Need-driven, survivors tend to be self-disparaging, depressed, withdrawn, mistrustful, rebellious, and conservative. Most are poorly educated, ill, and old. They are most likely to think things are changing too fast. The sustainers tend to be angry, combative people who feel left out of things. Unlike survivors, however, they have not given up hope. They are the least satisfied with their financial status of any lifestyle group and the most anxious to get ahead economically. Many sustainers tend to be "street wise" and often are involved in the underground economy.

2) The belongers, the largest single subgroup, numbering about sixty million people, or 25 percent of the population, typify what is generally regarded as middle-class America. They are traditional, conforming, conservative, moral, nonexperimental, family-oriented, and patriotic—the most old-fashioned of the VALS groups. Their key drive is to fit in, not to stand out.

3) The emulators, about thirteen million people or 6 percent of the population, are intensively striving, ambitious, competitive, and ostentatious, but they are also very hard-working, fairly successful, and ask more of themselves than do belongers.

4) The achievers are the thirty-five million Americans, about 15 percent of the population, who are at the top of the other-directed groups. The achievers have built "the system" and they are now at the helm. They are gifted, hard-working, self-centered, successful, and happy. They tend to be conservative and certainly oppose radical change.

These latter three groups constitute the broad middle of American society, constituting about 68 percent of the American population.

5) The I-am-me's are the youngest of the VALS groups, averaging under age twenty-five. These six million Americans, about 3 percent of the population, are in transitions from the outer-directed way of life, in which they were raised, to an inner-directed one that their lifestyles are pushing them toward. They are discovering new interests and setting new life goals. The confusion of this stage is evident. The I-am-me individual tends to be both contrite and aggressive, demure and exhibitionistic, self-effacing and narcissistic, conforming and wildly innovative.

6) The experientials are generally older than the I-am-me's. Numbering approximately eleven million, about 4.5 percent of the population, the experientials have removed themselves a good distance from the outer-directed lifestyles in which they were brought up. They seek direct, vivid experience, either through deep personal

involvement in ideas and issues or through hedonism and experimentation. They are very well educated and hold well-paying technical and professional jobs. Unlike achievers, however, they are politically liberal and have little faith in institutional leaders.

7) The societally conscious are fifteen million Americans, about 6 percent of the population, who are primarily concerned with societal issues, trends, and events. They are successful, influential, and mature. They are the inner-directed opposite of the outer-directed achievers. Though a diverse group, they share the belief that humans should live in harmony with nature and with each other. The nonmaterial aspects of life are more important than the material ones. This group is more comfortable with the world view of the ecologist than that of the free marketeer, who feels that enlightened self-interest will take care of all the problems.

8) The integrateds, perhaps only three million Americans, less than 2 percent of the population, are those who have attained a truly integrated outlook on life. They have put together the decisiveness of outer-directedness with the penetration of inner direction. Integrateds reflect both achiever and societally conscious qualities. They are both makers, movers, observers, and creators. They are open, self-assured, self-expressive, and often have a global perspective.

In general, political consultants will ignore the 32 percent of the American public at the "tails" of the standard distribution. They will be left out by a majoritarian subversion of the James Madison's carefully constructed balance of the conflict of interests. Political consultants are concentrating on the outer-directed belongers, emulators, and achievers that constitute 68 percent of the total population. Political consultants generally ignore the survivors and sustainers, who usually live in poverty, as well as the I-am-me's, experientials, societally conscious, and integrateds.

In the 1980s and early 1990s we are dominated by a neoconservative leadership that concentrates among the VALS achievers. This leadership embraces a comprehensive agenda in economic, cultural, and spiritual matters. The younger converts to achiever status are typically the children of the experientials, societally conscious, or integrateds of the 1950s and 1960s. They have created a new lifestyle not before seen in the appreciable numbers in the United States or any other country.

The Person-Centered Epoch

We are now working away from the paradigm of the rational man. The old acquisitive, conformist values will give way to "individualism, experimentalism, direct experience, naturalism, appreciation of diversity, and tastes." In our democratic capitalism, with a market-oriented economy, we find it appropriate and acceptable if advertising views its central problem in the late twentieth-century as selling values rather than things. On the other hand, to use the same merchandising techniques to manipulate the political process of our constitutional culture means that political messages will be used to convey warmth, emotional content, and a projected sense of reality that may be insincere and deceitful.

So long as they succeed in selling the product (the candidate), there are those who will view this adulteration of the democratic process as simply the process of evolutionary change toward a more efficient, cost-effective kind of politics. Others will see it as a way for the power elite to manipulate the central 68 percent of the voting population and to subvert our constitutional culture. The future of our constitutional culture will not be the same as it has been in the past. Some argue that we have little to fear because we are in the decade of decline of the other-directed belongers, achievers, and emulators. Some contend that in the 1990s we will experience a new class of visionary achievers. However, before we cross this threshold into a new tomorrow we must defeat the threat that the neoconservative power elite will use its influence with the centrists of the belongers, achievers, and emulators to change our constitutional culture into one oriented toward a Hobbesian world view designed to secure economic security. Operating with a psychology of fear, as Hobbes would say, of death, they will seek an alliance with the mob.

7. The Captive Public

Today's young Americans, aged 18 to 30, know less and care less about news
and public affairs than any other generation of Americans in the past fifty years.
— Times-Mirror Center for the People and the Press

Sound bites and symbolism, the principal fuel of modern political campaigns, are
well suited to America's up-and-coming young voters. Once political awareness was
linked to educational status. This is not the case among young Americans. According
to the Times-Mirror study the youngest element of the electorate is an easy target
for those seeking to manipulate public opinion. This generation votes less and is
less critical of its leaders and institutions than young people of the past. The corollary
to flagging interest in the news is a sharp decline in the younger generation's knowledge
of what is happening in the nation and the world. The day of the political consultant
has arrived. The death of our constitutional culture may be on its way. It is being
replaced by the Consumer Republic, in which the only meaningful participation is
choosing goods and services. Powershoppers are replacing precinct workers.

Revival of voter participation at a new level of semisovereignty—the chartered
metroarea level of governance—is essential if a more substantive kind of "pursuit
of happiness" is to have a fair chance. In a brilliant exposition titled *The Captive
Public,* Benjamin Ginsberg presents the disquieting thesis that mass opinion as a
major force in modern political life is a decidedly mixed blessing.[1] Conceding that
governments are more responsive to the opinions of citizens, Ginsberg shows that
opinion polling surveys, combined with the rise in the use of political strategists,
has enabled some politicians to "domesticate" mass opinion.

Ginsberg contends that governments over the last century have gained access
to a larger tax base, a more sizeable pool of military manpower, and a broader
base of political support. A key factor has been their ability to respond, and use,
public opinion. They promote the power of the modern state of the twentieth century.
Today, contemporary Western governments appear to listen and defer to their citizens'
views. However, the public opinion to which regimes now bow is not the natural
and spontaneous popular force that confronted their predecessors of earlier centuries.
Instead, the opinion contemporary rulers heed is, in many respects, an artificial
phenomenon that national governments and large businesses themselves create and
now make efforts to sustain. It is not the opinion of a participatory citizenry.

During the twentieth century Western countries constructed what liberal theorists came to call a "marketplace of ideas." They did so by subsidizing the development of mass communications, promoting mass literacy, and expanding freedom of speech and of the press. It was to be a forum within which the ideas of all groups would be freely communicated and free to compete for acceptance. A free market in ideas, like a free market in any other commodity, tends to work to the advantage of the most advanced or monied producers. The substitution of a market for the class organization of opinion has had the effect of promoting the ideological dominance of those classes that are economically and politically more powerful. They can better deploy the financial, institutional, and organizational resources needed to "market" ideas effectively. As a result, the lower classes became, over time, consumers more than producers of their own opinions, accepting many beliefs advanced by the upper classes.

In the early twentieth century the marketplace of ideas was sometimes dominated by the upper classes through brute force. During World War I the American government suppressed the opinions of supporters of revolution in Russia. The U.S. Congress and the president tried to prevent the distribution of leaflets designed to arouse public opinion against American intervention in Russia. The leaflets supported the government of Alexander Kerensky and were against the Bolshevik wing of the Russian Social Democratic Party. The U.S. government contended that the Bolsheviks would not take Russia out of the war and not impede our war effort against Kaiser Germany. The majority of the Supreme Court upheld the twenty-year imprisonment of the two defendants who had published the leaflet.

But Justice Oliver Wendell Holmes dissented. Holmes contended that government could permissibly limit speech only when threats to private rights were at issue. Holmes could find no such evil or intent in the leaflets in question. "Even if the necessary intent were shown," he said, "the most nominal punishment seems to me all that possibly could be inflicted."

> Persecution for the expression of opinions seems perfectly logical. If you have no doubt of your premises and want a certain result with all your heart you naturally express your wishes in law and sweep away opposition. To allow opposition by speech seems to indicate that you think speech impotent. Such as when a man says that he has squared the circle, or that you do not care wholeheartedly for the result, or that you doubt either your power or your premises. But, when men have realized that time has upset many fighting faiths, they may come to believe even more than they believe the very foundations of their conduct that the ultimate good desired is better reached by a free trade of ideas—that the best test of truth is the power of the thought to get itself accepted in the competition of the market, and that truth is the only ground upon which their wishes safely can be carried out. That at any rate is the theory of our Constitution. . . . It is an experiment, as all life is an experiment. Every year, if not every day we have to wager our salvation upon some prophecy based upon imperfect knowledge. While that experiment is part of our system, I think that we should be eternally vigilant against attempts to check the expression of opinions that we loathe and believe to be fraught with death. Unless we believe they so imminently threaten immediate interference with the lawful and pressing purposes of the law that an immediate check is required to save the

country. Only the emergency that makes it immediately dangerous to leave the correction of evil counsels to time warrants making any exception to that sweeping command . . . "Congress shall make no laws . . . abridging freedom of speech." . . . I regret that this conviction deprived the defendants of their rights under the Constitution of the United States. Justice Brandeis concurs.

Times, however, are changing. Struggle in the marketplace of ideas is waning. In twentieth-century United States, voting is the only normal or typical vehicle for the expression of mass political opinion. In other nations, mass marching, student demonstrations, wall-writing, pamphlet publishing, and many other forms of political involvement still play important roles in political life. It was once this way in the United States. It may become so again; the L.A. riot of 1992 foreshadows more than unrest. At the time of the founding of our constitutional culture, a natural, spontaneous form of mass political expression was the urban riot. There were draft riots in 1863, labor riots in the 1890s and 1930s, and civil rights riots even as late as the 1970s.

Robert Kuttner provides us with some valuable insight into the current state of our constitutional republic's use of the right to vote.[2] The universal vote is both the essence of political democracy and its most jarringly radical dimension. The tension is especially acute in the United States, a durable representative republic and a fiercely capitalist democracy. In the 1986 election, voting turnout as a fraction of the adult population was about 38 percent, the lowest since the wartime election of 1942. In the states, election voting rates were the lowest since 1798!

According to Kuttner, three factors explain low American voter turnout. The first is the American fear of the power of the state. The second is to do with social class and political party—the United States, in the words of historian Louis Hartz, was "born free of democratic institutions." Although we have encouraged the promotion of the United Way, and endowments for the arts, we have done little to encourage citizens to vote. America's record toward increasing registration and voter turnout is dismal. Finally, most of the other democracies have some form of proportional representation in their parliaments and other elected bodies. This provides some assurance to all voters that their vote "will count." We have the Voting Rights Act of 1965 designed to protect the power of a person's vote. Even without these incentives, the elimination of registration barriers probably would increase United States's voting turnout to the 75 percent range that we achieved in the nineteenth century. This is the current level of voter participation in Britain and Canada.

The idea that everybody gets to participate is the most wonderful and audacious thing about a constitutional culture when it has a participatory democracy. An organization called Human Service Employees Voter Registration and Education (HUMAN-SERVE), started up in 1983, ran a 1984 voters registration drive that registered millions of new voters, mostly minority and poor. The group promotes an idea dubbed "motor voter" registration, which has been adopted by Arizona, Iowa, Minnesota, Nevada, and Colorado. The idea is that anyone with a driver's license is automatically registered to vote at the address listed on the license. In its first year the program added 140,000 people to voter rolls in Colorado. Elsewhere, HUMAN-SERVE has promoted postcard registration—now in effect in twenty-three states, as well as election-day registration, long established in Wisconsin, Maine, and Minnesota. Sen. Alan Cranston has proposed federal legislation that would include public-agency registration such as motor-voter, mail-in, and election-day registration. George Bush vetoed this bill in July 1992.

Mandatory Voting

This book urges that mandatory "local" voting be required for those chartered metroareas that decide, with state cooperation, to obtain a new charter. This could be done under a form of reorganization by way of a federally aided new metropolitan reorganization act. Tax surcharges, similar to traffic violation tickets, could be imposed for those who did not comply with the voting requirement. Nonvoters could be charged a tax penalty on their annual tax return. "Hit 'em in the pocket book" works, as every politician understands. The aim would be to "habituate" the voter to participation by requiring it for municipal metroarea elections. By scheduling federal and state voting on the same days, high rates of participation in American democracy could be guaranteed.

Federally mandated citizen participation has worked.[3] Problematic as federally encouraged community participation may be, the record of its impact in cities that adopted federal Workable Programs for Community Improvement is clearly positive. Federally mandated community participation in this program was almost the only real access point for working class involvement in programs that affected the poor. Restoring community participation requirements would be a way for the working class to reenter local politics.

By way of the use of the polling process, modern Western states have converted mass opinion from an unpredictable, disruptive force into a somewhat controlled phenomenon. The public does cause changes in leadership. Nevertheless, it is clear that the power elite in effect selects the winning candidates by choosing to finance their elections. The power elite forms and molds public opinion by way of the surveying and public opinion process. Polls purport to provide reliable, scientifically derived information about the public's desires, fears, and beliefs. But poll respondents typically include a large proportion of individuals who "do not know," "do not care," or exhibit some other form of relative detachment or apathy. Polls in effect drown out those individuals with strongly held views. They are inundated in the great sea of those who are apathetic among the public. A government wishing to maintain merely the semblance of responsiveness can comply with the preferences reported by the polls and thus control innovation and imaginative change. Nonetheless, such change can still be forced by citizen networks using letters, strikes, protests, or other forms such as student activism designed to stir the public. Activism by its nature lacks "typicality."

The apathetic silent majority was the Nixon administration's answer to the protestors, demonstrators, rioters, and other critics who were using those forms of protest to seek major changes in American foreign and domestic policies. From the administration's perspective, the real virtue of the silent majority is, precisely, its silence. This neatly describes Hannah Arendt's concerns about how a totalitarian leadership gains control over a public with the power to vote.

From the perspective of political elites, the virtue of polls is that they make it possible to recognize and deal with popular attitudes before they are galvanized into opposition. Because of the current dominance of the market economy over our constitutional culture, differences between the paid pollsters' concerns and those of the general public are probably inevitable. There is no criminality here. Proprietary, profit-motivated polls will raise and deal generally with questions that are of interest to clients and to those who buy poll data. For example, the Times-Mirror's polls seldom pose questions about the propriety of the foundations of the existing order. Instead, respondents are asked to choose from among the alternatives already set up by the pollster.

A new kind of fascism may be emerging in the United States. The major media have considerable influence on political attitudes at the lower rungs of the social ladder. As a result, those who control the media get an exponential gain in power and influence over the political process. It is especially disconcerting that this power is combined with media financing and reporting of opinion polls.

The Reagan administration did everything in its power to end the "fairness doctrine" in broadcasting, the regulatory principle that mandated response time for points of view opposed to opinions broadcast by licensees on public airwaves. This delivered even more power to manipulate the masses into the proprietary hands of those who have enough money to out-bid others for television and radio broadcasting channels. In his 1905 *Decline of the West,* Oswald Spengler predicted that the abuse of power by the press and other media would be the death knell of the world's democratic societies. We could still prove him wrong by restoring reasonable access to the machinery that distributes information to those who have ideas but do not own the multimedia.

Voters' opinions and choices are often, though not always, the result of efforts by contending groups to build mass followings. Often this effort is in the form of an offer of material incentives sufficiently compelling to secure allegiance in the voting booths. ("Read my lips.") The VALS lifestyles approach to demographics enables candidates to center their electioneering upon the centrist 68 percent of voters. They literally ignore the demands or needs of the extremes. This loss of power by the minorities will result in the manifestation of control by the popular will of the majority.

Times-Mirror efforts to end the use of conventional labels like "liberal" and "conservative" are to be applauded. But the new VALS categories were used in 1988 by the political consultants to successfully manipulate journalists. By dovetailing their press releases to the trendy new Times-Mirror psychosocial profiles the consultants led the journalists by their handouts. Worse, the candidates follow the lead of successful media candidates and make little if any effort to inform the voters about the issues. Instead they appeal to the feelings and emotions that are said to motivate the new psychosocial categories.

It is interesting and encouraging to note that in the 1986 congressional campaign the average American voter, may have been stirred by distaste for the manipulative use of the telecommunications media. They voted against candidates who chose to "stay home" and let the political consultants and the media sell their candidacy. In general, such candidates did not fare well against a candidate who did try to get out in the field and "press the flesh," as Lyndon Baynes Johnson once called it.

Lionel Rubinoff, a Canadian professor of philosophy, has provided us with an eloquent statement, *The Pornography of Power,*[4] that is rich in philosophical insight.

An inquiry into the murky depths of human nature, it is concerned with two central ideas: progress and power. The idea of progress came from the idea of identifying values with pragmatic and hedonistic goals, goals that can be pursued only through the exercise of power. In the twentieth century there has been a corruption of the ideology of progress brought on by trying to achieve it. Today, the pursuit of truth, through science and intellectual inquiry, has been replaced by the quest for power.

Americans of the 1990s follow this dreadful pattern of conduct all too often. It is as though they believe that shows like "Miami Vice" are real life. In reality, the television show engages in more violence and killing in one weekly episode than the actual Miami Vice department does in a full year.

The media makes no subtle distinctions. All sensational news that appeals to the darker side of the spirit is treated as the same—the news of the day. For example, a man whose portfolio had a precipitous fall in value turned fantasy to action by going to the stock brokerage office and killing the manager with his handgun. It was featured in the news, though it was an extraordinary and nonrecurring event of a culpable, remorseful man. We lack a proportional sense of balance. The media does not feature the lives of the normal and typical as they do good deeds. To the media, that is not news.

Where is American culture headed? Leaders once had closeted, private lives. We are all fair game, today. Americans, today, have much to learn about the difference between "fantasizing" terrifying pornography, which it seems humans need to do to survive, or on the other hand "performing" it, which will be our doom. Americans have yet to accept the contradictory nature of human beings. We naively want impossible perfectibility. Europeans and Asians ask for less. Americans are often products of poor immigrant families living in a young nation. They need personal growth while seeking their nation's identity. They need to learn that any one person is capable of both good and evil. The problem is finding guiding principles that will cause the large majority of us to let evil be mere "imagination." This is because our moral values should transcend and restrain performance of natural, human, evil tendencies. We could broadcast a national reaffirmation of honor, integrity, loyalty, fidelity, competence, duty to speak, and more. This could provide us all with universal values, regardless of race, color, creed, national origin, sex, age, or other diverse cultural differences. This could be the beginning of a universally acceptable American creed.

Pornography is exploitation by description of tabooed activities with the purpose of inciting hallucinations or delusions for private, or worse, public, enjoyment. Anyone who watches American television for many hours a week is well aware of its pornographic exploitation of the imagination. The pornographic use of power is intrinsically an expression of irrationality, in the same sense that sex is an expression of irrationality. Pornography can be therapeutic when it remains fantasy. Rubinoff proposes that we face the absurd directly, by imagining it. Some humans accept ambivalence—good and evil—as a condition of humanity.

Like all other humans, we need self-control. In the past century we were tricked into denying our personal world of experience by learning to accept the idea that the spontaneous expression of irrationality is debasing. We have wrongfully been forced to murder the demonic within us in order to free the angelic. In fact, the more angelic we become in practice by way of repression and suppression, the more alienated we will become in spirit. As psychiatrist R. D. Laing, puts it,

If we cling to the good without the bad, denying the one for the other, what happens is that the disassociative evil impulse, now evil in a sense, returns to permeate and possess the good and turn it into itself. We have to begin by admitting and even accepting our violence rather than blindly destroying ourselves with it, therewith we have to realize that we are as deeply afraid to live and to love as we are to die.

The celebration of narcissism and the psychobabble of "self-actualization" are demonstrations of the capacity for evil in us all. The abuse of drugs is a celebration of this evil as people overindulge in appetites for pleasure, thereby reinforcing our demonic impulses. We should accept Rubinoff's main theme: the mystery and outrage of man's capacity for the enjoyment of evil is now coupled with modern-day ease and convenience. The result is that the ease with which the exercise and experience of power can inadvertently and surreptitiously be carried out contributes to evil ends. We must not only be capable of self-examination, we must find ways to accept that evil is part of us. By doing so, we, thereby empower ourselves to minimize the damage that it can do to each of us and our society.

Rubinoff raises again Plato's question: Is there a universal, *a priori* human nature underlying the behavioral differences that seem to divide cultures, societies, and possibly races? I argue that our modern knowledge of the human brain urges a unity of human nature. In what ways are we alike? For most humans the experience of virtue is accompanied by an experience of pleasure. Nevertheless, recently, happiness has become defined in terms of feelings of sensuality. Still, humans have been seen to get delight and satisfaction out of doing good. The pursuit of happiness that is implicit in our constitutional culture has historical antecedent in the humanistic world view of the Enlightenment.

The portrait of man as a creature of unreason comes at a time when man has already begun to doubt the truth of the humanist theory of rational man. The idea that evil owes its origin to man himself is far from being a radically new idea. Look to the classic description of man and the state of nature by our ever-ready mentor, Thomas Hobbes, in *The Leviathan:*

> In the state of nature . . . the life of man is solitary, poor, nasty, brutish and short. . . . In this war of every man against every man . . . nothing can be unjust (because nothing can be just). The notion of right and wrong, justice and injustice, have, there, no place. . . . Force and fraud are, in war, the two cardinal virtues. . . . In such a condition every man has a right to everything; even to one another's bodies.

Locke saw men left in a state of nature as realizing their need for a system of controls to ensure the survival of all. This communitarian theory became known as the contract theory of society, according to which morality is defined by its usefulness in maintaining social order.

Let us refocus our investigation toward the ethic of the power held by the elite. It is power and its uses that has been the underlying subject of this chapter's analysis of what it is to be human. Power is defined by the seductive terminology of fascism as a means that is reluctantly employed for the sake of a greater good. Hidden within these dulcet words is the power elites' joy of having power for its own sake—sheer pornography. German Nazis, the South American dictators, the Russian Communists, the CIA, all pretend, perhaps even believe, that they seize power unwillingly and for a limited time. They promise that just around the corner there lies a paradise where human beings will be free and equal. We know from the hard-earned experience of the twentieth century that those who seize power do not relinquish it. Cincinnatus, a good man called to power by the Romans, chose to return to his farm when he had accomplished the tasks of leadership. He was not the typical representative of the power elite. Power is not a means for most who have enjoyed its exhilarating force. It is an end. Before we capitulate to this sad state of affairs, we should attempt adoption of the ethics of the communitarian personality. Democratic capitalism is more compatible with it.

Such a perception of humans is in keeping with modern knowledge. Through the work of Freud, Jung, Erikson, Piaget, Maslow, and others we have come to realize that the communitarian personality, the social individual, can renounce the instinct of aggression in favor of a social conscience.

A recent defense of the irrationalists' version of the contract theory is found in Freud, who made it the basis for a psychoanalytic theory of culture and social control. Freud said that the real causes for obeying the laws of society are pragmatic rather then ethical. It is useful to sustain the illusion that our behavior is governed by ethical and religious considerations. But society must provide a variety of creative outlets to enable us to be aggressive without being destructive. Creativity is one of the primary forms to which aggression can be usefully employed. Freud argued for some form of capitalism as the most desirable form of economic order because it vents aggression in a socially acceptable way, through competition.

Freud's assertion dismayed the Marxists. Freud argued that by abolishing private property one would deprive the human animal, with its love of aggression and acquisitiveness, of one of its healthier outlets. Freud warned that too much repression by an unrealistic society could lead to an outburst of ruthless and destructive behavior. To Freud the chief source of this aggressive behavior is a primordial "death instinct" for self-destruction. He also acknowledged human nature as driven by an equally powerful instinct for self-preservation, which Freud called *eros,* the Greek word for love.

When Freud first began to reflect upon the implications of the death instinct, he conceived it as separate from eros. Later, however, he moved closer to the notion that they were really the same—distinct perhaps, but not separate. The implication was that every act of violence is implicitly an act of love, and every act of love is implicitly an act of violence.

A society that does not provide creative opportunities for the expression of aggression will find that some citizens are forced to choose other means of venting anger—war, crime, or other acts of barbarism. Many of these demonic acts, including some kinds of crime such as insider-trading rules violations and the recreational use of narcotics, will be wrongfully represented as essentially rational and even legitimate modes of behavior. Barbarism can become institutionalized in a pathological society through self-deception. The society becomes corrupt. There is nothing more dangerous to the immunological system and the health of a society than to build devious routes to the unconscious by pretending these evil ways are really a form of virtue.

There are many powerful people within our constitutional culture who strongly feel that most men need security, stability, and an overarching authority because of our conflicting needs. Today, these powerful Hobbesians are arguing that such was the original intent of the Constitution as promulgated by the Federalists, which did not include the Bill of Rights. Those who argue for this interpretation of original constitutional intent believe that most people do not want to plan for an uncertain future. They want to be free of the responsibility of planning. These elitists believe that what the majority ask is merely some sort of assurance that they are decently provided for. In this "trickle-down" scheme, the more energetic will work. This will produce a surplus that will raise the level of our ships of life, thereby enabling a sort of day-to-day enjoyment of life for everyone. The promise of security explains the power of Jerry Falwell, the TV evangelists, and the cult leaders of California and Florida. Still, we have an open society with a scientific outlook. Its unsettling quest for new knowledge forces some of our citizens—reluctantly—into freedom. Others eagerly reach out for the opportunity to risk. Nevertheless, because the fear of freedom is greater than the desire for it, men and women continue to engineer exotic avenues of retreat, to escape the dreaded demands of that freedom. Millions of our apathetic citizens know it would be better for them to settle for the security of totalitarianism than the uncertainty of rampant capitalism.

We need to reawaken the capacity of ordinary men to be creative with their fears. We need to discourage passivity and encourage autonomous action. The destruction of the possible human is the destruction of the creativity of ordinary men and women. This could be the greatest crime of our time. We must restore the capacity of the imagination to transcend despair. The early-1980s vogue of imagining the nuclear winter was an appropriate motivating force for the single-issue political activists who were attempting to bring about nuclear disarmament. Without it, they could lapse into apathy. However, the same idea may be a psychic disaster for ordinary humans, who are retreating to alienation, isolation, and withdrawal.

Virtue is a special kind of knowledge. The child learns to be virtuous by imitating virtuous parents or other good mentors. Society expects us to set a good example. American culture today is suffering from a widespread neurosis. Ordinary people see our society raping the natural beauty of the land in the name of progress. We surround every city with scrap heaps, garbage dumps, and junkyards. All are an expression of our leadership's indifference to the need for a sense of order, beauty, and justice. We have too narrowly focused our life pursuing the economist's goal of maximizing profits. We are in conflict with our nature. Happiness is the experience of harmonious interaction between one's behavior, one's nature, and the ecological world. Good humans, not sociopaths, need to have their existence coincide with their essence. Dostoevski has warned us that through the ritual of conformism to authority the individual can be reshaped into a potential psychopath. Freedom is demanding! Who seeks the loneliness that comes from demanding that others join in seeking change? We are timorous and need assurance that those who share feelings of moral outrage are capable of substituting imagination for acts of violence. Through the imagination, we can enter the life of the mind, where disaster can be encountered without experiencing it. In our minds, we can know how it feels to be hurt, beaten, and defeated. Through imagination we can critique the use of power, the abuse of power, without the experience of doing the evil of violent confrontation. Perhaps Bertrand Russell, the great philosopher, best expressed what I am saying: "Free men worship in spite of death. Man is yet free during his brief years, to examine, to criticize, to know, and to have the imagination to create. To him alone, and the world with which he is acquainted, in this freedom belongs; and in this lies his superiority to the restless forces that control his outward life."

Somehow we must break to pieces the gradualism of fatuous hope. Hope is merely ritual magic. It induces us to wait with folded hands. It is to the imagination, to man's capacity for creative thought, that we must turn if we are to understand fully the dimensions of freedom and the possibility of transcending despair. By turning to the imagination and the creative power of the human mind, we will achieve a transcendence that is a more hopeful source of salvation, rather than programs of social revolt and small-minded social reform. America's self-critical encounter with the finitude and limitations of the human condition would silently and forcefully bring the true dignity of Americans into being. I believe we could be a beacon for the entire world, a world that is searching for the dignity of man within the plight of the human condition.

The very basis of Christianity is a compassion that owes its origin to the historic murder of a god. That evil act has since become the basis for the eucharistic meal— a ritual act of love, atonement, and redemption. The imagination can save mankind from ultimate destruction.

Excessive Stress in Our American Metroareas

In 1977, the National Science Foundation concluded,

> Stress is a major problem in contemporary United States. It negatively affects the daily lives of scores of millions of Americans. It causes a bewildering array of psychological, physiological and social malfunctions. On an economic level the affects of stress probably cost the nation over $100 billion annually. Moreover, evidence available suggests that stress-related maladies are on the rise.

In 1983 Lawrence Galton reported several studies that showed that stress has almost doubled in the intervening years. Stress results from our perception of a need and our gearing up for the response. Stress can be looked upon as any disturbance that causes the mind and body to adjust. Not all stress is bad. Art and other significant social breakthroughs have resulted from stress and the response to it. The body organizes to make reasonable adjustments in response to stimuli, including stressors.

On the other hand, unusual stress can be injurious in diverse ways. In one famous medical laboratory experiment, two monkeys were placed side by side in chairs equipped to give electric shocks. One of the monkeys—and only one—could prevent the shocks to both self and its partner by pressing a lever. Under the psychological stress of such responsibility this "executive" monkey developed duodenal ulcers. On the other hand, stress has caused some people to reached high levels of mutuality, to lose the primary focus on self and turn to serving others. This has often strengthened their immune system and diminished their tendency toward illness.

Some studies suggest that meditation reduces anxiety and quiets the symptoms of the fight-or-flight-response, often activated by the type-A, power-motivated personality. Meditation may increase concern for others. Maturity, love, and detachment reduce stress and its potentially bad effects on one's health.[5] These findings say that one of the healthiest actions that high-powered, highly stressed executives could do is work to improve the welfare of their communities, for example, by leading the reorganization of government in their metroareas, which would also reduce the stress of their fellows. Today stress is generally medicated. One of the most successful pharmaceuticals of all time, Tagamet, relieves and helps heal ulcers. It would be better to prescribe instead healthy ennobling activities.

The Holmes/Rahe Scale

Thomas Holmes, a professor of psychiatry, and Richard H. Rahe compiled what is called the Holmes/Rahe life event stress scale. The most stress-provoking event proved, not surprisingly, to be the death of a spouse, Holmes and Rahe used that event to index all stress events, and gave it ranking of 100 in their stress-ranking system. Marrying proved to be half as stressful, still a very substantial amount of stress, with a ranking of 50. Others in the top ten were divorce, marital separation, a jail term, death in the family, personal injury or illness, marriage, discharge from a job, marital reconciliation, and retirement. In case after case studied by the researchers, the year in which several major life events occurred was followed by a year in which serious illness developed.[6] The researchers concluded that the greater the life change and burden of stress, the lower the body's resistance to disease and the more serious the illness that developed.

The stressors listed by Holmes-Rahe are all of a personal nature—the traumatic effects are internalized. This is because the vast majority of health-givers in our society deal with only one patient at a time. It is a bipolar relationship. These health-givers are ill-equipped to deal with external stressors, perceiving them as societal problems outside of the problem space—the patient or client. Most of the medical profession has little knowledge of public health problems. It would be a major mind change for them to accept that it would be better for everyone to cope with the cause of distress rather than provide Tagamet. Only public health healthgivers have the mindset to treat the whole society in a metroarea. We ought to take the public-health attitude toward mental health, defining pandemic external stressors such as crime in the streets, traffic congestion, delays of the law, and access to justice. The primary goal would be to diminish the stressor itself. In this way we would create a healthier environment for the general public. The result would be Americans who are happier and better able to play their roles in our constitutional culture and its marketplace of ideas, with its democratic capitalism for fairly allocating goods and services.

Modern men and women search for role models, mentors, gurus, exemplars. This chapter wrestles with the angels! It is a friendly and awful contest. In the United States we need to define a mature human personality who can deal with the freedom and liberty of our constitutional culture and free-market-oriented economy. Americans oppose the idea that there are known virtues every American should believe in and support. For many of us, the very idea of a consensus about the elements of a paradigm of personality development is un-American. The result is that once a child enters the common-school system, little effort is made to inculcate an ideal model of a good and virtuous human personality deserving of emulation. Unfortunately, this free-wheeling, "improvisational" approach to human personality development cannot be successfully aligned with citizen accountability and responsibility in America's constitutional culture. Nor can we reconcile it with the fair-play expectations of participants in the marketplace of ideas and the market economy of democratic capitalism. We are getting good Americans by chance.

The United States has, to date, failed to prepare its doctors, lawyers, clergy, businessmen, political leaders, and other community leaders to understand their roles. The result is daily reports of disasters arising out of failures to act according to ethical values required by our constitutional culture and democratic capitalism. It has not been all bad. We have been blessed by the presence, for example, of George C. Marshall, who understood the limited role of a military man serving civilian government. On the other hand, we have the disasters of a well-intentioned Admiral Poindexter, head of the National Security Council, who feels he "owes no apology" for his acts of extreme moral turpitude done in the name of patriotism.

Dr. Michael Gazzaniga, professor of psychology and neurology at Cornell University Medical Center, argues in *The Social Brain* that the brain is more a social entity than a psychological one.[1] Modern minds probably have a different capacity to accept magical beliefs than that of the humans of early Mesopotamia and Egypt. In those days "voices" were heard and "gods" were seen throughout the human environment, according to commentators such as Jaynes. Of course, that continues to be true even today in some corners of the world. The natives in the Cameroons recently experienced a nearby lake's inexplicable release of an unseen cloud of death. Western scientists know it is a large release of carbon dioxide, but have not been able to explain this to the illiterate natives whose loved ones have been "killed by the gods."

From childhood, the external environment shapes how we use our brains. Though religious institutions have not conceded it, the twentieth-century human mind is radically different from that of the days of the Old Testament in Egypt and Babylon. The human brain's unique capacities and insistence on making inferences from observed events are responsible for the disparate constructs of creation and other personal beliefs that some people hold today. In a diverse culture such as the United States, people with diametrically opposed beliefs are asked to be friendly neighbors. This is difficult. The problems created by the different views of monotheism, Christianity, Judaism, Islam, Buddhism, and other faiths make it difficult to maintain peace and order in our cities. We all need to recognize that our brains are alike in their general potential.

The human species must have a belief that guides, controls, and dictates behavior. We all develop one about ourselves. Even B. F. Skinner, who propounded his own perception, had one. It is a short jump to imagine how to develop one about suprapersonal events as well. Call it God, the Christ, Mohammed, or quantum mechanics, they are all beliefs that allow for human action. According to Michael Gazzaniga, modern man will have to figure out how to transcend current religious beliefs and move to a system that creates interpersonal understanding instead of indifference, even hate.

Viktor Frankl, a gifted psychiatrist who survived Nazi concentration camps, stated in *Man's Search for Meaning* that the last of human freedoms is to choose one's own way.[2] If there is meaning in life at all, then there must be meaning in suffering. Suffering is ineradicable. Without suffering and death, human life cannot be complete. The way in which one takes up his cross—even under the most difficult circumstances, can add meaning to life. Here lies the chance to make use of or to forego opportunity to attain moral values. What humans actually need is not a tensionless state but rather the striving and struggling for a worthwhile goal, a freely chosen task.

In his book on the twentieth-century encounter of the world's three great religions Malachi Martin calls for religious leaders to accept the modern understanding we have gained about the human brain. We live in a time of mental crisis because of conflicts generated by religions. Our religious leaders have failed in the ecumenical objective of reaching the common ground by which the world's great religions could sustain belief while taking comfort from each other. Today there is a destructive force arising from religion that unleashes such hate that zealots bomb abortion centers to support their chosen belief. This is a classic example of the serious social unrest arising from the failure of religions to adapt to the modern view of what a human is biologically and neurologically as a man or a woman.

Through the centuries China has benefitted from the teachings of Lao Tze and Confucius. Both philosophers taught high ethical standards of conduct to both citizens and leaders. Perhaps the most paradoxical of Lao Tze's teachings to a leader is the idea of inaction or noninterference. About the governing of a nation, he said, "Of the best rulers, the people only know they exist. The next best, they love and praise. The next, they fear, and the next, they revile . . . but (of the best) when their task is accomplished, their work done, the people all remark, we have done it ourselves." May America's future be blessed with the best leaders.

The most distinctive of the Taoist idea of the ideal personality is its emphasis on transcendence. According to Lao Tze, the mature personality transcends not only the conventional concerns about personal gain, fame, success, social approval, or disapproval, he or she also is free of worries about life and death. Both are thought of as aspects of the natural process of self-transformation.

Lao Tze said, "The true man of ancient times knew nothing of loving life, knew nothing of hating death. He emerged without delight; he went back in without a fuss. He came briskly, he went briskly and that was all." The mature personality is one who completely identifies with the universal mind, who lives actively in this phenomenological world and yet transcends it. Still, he or she is not fully human until he or she becomes fully aware of being not only a member of his or her society but also a denizen of the universe, and acts accordingly.

The Mature Personality Paradigm

Between 40 and 60 percent of our growth in population is attributed to both legal and illegal migration from new minorities. Hispanic-Americans from Latin America, blacks from the Caribbean, and East Asian immigrants are all seeking a new life of opportunity and liberty. A clearer perception of our constitutional culture and democratic capitalism for these new arrivals would be a saving grace for us all. The impact of this major new wave of immigration is disparate and may be surprising.

Asian-Americans use a personality development process that is more suitable to the open society of our constitutional culture. They seem quick to understand the responsibilities as well as the liberty expected of a communitarian personality. Other immigrants are having more difficulty with assimilation. Newly arrived Asian-Americans are advancing much more rapidly then other new minority immigrants. We are experiencing real friction arising from the Asian-Americans' success. This has resulted in violence from blacks, Irish Catholics, and Hispanic-Americans. This is because there are differences in attitudes toward the work ethic, family solidarity, and the desire to improve oneself through assimilation.

The Asian-American population is now exploding. According to the census bureau, it grew an astounding 125 percent between 1970 and 1980, to 4.1 million, though people of Asian extraction make up only 1.8 percent of Americans. It is likely that their influx is having an effect on American society as important as the migrations from Europe a hundred years ago. Today more than a third of Asian-Americans live outside Chinatowns, in the East, South, and Midwest. The term *Asian-American* is probably a misnomer in the context of cross-cultural influences. It now refers to over 900,000 Chinese from all parts of China, along with over 400,000 Vietnamese, 800,000 Filipinos, 700,000 Japanese, 500,000 Koreans, 400,000 East Indians, and a huge assortment of everything else from Moslem Cambodians to Catholic Hawaiians.

Asian-Americans attract attention because of their new prominence in several professions and trades. In New York, Korean-Americans run an estimated 900 of the city's 1,600 corner grocery stores. Filipino doctors outnumber black doctors and have become general practitioners in thousands of rural communities that had lacked physicians. Americans of East Indian extraction own eight hundred of California's six thousand motels. In parts of Texas, Vietnamese-Americans control 85 percent of the shrimping industry. However, they only reached this position after considerable violence against them.[3]

Most significant for the future is the entry of Asian-Americans into universities. At Harvard, MIT, and Julliard the percentage of Asian-Americans far outstrips their percentage of the American population, ranging from 10 to 30 percent. In the current, largely foreign-born Asian-American community, 33 percent of people over twenty-five graduated from college, compared with 16 percent of the general population. For third-generation Japanese-Americans, the figure is 88 percent! President Reagan called Asian-Americans "our exemplars of hope and inspiration."

Still, these stories do not come to grips with the many problems of adjustment Asian-Americans, like all immigrants, have to deal with. They range from the absurd to the deadly serious. Many Asian-Americans face racial violence. Recently, groups of Cambodians and Vietnamese in Boston were beaten up by white youths. There have been incidents in New York and Los Angeles as well. Asians live almost exclusively in metroareas, where average incomes are higher. They usually have more people working in each family. Yet because of language difficulties and differing professional standards in the United States, many new Asian immigrants initially work in jobs for which they are greatly overqualified. This results in some envy, fear, and anger by coworkers as their Asian colleagues are promoted faster in the interests of the business firm.

Universities are actively, though judiciously, discriminating against the pressure for admission on an equal status by the Asian-American immigrants. The discrimination is understandable. Many Asian-Americans are seeking to be college and university teachers. Yet often they lack the oral language skills required despite the fact that they can write English well.

Thomas Sowell argues in his book *Race and Economics* that Asian-Americans and Jewish-Americans both have excelled by developing self-sufficient community organizations. They combine their skills through networking and emphasize the need for education. They have sought success through economic advances instead of political action. Autonomy and self-sufficiency seem to be traits they emulate. The first element of this self-sufficiency is family. Most obviously, it provides a secure environment for children. Second, it pushes these children to do better than their parents. Finally, it produces a significant financial advantage. Asian-Americans have often headed into family businesses as their first rung toward success. All the family members pitch in with long hours to help them succeed. The second element of Asian-American self-sufficiency is its development of powerful community organizations. Clan organizations are formed along family lines, mutual-aid societies, and revolving-credit associations, to aid others in starting businesses.

All this achievement by immigrants, who often came to the United States only a few years ago with nothing, highlights the continuing difficulties of black Americans. Although blacks have made extraordinary progress in the past hundred years, they must adapt to new and different cultural values if they are to raise themselves out of the underclass in a market-oriented society.[4] Our constitutional culture provides them with the power to fight for equality in political and civil rights, which they do not yet have. Still, it does little if anything to provide them with the cultural values that will aid black parents in developing mature personalities among their children, so they can cope with the hostile racist environment that still prevails. In the market-oriented economy, political and civil rights are only indirectly related to economic success. The pervasive hypocrisy of our constitutional culture markets an image of equality and human rights while looking the other way. Massive social institutions work to impose grinding racial discrimination that is far more than some humans can bear.

Black leaders found in medicine, the church, sports, the law, theater, music, teaching, and other professions provide us all with the vision of a better America. In the 1960s, courageous black Americans, joined by empathic whites and other races, launched the civil rights movement, which has been one of the most effective mass movements for social justice in human history. In this the United States has been far more successful than India has in its efforts to free the untouchables. There is much strength and power in the personality of black Americans. Still, black Americans today face deteriorating conditions, in sharp contrast to many other American groups. The incidence of poverty among blacks is triple that of whites. The tragedy is the unemployment rate of black male youths—consistently double that of their white counterparts. We have reached the point where more than half the black children born in this country are born out of wedlock, most to teenage parents. In 1982 the probability of being murdered was six times greater for black males than for whites. The high school dropout rate in many metroareas is more than 30 percent and in some 50 percent. These problems reflect the current state of mental depression, or, worse, disabling despair overlaying rage, that is pervasive among many poor lower-class and lower-middle-class black Americans, especially males.

Nevertheless, in the 1990s, black leadership can take group action. Progress is effected not only by public policy and the racial attitudes of society as a whole, but also by a group's capacity to exploit its own strengths. Black people have traditionally understood that intellectual development is the key to success in American society. Desegregation was expected to help greatly in this respect. It was believed black self-esteem and self-identity would improve if blacks could compete in the classroom with all other Americans. Yet, three decades after *Brown* v. *Board of Education,* real problems in the intellectual performance of black people remain. The statistics are a result of the deleterious effects of poverty: poor prenatal care, early-year malnutrition, the lack of well-baby clinics, and poor early child development training. Parental cultural support for intellectual attainment among poor blacks is also lacking.

The expenditures of public and private funds on prenatal care, well-baby clinics, day-care centers, and prekindergarten training for all those below the poverty line will produce handsome dividends for the entire nation. Immediate expenditures on these child-development items are more important than most of our national defense expenditures. We face a coming generation, who, if not promptly and consciously acculturated to support our constitutional culture and democratic capitalism will, in a few decades, become a permanent underclass brutalized by functional illiteracy. They may become the mob that supports happy fascism.

The Healthy Alternative

We need to encourage autonomous persons to network their way to working consensuses for their competing groups. We could do this by way of dialogues toward workable programs for community improvement brought about by compromise and self-motivated "bottom up" planning. American metroareas are more like a brewing bacterial ferment creating a healthy pot liquor than a melting caldron that creates a new alloy. We need to recognize Abraham Maslow's contention that all men and women share certain basic needs arranged in a hierarchy. Maslow asserts that there are five levels in the hierarchy of basic psychological needs that we seek to satisfy within the universal human need for intellectual and spiritual development:

1) Psycho-physiological needs. To survive, people need a minimum of food, clothing, shelter, and rest. These represent the most elemental needs;
2) Safety or security needs. When the above psychological needs are satisfied, people want to keep and protect what they have. They try to stabilize their environment for the future;
3) Social needs. The environment having become more stable, people seek to be part of something larger than themselves. They have social needs for belonging or sharing and association, forgiving and receiving friendship and love;
4) Ego needs. These are many but fall into two basic groups: self-esteem (needs for self-confidence, independence, achievement, and knowledge) and reputation (needs for status, recognition, appreciation, and respect);
5) Self-fulfillment needs. Growth, self-development, and self-actualization are the capstones of the other needs. Humans want to realize the full range of their intellectual, imaginative, and creative potential as human beings.

A satisfied need is not a motivator for further transcending behavior. As Jung has said, humans often commit a form of psychic suicide by satisfying a driving goal. No longer having a motivating force, a person may plateau at one of the earlier levels.

There is a catch-22 for free marketeers. Social, ego, and self-fulfillment needs cannot be satisfied easily by the typical marketplace of consumer goods and services. So, men and women are increasingly turning from economics to political action, the arts, community action, and other forms of creativity, such as the crafts. Sadly, more are turning to drugs, cult religions, and consumerism as a way to "turn off" society.

Today's crisis is a crisis of trust stemming from the long decline of America's leadership; it is corroding our sense of community. The crisis is due to a paradigm shift: we are experiencing a change in our expectations. The old institutions are using all their tools to relate our ego needs to the material things that the market economy has become accustomed to supplying. By giving people more power to involve themselves in the political process, instead of limiting them to an ineffective vote, a spiritual regeneration could occur.

Normality is the maximal use of maturity, or it could be an ideal of "good" human functioning. Therefore let us first set out a respected theory of personality to provide us with some underlying concepts and terms to act as a basis of discussion of the kind of human who might successfully pursue happiness. B. R. Hergenthaler's abstract of Erik Erikson's theory of personality does this job best.[5]

Erikson's Theory of Personality

Erikson sees life as consisting of eight stages. The first five stages parallel Freud's proposed psychosexual stages of development in terms of timeline, but in terms of what happens during these stages, Erikson's stages are very different. The last three stages are Erikson's major contributions to psychology. Each stage of development is characterized by a crisis. The word *crisis* is used by Erikson in the way it is used by medical doctors, that is, to connote an important turning point. Each stage is named according to the crisis that arises in it. Erikson says that when the crisis characterizing a stage is resolved positively, a virtue emerges in one's personality; this is usually developed in the next stage.

Basic trust and basic mistrust. The first stage lasts from birth through the first year and corresponds closely to Freud's oral stage of psychosexual development. If those who care for an infant satisfy his needs in a loving and consistent way, the child will develop a feeling of basic trust. But if the caretakers are rejecting, preoccupied, or indifferent, and satisfy the infant's needs in an inconsistent manner, the baby will develop the feeling of mistrust. The basic trust versus basic mistrust crisis is resolved when the child develops more trust than mistrust. It is the ratio of the two solutions that is important. A child that trusted everybody and everything would be in trouble. A certain amount of mistrust is healthy and conducive to survival. Still, children with a predominance of trust will develop the courage to take risks and not be overwhelmed by setbacks. The virtue achieved by successfully passing through this stage is hope.

The emergence of the virtue of hope. This is the second stage, from age one to age four. Erikson defines hope as the enduring belief in the attainability of fervent wishes despite the dark urges and rages that mark the beginning of existence. A trusting child dares to hope, which is future-oriented; the child lacking trust cannot hope since he must constantly worry whether his needs will be satisfied. He is, therefore, stuck in the present.

Initiative versus guilt. This stage occurs from about the fourth to about the fifth year. It corresponds to Freud's phallic stage of psychosexual development. During this stage, the child has more detailed motor activity, more refined use of language, and a more vivid use of imagination. These skills allow the child to initiate ideas and actions, to fantasize, and to plan future events. In the preceding stages, the child learned he is a person. Now he begins to explore what kind of person he is and what kind of person he can become. During this stage limits are tested, to find out what is permissible and what is not. If the parents encourage the child's self-initiated behaviors and fantasies the child will leave this stage with a healthy sense of initiative. But if parents ridicule the child's self-started behavior and imagination, he will leave this stage lacking self-sufficiency.

The virtue achieved by successfully passing through this stage is purpose. Erikson defines purpose as "the courage to envisage and pursue valued goals uninhibited by the defeat of infantile fantasies by guilt and deforming fear of punishment." A child who has met the crises of the first three stages positively has the virtues of hope, will, and purpose.

Industry versus inferiority. This stage lasts from about the sixth year to about the eleventh year. It corresponds to Freud's latency stage of psychosexual development.

Most children attend school throughout this stage. It is during this stage that the child learns the skills necessary for economic survival. If there is a positive response to this crisis, the child learns the technological skills that will allow him or her to become productive members of his or her community. In the United States, school is where children are trained for future employment and adjustment to their culture. Since in most cultures, including our own, surviving involves the ability to work cooperatively with others, the social skills are among the important lessons taught by schools. According to Erikson, the most important lesson that the child learns during this stage is "the pleasure of work completion" by way of "steady attention and persevering diligence."

From this lesson comes a sense of industry that prepares a child to look confidently for his or her productive role in society among other people. If the child does not develop the sense of industry he or she develops a sense of inferiority, causing the child to lose confidence in his or her ability to become a contributing member of society. Such a child is more likely to develop a negative identity. The child may also overvalue the hierarchical importance of his or her role in the workforce. For such a person work is equated with life. He or she is blinded to many other important aspects of existence. Many of our "workaholics," "over-achievers," and "obsessives" plateaued at this stage of their development.

The virtue achieved by successfully passing through this stage is competence. Erikson says that competence is the free exercise of dexterity and intelligence in the completion of tasks, unimpaired by infantile inferiority, which comes from ridicule or lack of concern by those most important to the child.

Identity versus role confusion. This stage occurs between about twelve years of age to about twenty years of age. It corresponds roughly to Freud's genital stage of psychosexual development. Erikson is best known for the description of this psychosocial stage. It contains his now famous concept of "identity crisis." During the 1990s we are at a very critical problem stage in our national development. This is true not only for the adolescents of the American "underclass," but also for the neglected "overprivileged" children of America's professional couples, who are often too preoccupied for proper parenting. This stage is the transition from childhood to adulthood. In the preceding stages, children learn who they are and what it is possible for them to do. During this stage children ponder all this accumulated information about themselves and their society. Now children commit themselves to some strategy about life. In this way they gain an identity and become an adult. Gaining a personal identity marks the satisfactory end of this stage of development. Still, the stage itself is a time of searching for an identity without having one. Erikson called this period a psychosocial moratorium, in his words, a prolongation of the interval between youth and adulthood. In recent decades, the United States has been making a tragedy out of this prolonged transitional period. For too many of our youths becoming adults is an aimless adventure. There is a shortage of appropriate role models, a surfeit of Mick Jaggers, Dennis Levines, and Sean Penns.

Erikson used the term *identity,* sometimes *ego-identity,* in a variety of ways.

I can attempt to make the subject matter of identity more explicit only by approaching it from a variety of angles. At one time, then, it will appear to refer to a conscious sense of individual identity, at another point, to an unconscious striving for continuity of personal character, at a third as a criterion for the silent beings of the ego-synthesis, and finally as a maintenance of inner solidarity with a group's ideals and identity.

If the young adult does not leave this stage with an identity, he or she leaves it with role confusion, or, worse, with a negative identity. Role confusion and negative identity is characterized by the inability to choose a role in life, and so prolonging the psychosocial moratorium indefinitely. One may make superficial commitments that are soon abandoned. Negative identities are all those things a child is warned not to become. For Erikson, role confusion and negative identity explain much of the unrest and hostility expressed by adolescents in this country.

The virtue achieved with the creation of identity is fidelity, defined by Erikson as the ability to sustain freely pledged loyalties despite inevitable contradictions of value systems.

Intimacy versus isolation. This stage is also called early adulthood. It lasts from about twenty to about twenty-four years of age. For this psychosocial stage and those following, there is no corresponding Freudian psychosexual stage of development. Freud once defined a healthy person as one who loves and works. Erikson agrees with this definition.

The virtue achieved by successfully passing through this stage is love, which Erikson defines as the mutuality of devotion forever subduing the antagonisms inherent in divided function. Only the person who is secure in his identity can risk merging himself in a love relationship with another. A young adult with a strong identity eagerly seeks intimate relationships with others. People who do not develop the capacity for productive work and intimacy withdraw into themselves, avoid close contacts, and develop a feeling of isolation. Some compulsively and obsessively pursue their personal dreams and become poets, artists, inventors, writers, and great scientists. They are rare forms of adaptation. This discussion is a pursuit of a normal state for ordinary people.

Generativity versus stagnation. This stage, also called middle adulthood, occurs from about twenty-four to about sixty-five years of age. If one has been fortunate enough to develop a positive identity, and to live a productive happy life, one tries to pass the circumstances that caused this effect on to the next generation. This can be done by interacting with children. They need not be one's own, nor must it be done directly. It can be done by producing or creating things that will enhance the lives of those in the next generation. Erikson calls this generativity. The person who does not develop a sense of generativity is characterized by stagnation, boredom, and interpersonal impoverishment.

If the ratio of generativity to stagnation is favorable, one leaves this stage with the virtue of care, defined by Erikson as the widening concern for what has been generated by love, necessity, or accident. Care overcomes the ambivalence adhering to irreversible obligation.

Ego-integrity versus despair. This stage occurs from about the age of sixty-five until death. It is called late adulthood. Only a person who can look back on a rich, meaningful happy life does not fear death. Such a person has a feeling of completion and fulfillment, Erikson's ego-integrity. The person who looks back on his life with frustration experiences despair. Strange as it may seem, the person experiencing despair is not as ready for death as the person with a sense of fulfillment. He has not yet achieved any major goals in his life. The eight stages are progressively related to each other, but the eighth stage is directly related to and can fulfill the first. The eight stages of development are interrelated in a circular fashion. For example, the adult attitude toward death will directly influence the young child's sense of trust. If the individual has more ego-integrity than he does despair, his life will be characterized by the virtue of wisdom, which Erikson defines as detached concern with life in the face of death.

For Erikson the outcome of every crisis resolution is reversible. For example the person leaving the first stage of development without basic trust may later gain it, and the person having it may lose it. *Erikson considered a person healthy if he successfully traversed the eight stages of life and thus got the virtues of hope, will, purpose, competence, fidelity, love, care and wisdom.* If a person does not gain these virtues his or her ego is weaker than it otherwise would be; therefore his or her ability to cope with life and its vicissitudes is weakened.

The Able Mind

According to Charles Wahl, clinical professor of psychiatry at the University of California at Los Angeles, the antecedents of the able mind are the same as those of the normal person: knowing and liking oneself, having evolved through a cherishing and loving environment with persons who have manifested positive cathexes to learning and problem-solving.[6] According to Wahl, the able mind:

- Reads quickly, retains easily, and recalls past learning whether aural or visual. Learning through the other senses of smell, touch, and taste are also maximized, though less so in urban areas.
- Can think for long periods of time without fatigue. As Wahl states, Newton once said that he created the Newtonian laws by thinking about them incessantly. The Japanese once said, "A concentrated mind can pierce a rock."
- Has unimpaired curiosity; is not guilty about doubts.
- Is free from narrow constrictions of convention and from overpowering need of peer or superior approval.
- Has ego ideal, rather than super-ego.
- Is psychologically minded.
- Perceives parents as persons, not personages.
- Sees that life is in proportion, not with narrow tribal or magical-religious constraints.
- Makes the smallest use of magical-thinking possible, except perhaps in aesthetics and humor.
- Makes the smallest use of repression (not suppression) as a coping device. Also makes very small use of the mechanisms of "denial" and "undoing."
- Has *Weltanschauung*—a sense of fair and reasonable well-being. "Has it all together."
- Can accept death, hence can live, as Spinoza said. Time is prized and the mind is used for thinking about physical rather than metaphysical things.

Given acceptance of Wahl's antecedents of the able mind as the same as those of the normal person, it is desirable to set forth the antecedents of normal mental functioning:

The characteristics of normal versus neurotic mental functioning

Neurosis	Normality

1. Person displays significant problems in love and in work and is blocked either in intention or execution in these areas.	1. Love proceeds continuously from:
	  (a) self-love
	  (b) love of collaterals and family
	  (c) love of tribes
	  (d) species love (all men are brothers)
	  (e) all life.
	Work is characterized by nonconflict progression, zest, self-actualization, perseverance, creativity.

2. Irrational thinking. Predilection for fantasy or magical-thinking rather than secondary-process thinking. There is limited use of and reach of the mind. There is a heavy use of repression as a coping mechanism. There is a limited recall of the past.	2. Full reality testing. No inhibitions to curiosity or learning. Minimal use of mystical, archaic, magical-religious or superstitious thought. There is an active capacity to problem-solve, a full use of concept formation, ability to extrapolate and generalize, to employ third order abstractions, i.e., the full use and reach of the mind.
3. Low self-esteem. High degree of conventionality, bigotry, and tribalism.	3. High self-esteem. Cosmopolitanism. High tolerance for others and the habits, patterns, and folk ways of others.
4. Hans Sachs. The neurotic reacts to people and situations in the present as though they were people and situations in the past without observing that he is doing so.	4. Realistic response to every new situation unencumbered by past experience and a complete absence of familiarizing his environment.
5. Limited or few coping mechanisms. Inflexibility of response, personality essentially constricted in character.	5. Wide range of coping mechanisms. Flexible response. Wide-ranging and flexible character.
6. Intense, unremitting self-engrossment.	6. The opposite of self-engrossed. A deep self-capacity for species rather than tribal identification. Wide-ranging attention to self and others.

7. (a) Absence of *Weltanschauung.*
(b) Morality is irrationally and culturally derived without logical scrutiny or thought.
(c) The personality is constricted and guided by an irrational superego.

7. (a) An active *Weltanschauung.*
(b) The patient is ethical rather than moral, and the ethics are rationally derived.
(c) The personality is broad and flexible and is guided by adherence to an ego-ideal that is consciously derived.

8. Thanatophobic and hypochondriacal. High somatic compliance. Numerous psychosomatic symptoms.

8. Persons can deal with the concept of death of finitude. "Neither wishes death, nor fears it." Experiences very little somatic compliance.

9. High use of symptom formation in anxiety binding. Especially prone to patterns of depreciation and manifests disproportionate response to stimuli. Impaired self-regard.

9. Relative absence of symptoms. High self-regard.

10. Anti-hedonic effect.

10. High capacity for zest, joy, and happiness, irrespective of situational factors.

11. Outer-directed; low self-regard.

11. Inner-directed; high self-regard. Has 51 percent of stock in one's own corporation.

12. Stunted curiosity, not psychologically minded, inability to appreciate another's point of view, lack of empathy.

12. Free-ranging curiosity, is psychologically minded, can deeply appreciate a point of view of someone quite different from himself. Empathy.

13. Blunted use of capacities for work innovation and creativity.

13. Full use of capacities for same.

14. Learning is forced by authorities, is resisted or is unsuccessful, inefficient, and spotty. Tasks rarely are completed.

14. Learning is interesting and easy; addressing learning tasks can be concentrated. Tasks can be persevered into a successful conclusion.

15. Difficulty in human relationships, deeply limited by arbitrary capacities such as age, tribe, ethnicity, and economic and educational levels. Very narrow range of persons to identify with, and continuously responding to present people and situations in terms of unresolved problems in past relationships.

15. Success in relationships. Love and high regard both for self and others through all dimensions of relatedness. Successful, happy, stable relationships with others, on both an intimate and casual basis.

16. Neurotic. Has problems in both the intention and execution of love and/or a choice of impossible, unworthy, and unstable love objects. "Choosing the club to beat oneself to death with."

16. Can love and be loved and objects chosen are worthy and reciprocal in response.

There are several other antecedents for the development of an able mind:

- A secure family always cherishes the subject but differentially applies approval. The child is raised by positive reenforcement, rather than aversive conditioning. Learning is characterized by rewards of achievement and a genuine showing of interest.
- Socializers supply graded tasks so the child can grow up in sequence.
- There has been freedom from enduring states of want, economic, social, and sociopolitical.
- The child has known pleasure of gratifying curiosity and of having it rewarded.

Wahl's last area of concern is the quality of life known as happiness. Being a subjective state, happiness is the most difficult to describe. Wahl outlines it by a series of paradoxical statements from different sources. Aristotle defined happiness as consisting in "the fullest use of all one's faculties and capacities in an environment that affords them maximum scope." Happiness is not simply an absence of dysfunctional symptoms nor is it only the product of a happy socialization. A deep and morbid conception of the human race is an extrapolation on to fate of the Greek idea of Hubris. They thought that the gods secretly envied humans and their happiness and therefore did not permit them to have too much of it. Publius Syrus said "Irritare est calamitatem cum te felicitem voces"—"To call yourself happy is to provoke disaster!" We see the same idea in Jewish superstition, the Kinnehora, or in the dynamics of the success neurosis. One really has to like oneself, and to have been liked by others, not to feel guilty about being happy. Some psychiatrists know a great truth. Namely, that if we have every conceivable thing that is supposed to conduce to happiness—youth, beauty, wealth, love, task, respect, fame, health, renown and longevity—it only adds up to about 65 percent of what we require for happiness. The rest must be internally derived. Describing happiness, Freud said, "The goal of analysis is to exchange neurotic unhappiness for general unhappiness, which is the lot of mankind." Americans reject this mordant view.

One objective of this text is to reject Freud's dolorous world view, to follow instead our founding fathers in seeking a more healthy paradigm. The process of pursuing happiness is worth the effort and is more enlightening. The antecedents of happiness consist of not personifying causation. This enables the happy person to be content with relative contentment, to not feel that a happy state is one devoid of tragedy and misadventure. Ecclesiastes says, "The race is not to the swift nor the battle to the strong, nor, yet bred to men of understanding, but, time and chance doth with us all."

Ashley Montagu is a good starting point for understanding the pursuit of happiness.

Most Americans lead a somewhat selfish existence, narcissistically developed by their own self-interest, which eventually leaves them out in the cold. . . . We are a culture of success. We must have the right kind of car, marry the right kind of spouse . . . in the hope of finding happiness, in the hope of finding the cure for what is making us miserable and unhappy. . . . Americans are out for success—specifically, a success measured by external validations. . . . There are no games or sports in America. You play to win. As Vince Lombardi said, "Winning is not everything, it's the only thing." . . . You should play because it's fun, and you should do your best, hoping your opposite numbers will do their best. It doesn't mean you do not like to win. Of course, you should like to show that you have great skill . . . for the pleasure you take in that skill. . . . Young people need the necessity of making something of themselves. . . . It is within your power to make yourself happy or unhappy by setting yourself such goals as are within your range, and that you will enjoy achieving. . . . We're all born social creatures . . . we humans are dependent on others for our growth and development. . . . Interdependency with others is necessary. It's not merely conferring benefits in a creatively enlarging manner. While you're conferring benefits upon the other, the other is gaining and reciprocally conferring benefits on you. . . .

Loneliness is an endemic disorder in America. There's something not quite right about someone who lives alone and likes it. . . . You can be successful only if you are a warm, loving, relating human being who takes the whole world into his or her orbit. You can't do everything, obviously, but you can do something. . . . . I have lived 81 years, and have had a great deal of experience with this sort of conduct toward others. I had to learn to be this way. . . . We remain educable throughout our lives. . . . For most human beings I would no longer speak of aging. I would speak of growing. . . . If you've become a nasty, hostile, aggressive creature, that doesn't mean you can't change into a warm, loving, human being! How do you do it? Simply by acting as if you were a loving human being . . . it's the demonstrative act toward others in which you communicate a profound involvement in their welfare. . . . If you go out and look for happiness you won't find it. Happiness is something that comes by way of some pleasant experience when you have done something that has been very helpful to someone else, has given someone else a great deal of pleasure.

Gurus do help. Montagu has been a truth-teller to many. We have been blessed by his presence. Our roots play a major role in happiness. Family, close friends, knowing the territory, all give us a sense of security and comfort. It is not only love and responsibility to others, but reciprocal love and responsibility from others to us that makes us feel good.

Drugs and the Existential Vacuum

Addicts and pushers have made one patch of Zurich, Switzerland, into the crossroads of drugs in Europe. A few hundred yards from a shopping center,on average two thousand people per day mill around the old Zurich bandstand to buy and sell drugs. Weekends the average swells to four thousand per day. Dealers openly advertise their wares. Zurich authorities believe that addicts are not criminals but sick people who need help. Yet, all the many social services simply make things worse. Some feel that they make the addicts more dependent on drugs. In 1990, drug-related deaths in Zurich are up 80 percent over the previous year. The Zurich market is an example of an abysmal market failure in a part of the world that should be able to control it.

In the United States our market economy produces about $40 billion in illegal drug sales. By comparison, Americans spent $38.6 billion on prescription drugs in 1990. Our intensive war on drug crime is a dramatic attempt to make a big bang while avoiding the real problem. I do not take up the war against drugs in my chapter on crime. This is because drug use is a social problem, only secondarily a criminal problem. True, about 75 percent of drug sales are to people who have been previously arrested or convicted of crimes. But the United States's sharply rising crime rate soared before drug use became so widespread. The nation's leadership would rather build prisons and diminish the rights of all citizens to try to win the drug wars than use major changes in social policies that would work. Here are examples:

Attack the demand side. Make buying and using drugs a federal crime. Possession and use of selected controlled substances could be made a federal minor misdemeanor in the first year, a major misdemeanor in the second year, and a felony thereafter, with mandatory jail sentences. Phasing in the degree of criminality of drug buying would give the addicts time to change. Do it. Columbia is planting poppies. Heroin is on the way here.

Attack the supply side at the source. Bolivian and Peruvian diplomats have offered to help the United States use agricultural subsidies to buy up the coca-growing fields. We could sharply diminish the supply by buying the coca leaves at the lowest possible price, thereby choking off the cocaine at the source. Similar measures could be considered for the fields of opium poppies in Thailand and elsewhere. It would be necessary to send agricultural extension workers to the fields to show the farmers other cash crops that they could grow and market. Columbia is another sort of problem. Intervention may be necessary.

Use the death penalty for three-time convicted drug dealers and their first-degree accomplices. Ten-year mandatory sentences could be used for first-time drug dealers, who should be provided with therapy and vocational rehabilitation. These draconian measures should be reserved for the worst of the lot, those who are training the runners and are hardened criminals that are incurably dangerous to others.

Adopt a national health plan. This would make low-cost prescription drugs such as Xanax and Sinequon available for anxiety and depression. This would sharply drop the retail price of cocaine and heroin. Those who live in an existential vacuum are always going to seek relief from the suffering and despair of a life without meaning.

Change social policies to provide ways out of the existential vacuum and ennui, currently ignored by our political leadership. A realistic sense of optimism must replace the tragic sense of nihilism about man's predicament. Security found in paradise is closed to man forever. He must make choices. No instinct tells him what to do, traditions have lost their power, often humans do not even know what they wish to do. Instead of choice, many choose to do what other people do. This peer pressure is particularly acute in adolescent and early college years. The existential vacuum manifests itself mainly in a state of boredom, or worse, anxiety and depression followed by despair. Vicktor Frankl, a founder of the school of logotherapy (cognitive therapy) reported that among his American students 60 percent exhibited a marked existential vacuum.[7] Not a few suicides can be traced back to this existential vacuum. Opting for drug use is a form of psychic suicide. The power of chemicals is substituted for human thought and brain power. Temporarily, selling drugs is opting for economic suicide in the sense that the runner is choosing to opt out of conventional society and whatever job opportunities it offers. Selling drugs pays well. If our society wants to foster a healthy outlook to replace the mass neurosis of nihilism we need to set up a field of tension where one pole is represented by meaningfulness that can be fulfilled and the other pole is represented by a means to fulfill it. Today, drugs, alcohol, and sexual promiscuity are the escapes from this void.

The war against drugs will fail until our society unites behind the ideas that man is responsible and must actualize the potential meaning of his own life. *Each human can discover this meaning in life by 1) creating a work or doing a deed, 2) experiencing goodness, truth, beauty, nature, culture, and the love of another, and 3) learning a positive attitude toward the inevitable suffering experienced in life.* Consider the lack of opportunity to achieve the three actions above in the life of the ordinary black male in a poverty ghetto. Our hypocritical society sets up these Americans for a fall into the existential vacuum. For many, drugs are the answer.

Our basic guarantees of freedom and equality are under attack as we find the government sacrificing our fundamental rights to battle the dragon of drug-related crimes. Ralph Garland, a prominent Georgia criminal attorney, says that America's political leadership has not stood up for individual freedom in this country, that the criminalization of drug activities has totally collapsed the system. Some have characterized the current war on drugs as a war on the Bill of Rights that does nothing to solve the problem. We are preparing the ground for a totalitarian leader to protect us from disorder. Things could get worse.

Brave New World

Consider the designer drug alternative. Few Americans are aware that the most successful totalitarian government in history was that of the ancient Incas of the Andes. The dominance and control of the ruling class was maintained by drugs and alcohol. The people were kept numb, docile, and working with coca leaves and beer. Of course, the Incas' government had the advantage of the lack of extended collective memory of wrongs done by the leaders because there was no writing and memories were under official control. So to all appearances the Inca leaders were demigods who governed wisely.

In comparison, the twentieth century experienced a major literary event when Aldous Huxley wrote *Brave New World*. It depicted a modern totalitarian state that was in some ways similar to the Incan empire and fulfilled Thomas Hobbes's dreams. In December 1985 the *Futurist* interviewed Huxley's son, Matthew, and an official from the National Institutes of Health. The dialogue is about his vision of the future in America. Huxley thinks that *Brave New World* was a warning. The story depicted three ways to control the population: soma, sex, and psychobiotechnology. Today, recreational sex and games are in a state that one might say, "The party's over." AIDS is a very lethal threat that is just entering its years of pandemic terror. Huxley fears the threat of AIDS will provide government with a public sympathetic to more controls through public health measures. As to soma, the technology for creating it, in effect, "designer drugs," is well in hand. It is not yet legally developed and dispensed, much less used as a method of social control, but it is here and traded sporadically on the streets. As for biotechnology, today's five billion people, and still growing, indicates that such staged and genetically engineered IQ levels in the population are a long way off. Still, Huxley thinks a problem of the first order, challenging us now, is matching population growth with our ability to maintain social and political organizations, so we can manage to maintain peace and survival. Today it is certain that we must be on guard against the development of socially sanctionable drugs. Huxley is certain they can be developed. Whether they should be developed is the question. In 1987 Walker Percy's novel *The Thanatos Syndrome* warned of the possibilities implicit in such a drugged population. Clearly we have already reached the time when drugs could be used to "turn-on" and "tune-out" the population. It is a superficially appealing way to diminish stress in the pursuit of happiness. We must listen to Huxley when he says, "The marriage of the silicon chip with automated tools (from speech typewriters, to computer designed assembly lines) will cause an absolute transformation of our society. It will vastly limit the opportunity for meaningful work . . . I think we are in for some serious trouble."[8]

Part IV: World Cities and American Metroareas

Preface

The municipal infrastructures of hundreds of earth's cities are being overburdened by a burgeoning of world population that intends to live in cities. Horrendous public health problems are in the offing. Modern Americans may soon grasp the reality that the brains of the billions of humans who inhabit the earth are the true battleground of geopolitics. If so, we could be on the way to developing mature human personalities in the United States that can cope with these very pressing global problems. The metropolitan explosion is a force to be harnessed with the creativity of autonomous humans working together, not by the police-state tactics of draconian truncheons that will be used by fear-dominated, neofascistic economies. The rapid growth of giant cities in both the lesser-developed and highly industrialized countries is the frontier of our being. Men and women with fire in their minds could rebuild the spirit of the world by a massive construction and reconstruction of the sewers, waterways, water systems, bridges, and transportation systems of the metroarea environment of most humans.

A highly respected economist, Alan Blinder, says that America's crumbling highways are giving the nation's economic productivity a "flat"! America has failed to maintain and expand its public capital stock—the municipal infrastructure. Subdivisions are halted because we lack sewer capacity. Airlines cancel flights, or have their planes hover in the air because we lack runways. Bridges are worn out. We failed to separate storm (rainwater) from sanitary (putrid water) sewers. As a young nation, we have seriously erred. We have given primacy to the private sector, and the military sector, while starving the metroareas. Blinder quotes researcher David Aschauer to show that this wanton neglect of our metroareas has been a driving force behind the decline in productivity of our manufacturing and service sectors of the economy. The amount spent on the infrastructure has been decreasing. Over the past twenty years annual spending has fallen from 2.3 percent of the gross national product to only 1 percent. More than 60 percent of the nation's highways need to be resurfaced. Somewhere in the United States a bridge collapses every day. In New York City two water mains collapse daily.

The issue is not only safety and sanitation but also national productivity. If democratic capitalism is to work well it needs a flow of funds to the true merit goods of the public sector: the municipal infrastructure. I hasten to add that this includes education, recreational parks, libraries, public hospitals, and other human services. This is because we are a constitutional culture that is forming a new kind of metroarea for the "knowledge" workers who populate the information economy. Knowledge workers come together in our metroareas for economic opportunity, and recreational, cultural, and religious pursuits. In effect, as individuals they seek the opportunity to grow and improve their spiritual potential. They need a good environment in which to work and play and pray. At this time we have many serious public health problems that are imposing great stress on these knowledge workers: handguns, murders, excessive waste of the military, the homeless, to name a few.

In this section I will provide some proposals for radical changes in our public policies designed to head us in the direction of using tax policy as an incentive. These policies will result in more active participation by our citizenry in both governance under our constitutional culture and within democratic capitalism. To prepare for those chapters we need some discussion of the place of public expenditures in the ethos of our myth-laden political economy. We have done a very bad job of educating the American public on the high value that citizens ought to place on public expenditures for the municipal infrastructure. These serve everyone within over three hundred urban areas, where nearly 95 percent of our population lives. Our media have misled the public into believing that such public expenditures are a waste of money. A national reeducation on these matters should probably start with our journalists.

9. The Population Bomb

Our Spaceship Earth is a global ecological system, lost in space, on autopilot, without "Star Trek" 's Mr. Spock or Arthur Clarke's David Bowman to save us. America is in a drug-induced stupor. Enjoying its self-congratulatory mood, the United States is on a consumer binge. The world painfully waits for us to overcome this self-indulgence and face our responsibilities as the self-avowed leader of a humane society that takes rights seriously. The hourglass is inverted, the sands of time are running out. During the next few decades we face temporary overpopulation of our planet. We are experiencing the virtual urbanization of the whole world. Now even remote rural areas will be connected by telecommunications to urban cultures and their rich diversity. The unprecedented growth of some global megalopolises will cause heavy-handed fascistic central planning to cope with the impending certainty of social disorganization. Or, worse, there will be severe public health problems of unprecedented magnitude. Tragic and disastrous social disorganization, caused by the AIDS disease, has riddled Uganda, once the pearl of Africa. It is a harbinger of what will come unless international cooperation supplants religious and national confrontation. The current pace of change is hard for the human mind to grasp. For example, Mexico City could have a population of 26 million to 33 million by the year 2000.

Mexico City

Mexico City! Grand, cosmopolitan, proud, beautiful Mexico Districto Federale. This ancient metropolis has grown to about 19 million people and will soon surpass Tokyo as the largest city on planet Earth. Anyone who visits Mexico City will experience a thrill at the mix of ancient Aztec ruins and Spanish cathedrals with modern architecture and the extraordinary murals of Mexico's world-famous artists. This city built on the dried-up bed of Lake Taxcoco is now edged with many miles of slum hovels. The first thing one would see if arriving by air is a perpetual, ugly gray-brown blanket of smog that shrouds the entire city. Mexico's growth to number one as a world-class city is impelled in large part by jobless peasants streaming in from the countryside at a rate of about a thousand a day.[1]

As novelist Carlos Fuentes has said, Mexico City is the capital of undevelopment, the capital of pollution, and the capital of slums. This is the city builders' dream turned to a nightmare. It is a warning to the other great cities, particularly those in the Third World, but also to New York or Los Angeles. More than 2 million of the city's people have no running water in their homes. Ninety-five percent of the inhabitants have access to water, but for many of them it is by way of one faucet shared by an entire block. More than 3 million residents have no sewage facilities. Tons of waste are left in gutters or vacant lots to become, through leaching, part of the city's water and dust. One Mexico City newspaper wrote, "If fecal matter were flourescent, the city wouldn't need lights." Mexico City produces about 14,000 tons of garbage every day, but processes only 8,000. The rest gets dumped in landfills or is left to rot in the open. The result is a rat population far in excess of the human. The daily byproduct of chemical air pollution amounts to 11,000 tons. Normal breathing is estimated to be the equivalent of smoking two packs of cigarettes a day in clean air. The combination of chemical and biological poisons kills 30,000 children every year by way of respiratory and gastrointestinal diseases.

The undefended two-thousand-mile frontier between Mexico and the United States is the only place in the world where a wealthy industrial nation borders on a poor and overcrowded one. The official total of legal Mexican aliens in the United States stood at 596,000 as of 1981. It is nonsense. Some demographers estimate the numbers in the millions. Usually, says one, "about two thirds of the Mexican peasants who can't survive on the land go to Mexico City and to the other of Mexico's cities. One third somehow make their way into Texas, California, and on into the cities of the United States. If those proportions were ever reversed, we'd be in terrible trouble."

Still, Mexico City is not a vast pile of urban rubbish. It is a world-class star, a stylish city of the Western hemisphere. It is a city of broad boulevards, gleaming modern office buildings, sparkling fountains, scarlet flower beds, and noble, baroque churches that welcome one and toll every morning with a resonant litany of bells and chimes. Mexico is blessed by eleven major daily newspapers and six television channels. The shops in the Zona Rosa, near the Paseo de La Reforma, were a glitter comparable to that of the most fashionable areas of Paris or New York City before the terrible earthquake. The pace of renovation has been amazing.

That is the Mexico City of the rich and the tourist. Then there are the others, as in any city—artisans, bakers, housewives, secretaries, cops, and robbers. Those who have jobs are among the lucky. Unemployment runs to nearly 40 percent. Many have part-time jobs, thus, the official unemployment rate is 12 percent. To some, the answer lies in burglary and theft, which rose 35 percent in the early 1980s. Below many layers of workers come the *pepenadores,* the rubbish pickers. By picking through the trash of the landfills, they hope to find resalable bits of metal or plastic to survive. Below even these garbage pickers are those who can do nothing but beg.

At the Zocalo, the central square, with its monumental cathedral and the presidential palace, one finds the balding man in his tattered suit. A haggard woman with a baby in her arms stands next to him holding out an empty tin can. Beyond, in the dusky air, sits one of thousands of silent Indian girls known as "Marias." This one holds out a thin, brown palm, but nobody stops. The tidal wave of peasant migration into Mexico is impelled by an immense wave of irrational, irrepressible hope, mainly by Indians who believe in change. Yet, there is a stolid anger seeping under the surface. In Mexico City there is the shadow of ideology, both religious and secular. There is also the shadow of corruption and the shadow of inertia. The problems are always growing faster than the solutions. In an ideal world, the problems of Mexico City could be solved. Overpopulation could be checked, even quickly and harshly, as is being tried in China. Air pollution could be reduced as in California; and government could be decentralized as in West Germany. But between the idea and the future there is reality and the humans who discourage positive action.

Consider the birth rate. The United Nations has given Mexico $24 million since 1972 to finance birth control. The government has spent it properly. Educational family-planning programs have caused a drop in the city's birth rate from about 43 per thousand in 1970 to 31 per thousand in 1980. Still, this was largely offset by improved medical services producing a corresponding drop in the death rate. Abortions are banned, unless the mother's life is in danger or she has been raped. Yet about a million Mexican women have them performed illegally every year. About 10,000 of these women die in the process. Knowledge of contraceptives is minimal in the nation. *Mimodo* is a term often applied to the various aspects of life in Mexico City. It means literally, "no way" or "nothing can be done." That attitude could engender the breakdown of this great city. While the Reagan administration concentrated its attention on Nicaragua, Panama, and El Salvador, we jeopardized Mexican recovery and revival after the earthquake. It is folly. Mexico City alone is more than twice as populous as El Salvador and Nicaragua combined. Mexico is also afflicted with more than twice as many problems and much closer to the Texas border. Mexico's economic and political health is so frail that a crash program of domestic and foreign investment is needed now. Inflation hovered recently at around 100 percent. It is certain that the United States should take a more activist role in Mexico. We are Mexico's biggest trading partner, primary recipient of its flight of capital, and a haven for millions of destitute Mexican citizens trying to escape and survive. A bilateral commission of American and Mexican leaders should be set up by both nations' presidents to work out a new economic and political relationship. The Nicaraguan affair is a trifling diversion in comparison. Mexico is the greatest foreign policy and security challenge facing the United States for the rest of the century.

Runaway Third World Growth

For some time projections have shown that the population of India will be about one billion people by the year 2000.[2] Of that, 350 million will be living in cities, three times as many as lived in Indian cities in 1986. In the major metroareas, Bombay, Delhi, and Calcutta, pockets of glistening skyscrapers are surrounded by squalid slums. Bombay has about 200,000 pavement dwellers. Each day about 350 more people arrive. The result is frightening overcrowding, with all the expected problems of dire poverty: traffic congestion, wandering, loitering unemployed, crime, filth, and unrelieved misery. A twenty-four-hour supply of clean drinking water does not exist in any city in India, nor is it likely to in the foreseeable future. India's roads are unplanned and outdated. Lacking in public transportation, severe deficits of available resources exist in education, health, and communications.

Brazil remains buoyant because of its confidence in growth.[3] Still, in the *favelaes* of Rio de Janeiro and Sao Paulo there is no water. It must be carried a distance. Stealing is a way of life to stave off hunger. Tens of millions of Brazilians live in slums. Hundreds of thousands of youths will do anything—anything—to survive the terrifying life of the streets of the major cities. According to Joseph Ramos, assistant director of the Latin American Economic Council, about 80 million Latin Americans live in extreme poverty. Most of them live in the metroareas.

In the later 1980s Mozambique's roads were thick with people. More than 1.5 million have abandoned their homes in the face of war, drought, and economic decay. Mozambique leads the human suffering index of the Washington-based Population Crisis Committee. For all Africa, Mozambique is a severe disappointment. With its fertile soil, rich mineral resources, and long coastline, it was to have been the best example of what black-ruled sub-Saharan Africa could be. Instead it is a vast zone of human suffering. The foreign debt cannot be serviced by exports. The illiteracy rate is 75 percent. Under colonialism, the Portuguese occupied every position that required any skill, so when independence came and the vast majority of Portuguese left, control of society fell into the hands of people without the necessary skills. Then, the illiteracy rate was 93 percent. The number of native college graduates was less than twenty. In 1976, nine million tons were shipped through the port of Maputo. Now less than two million are handled. A Maputo businessman laughs, ironically, "If you do not know what you are doing you go bankrupt. . . . Same with a country."[4]

Marseilles is a city at risk of being the victim of de-colonization. France's overseas empire gone, its former subjects are crowding into the city. It is racially tense, and a stomping ground for the neofascist National Front. Local elections, in 1985, showed alarming gains for the National Front feeding on fears of immigrants. Given the predilection of white officials and gangsters for fraud and murder, the city seems to have little excuse to blame immigrants for the crime rate. The Arabs do not assimilate. They are many, and have turned the center of the city into a casbah, selling carpets, suitcases, tea, oriental cakes, prayer books, and illegal drugs. The city is drifting, without a plan, into a chaotic future.[5]

Singapore is the vibrant success story of twentieth-century fascism. This world-class metropolis is an intense amalgam of races and cultures. There is a population of 2.5 million, mostly Chinese, then Malays, Indians, Pakistanis, with Europeans at the bottom of the list. Shopping is a voyage of discovery through the world's most desirable goods. Reality is a small piece of land—the toe of Malaya—1 degree north of the equator. Annual per-capita income is $7,000, ahead of Ireland and Israel. Most of the population lives in high-rise, high-density warrens that would have vandals, violence, and drugs if in the United States.

Yet, in Singapore, vandalism is almost unknown. Criminals (ignoring for now white-collar criminals) and drug dealers are rare. Printed in red letters on tourist cards is the notice, "Warning—Death for Drug Traffickers." Jaywalking and littering are abhorred. Dropping a cigarette butt on the street is subject to a $250 fine. An extremely high rate of savings is compulsory. Citizens are required to spend a high percentage of their income on housing; the amount required is in accordance with their station in life. The Singapore river is dredged regularly for sanitary reasons. Health inspectors regularly check food stalls to ensure compliance with standards of cleanliness. The *muezzin* call the Muslim faithful to prayer five times a day. A Hindu temple in the midst of Chinatown is open for worship. Religious freedom prevails.

Singapore is a place of business. Tourists stay for about three days, for there is little to do. The government maintains strict order in the place of work and productivity. It is a story of success of capitalism, but not democratic capitalism, nor of a constitutional rights–based culture. Singapore is small, the lines of communication are short, from only one level of government to the neighborhood. Singaporeans worry that they are overregulated. Break dancing is outlawed. Roller skaters are confined to a specific area. Cars cannot speed. Teenagers cannot deface the walls. Hard-headed courts use imprisonment without hesitation.

Lee Kuan Yew, the illustrious founder and prime minister of Singapore, encouraged transitional leaders to develop as he neared retirement. Yew argues that Asian culture finds the democratic experience a hindrance to growth because the agricultural society cannot be reconciled with the demands of urban citizens. Yew argues that China governs by recruiting rural soldiers and keeping the cities in check. China cannot enthuse the urban intelligentsia. Somehow the urban people must be drawn into the system not only to run enterprises but also the cities and towns. Yew sees India as a debasement of democracy with votes dependent on caste, religion, language, primeval pulls on ancient loyalties, and cash. Yew states that for the development of the kind of democracy we associate with Britain or America you need certain cultural impulses such as a tolerance of different views, a willingness to accept for the time being that opposites may prevail while one tries to win over a majority the next time around. Still, Yew feels that modern industrial society needs participation for success. Participation of the workforce will inevitably spill over to government, if reinforced by the media, and with exposure to other cultures. Still, at the same time in Asia old patterns prevail—Asians look to the magistrate to solve the problems.

Yew says he was an authoritarian, but that if he had not taken the initiative, nobody would have. Who is going to stop people smoking in public places when there is no antismoking movement? Yew follows his head, not his heart, in governing Singapore. Still, Yew's replacement, Goh Chok Tong, has a less stern, more open style. Tong hopes to lead Singapore into a more entrepreneurial and flexible future, less dependent on central planning. Singapore must live by its wits and through the processing of goods and providing of services. No economy can afford to ignore the rest of the world, but for Singapore trade is the essence of existence. The metro-areas of the United States would be wise to heed, as they enter the global economy of today and the future, to compete with a Singapore.[6]

These vignettes of various world cities and their countries emphasize that the world has entered a time of crisis. The rise of mass-based civilization may be an incipient brutalization of the culture of the earth's highly industrialized nations. There is a spreading of ignorance, the promotion of trendy, brain-numbed mediocrity, that may cretinize creativity and destroy precise and highly imaginative thought. All this is done in the name of preserving law and order and promoting consumer egalitarianism.

The quality of the municipal infrastructure is being ignored! The immense capital requirements for sewer lines, water lines, streets, housing, and everything else will be necessary to prevent pandemic AIDS, cholera, typhus, and tuberculosis, which are no longer even being measured by the industrialized countries. Calcutta, Mexico City, Lima, and others, are already crying the sorrow of the global shame we will experience as those in dire poverty—the homeless—roam the streets. Either horrendous public health problems are imminent or draconian fascism will be used to cudgel the poor into terrorized civility. The biospheric envelope of atmosphere, water, and topsoil is the container of the inhabitants of earth. For human culture to survive, we must enter a new contract with nature. Survival is dependent on significant attitudinal changes.

Every human must come to understand the results of urbanization. Urbanized society, in which the majority live crowded together in towns and cities, represents a new and fundamental step in man's social evolution. There is nothing, today, that will have a more profound effect on the political, social, and economic interaction of humans than the rapid urbanization of the human race. Today urbanization is linked to the emergence of AIDS in Africa. Research indicates that AIDS is not new. Large-scale migrations to cities of Africa are associated with the emergence of AIDS as an amplified disease. Altered lifestyles appear to have converted a somewhat rare disease of remote villages—the so-called "slim" disease—into the AIDS ailment that is spreading throughout the world, according to Francois Claval of the Pasteur Institute of Paris. Villagers may have known about the disease for many years. Much time has gone into the evolution of the genetic materials of the two viruses currently identified as causing the disease.[7] The effect of AIDS on lifestyles and moral codes is yet to unfold.

The Worldwatch Institute warns that people living in cities increased from 600 million in 1950 to 2 billion in 1986. More than 50 percent of the world's population will live in cities by the year 2000.[8] The multitudes find the city a better place to live than elsewhere. Over 250 cities in the world ecosystem have populations of 500,000 or more. Nearly half are in the developing countries, sometimes called, erroneously, underdeveloped. What is it these cities hope for? As long as the human population expands, cities will expand too. If India's population grows as U.N. projections suggest, the largest cities in India in the year 2000 will hold between 36 million and 66 million inhabitants. It is tragically obvious that the only way to stop urban crowding in the underdeveloped nations is to reduce the overall rate of population growth. The conflict between seeking economic opportunity in our cities and the unwillingness to shoulder the social responsibilities of being citizens in these same urban spaces can no longer be endured. Spaceship Earth suffers under the neglect of responsible stewardship. We have pursued economic betterment through increased consumption without regard to the effect on the urban ecosystems where most of us live.

Unfortunately, Americans, who live in some of the most efficient metroareas in history, seem oblivious to the threat to their democracy implicit in the trends of the metroareas of our developing nations. Citizens of many world cities are not concerned about ecology—they are fighting for survival. In the future, earthlings will look back with some bitterness on the narcissism of Americans who concentrated their attention on consumer materialism while the world cried out for their leadership. The conflict between seeking economic opportunity in our American cities and the unwillingness of U.S. leadership to shoulder the global responsibilities of being citizens of the planet earth can no longer be endured.

In the new global economy all metroareas are in competition with each other. The metroareas of the world compete with, and simultaneously depend on, one another. Paradoxically, specialization may be the key to both competition and interdependence. The past, present, and future roles of metroareas are evident in their interdependence with nearby metroareas of the hinterland of their region. It is a truth infrequently observed that a city usually sends its largest outflows of travel and information to the metroarea on which it relies most heavily for specialized services that are not available locally. Thus, knowledge of the industrial mix, the way jobs and people and land interact with their region and the globe, is essential. American academics study international commerce when they should be studying the relationships between earth's metroareas.

Family Planning

In 1986, on the fortieth anniversary of the United Nations, thirty-five sovereign states representing over half the world's population presented to the Secretary General Javier Perez de Cuellar a statement on population stabilization. They said that the time had come to recognize the worldwide necessity to arrest population growth. Each country needs to adopt the necessary policies and programs consistent with its own culture and aspirations. The states said that all nations should participate in setting goals and programs for population stabilization. Measures for this purpose should be voluntary and should maintain individual human rights and beliefs. The states noted that today there are 76 million more annual births than deaths. If present rates continue, by the year 2000 there will be 100 million more births than deaths each year. A billion people have been added in the last thirteen years; the next billion will be added in only twelve. The signatory nations included the People's Republic of China, India, Japan, Bangladesh, the Philippines, Thailand, Egypt, Korea, and many small nations. The absence of the old Soviet Union and the United States in this call for social justice and responsible management of population growth directs our attention to the failure of leadership of these nations. The absence of Pope John Paul's signature is a sad commentary on the archaic policies of that highly influential moral force.

The reports on population planning are not encouraging. Until the rate of world population growth slows markedly, improving the human condition will be difficult. Beautiful Kenya! It is a world treasure of flora and fauna desperately battling against an astonishing 4 percent annual increase in population as of 1987. Kenya is destroying its nature preserves and has failed to stop increased poaching of wild animals for food as humans compete with animals for land. President Arap Moi has sharply increased family planning outreach workers, but the funding is woefully inadequate as the world concentrates its attention on the much more glamorous arms race. Moi is turning toward dictatorship and a command economy as he copes, desperately. In black Africa, national fertility rates have increased in the past decade. The average number of children born to a woman in Kenya is now eight. Combined with a declining infant mortality rate due to improved medical services, Kenya's population could increase from 22 million today to 83 million in 2025.

In Bangladesh the fertility rate figure is 6.3, which means that 266 million people, nearly three times the present population, may be squeezed into an area the size of Wisconsin by 2025. At the national level, some countries have performed admirably. Twelve countries in Europe have brought population growth to a halt.

Most important, China, home to 22 percent of the world's people, has reduced its annual population growth to just over 1 percent, comparable to that in some industrial countries. In a nearly desperate effort to break the momentum of its population growth, China has shifted to birth planning and the adoption of birth quotas at the commune or production team level. Its national goal is now one child per family. Awards are issued to those who make the "glorious pledge of no more than one child in their family."

India, the world's other population giant, is getting its family planning program back on track. Without decisive action, India's population of 715 million is projected to grow by another billion people before stabilizing. There is some good news. In the ten years since the United Nations sponsored the International Conference on Population in Bucharest, the annual growth of the world's population has declined from 2 percent to 1.7 percent. But the World Bank estimates that in 2025, a date within the foreseeable lifetime of most Americans under 30, global population could increase by 60 percent, to about 8.3 billion. Of that total, about 7 billion will be residents of the undercapitalized, undernourished third world.

Although the economic crisis of the 1980s has been exacerbated by economic mismanagement, its roots lie in the depletion of global resources, both nonrenewable and renewable. In the mid-1980s, we were experiencing a temporary oil glut due to overproduction. Nonetheless, depletion of oil reserves, with its effect on world oil prices, is the threat to world economic stability during the 1990s. And glowering over us all is the more serious long-term threat of depletion of topsoil resources. Land is being gobbled up by subdivision extension of our world's urban areas and by the adoption of chemical agricultural practices. These practices lead to excessive soil erosion and the abandonment of arable land. We are, in a sense, eating the seed corn and burning rather than cropping the forests.

In the United States, the crop surpluses of the early 1980s, sometimes cited as a sign of hope, are partly the product of the mining of soils. In Africa, falling per-capita food production has since 1970 slowly but steadily dragged that continent into a crisis. In many areas grasslands are disappearing under the grazing appetites of excessive numbers of cattle, sheep, and goats. This desertification, the word that describes the conversion of productive ranch land into desert, has become part of our international lexicon. World Watch Institute, in *The State of the World, 1990,* estimated the worldwide net loss of top soil from cropland at 24 billion tons annually. Worldwatch has since raised that estimate to 25.4 billion tons, based on fresh data from the United States and China. A sustainable society is one that shapes it's economic and social systems so that natural resources and life-support systems are maintained. Today we study the archeological sites of earlier civilizations that did not do so, depleting their soils, mismanaging their irrigation systems, or otherwise embarking on a path of counterproductive development. The world economy has moved onto a development path that is unsustainable. The planet can no longer "muddle through."

Forests are a renewable energy source. In the United States, where forests are widely underharvested, or not harvested at all, firewood now supplies twice as much delivered energy as nuclear power. Efforts to protect the world's forests are not faring well. Each year they shrink by an area roughly the size of Hungary. A notable exception is South Korea, which has successfully reforested its once denuded mountains and hills. Elsewhere, because of overcutting and clearing for farming and grazing, the world's forests are shrinking by nearly 1 percent per year.

Gene-pool diversity is losing ground. The loss of genetic diversity results when plant and animal species disappear. It is a principal threat to a sustainable world society. Clearing tropical forest, with the loss of richness in flora and faunae, can eliminate complex, uncatalogued species. Many have yet to be evaluated for their potential commercial value.

Traditionally, African societies enjoyed many human rights enshrined in the United Nations covenants. The post-independent African states, which are larger than the precolonial empires, face new challenges affecting these rights.[9] Today, in Africa, there is both malaise and underdevelopment. There are more limited opportunities, creating a class of migrants and refugees, and a growing population, all pressing the state for services it is ill-equipped to provide. Generally, there is an inept search for viable political and economic institutions to manage the muddle. Human rights are sacrificed in the struggle for power. For most of Africa's leaders, human rights are a topic of debate at the United Nations, and an instrument to be used against vestiges of colonial rule and European domination on the African continent. But human rights are not a universal set of standards to be applied to themselves. Generally, the arguments of African leaders run somewhat like this one:

We, too, would like to provide our people with the rights of liberal democracies. But that is easier said than done. After all, the most basic human right is the right to life itself. In my country people die because they do not have clean water, enough good food, or basic medical care. Those are our priorities. If we have to silence or imprison those who would seek to undermine our unity and our goals, then so be it. So goes the voice of leadership in Africa.[10]

Africans themselves are now concerned that curtailing human rights to get national unity and development has not met the test of time.[11] Nigeria and Senegal are two exceptions to the general trend in Africa. In both states the political leadership has tried to develop institutions that respect basic civil and political rights. In each case, the leadership feels the processes of nation-building and development are better served by observing human rights. This may be a challenge to those African leaders who cite the inherent dilemmas of human rights as reasons for denying them. Both Nigeria and Senegal have relatively heterogeneous populations. Both states are undeveloped. They suffer from pervasive poverty, and have bureaucracies whose members are geared to nepotism and urban living. Corruption in Nigeria is extensive. It risks destroying Nigeria's success in beginning an open, competitive political system in which civil and political rights tend to be respected. At the state and federal level there are many examples of efforts to provide free education and better and less expensive medical care. But rampant corruption has led to gross mismanagement of government funds and has diverted needed resources away from development.

Senegal differs from Nigeria and other African nations. Senegal's association with France dates from the seventeenth century. During that time, a native elite developed that not only shared the egalitarian and liberal views of the French Revolution and enlightened French philosophers but also participated in French political affairs. The post-independence generation began to have serious misgivings about the extremely close relationship between the Senegalese political elite and France. In the 1970s, students with Islamic roots began to identify more closely with one another in trying to set up a Senegalese intellectual and philosophical identity independent of France. Senegal shows that respect for basic rights and the achievement of nation-building and development are not mutually exclusive goals. It shows that enhancement of civil and political rights through a progressive opening of the political system to criticism and multiparty participation can help overcome potential social unrest caused by economic and development problems. Africa is not alone. Other major areas of the world have also remained in this stage for a dangerously long period. For now, the key to the continent's future is the Union of South Africa. There can be no lasting solution for Africa as a whole until a multiracial society in South Africa has been created.

Bolivia, Chile, Ecuador, and Peru have experienced a decline in per-capita food production for more than a decade. Per-capita grain production has fallen by roughly a fourth over the past fifteen years, for much the same reasons as those in Africa—rapid population growth, widespread soil erosion and desertification, and lack of leadership interest in agricultural development.

Another major area of the world at risk is the Indian subcontinent. Annual population growth ranges from 2.4 percent in India to 3 percent in Bangladesh, Nepal, and Pakistan. With 960 million people and a growth rate more than 2.2 percent per year, the subcontinent has not yet made it to low birth rates. The failure of family planning may result in the destruction of national cultural heritages as the fight for survival spreads ignorance and disease.

The effect of these population pressures around the world is that mounting economic demands are leading directly to the deterioration of resources upon which we depend for increasing value-added world economic productivity. We are borrowing against the future in more ways than the Reagan/Bush administrations' awesome deficits. Besides the decimation of the world's forests for firewood and for timber exports, and the destruction of forests by acid rain in the industrial countries, the failure to invest enough in emission controls for coal-burning power plants in Poland, Czechoslovakia, West Germany, and the United States is helping keep current electric costs down, but at a cost of severe damage to our forests.

In a world where broad-based advances in knowledge have led to a high degree of specialization, the need for interdisciplinary research has increased. Even its pursuit has become intellectually more demanding. This challenge was boldly recognized in September 1984 at a meeting of the International Council of Scientific Unions in Ottawa, Canada. Members from some twenty scientific unions and seventy-one national academies of science passed a unanimous resolution urging a worldwide project to study the interaction of the earth's physical, chemical, and biological processes. Unfortunately, there is no overarching body of rational theory that integrates economic trends and ecological forces. Economic analysts turn to their highly developed theory and ecologists rely on well-established ecological principles. There is no easy way to integrate the two approaches, except common sense. If we are interested in food price trends after the end of the century, we should be looking at soil erosion rates today. However, such a long time horizon does not have a good fit with either short-term profit maximization or central economic planning's goals. But the less soil we have, the more food will cost. Many countries with rapidly increasing populations are merely keeping pace with the global rate of economic growth. Some are experiencing declines in per-capita income because their rate of population increase outpaces their economic growth.

Fresh per-capita potable water is on the decline. Supplies of fresh water are constraining both agricultural and industrial expansion. Food is being produced in key agricultural regions of the world by overdrafting our water supplies. For example, in the United States the depletion of the Ogallala aquifer in the southern Great Plains and the diversion of water from irrigation to Sun Belt cities in Arizona, California, and Florida have led to an unanticipated 3 percent decline in national irrigated areas since 1978. Aquifer depletion is now taking its place beside oil depletion and soil erosion as constraints on growth in world food production. The depletion of aquifers or ground water by overdrafts are also rampant in China's northern provinces, in the south Indian state of Tamil, and in the Soviet Central Asian republics.

Population-Induced Climate Change

Meteorologists have traditionally dismissed the notion that large-scale human population clusters could induce climate change. They argued that the forces driving global atmospheric circulation would overwhelm any local, human-induced alterations. Drawing on relevant information from several fields, including agriculture, ecology, hydrology, as well as meteorology, we can now piece together the fact that population-induced local climate change is under way in Africa and the Amazon basin.

For example, as the Amazon rainforest is converted to cropland or grasslands, the share of rainfall that runs off increases. This swells streamflows while decreasing evaporation and therefore the amounts of water in the area's hydrological cycle. The net effect is to lower average rainfall, particularly in the western reaches of the basin. The evidence is persuasive that for the first time we may be on the threshold of man-induced climatic changes. Most of us are aware that a buildup in atmospheric carbon dioxide will warm the earth, a process dubbed the "greenhouse effect." This is the idea that we are upsetting the balance that evolved over long spans of geological time through the short-term (about one hundred years) emission of fossil fuel byproduct hydrocarbons into our atmosphere. The results are multifarious. The rise in sea level anticipated with a doubling of atmospheric CO_2 could range up to 5 to 7 meters over two centuries. With sea levels that high, vast areas of rice land in the flood plains of the Ganges, Yellow, and Mekong Rivers would become untillable without dikes. Such structures would be among the largest public works projects ever undertaken, requiring vast amounts of capital and labor. For a low-lying country such as Bangladesh, where 13 million people live less than 3 meters above sea level, the significance of such a rise is too obvious. Recently, Bangladesh, in a great show of national spirit, used human labor to build a dam to conserve fresh water in the estuary. Yet, few nations are following South Korea's example by planting more trees that consume CO_2, counterbalancing the "greenhouse effect."

The Global 2000 report was an American interagency governmental report prepared in response to a directive by President Carter.[12] Generally it has been ignored by the succeeding administrations. Carter's purpose in requesting the study was to collect knowledge about the long-term implications of present policies and programs. The report sought to establish a base for longer-range planning. To the free marketeers

Population Statistics*

	Country Pop.	Rate of Growth[1]	Cities Pop.[2]			
	Mid-1981		1975	1980	1990	2000
Egypt	43.2	2.7%				
Cairo, Giza, Imbaba			6.932	8.391	11.975	16.398
Zaire	30.1	3.5%				
Kinshasa			2.049	2.957	5.550	9.1126
Mexico	69.4	2.7%				
Mexico City			10.942	13.878	21.631	31.61
Argentina	28.1	1.6%				
Buenos Aires			9.332	10.375	12.334	13.978
Brazil	124.7	2.3%				
Sao Paulo			9.965	12.494	18.662	26.045
Rio de Janeiro			8.328	10.016	14.149	19.383
Peru	18.1	2.6%				
Lima, Callao			3.901	5.157	8.315	12.130
China	1044.8	1.6%				
Shanghai			10.888	12.002	14.855	19.155
Peking			8.487	10.216	14.218	19.064
India (including Sikkin)	692.9	1.9%				
Calcutta			8.077	9.583	13.740	19.663
Greater Bombay			7.094	8.722	13.113	19.065
Delhi			4.489	5.704	8.961	13.220
Madras			3.748	4.658	7.103	10.375
Indonesia (including East Timur)	159.4	2.1%				
Jakarta			5.593	7.191	11.452	16.933
Pakistan	89.0	2.9%				
Karachi			4.465	5.971	10.206	15.862
Philippines	50.0	2.4%				
Manilla			9.444	5.593	8.637	12.683
Thailand	48.9	2.3%				
Bangkok, Thonburi			3.277	4.258	7.031	11.030

*Population figures are in millions.
[1]The Environmental Fund was compiled by Laura Rosen and Dawn Hill under the direction of Robert Cook.
[2]*1977 Compendium of Social Statistics.* (United Nations: New York, 1980.)

of the Reagan/Bush administrations, planning is anathema—except for the military. Everything else is left to the operation of the marketplace as an ideological commitment. In spite of its weaknesses, the Global 2000 Report to President Carter presented an important and useful picture of the future.

Fortunately, since 1983 its viewpoint has been advanced by the work of the

World Watch Institute under the directorship of Lester Brown. According to the Global 2000 report, present efforts to meet human expectations and basic human needs should be modified between now and 2000. The policies in place may undermine the biosphere's ecological capabilities to meet basic needs on earth by early in the twenty-first century because of a destruction of the ecological balance of the globe.

This book intentionally deals with a short time horizon—only twenty to thirty years—because the problems set forth are emergent. The continued urbanization in the less-developed countries (LDCs) will result from the failure of those countries to restrain general population growth and its destabilizing effect on the economy and ecology of those regions. The forecast is social disorganization and pandemic public health problems. For the LDCs, the Global 2000 report projects dire consequences. The report sees increasing social disorganization, urban poverty, spreading disease and pandemic public health problems, psychological alienation, and a rising inability of ordinary humans to cope with the problems of food, clothing, and shelter. Resorting to antisocial behavior will become a persistent and growing problem. The report presumes that massive poverty will occur in the worst of the world's major megalopolises. Table 1 details population statistics for major cities in the LDCs. Many of the countries concerned are beset already with serious problems of poverty, unemployment, and serious ecological instability. Urbanization trends—with their effects on culture and civilization—show significant social and cultural change within those countries that are experiencing the largest increases of their major cities. We want to consider the potential effects of advancements in the science of agriculture and of political programs for reform in land use and tenure. Still, it is possible that the future economic development of less-developed countries may result in dispersal and ruralization of their populations. But this would require some form of democratic central planning. This is presently opposed by the governments of the United States of America and other leading Western nations. Therefore, it is more appropriate to presume that social disorganization and public health problems will result. These huge cities of the future will be more like the disastrous urban conditions of London, described by Charles Dickens in the nineteenth century, or Barbara Tuchman's descriptions of the time of the bubonic plague, than "the city beautiful" of urban planners.

The most rapidly growing sector of these huge cities will likely be in the uncontrolled settlements. These are squatter cities where large numbers of the poor will live without access to basic public services such as potable water and sewage disposal. This is already happening in Cairo, Kinshasha, Mexico City, Calcutta, Jakarta, Manilla, Lima-Callao, Shanghai, greater Bombay, and elsewhere. Raw sewage, air pollution, lack of housing, poor and crowded transport, inadequate fire protection, and spreading diseases such as cholera and typhoid, will present increasing difficulties for these cities.

Cholera and Other Epidemics

In 1991, it was reported that the cholera epidemic in Peru has started the international spread of the disease. It is now present in other countries of Latin America. A few cases have been seen in the United States. Truly astonishing is the Peruvian government's success in diminishing the death rate from the epidemic. Less than

1 percent of the roughly 250,000 who got the disease died. In West Africa during early 1970s the death rate in a similar outbreak was between 20 and 30 percent. Still, the cholera will return to Peru in weakened form for some years. This is cholera's normal course. The solution is getting water and sewers to people so they can wash. Instead the breakdown of the public health infrastructure will probably result in social disorganization and riot that will lead to heavy-handed fascism. We can expect further degradation of the surrounding countryside. Immediately outside the cities, firewood gatherers, animal grazers, and charcoal-makers will strip the land of accessible trees, shrubs, and grasses. As the area degrades due to soil erosion and barren land spreads there are likely to be losses of indigenous plants and endangerment of animal species. The aggravated soil erosion will increase the risk of serious flooding.

In contrast, the industrialized nations will be forced to make major choices about the essentialness of their future energy and resource-exploitative industries. There will be major changes in production technologies. The era of rapid growth for industrialized nations was fueled by low energy costs and high consumption. This has been particularly true in the use of clean, inexpensive, abundant petroleum fuels. We are near the end of that exploitation. Designs of industrial buildings, office buildings, high-rise apartment buildings, and retail centers are turning rapidly to the conservation of resources, especially energy. In addition, the use of building materials that consume large energy to produce them (e.g., aluminum) is being discouraged. We will turn, too slowly, to a conservation ethic in the use of both energy and materials to attempt to improve environmental quality in the twenty-first century.

We must note that the population projections for the LDCs have presumed a continuing reduction in the infant mortality rate. Perhaps there can be doleful optimism on that matter. Instead of declining, the infant mortality rate in the LDCs may sharply increase as the world's city environments degrade. The causes of high infant mortality rates are well known and closely linked to environmental conditions. Diseases most often fatal during early childhood in developing areas (e.g., Latin America) are fecally related or airborne contagious. Intestinal parasites and various infectious diarrheal diseases are probably the most devastating of the fecally related types, especially among infants. In Egypt, Iran, and Venezuela the monthly incidence of diarrhea among preschool children is estimated to be 40 to 50 percent.

Deaths from infection nearly always result from a combination of undernutrition and the infection. Therefore, Malthusian grave dancers can take macabre pride in attacking some projections of population increase in the major world cities, especially in the LDC countries. Birth control and family planning ought to be more acceptable choices than the spreading of grief, mourning, and despair over the poor populations of the world.

The record of international cooperation among sovereign nations has a discouraging aspect. Solutions to many global environmental problems are related directly to economic developments and population stabilization efforts. Therefore public or private programs to address global and environmental problems inevitably become involved in some of the world's most difficult and complex social, political, and economic problems. The position of the Roman Catholic Church and the Reagan/ Bush administrations on birth control shows how gracelessly blind faith avoids social confrontations. Yet, the problems are here, brought on by more demand from more humans than the world has learned how to supply. We await the crises that will cause a humane, rather than a merely prayerful, response to a world in peril.

It will add a useful prospective to the discussion of the future of our terrestrial environment to consider the following table of use of the earth's total area.

Table 2

Human Land Use

(world's total area = 510 million square kilometers)

Urban areas	1 percent
Irrigated arable land	1 percent
Other arable land	2 percent
Open forest & range land	2 percent
Closed forest land	5 percent
Desert	2 percent
Other ice-free land	12 percent
(Subtotal 25 percent)	
Fresh water rivers & lakes	4 percent
Oceans	71 percent

(Source: Global 2000 Report to the President, Technical Report, vol. 2, 1980.)

Desertification is the most dramatic change. If unchecked, the process of annual desertification will add 140,000 square kilometers to the roughly ten million square kilometers of desert already on earth. This process will increase the world's desert by the area of Nevada and New England combined. At the other climatic extreme, some humid tropical rainforests will be deforested for cultivation, thus reducing the amount of the earth's surface covered with closed forests from a fifth to a sixth.

Declining Soil Quality and Birth Rates

China is a beacon of hope. It provides leadership for the entire world in aggressive birth-control programs coupled with primary attention to improving agricultural productivity. In contrast, Pope John Paul, Ronald Reagan, George Bush, and others actively oppose attempts to improve family planning in the world. The prospect of declining soil quality is very serious, when placed against a backdrop of increasing population density in urban areas and on arable land. Birth rates will not decline to replacement levels anytime soon. Therefore, arable land will be very intensively cultivated in the attempt to feed more mouths. Note the glaring defect in human conduct here. Social mores need to be changed and adapted to meet human needs.

As economist Julian Simon points out in *The Economics of Population Growth,* human beings throughout history have devised many ingenious ways to meet the growing needs of increasing population. With good management, good soils, favorable climate, agricultural systems can be highly productive for centuries to come. But other more fragile renewable systems in certain regions of the world (such as tropical rainforests) are not so favorably endowed. There, a descending spiral of excessive demands on the system results in degradation of the resource base. Diminishing productivity is the rule rather than the exception. For example, salinization and water-logging of irrigated lands played a major part in the decline of the ancient Sumerian civilization. That soil, ruined by two thousand years of Sumerian irrigation, has not recovered to this day.

It is a tragic truth that modern instances of serious deterioration of resource systems are too easy to find. For example, in Sahelian Africa, south of the Sahara, a vicious cycle of poverty, accelerating population growth, and excessive demands on the environment is leading to expansion of desertification. Here, and in many other places in South Asia, the Andean region, Central America, and on islands such as Haiti or the Malagasy Republic, efforts by growing numbers of people to meet their need to survive are damaging the very cropland, pasture, forest, and water supplies on which they must depend for their livelihood. There are still large uncultivated areas in the world, such as the vast savannas of Brazil, the western provinces of China, and Siberia in the former Soviet Union. But the ability of much of this land to be used as a crop or range land is still problematical. Their delicate ecology requires humans to have the education, commitment, and energy to adjust to the peculiar demands of the land of those regions. Perhaps most important, much of the unused land still available is far from people and from the network of public facilities and private businesses needed to support modern agriculture. America's history teaches us that Americans had to give away land to entice the capitalists to provide the means to construct the railroads that served the farmers and the small towns of the wilderness. We should not forget how America used the Homestead Act with its 160 acres for squatters to encourage peasants from Northern Europe to migrate. The United States gained the great skills of those farmers.

Economist Julian Simon's definition of "long term" in *The Economics of Population Growth* is thirty to two hundred years or more. Positive trends that will ultimately assert themselves over such a time span are not acceptable in the dreadful short run in the LDCs. There we have a failure of leadership now. In the only global system we have, the leaders of the industrialized nations are looking the other way. The Simons of the world, as economists will do, say that technological improvements and the application of management skills in water and soil will occur simply because they are available. But, they fail to consider the social opposition of amiable optimists like Ronald Reagan and wrathful religious fanatics like Pope John Paul.

By 2000 the world will be more vulnerable to low-probability, high-risk events. Food production will be more vulnerable to fluctuations in climate and to disruptions in the supply of energy for fertilizer production, farm machinery fuel, and irrigation. Loss of wild progenitors of major food crops could lead to increased difficulty in maintaining pest and pathogen resistance in the high-yield hybrids. A major shift to nuclear power could make the energy sector vulnerable to terrorism and accident. A major shift to coal could be a serious problem in increasing acid rain and the development of a possible CO_2 envelope over the biosphere.

Several developments are anticipated that could affect all three major media of the earth's biosphere, air, land, water. The release of toxic substances, including pesticides, insecticides, and solid and liquid waste is being more effectively controlled in the industrialized nations. Still, under present policy, growing amounts of these substances will enter the air, land, and water in the LDCs. The *National Geographic* has reported very heavy use of pesticides and insecticides and chemicals on vegetables, fruits, and other produce shipped to the United States from Mexico and the Caribbean. The levels are so high that the workers in the fields are sickened. We must wash our produce at home even more carefully than in the past. Low-level radiation materials will be released in increasing amounts into all three environments of the biosphere. The oxides of nitrogen and sulfur, outputs from fossil-fuel combustion, will increase atmospheric concentrations, further acidify rain that may alter chemical balances of our surface waters over wide areas. Some of these chemical elemental residuals result in environmental problems on a global scale. Such problems require global cooperation.

There are those who look into the future seeing human progress rolling ahead in keeping with past trends. Simon is a proponent of this view. "The main fuel to support the world's progress is our stock of human knowledge. The world's ultimate resource is skilled, spirited, and hopeful people exerting their wills and imaginations. People who provide for themselves and for their families, and by that inevitably providing for the benefit of us all."

I differ with Simon's world view primarily on the inferences drawn from the dynamic relationship between renewable and exhaustible resource systems and human beings throughout history. Also, I hold that analysts such as Simon err by treating all human beings as exactly alike. Potentially we are the same. But cultural training brings about ethnic differences that result in different attitudes and capabilities. It effects the willingness to make hard decisions to carry out arduous tasks. France could not have carried on the Battle of Britain. It preferred the waters of Vichy to the waters of Dunkirk. Iranians of the 1990s are different from the Japanese in ways that affect their willingness to use knowledge and to be cooperative, competitive, and productive. Simon acknowledges at the outset that his general analysis is only a partial one when he says, "I am not saying that all is well now." He acknowledges that today children are hungry and sick; people live lives of physical and intellectual poverty, and lack opportunity; new pollution is present that we do not understand.

The highest praise that we can give Simon is that his sense of optimism should prevail over the despair of the gloomsayers. The fault with Simon is that he attributes America's success to the energy, common level of knowledge, and productivity of its people, and the market economy. This is only a part of the truth. American success also came from the forests, fossil fuels, rich soils for agriculture, abundant water, and minerals (now depleted) given the United States by Nature. We were a relative Garden of Eden when compared with nations like modern Greece, Chad, Paraguay, and Bangladesh, among many others. The record of a rich nation like the United States with an abundance of natural resources and a strong commitment to environmental protection hardly typifies conditions throughout the world.

The feeling underlying Simon's thought is that an economic rational man using the land in an environment of scarce resources can allocate resources efficiently to enhance human productivity. Simon ignores the ecological theme, but it is one borne out by centuries of human experience in other regions of our good earth. Today either human beings find a way to live in harmony with natural systems or they will kill the land. At the very least they will destroy its productivity for decades. It has taken the Israelis two generations of toil to restore productivity to the Palestinian lands ravaged by centuries of exploitative farming techniques. People can starve while we await the restoration of eroded lands. Wishing won't make it so, nor will a free market. It will require new forms of cooperation, competition, and a melding of economic analysis with an ecological understanding of the global ecosystem.

New Growth: Rebuilding and Restructuring World Cities

In April 1992, Peter F. Drucker, global guru to business managers, strongly urged world leaders to replenish and upgrade the municipal infrastructures of our world cities. Drucker sees this as ample potential for economic growth.[13]

The means can be marshalled to restructure these cities so they provide a hopeful life with a good future for their citizens:

- Adopt both long-range capital improvement programs and crisis management of emergency problems;
- Restructure metroarea government to provide fewer governmental units;
- Provide metroarea-wide authority over municipal services such as water, sewage, pollution abatement, housing, and crime control. In effect, create metropolitan reorganization and regional planning and budgeting;
- Prioritize capital improvements:

     first, to population control;
     second, to housing;
     third, to massive public health programs, including adequate clean water
          and sanitary sewage;
     fourth, to low-energy technology (the bicycle is an example, fiber optics
          another; highly skilled resources management is an essential keystone
          to such a plan);
     fifth, inventory existing conditions to provide the data and maps necessary
          for rational planning; and
     sixth, go toward universal urban education.

     More important, it is a time for more of an emphasis on the pragmatic, problem-solving, creative use of resources. Using appropriate and available technology at reasonable prices should be the overall goal. Mass education should not be designed to produce effete intellectuals but engineers, technicians, and paraprofessionals. Graduates of the colleges and universities must be provided with incentive to stay or return to their native countries instead of emigrating to the West.
- There must be the acceptance of social restructuring—loss of tribal power— for the building of a cooperative society rather than the social ills of alienating the outsider immigrants. The proper use of television, radio, and other educational media could promote fair play, competitiveness in the marketplace, and cooperation in social and public works activities.

The LDCs must adopt more rigorous social norms if they are to get good-faith loans and grants from the industrialized nations. As businesses throughout the industrialized world are accepting auditing according to generally accepted accounting principles, so the LDCs must accept responsible accountability in the use of funds if they are to gain approval of loans and grants. Meanwhile, the industrialized countries have much to learn about the appropriate priorities for making such capital transfers to the LDCs.

Today there are global financial markets without a world medium of exchange. The Bretton-Woods system of fixed exchange rates has been replaced by a "devil may care" electronic system of world financial markets. The American dollar is forced to be the world's reserve currency. There is no global central bank that works. The Bank of International Settlements moves from crisis to crisis. From 1985 to 1990 there was a chronic crisis of LDC debtor countries having extraordinary difficulty meeting their interest, let alone principal, payments on outstanding debt. Castro proposed that they repudiate the obligations. The decline in commodity prices resulting from the overproduction of nations desperate for hard currencies has worsened the ability of the LDCs to meet their obligations.

There are calls to construct another international monetary system that will be congruent with one theory or another. These monetary policies are mere paradigms obscuring reality. The irony is that these theoretical ideas come too late. As Walter Wriston, former chief executive officer of Citibank, has stated, "We already have a new system in place."[14] This new global monetary system was not built by politicians or economists. It has grown out of technology. The men and women who have tied the world together with telecommunications and space satellites did not fully realize that they were building the infra-structure of the new global marketplace. The convergence of computers with telecommunications has produced a twenty-four-hour global trading system in almost all world currencies except the ruble. This has created a new international monetary system that Wriston calls the "information standard." Political, regulatory, and economic concepts in this changed context have lost some of their relevance.

Unlike prior arrangements, this standard is not subject to effective political tinkering by sovereign nations. It is an invisible form of supersovereignty imposed by the invisible hand of economic discipline on all nations. Throughout history, kings, Roman emperors, and national leaders, have been nervous about people learning too much too quickly about the way a political process debases their people's savings. The Amsterdam bankers of the seventeenth century became unpopular with the contemporary states by weighing coins and publishing their true metallic value. This was often much less than what was represented on the face of the coins. That same principle has now been expanded by technology. The "global information standard" makes and publishes judgments about every currency in the world every minute and every hour of every day. This state of affairs does not sit too well with many sovereign governments. They correctly perceive that the new information standard diminishes the very nature of sovereign power. Today, instead of weighing metal coins and publishing their intrinsic worth, telecommunicating global markets weigh the fiscal and monetary policies of each government that issues currency and asserts a market opinion of the value of the currency. The markets' values are instantly seen by the traders in Hong Kong, London, Zurich, New York, and other world class cities. Major countries that have announced inappropriate monetary fiscal policies to meet the problems of the day have seen their foreign exchange reserves vanish in a short time. There is no longer enough money in the central banks of the world to hold to an unrealistic exchange rate in the face of bad economic policy.

Solving the Debt-Funding Problem

Outsiders have come up with novel and yet workable solutions to these threatening, worldwide problems. Herman Kahn in *The Coming Boom* proposed unconventional financing that would be practical and workable.[15] Kahn proposed that the LDC debtor nations be provided loans at low, fixed interest rates comparable to a long-trend real interest rate of, say, 3 percent per year. Kahn then called for annual adjustments of the principal of the loan using some appropriate index to account for the domestic inflation of the debtor nation. This would have the ameliorative effect of setting interest rates at a realistic level, which could be repaid. This would not unduly burden the balance of payments of the debtor countries and simultaneously protect the creditor by maintaining the integrity and value of the principal. The nations with the discipline to maintain a favorable balance of trade could make payments on the principal. This would be especially true if trade expanded. Obviously, any nation like Israel and Argentina that did not control the price deflator in their gross national product and the upward movement of their consumer price index would find their bonds unmarketable in the telecommunication markets of the world. Longer-term investments such as regional water and sewage facilities, dams, solid waste disposal plants, and mortgage bonds could be worked out under the same system.

World-Class Cities

In 1950, Patrick Geddes, a pioneer in city and regional planning, recognized that there are certain great cities in which a disproportionate part of the world's important business is conducted. Geddes christened these cities the "world cities."[16] The "world cities" are, first, usually the major centers of powerful national or regional governments. Sometimes international authorities are located there, too. Hong Kong, Singapore, and Sao Paulo are exceptions. Usually, there are government agencies of all kinds. Around these gather a host of institutions whose main business is government: the big professional organizations, trade unions, trade associations, and employers federations, and the headquarters or regional headquarters of major industrial organizations and corporations. Second, these cities are usually also national centers or regional centers of trade serving a large hinterland. Characteristically they are great ports (and airports) that distribute imported goods to all parts of their country or region, and, in turn, receive goods for export to the other nations of the world. Radiating from these transportation hubs are roads, railways, seaways, and air routes that focus on the metropolitan city. Third, traditionally the world cities are the leading banking and financial centers of their region or the national state in which they stand. They are a focus of telecommunication facilities.

Because of their centering of government and trade facilities, these places early become meccas for professional talent. World-class cities have a distinctively high-skilled medical profession and a legal profession gathered around the courts of justice. The better universities grow there for better teachers are drawn to world cities. One often finds great national libraries and museums in such world-class cities. Because the telecommunicating facilities so necessary to the banks and financial services are located there, the world class cities become places where information is gathered and disseminated. Book publishers, magazine publishers, and major newspapers, and with them their journalists and regular contributors, cluster in these cities. Because of the attractiveness of the ambience added by this activity with the clustering of cultural pursuits, as a rule the richest members of the nation or region also choose to locate in these areas. In this affluent age luxury shops, boutiques, great department stores, superregional shopping centers, festival centers, and a host of specialized shops that cater to every demand find a market in these cities. The range of industry is widened to provide the traditional luxury articles forged by master craftsmen and artists for the rich. Often craft centers produce "knockoffs" that become articles of popular consumption. The manufacturing takes place on the assembly line of vast factories within these cities' lofts, and in the cottage industries of their suburbs.

To date American taxpayers have been reluctant to foot the bill, thus they have few world-class cities. Amsterdam, the Netherlands, provides us with an example of a smaller world-class city that is also an open city that promotes the autonomy of individuals in an atmosphere of tolerance laced with responsibility. Americans would do well to study such cities. One also should understand that a few urban complexes, the Randstad or the Ring city of the Netherlands, and the Rhinewar complex of the former West Germany, developed a special form that may be of great interest to the world cities of the LDCs. Instead of concentrating all the metropolitan functions into a single, highly centralized giant city, these areas have managed through accidents of history to distribute these functions among several smaller, specialized, closely related centers. This "polycentric" type of metropolis may have special interest for the planners of those countries now forming new world cities for the human race.

In spite of their poverty and their great difficulties in gathering capital, LDCs can create future metropolises that will improve upon the past. For example, fiber optics and microcomputers will lower the costs of setting up a communication system far superior to the very expensive infrastructure and social overhead that is in place in the cities in Europe, the United States, and the old Asian cities. Our increased knowledge of the relationship between energy conservation and pollution will enable many of these cities to develop the use of mass transit, bicycles, and pedestrian walkways in such a way as to provide convenience for the population along with lower pollution factors.

Toronto

Toronto is a metroarea of 3.4 million people, bigger than Houston, older than Chicago, and its people do not know where the graffiti and debris are to be found. Toronto is a big, cultured, sophisticated, ethnically rich, inviting city, without a Bronx, Watts, or Cabbagetown. It is a city where thirty-three-year-old subways and subway cars are nearly as clean as on the day their service was inaugurated. Toronto cleansweeps every residential street once per week. Crime is not a psychic preoccupation. There were just thirty-seven homicides in 1986. Women feel safe to walk unescorted in most parts of the city. The poor and disadvantaged have not been warehoused in ghetto enclaves. Instead, they are mixed into metropolitan neighborhoods as the United States once did in Washington, D.C., Charleston, South Carolina, and other eighteenth-century cities. All in Toronto. of course, is not to the good. Yonge Street, north of the downtown, is home to prostitutes and a few adult bookstores. Large cities will have their lewd zones.

Toronto is a true city of neighborhoods. As writer Howard Witt of the *Chicago Tribune* says, "Chicago boasts of its ethnic diversity, but its neighborhoods often seem delimited by strained fault lines. Toronto's tend to flow seamlessly and cheerfully, colorfully on into another." Downtown Bloor Street is home to the city's most fashionable stores. Within a few blocks many of the University of Toronto's buildings are next to the Annex, an old Ukrainian neighborhood. Beyond the Annex one finds neighborhoods turning Indian, then Haitian, then Korean. Toronto, like Canada, is pancultural. Beneath the downtown center core runs Toronto's famed network of concourses interconnecting centers of shopping, administration, finance and professional services. It is a welcome protection against winter's cold blasts. Towering above the city is the CN Tower, 1,821 feet high, "the tallest free-standing structure in the world."

Toronto is a city that works well is an area that opted for metropolitan reorganization more than twenty years ago. Toronto now is a metroarea. There is local representation, and, more important, actual participation. The sensible Canadians of Toronto have accepted metropolitan planning and budgeting because they know it is better than "that government that is 'best' because it governs least."

American metroareas need to follow the example and reorganize themselves. Perhaps the federal and state governments can provide some leadership by restructuring the taxing system. Meanwhile, American citizens, blithe spirits that they are, go on about the business of playing soldier and being happy consumers without a care for the world of which they are a part. America needs to refocus its energies toward the development of the major cities of our developing nations. The world can experience a boom in productivity as it supplies the needs of these cities. It is little noted and hardly remembered that the rapid growth of the United States and its cities during the eighteenth, nineteenth, and early twentieth centuries produced major markets to buy the goods supplied by the Industrial Revolution of Europe. The United States has a similar opportunity, today, if the world can learn to coordinate its capital markets, its suppliers, and its trade markets as a global system. An exciting time could be ahead for American youths as they spread throughout the world carrying in their minds skills and talents to aid in the building of good cities in these burgeoning LDC metroareas and showing why our constitutional culture with its workhorse democratic capitalism work so well.

10. American Chartered Metroareas

Urbanography has gone awry. American families and their cities are among the rock-and-roll consumers sleepwalking their way toward a fascist state. We could take a more visionary view and hope that the primal force is using federal and state supremacy as the mortar and pestle in which to grind American ethnic diversity into a new compound, the possible humans. The challenge is—Can we handle the tomorrow of the information society in our metroareas?

After the 1970s, the riots stopped and the Cassandra predictions turned into puzzlement as the conundrum of stagflation set in. Inflation increased public employment costs and brought slower growth, especially in the "mature" economies of older cities. This led to a shifting of urban government expenditures away from capital investment and toward short-run services and maintenance. Today, George F. Peterson points out, for example, that New York City's present rate of replacement of water mains presumes an average life of 296 years. In Los Angeles, street repairs imply a 130-year cycle of replacement. East St. Louis schools would require $40 million for repair and replacements to meet current state sanitary standards, a sum two hundred times the current annual expenditure of that school system's budget for repairs. Imminent collapse is not threatening, but pessimism about the future of American cities seems warranted. Today, the riots have started, again.

Most American cities have an unusually high degree of seemingly effortless cooperation about most things essential. Compared to Calcutta, Bombay, or Caracas, America's metroareas are a modern invention that works well at supplying water, sewage, and energy. More tax money is not the answer, although restructuring the taxing power for our metroareas is of critical importance. Our most critical problems are attitudes, a lack of cohesive ideals, an absence of unified future orientation. In sum, there is a sorry absence of what humans need the most, a noble purpose for their lives.

Los Angeles is a megametroarea that may be our future.[1] It is carrying on an admirable fight to overcome the chaos of a past without a plan. Los Angeles created the super road, annihilated the sidewalk, and destroyed public transportation. Young cities such as Houston, Phoenix, and Denver continue building metroareas, growing in the Los Angeles mold, with many subdivisions, commercial strips, and shopping centers built by Los Angeles-based developers. Suburbias from Cleveland to Long Island to Seattle show southern California roots. Even Europe has experienced "creeping Californization." Pierce and Hagstrom, authors of *Urban America—50 States Today!* (1985), found residents of Jerusalem's suburbs fighting strict local zoning controls, trying to build California-style homes on mountainsides and demanding roads to make it easier to accommodate their cars. Urban "experts" the world over have condemned California's sprawl as wasteful and dehumanizing. Who says they are wrong? Nevertheless, to people around the world the image of southern California has become synonymous with individual liberty, unprecedented personal mobility, affluence, and "the good life."

Los Angeles' growth differs from that of other major cities. This de facto capital of the major state of California has figured out a new angle to the big-city growth scenario. Population experts predict that the population of Los Angeles County, the 7.8 million people in Los Angeles and its eighty-three contiguous cities, will arrive at the year 2000 with only 10 to 12 percent more people than it has now. While skyscrapers are shooting up in downtown Los Angeles and the local economy is prospering, population growth is just inching ahead. Nevertheless, Los Angeles is echoing the great cycle of many large American cities. Its suburbs are sucking up white families, taking them from the central core, and, in turn, using vacated spaces within the central city as a magnet for new residents and industry from outside the area.

L.A.'s emigres tend to be middle-class whites, but the few white immigrants are affluent. There are the minorities: Mexicans, Filipinos, Koreans, blacks, Vietnamese, and other racial and ethnic groups. This demographic hurly-burly is giving the area a new ethnic cast. Kevin McCarthy, a demographer at the Rand Corporation, sees only Honolulu, Hawaii, as comparable. He says, "There is a transformation of the Los Angeles basin into the first continental, multiracial and multiethnic metropolis in the United States. It is emerging. Whites will no longer be the predominant majority." Assimilating the immigrants requires that Los Angeles County keeps the non–high-technology economy dynamic. A casual observer quickly senses the area's growing international flavor. McCarthy says, "I believe the newcomers are a net plus. They're good for industry, no question, they have the work ethic and are seeking upward mobility. They are also a locus for the infusion of foreign capital. If you're from India or Korea or Taiwan with money to invest in the United States, and you have relatives in L.A., you're not going to invest it in Pocatello, Idaho."[2]

The lifestyle experience provided in individual metroareas varies widely. Overall, the growth of individual metroareas, cities, and suburbs depends on the interaction of many general trends, with significant localizing characteristics. Risk management avoidance theories assert that people or business firms are moving away from central cities to suburbs or from certain metroareas to others to avoid negative external attributes such as crime or high energy costs. Positive attraction theories also state that people or business firms are moving from central city to the suburbs, or from some metroareas to others, to obtain desired amenities, from lower density to better employment opportunities. Finally, there are certain government policies influencing the location of public and private investments, households, and economic activities that are biased in favor of suburbs and against central cities. Ascribing central city decline to intra-metropolitan factors is wrong. Neither city residents nor governments have the power to change their situation.

Positive action by democratic capitalism is necessary if our constitutional culture is to survive. The federal government must step in to provide incentives for the joint federal/state chartering of metroareas under reorganization statutes. The objective will be to empower local citizenry to deal effectively with the problems, such as affordable housing, rather than to continue the apathetic malaise. It will be like "pump priming." One of the most important social functions of large cities has always been helping poor households upgrade themselves. Most of this is done by the operation of the free market providing access to jobs, training, formal education, housing, health care, and cultural opportunities.

Some urban studies show that biased public policies have contributed to recent big-city losses of population, jobs, income and tax deprivation.[3] Such biases have caused consumers and investors to diverge from more efficient use of our metropolitan land areas and municipal infrastructure. Downs, Bradberry, Small, and others recommend the following changes to remove anti–central city biases:

- Provide the same tax benefits, including depreciation, for renovating existing property as for new construction.
- Make federal water and sewage aid available for both renovating existing systems as well as building new ones.
- Change federal funding for public transit and highway maintenance to provide for the same fraction for new highway construction as for highway and bridge maintenance and renovation.
- Place a cap on home ownership tax incentives by substituting a standard rate tax credit for the present homeowners deductibility of mortgage interest and property taxes.
- Eliminate the federal tax exemption for interest on industrial revenue bonds except those that are used to construct or renovate plants or new jobs in inner-city enterprise zones.
- Enact a federal prohibition of local rent controls or provide federal penalties against cities that adopt them by denying them grants for rehabilitation, sewage, and water grants-in-aid.
- Adopt a voucher system to attack racial segregation in public schools. This will encourage families and their children to attend schools located in neighborhoods of their choice, although they may not live there. Encourage the use of public transportation systems by the school children by changing the daily school hours away from the peak demand of other users.

There is a great need for areawide solutions that require metropolitan reorganization. A chronic problem in bringing about metropolitan governments has been the ignorant, self-serving opposition of local newspapers. Metropolitan governments have not been politically popular as a goal among local newspapers in the United States. Since 1950, only six major city-county consolidations have occurred: the parish of East Baton Rouge and the city of Baton Rouge, Louisiana; Jacksonville and Duvall County, Florida; Lexington and Fayette County, Kentucky; Nashville with Davidson County, Tennessee; Indianapolis and Marion County, Indiana; and Columbus and Muscogee County, Georgia. It can happen elsewhere. As a lawyer in Nashville said, "It was difficult but we got them to unite on the garbage first." Possible alternatives to chartered metropolitan governments would be incorporating large district metro-authorities for essential services. Another would be metropolitan tax-base sharing.

Many southern and western cities are healthier and have a better distribution of blacks in housing than many northeastern and midwestern cities. This is in part because southern and western states do permit cities to annex surrounding territory more readily than the northeast and midwestern cities. The idea of unitary, chartered metropolitan government would remove the fiscal advantage that residents of high-income outlying jurisdictions have gained by voting with their feet to insulate themselves from low-income taxpayers. Loss of local control and a decrease in the variety of public-service offerings in the metroareas may occur. On the other hand, who needs variety in the supplying of potable water, mass transit, sanitary sewage, and the disposal of solid waste?

Chartered metropolitan governments would save money. There are acknowledged economies of scale for certain services that can save money using metroarea-wide governmental authorities. The savings would result from metropolitan governments focusing on providing capital-intensive services such as clean water, sanitary sewage, and solid waste disposal. There are also economies in providing other areawide "natural monopoly" utilities such as more sophisticated police, firefighting, and public health prevention services. More radically, some banking and communication services such as payment of utility bills could be conducted more efficiently by a metropolitan district governmental agency. In the more labor-intensive services such as police and fire protection and road maintenance there are advantages to local control in the provision of some services such as patrolling the local beat. Minneapolis/St.Paul provides us with a good example of metropolitan cooperation.

Minneapolis/St. Paul

St. Paul (population 270,000 in 1980), the smaller and more easterly part of the Minneapolis/St. Paul complex, is the state capital, a major port, and a stockyards city. It is important in railroad, publishing, and insurance. Symbolic of St. Paul may be George Latimer, the erstwhile labor lawyer who served as the city's engaging and energetic mayor in the late 1970s and early 1980s. Latimer put St. Paul at the forefront of the most advanced urban experiments, including a district heating system and energy parks of energy-efficient light industry and housing. Resorting freely to federal subsidy programs, he pulled St. Paul out of its urban doldrums with a spectacular town-square project featuring office towers, retailing, a hotel, and a dramatic four-level, glass-enclosed greenhouse public park. The Lower Town area attracted a $100 million redevelopment project headed by the famed Chinese-American city planner Wei-Ming Lu.

Minneapolis (population 371,000 in 1980) is a flat prairie town that got its start as a miller of the West's wheat. She is larger and traditionally more sophisticated than St. Paul, a more important banking and finance center in general, and more Scandinavian in population. There has been a wave of historic building in Minneapolis since World War II, fostered by the Businessman's Downtown Council, formed in the 1950s. The result is the pioneering pedestrian-transit Nicollet Mall, designed by Lawrence Halpern, and a flamboyant Federal Reserve bank building by Gunnar Birkirtz. There are restored old industrial buildings, renowned museums, and the fifty-seven-story Investor Diversified Services tower by Philip Johnson, the tallest structure between Chicago and the Pacific. It features a multistory crystal court, where one finds the convergence of Minneapolis's twenty skywalks, which protect against the ferocity of Minnesota winters.

Tax base sharing has been done only in the Minneapolis/St. Paul metroarea. The joint cities' plan allocates 40 percent of any increase in each member city's commercial and industrial taxbase to a metropolitan pool. The pool is then distributed among 195 municipalities and school districts according to a formula based on population and relative fiscal capacity (as measured by assessed value per capita). The net effect on a tax base of any community depends on how fast its commercial industrial base is growing, how big its total tax base is, and its population. The Minnesota plan took affect in 1974. By 1978, the shared base had grown to 11 percent of the total value of areawide commercial and industrial property. In spite of the small size of this total, the plan has already reduced disparities in tax bases and rates in the metroarea. The plan appears to redistribute resources toward communities with low fiscal capacity or high concentrations of the poor and elderly, although service needs are not reflected in the distribution formula. The major beneficiaries have been the central cities of Minneapolis and St. Paul, where the total amount of redistribution is still small. That may be a political advantage. At the program's start it provides only modest—therefore palatable—gains and losses to the individual political subdivisions of the metroarea.

Metropolitan tax base sharing unifies a central city with the entire surrounding market area. It allows the city government access to revenues generated in parts of the area that are still growing. But it also retains complete local control over which services are provided, the tax rates, and the land use. It operates from year to year, automatically, so intergovernmental transfers do not require annual legislation. This is a major political and planning advantage. One aim of this book is to recommend policy changes to deter the decline of our central urban areas. American metroareas ought to look to Minnesota as a possible ideal of successful democratic capitalism. In Minnesota the political structure remains open, issue-oriented, and responsive. Questioning how and why things are done—up to the highest level—is not only tolerated but encouraged.

The state government has been a national leader in delivering good services to people. The quality of delivery has been so high that Minnesota's citizens and corporations have been willing to pay a rather high tax bill. Few states have exceeded Minnesota in the quality and extent of education offered in schools and colleges. No other appears to provide health care of comparable quality. What does this state have going for it? Minnesotans appear in fact, as well as theory, to control their destiny. There are few invisible powers lurking behind the seat of government. This is not plantation management with a "good old boy" network subverting the governmental process. It is a democratic society with a dynamic process of governing itself. Of course, the special-interest groups such as the railroads, private power companies, insurance companies, labor and business groups, and religious organizations lobby in the legislature, but none is consistently successful in promoting its interest over the common weal. However, other states should not be compared unfavorably with Minnesota. Minnesotans have had a long period of affluence and stability and homogeneity of population.

In 1980 Minnesota was still only 3 percent black and Hispanic and 1 percent Indian. Minnesota has not had to divert substantial resources to achieve racial integration or cope with racial strife. Minnesota is a state in which government has traditionally been an instrument for achieving public good, not an oppressive or patronage-ridden mechanism. From its first years, Minnesota's dominant ethnic strain has been northern (Scandinavian, German, Yankee) and her leading religions Protestant. Republicans have won 30 of 35 elections for governor. Still, Minnesota's Republicanism has been remarkably progressive. The fathers of modern Minnesota politics are Harold E. Stassen and Hubert H. Humphrey. They took politics out of the back room and engaged thousands of men and women in political activity, among them Warren Burger, future chief justice of the United States. Men such as Stassen and Humphrey developed a governmental process that has been a superior instrument of the peoples' will. The result of this responsiveness by an established political party is that Minnesota citizens have avoided the use of the initiative and the referendum and other populist devices used by people to check governments they do not trust. This has left responsibility squarely in the hands of the regularly elected and responsive legislature. Minnesota's government is one of the most powerful and sensitive to public demand in the country today.

The leaders of the prestigious national and international firms in Minneapolis and St. Paul live on the edge of two worlds. On the one hand, there is the small-scale, nineteenth-century America that begins with the farmers and small businesses, without a single dominant industrial interest, and the Great Plains. On the other there is close touch with the sophisticated Eastern world of high finance and complex organization. By moving in both worlds the leadership maintains an unpretentious quality (many answer their own phones) while adapting their economy to professional management and organization. For thirty-five years the famous Dayton-Hudson department stores chain has been giving 5 percent of its pretax profits—the maximum portion of corporate income tax that is deductible—to community causes, social action, or the arts. Businesses in Minnesota feel and act as socially responsible, communitarian personalities.

Nicollet Mall, long a model for what cities can do to keep their retail centers pumping, turned twenty years old in 1986. Its age is showing. The pedestrian walkways wear many patches and some planters contain dead trees. Observers have stated that the leadership of the business community, the ones with a real community obligation, have begun to diminish in numbers. Leadership at City Hall was said to be inexperienced. Developers have taken over the leadership role. The politicians do not know where to turn, so they do what the developers tell them. What the developers tell them is in the developers' interest only. The numerous store closings at Nicollet Mall have awakened local leaders to the need to reinvigorate the city showpiece. In a sense, this is a normal state of flux. A process is going on which may or may not lead to a consensus. They are seeking the right mix of new retailers who will provide the sophisticated atmosphere that the city is alive and that it is entertaining and fun. Having one's books in order doesn't guarantee retail success.

In 1977 a group of corporations, including Dayton-Hudson, 3M, and General Mills, formed the Minnesota Business Partnership. Its function is to involve chief executives and senior managers as partners with state government on issues of broad import to Minnesota, not just business's particular interests. This has resulted in more orderly growth and improved Minnesota's competitive interstate position on economic development issues.

Twin Cities unity is achieved on governmental fronts by timely intervention of the area's progressive Citizen's League, a voluntary organization of citizens task forces that have addressed every issue from sewer lines to justice. The Citizen's League is the godfather of the Minneapolis-St. Paul Metropolitan Council, to which the state legislature in 1967 awarded a tax base of its own. There are governor-appointed members in control of metrowide agencies that handle sewers, transportation, airports and parks. Short of a full-fledged metropolitan government, this may be the country's best model of metrowide coordination of services and areawide decision making. In 1976 the council gained the power to write the nation's first mandatory land-use planning law for an entire metropolitan region. This was the result of Citizen's League's education and timely state legislative action. Never willing to rest on its laurels, the Citizen's League was still stirring the pot in 1980 with a remarkable idea—urban competition between private and public organizations to carry out government services. Any monopoly institution, it was argued, inevitably becomes top-heavy and bureaucratized and thus insensitive.

Property taxes were driven down sharply in the 1970s, from around 2 percent of market value to less than 1 percent. The citizens grouse over the sales and income tax levies, but this dissatisfaction rarely reaches crisis levels because of the high quality of state and metroarea services. There is also no patronage system to arouse citizen's ire. Minnesota ranks only twenty-first in income and twenty-third in population nationally, but it may set up a model for the future of American families and their culture.

The University of Minnesota is the mother institution of one of the nation's outstanding medical schools, which now cooperates with its high-profile rival, the famed Mayo Clinic at Rochester, Minnesota. The hope of many Americans is that we will see interdisciplinary research to solve our common problems. Minnesota leads the way, again, with the Humphrey Institute, which has declared its intention to operate across all disciplines and professions of the University of Minnesota to combat "specialized" achievement, "the chief bottleneck of our society." It is working on a mid-career program for politicians, administrators, and journalists that would be "a mind-stretching inquiry into the nature, techniques, purposes and ethics of leadership in the late twentieth-century city, state, nation and international order." It is hoped the institute will encourage scientists and academics to be a part of this because so many of our intellectuals are cut off from the mainstream of life.[4]

Raw poverty and slums are fairly rare in the Twin Cities. There are social problems aplenty—poor whites, blacks in the inner city, Indochinese refugees, and, finally, Native Americans, who have their greatest urban concentration in America in the Twin Cities. One finds the heaviest Native American concentrations on or near Franklin Avenue. It is a neighborhood that belies the city's squeaky-clean, progressive image. Here one finds a startling array of social maladies: massive unemployment, alcoholism, vagrancy, knifings, rapists, and chronic welfare dependency. On the other hand, Franklin Avenue is also the home of the American Indian Business Development Corporation, an organization devoted to economic development that is building a major shopping center in the Franklin Avenue area.

The United States, with its over three hundred metroareas, is too big and too diverse to think of in terms of one "city of the mind." I will use Richard Boyer and David

Savageau's excellent work, the periodic *Places Rated Almanac.*[5] Since my objective is conceptual rather than factual, the 1985 edition will suffice. In this edition 329 U.S. metroareas were compared on the basis of climate, housing, health, crime, transportation, education, the arts, recreation, and economic outlook. Generally speaking, smaller metroareas ranked better on the indicators concerning crime, housing and economics, while the larger areas scored higher on the availability and quality of facilities. In overall rankings, *Places Rated* privileges those areas that show steady strength in all categories, although they might not have any dramatic, first-place showings. To emphasize the facilities and indicators of quality of life that were used in this rating system, table 3 lists the scores and general ranks of the *Places Rated's* top twenty metroareas. Thereby one can see the wide range of the ratings over these rankings. High-ranking metropolitan cities are combinations of a wide range of rankings in the individual categories.

Many of *Places Rated's* high-ranking metropolitan cities are combinations of superior and dismal rankings in the individual categories. New York City is an excellent example of an uneven performance. The "Big Apple" has first-place performances in health care, transportation, and the arts. But the city has a miserable showing in housing (312th) and crime (329th), for which it is last. High housing costs and real estate values along with dangerous streets, for many people, cancel the wondrous facilities that this world-class city has to offer.

Table 3
America's Top 20 Metroareas—1985

Metroarea	Cumulative Score
1. Pittsburgh, PA	716
2. Boston, MA	752
3. Raleigh-Durham, NC	753
4. Philadelphia, PA-NJ	774
5. San Francisco, CA	774
6. Nassau-Suffolk, NY	786
7. Louisville, KY-IN	840
8. St. Louis, MO-IL	845
9. Rochester, NY	860
10. Norwalk, CT	889
11. Dallas, TX	898
12. Seattle, WA	919
13. Atlanta, GA	921
14. Knoxville, TN	928
15. Buffalo, NY	931
16. Baltimore, MD	932
17. Washington, DC-MD-VA	933
18. Cincinnati, OH-KY-IN	938
19. Burlington, VT	941
20. Syracuse, NY	950

Most metroareas that performed best in the 1985 edition are east of the Mississippi. Many are found in the Northeast. The states of New York, New Jersey, and Connecticut are especially strong in highly ranked places, as is the multistate region of the Ohio Valley. The South and the West (excluding California), despite significant population growth in the last twenty years and generally favorable economic indicators, do not show their presence with frequency among the top places rated. This is because American democratic capitalism shows little interest in developing community facilities in the early stages of city development. Developing communal facilities is not for the nouveau riche.

Let us turn now to other ways of looking at how cities function for humans. If the human condition is to seek meaning in life for the individual, we should avoid totalitarianism, increase individual opportunity, and encourage the activity of a marketplace of ideas within our metroareas so we can interact for the betterment of man. More thought must be given to the idea of the symbolic reality of urban images and themes. These metaphors must be acknowledged. The idea of an educated city was made unforgettable, early, by means of the Greek "school without walls." Lloyd Rodwin and Robert Hollister have provided us with a very penetrating interdisciplinary survey of metroareas in their *Cities of the Mind,* which provides valuable insight into the way many of our academic disciplines see American cities, past and present.[6] Some of the following pages are drawn from that source but modified and intertwined with my ideas.

Cities of the Mind provides an explanation of the metaaspects of the various urban studies in the social sciences through the lens of the thematic urban image. They deal with the theme of powerlessness of our metroareas in legal concepts. Others comment on the evolution of the descriptive and mathematical perspectives in urban geography, or sociology's jungle, bizarre, organismic, or machine images. They present the methodological emphasis on behavior in economics and the like. All together, the book represents the effort of specialized intellectuals seeking some thematic form or image that is in each case only a partial analysis. It is argued here that there is a sort of a fugue, a blurred vision, of what it is to be an American. We have incoherent ideas, lacking in unity, fostered and promoted by the media. In all cases, still, American psyches do press on. It is a part of their psychic perception of self that they have a feeling for the place in which they live. For some modern humans there is even a global city of the mind. For these humans there is a perception not only of the metroarea in which each resides, as well as of those they have visited, but even of those they have never seen. All are there "in the mind" through the wonder of technicolor telecommunications. American metroareas are a part of our perceived psychic reality. Therefore, there cannot be a common definition of this "image" of the city in our psyches.

The Web or Network Image

The web image emphasizes the interrelatedness of the parts of the city and the exchanges or other interactions through which these relationships are started, maintained, or severed. Here, the emphasis is not on the container in which the game takes place, but on the ways in which interactions are structured rather than merely occurring randomly or by accident. The picture here is one of a process that may be more compatible with my view of the human animal's brain as a gland and the way it works. Yet the power of satellite cities to control their destiny has been weakened in those cities that are near large, important metropolitan centers such as Boston. They have been caught in the web. Although close to a regionally and nationally important metropolitan center, each satellite has developed out of historical economic and social conditions that are unique. These satellites are not merely the result of proximity to a large city. Boston is the point of central tendency for a dense population mass, and has been since colonial times. Nevertheless, Massachusetts government has failed to find the common interest that would promote a cohesive communitarian spirit among citizens of greater Boston. The city politicians that fragment metroareas such as greater Boston are faced with a continuously high perception of risk in decisionmaking. Following self-interest, the only rational response is usually the protraction of the decision process, allowing some important political conflicts to stretch out over long periods. The result, throughout the nation, is a strong tendency to "gridlock." We await the "crisis" of the sewage, the water, the police, the schools. This prevalent decisionmaking style can create greater long-run unpredictability as the successive stages of a conflict accumulate. They become more complex and volatile, more stressful. The result is that the citizenry withdraw from the process, choosing, instead, alienation, apathy, and containing their anger, increasing urban stress. As part of this process of accumulation, the resentments and frustration of local political groups also gather. This accumulation helps the conflict to become intertwined with other significant community disputes.

Douglas Yates argues that cities are not only difficult to govern, they are, in fact, ungovernable under present charters and taxing powers.[7] In Yates's view, the sheer multiplicity and complexity of the issues facing urban political decisionmaker helps create a decision environment that is somewhere between uncertain and deficient, despite the intrinsic capabilities of the decisionmakers. Though they have frequent guidance from external sources, the political systems of the balkanized metroareas consistently find it difficult to create, implement, and continue programs of public policy. America's political processes are immature and fail to provide a workable environment for the human inhabitants of cities. Citizens should be able to take a long view of the problems of urban municipal services management. Planning for these places should be based on a proper assessment of their place in the metropolitan and regional economy and polity. Politically, the central cities are increasingly isolated. They are hemmed in by dozens of self-protective suburbs. Their electoral clout, once a potent force in state politics, has been reduced through population loss. Throughout the United States the "satellites" within the Census Bureau's metropolitan statistical areas (MSAs) and also the major central cities of the larger metroareas have become just another group of political units among many.

None of these cities have much to say about their futures. How can we promote a greater sense of political interest and efficacy—among both leaders and citizens— when both state and federal government authority are taking more and more responsibility for programs that reach deeply into the fabric of urban life? I argue for strong federal involvement in chartering metropolitan reorganization. The federal government should provide tax incentives for the chartering of metroareas, the boundaries of which would be synonymous with their MSA boundaries, with zoned, geographical, proportional representation to protect village and neighborhood power, so home rule would provide empowerment of the people to make participation meaningful. It would improve the networking.

After World War II, America evolved an image of the city as a competitive model of special interests, independent groups vying for their share of the expenditures, interacting for the common good. This was a competitive market model seeing political conflict in cities as benign. But it ignored the problem of alienation, apathy, and the possible use of competition between the groups as a way of venting stress. In the 1950s a new generation of politicians came to the fore. They put together coalitions of ethnic-stock voters, small business people, labor unions, downtown business leaders, newspaper publishers, and the civic elite. They got behind the idea of city government working toward the city beautiful. To many, the image of the city as a competitive market in which individual interests of city residents were expressed through political organizations resulted in campaigning focused on the goals of "products" such as neighborhood rehabilitation, sewage improvement, and public transit.

This approach conforms to a perception of the public interest that recognized the importance of the human personality. This was an incisive intellectual break with the image of urban politics that had been fashioned by political scientists during the Progressive era. The change was made by persons such as Edward Banfield and Martin Meyerson, and others. Banfield raised questions about the Progressives' interpretation of the concept. He pointed out there are two ways to see the public interest. One is the understanding of the Progressives: the public interest is what is common to the public, as a whole. However, Banfield noted, there is an equally legitimate interpretation of the public interest, namely, the total of the individual interests of the city's residents. In his *The Unheavenly City* and its sequel, *The Unheavenly City Revisited,* Banfield argued that the most serious problem in American cities is the product of large concentrations of blacks (and Hispanics) who believe themselves to be—and are considered by influential elite to be—the victims of racial oppression. The victim mentality does not serve them well. It causes them to concentrate on reparations and the past rather than to be individuals who are future-oriented and getting on with life as it is. Such beliefs can lead to riots, as they did in the 1960s and in 1992. Banfield predicted they would continue to do so for some decades to come. Worse, the belief by important segments of the middle and upper class that blacks are systematically oppressed by American society can undermine the stability and the character of the nation's political system, if nothing is done about it. Yet, many measures which could address the problems of the blacks and Hispanics in the lower classes subjected to poverty are not currently politically feasible.

Gunnar Myrdall wrote about this in his 1930s opus on race relations in the United States, *The American Dilemma.* We have a very serious, long-term dilemma. Because under the current state of the art, there is no reliable way of determining which of these poor people, unemployed workers or criminals, are victims of circumstances, and which ones, on the other hand, are members of the incorrigible lower class which has been around from the times of Babylon. It is a dilemma, for if we pursue some of the "liberating" policies that have contributed to the cities' current unruliness, such policies will give free rein to members of the incorrigible lower class. This would require those governing to abstain from "openness" to avoid some of the harsh measures—who wants police brutality? Also, who wants the wrong of an adverse impact on the noble and worthy poor? Why should they be subjected to limits on their liberty and freedom because of the conduct of their incorrigible neighbors? Mayor Wilson Goode of Philadelphia was done in by this dilemma due to his ill-fated attempt to use the "firepower" of the state against the incorrigibles. Tragically, death and home destruction was wreaked upon good and decent people.

The United States needs to acknowledge that prior convictions of criminality plus jury findings of incorrigibility should result in second-class citizenship. Banfield and others have pointed out that many policy proposals that have the greatest political appeal are quite unlikely to have their intended results. The failure of such programs is unfortunately being taken as a confirmation of the ineptitude of the American system by politically important groups and the media. They are spreading the fascistic belief that we must sacrifice our freedom and the democratic character of American society to alleviate these problems. It is this threat to free institutions that is a central problem of American cities. Banfield's conviction that the stakes are high explains his tone of alarm. Banfield, like a Puritan preacher, seeks to set his congregation on the right path by vividly portraying the torments of hell. Banfield, in describing the city as a source of chaos in the American political order, sought to convince his readers that they could no longer ignore the unpleasant fact that some inhabitants are anything but angelic. Nor can we continue to ignore their needs and wants. If we do, we will turn America into the unheavenly city. Nevertheless, it is important to note that Banfield's book does end with an expression of hope. Banfield draws a quotation from Cotton Mather's "Theopolis Americana": "Come hither, and I will show you an admirable spectacle! 'Tis an heavenly City . . . a city to be inhabited by an innumerable company of angels, and by the spirits of just men. . . . Put on thy heavenly garments, for America, the holy city!"

Americans ought to be far more willing to make fundamental alterations in the structure of city governments and the size and shape of chartered metropolitan governance districts. Such changes would not tamper with the institutions of national government. Entire city charters have been and can be scrapped. New charters can be adopted with relatively little hesitation. On the other hand, great caution is appropriately exercised in amending, let alone rewriting, the U.S. Constitution. Reorganization of our metroareas and more direct participation by citizens, particularly at the local level, is essential for the survival of our constitutional culture. The situation requires immediate action by our federal government to enable reorganization of metroareas under new state charters with wide and deep powers of local governance as well as tax-sharing powers. Let's consider one urban problem—transportation— as a way of looking at solutions and our inaction.

Transportation

Intraurban transportation in our metroareas has been decaying in quality for decades. It was not simply the expansion of the ownership of automobiles and the construction of suburban shopping malls that sent the downtown areas of our satellite towns in suburban counties, along with the central cities, into a decline. With the expected increasing expense of operating private automobiles, the revival of older neighborhood shopping centers may make good sense. Often the highway rights of way and other municipal infrastructure to get to these small and middlesized communities is already in place, awaiting conservation and enhancement. Unfortunately, up to the 1990s we have ignored the valuable "sunk cost" of societal investment in these older highways. Instead, we build huge regional malls that require the taxpayer to expend billions of dollars to supply the connecting roads and other adequate municipal services. Growth calls for most of the new regional malls. Still, it does not justify the failure to improve connections to the nearby villages or small towns that suddenly become abandoned. This cannot be termed orderly growth.

Also, today, in many of our large metroareas we are experiencing much waste of energy through journeys to work from the inner city to the suburbs and excessive crisscross commuting back and forth across the circumferential beltways. Many of these commuters could diminish traffic congestion and urban stress if metrowide planning was used to improve the secondary road system for short-haul commuting by car or, better yet, by bicycle. The suburbs are becoming very important work locations in our service-oriented economy. But the cost-effective, energy-efficient transportation network is still to be worked out.

The 1980 census reported that 20 million Americans commuted daily from one suburb to another. About 14 million traveled from suburbs to downtown cities. Today's suburban highways are so overcrowded that once-easy five- and six-mile commutes now take forty-five minutes of stop-and-go driving in bumper-to-bumper traffic over two-lane country roads that still run past farms and cow pastures. There are serious difficulties in the short trip that is necessary to gain access to the radial spoke highways or the concentric circle beltways. At least they provide higher-speed movement to and from the home for the urban workers. Most city planners continue to think of access to and from the downtown, while the transportation needs are soaring in the crisscross traffic near and around the suburban urban villages. Most urban village cores are being created by private developers in unrelated and uncoordinated ways. Each local political jurisdiction acts as if it were an island unto itself. Regional planners and local governments work under a serious handicap in trying to alleviate the suburban traffic problems caused by this lack of coordination.

The answer is not the construction of subways or elevated trains, except in part. Many people who ride fixed mass transit systems, in cities like San Francisco, Atlanta, or Miami, are those who used to ride the buses. The construction of decent bus highways—or bus highway lanes—would have been much cheaper for everyone than the construction of our mass transit subways and elevated rail systems. Nevertheless, fixed rail transit remains a gleam in many a downtown businessman's and politician's eye, not to mention those of the career-building transportation planners and engineers. Even Los Angeles, the capital of California's "car kingdom," wants to build an eighteen-to-twenty-mile "metro-rail" subway system costing $3 billion. Consider the fantastic reality of Atlanta's new MARTA system. The fare box brings in only 35 to 40 percent of the annual operating budget. The budget ignores reasonable amortization of the capital costs because such costs are not included.

Solutions to the transportation problem are quite difficult to find because the new urban-village nodes of activity—large retail, office, and industrial buildings widely separated by parking lots and landscaped areas—lack density, so only a few people will find it convenient to walk from a given bus or subway station. Furthermore, office workers must have a car during the day if they want to visit a client or go out to lunch. This leaves us with our automobiles and the clear need to find a way through to a system of peak-hour surcharges to force ride sharing. We need to seek the cooperation of both employees and management for staggered work times. Coordinated planning of nearby office complexes and industrial parks could be forced by shifting the cost of interconnecting highways and access points upon the developers. They would find a way to pay for the transportation improvements by user charges. Such costs are currently being borne by the public. Furthermore, the technology is already here for computer billing of automobiles that pass transportation access points at places of high congestion. These user charges could force down traffic congestion through monthly billing to those whose cars pass the point at peak hours. This could result in a great increase in kiss-and-ride and ride sharing. This could also alleviate much of the loneliness and alienation that are a part of the metroarea for many urban workers. Commuters would have the time to strike up friendships with those they traveled with regularly.

In 1975 Singapore introduced a simple auto license sticker to charge low-occupancy cars entering the crowded city center at peak morning hours. It immediately cut congestion 40 percent. A small force of traffic police at entry points kept drivers honest at low cost to the city. Hong Kong undertook a more elaborate electronic road-pricing experiment. From 1983 to 1985 cars were equipped with small solid-state electronic license plates that automatically identified them to sensing loops in the road connected to a central computer. The computer reported the tolls and billed car owners each month. The system permitted flexibility as to which roads to toll and what to charge. Politically, it failed, probably because it was not properly explained to the public. The Hong Kong motorists came away unconvinced that their fees would be offset by lower taxes. Some objected to having their routes monitored by computer. This is in spite of the greater intrusiveness that already exists in bank and telephone records. As expected, some scofflaw motorists defeated the system by covering over their electronic license plate and disabling it. This called for a small force of traffic police at entry points to spot-audit automobiles for such abuse.

The New Jersey Port Authority plans to affix license plates that will assess tolls on about three thousand buses passing daily through the Lincoln Tunnel. Greater Atlanta will install a similar electronic billing system for the users of a new highway that was built primarily to relieve traffic congestion at peak hours. These electronic toll collectors are faster and less grumpy than human toll collectors. The system can provide an accurate reading of vehicle speed, traffic volume, and lessen pollution and time constraints. Working on the supply side, European bus transport has caused significant shifts by moving toward using smaller buses. They encourage free enterprise by small private operators who receive no subsidy to make bus transit more efficient. This eases the heavy dependence on the mammoth, full-size buses. They have cut into the state-owned monopoly on bus service. The small, private operators, who receive no subsidy, now account for two-thirds of all bus trips within some European metroareas. This was a switch to an open, competitive model. The national bus system was denationalized and many new private companies planning to use minibuses are now competing with the traditional single- and double-deckers. This could significantly change the bus transport system in Europe. The United States has shown an inflexibility, an avoidance of change, by failing to break the hold of municipal employees and bureaucrats over mass transit systems. Europe and Asia are leading the way.

Ways must be found to furnish technical and other services without further eroding the sense of competence that local decision makers have. We need to make metroarea elected officials more secure in their political bases while at the same time reforming and reorganizing into the larger metropolitan districts. The metroarea will need some "at large" elected representatives, but they should be in the minority. Most officials should be proportionally elected from an adequate number of local zones, boroughs, cities, and villages to assure local representation on the governing boards of the metroarea municipal service agencies. Cities must not wait upon state or federal resources or on the prospect of major new private investment for cost-effective development and conservation. By the year 2000, less than ten years from now, over fifteen million people will be added to America's urban settlements. This is equivalent to about fifteen cities the size of Cincinnati.

Hans Blumenfeld, Greater Toronto's famous planner, asserted that it is a fallacy to believe that in a big metropolis there can only be one choice between, on the one hand, crowding together with high densities and poorly designed, inadequate land-area ratios, and, on the other hand, spending too much time traveling to work. Blumenfeld showed that using a travel rate of thirty miles per hour, which is quite possible for both private and public transportation, the total area within one hour's distance from the center could accommodate fifteen million people in single-family housing on lots of sixty by one hundred feet. It would accommodate all business and industrial uses, provide the municipal infrastructure, streets and utilities, and still leave a thousand square miles for recreation and open space. In effect, we can achieve better cities by having developers work within the rules of land-use controls developed by the citizen planning agencies.

The modern metropolis does not require extremely high residential densities or excessively long journeys to work. The problem lies in achieving a rational distribution of the land-use components with a suitable organization of transportation facilities to connect them. The very reason for the existence of a city is that it puts enormous numbers of diverse households, businesses, churches, foundations, nonprofit organizations, and other decision units in close proximity so they may interact in fruitful and efficient ways. The city should be a vast web of interdependence. By active participation citizens can help the government with zoning and building code compliance. They could take care of themselves with low-cost loans to the elderly and other low-income people who may otherwise have to defer maintenance and cause spot-blighting in a neighborhood that is otherwise sound.

None of this will occur unless government is a partner in progress with the neighborhood residents. Neighbors need to have confidence that the municipal infrastructure will not deteriorate while they are seeking to improve the properties in the neighborhood. American metroareas have significant problems concerning local public finance. Large diseconomies result from the uneven apportionment of taxes and the provision of services. Low-income individuals are concentrated in political jurisdictions that, by virtue of a low tax base, require a higher burden of taxation per capita on the residents. These same enclaves also provide lower levels of service than is true for higher-income communities.

The conservatives in power are suspicious of social engineering for good reason. Profligate spending by the military, on the one hand, or badly designed and poorly located public housing, on the other, is a waste of public goods. But, free marketeers are, in fact, unconcerned with poverty. They have a theological faith in the efficient workings of the market to overcome individual suffering. Somehow the "magic market" will solve the problems before Hannah Arendt's mob responds to a demagogic charismatic leader who will show us all the way out of this constitutional culture that stands in the way of laissez-faire capitalism. The growth of our metroareas is a repeat of past errors.

Urban Villages

We are forming many potential villages within each large metroarea. They are connected by networks of communication and transportation corridors. This has exciting possibilities for increasing the vibrancy of life for our constitutional culture, and for democratic capitalism as well. Today it is also making worse the chronic problem of economic class segregation in our metroareas. The high-rise office complexes and regional shopping centers are creating concentrations of lower-paid service jobs in these suburban village cores. These jobs are too far away from the dwellings of the job holders. It is quite impractical to travel to work without great hardship. This reverse-commuting and crisscross traffic are common phenomena of the urban villages. Such systemic malfunctions are largely ignored by urban transportation planners. Instead, they establish additional beltways to create more nodal points of activity at the crossroads of beltways and radial transportation corridors.

Another reason for the resulting emergence of urban villages has been changes wrought by transportation patterns. It has been described as the development of star patterns (radial transportation corridors connected by circular urban beltways). It is a result of Americans' preference for the internal combustion engine of automobiles and trucks. The truck can travel from door to door, unlike fixed rail transportation. A third reason has been the recent telecommunications advances, notably the dramatic drop in long-distance telephone costs. More and more day-to-day work is being done over the telephone. Fax it. We use not only cheaper long-distance telephone rates, but overnight mail, fax telecopiers, and computer modems. These allow communication without physical proximity. To date this new appearance of urban village cores at the nodes of major highway crossovers of the urban roads and the radial interstate highways is benefiting only the middle and upper class. Little if any provision is made for housing lower-income urban village workers.

Most of America's urban villages are growing, white, upper-middle-class areas. Executive and business owners making the decisions about office locations and "clean" industrial sites usually decide to bring their offices or industrial plants nearer their homes. The result is that clerical, light assembly, and service employees take long— also often expensive in money and time—car or bus commutes to the suburbs from the city home they can afford. With one (usually two) transfers, many bus passengers take anywhere from an hour to a two-and-a-half-hour ride twice a day. More sophisticated suburban businesses are offering bounties for new employees by the way of higher wages. More effectively, they are providing shuttle buses for a nonstop commute to the home areas of many unskilled workers.

Lower Cost Housing for a Better Life

In the United States, construction of new, lower-quality housing that would be safe, sanitary, and decent is prevented by class-biased enforcement of zoning laws and building codes that require higher-quality units. Therefore, new housing is "not affordable" for most moderate-income and all low-income households to buy or occupy without direct subsidies. Furthermore, the buyers of new suburban housing often do not pay the full social costs of the units they enjoy. The cost of creating the new streets, sewers, water systems, parks, and schools in their subdivisions are spread over all the taxpayers in their jurisdictions, not just those buying homes in that subdivision. There has even been a tradition of chaotic planning of our suburbs for decades. During the past forty years we have built millions of acres of new subdivisions with inadequate sanitary sewage, below-standard roads, an absence of parks, and insufficient clean water supplies. This results in much lower real estate taxes than for the inner city, but suburban homes are accordingly underserviced in terms of public health standards. The clamor for adequate service has resulted in inevitable increases in taxes accompanied by the braying chorus of those jackass journalists who view all tax increases as wasteful.

Manufactured housing is a cost-effective, attractive alternative to the housing stalemate. One of the fastest-growing sectors of our economy, manufactured housing has been stymied by a lack of uniformity of regulatory controls at the state level. A recent study by the National Association of Home Builders' Research Foundation found that thirty-five states permit industrialized housing. However, the laws vary so widely that they discourage manufacturers from expanding their markets and introducing new materials and assembly methods. Unfortunately, manufactured housing is, generally, barred by the local growth-control officials who are culturally prejudiced against them. A few states have adopted uniform statewide building codes to prevent this local prejudice. Manufactured housing builders in the United States have proven over and over that good-quality, beautiful neighborhoods in the suburbs can be built at costs affordable to low- or moderate-income families. Nevertheless, the manufacturers keep a very low profile because of the cultural bias opposing such housing. Modular housing is an example of the opportunities that exist for some military contractors if we were to carry out a more peace-oriented international policy. So far the federal government has actively opposed policies to make sites available for manufactured housing at convenient locations. Up to two hundred companies actively manufacture modular housing. They produced an estimated 64,000 homes in 1985. About 80 percent of the output is trucked across state lines. While a five-state market is the norm, 17 percent ship to ten or more states, each state with differing administrative procedures.[8] There should be a call for master planning that would encourage the construction of "five star" carefully planned mobile home parks. The quality and capacious convenience of the mobile home is a superior housing value to anything else offered for the low- to moderate-income urban worker. It could sharply diminish commuting time and concomitant pollution problems. The crisscross traffic around the urban fringe and near-city-to-outer-city journeys to work to commute have created new transportation problems that clearly call for a re-organization of our metropolitan planning districts. Developers are among the more enlightened. They favor the new spirit of private and public cooperation. They realize that the alternative could be government-ordered construction moratoriums or rationing of sites to the highest bidders through the intervention of state bureaucracy.

Most planners are in agreement that if the government would work more closely with developers serious transportation problems could be lessened. The problem is identifying what we mean by government. Some local governments resist developers by trying to avoid rapid growth. They are scattered, nineteenth-century fiefdoms trying to ignore far-reaching twenty-first-century issues. Metropolitan Atlanta has forty-six cities and eight counties within its Atlanta regional council, and eighteen counties within its federal standard metroarea. Greater Los Angeles has well over one hundred cities and five very large counties. Coordination by ad hoc committees from so many jurisdictions is ludicrous. Yet it is what conservative political thinkers, and those who are ignoring the problem, indicate that we must continue to expect. St. Louis County, Missouri, had a referendum to try and reduce the number of communities within the county from over ninety to a few more than twenty. Hopefully others will follow. Certainly the best answer is for the federal government to provide tax incentives for a complete reorganization of the metroarea government along metropolitan district boundaries. The growth of urban village cores around the nodes of our transportation corridors spills over several governmental bodies.

Contrary to what many voters think, well-to-do suburban communities do not rationally control growth when their neighbors can act independently. Beverly Hills, California, found that the Four Seasons Hotel wanted to build a high-rise hotel on Wilshire Boulevard near Rodeo Drive, in the heart of the city's commercial Golden Triangle. Research reports on building density and hotel-generated traffic congestion were so controversial that the city council opted to refuse to vote on the question. They chose a referendum that resulted in the Beverly Hills voters defeating the ordinance changes that would be needed for the hotel to be built. This action eliminated the possibility that another major hotel would open in their city. Victory? The result was that the Four Seasons hotel developer found a location literally across the street from the Beverly Hills city line. Beverly Hills lost the new hotel's sales and occupancy tax revenues, but will have the traffic congestion anyway.

The continued balkanization of our metroareas is against the public interest. Small, local governments are incapable of dealing with orderly growth under the pressures of demands for more jobs and higher-density land use. Probably the best short-term solution is the creation of strong, effective, large-area agencies with chartered metroarea governmental powers over single, specialized functions such as sewage and water services and crime detection and prevention. Fire protection of high-level complexity, transportation planning, and land-use planning and zoning are also large-area problems. The jurisdictions would correspond to the economic and psychological boundaries of the metroarea-wide economy. There could be proportional representation and local home rule over neighborhood activities such as local parks, local police patrolling, and health services. In this way, the urban villages that sprout up in response to the cultural, economic, and psychological demands of the metroarea residents would become centers of cohesive networks within one large metroarea. As the citizens work, play, and seek to sustain their creative and spiritual potential, they would be networking in their neighborhoods.

I have been intentionally vague about defining the levels of authority and how power would be diffused under this chartering reorganization. More than one model should be adopted for our metroareas due to our cultural diversity and the differences in lifestyles sought by humans as they pursue happiness. The essential change is that the federal government should pass a "metropolitan reorganization act" that would empower states to jointly charter metroarea-wide governments that would become eligible for federal funding. We should use the incentive of value-added tax (VAT), coupled with mandatory reduction of real estate taxes, and federal planning aid.

Metro Consolidations

The great success of the consolidation of our school districts under the leadership of James Conant, with Admiral Hyman Rickover acting as the cheerleader, is our harbinger and guide. The nation shrank the number of school districts nationwide from 100,000 in 1940 down to 15,000 today. We did this on the basis of the curricular enrichment benefits. By consolidating we provided fast tracks for meritorious students and special remedial classes for those with deficiencies. These were made possible by the economies of scale due to the elimination of smaller, inefficient school districts. But this consolidation was not easy. The hostility and resistance of mothers, majorette clubs, and football booster organizations, along with the coaches, band directors, and high school principals, was intense. Nevertheless, federal incentives and the use of the state's sovereign power did bring about this sweeping change.

Perhaps, we should take on a less than incendiary issue, such as garbage, as our first real step for mankind on earth. Areawide solutions for capital-intensive services such as the gathering and processing of solid waste are a major first move. Connecticut has led the way with six or seven regional solid waste facilities. It has required municipalities, industries, and large facilities to join with others in sharing the cost of shipping their solid waste to these concentration points. Large economies are realized through the process of disaggregating the waste and debris from valuable byproducts. There is also much more efficient management of pollution. Regionalization results in being able to afford more highly skilled personnel to solve the difficult, highly technical problems of this somewhat mixed, sometimes dangerous solid waste.

Sewage and potable water are also prime candidates for the first, second, and third phases of metrowide planning that will result in real savings. There are no such real benefits involved in consolidating local police, fire control, and other highly labor-intensive services. On the other hand, there are real cost advantages through consolidation of specialized crime forces such as detectives, SWAT teams, and arson experts. Such highly qualified technical personnel may work more efficiently over a larger geographical area than in the small political jurisdictions within American metroareas.

The idea of having metrowide transportation management associations (TMAs) to find solutions to local transportation problems is past the time for adoption. Transportation management associations can organize ride-sharing and van pools. They can promote staggered work hours and lobbying for government-funded improvements. Some can expand their role into child care, private police for urban villages, and other services for the geographic area. It is imaginable that the TMAs— born of the traffic congestion crisis—could mature into an echelon of partners in progress between businesses, neighborhoods, and governments. They are well suited to the realities of emerging urban villages that cross over local political jurisdictions.

11. American Metroareas—
The Best Hope for Human Rights?

Can American metroareas be good places to live? Yes. In the early development of the political thoughts of Democrats and Republicans, both were in the liberal traditions. Here, liberal is compared with right-wing aristocratic conservatism of Europe were there was no place for "cities" found in the minds of the liberal society. Still, cities have had powerful, psychic power. Cities have sometimes been seen as the essence of freedom. A German proverb says, "The air of the city makes one free." Also, cities are seen as a danger to freedom. Cities have been touted as a source of individual development and fulfillment. In contrast, they have been seen as the source of atrophy of individualism and the increase of nonchalant, blase attitudes. Cities have been characterized as an expression of bourgeois rationalism, on the one hand, and as threatening passionate excesses through majoritarian politics, which could destroy that very rationalism. Cities have been classified as an integral subdivision of a free society, and as a part of the state. Cities have been analyzed as purely economic phenomena and as creations of the mind.

The principal conundrum is that metroareas are entities intermediate between the state and the individual. Within the United States, with its dual state and federal sovereignty, we have an added level of complexity. This third level of quasisovereignty, the metroareas, should be chartered by joint act of the federal and state legislative bodies. Because of the evolution of the human brain, our educational levels, and the telecommunication media's effects, chartered metropolitan districts could be a way for direct democratic participation without disturbing the traditional state and federal relationships. There would be the diffusion of power and a more active expression of citizens rights at the local level.

I believe that, at least at first, local district voting should be mandatory within such chartered metroareas. It is a necessary tutorial for responsible citizenship. Thus this "bastard child," the third-level orphan, our metroareas, could be the way to revive citizens' participation and overcome the apathy and alienation which now dominates the body politic. This idea is contained in the images we have of the metroarea as an organism. The first influential organic imagery was contained in Emile Durkheim's classic, "The Division of Labor in Society" (1893). Durkheim analyzed modern society's organic solidarity. The progress in knowledge in biogenetics and biochemistry suggests that the analogy of the metroarea as an "organism with networks" to other metroorganisms has real usefulness. The relation of our metroareas to the region and the nation may be likened to the brain's relation to the human body. The issues of external dependence and systemic linkages reemerge in the study of urban problems.

Organic imagery may combine with machine imagery in a macroscopic approach to the metroarea. This imagery portrays the area as neither the city of vice nor the city of virtue. Bazaar imagery continues to be activated by the many network studies of the metroarea. This image increases our perception of the interdependence of metroarea inhabitants. The sociologists' images are valuable because they enable us to understand that the metroarea is a state of mind. Economic forces do not deterministically control the pattern of land use in a metroarea. Economic issues and actions are influenced by cultural images and historic symbols. They play a critical role in directing population into certain areas of the MSA and resisting business encroachment into other sectors of the metroarea.

Some sociologists have focused on the local neighborhood as a central structure —a sanctuary—that reduces the danger and the uncertainty of the urban jungle. Because of the jungle of the metroarea, we create neighborhoods in which we feel that people like us are located. We give these areas names, like Grant Park (Atlanta), Georgetown (Washington, D.C.), and Nob Hill (San Francisco). They become safe places in which to shop, work, play, and reside. These enclaves can be a concrete realization of social values and the cultural ideas that shape the social diversity of our differing metroareas. Still, as we start to huckster the differing "brand images" of our metroareas, we should not ignore the cries of a modern Jeremiah, Lewis Mumford. He called attention to our new barbarism—the multiplication of bathrooms and the overexpenditure on broadly paved motor roads and, above all, the massive concentration of human attention on fashion.

Today, our psyche foresees an image of a metroarea given over to a multitude of roundtables. There, discussions could occur among conflicting neighborhoods and conflicting interests. Such colloquies could be held with a hope of identifying the common ground and a willingness to make commitments. Such an image, although consistent with a view of many organizations at the neighborhood level, suggests looking at the cityscape from the street level instead of from the skyline of the power elite. People, not machines or abstractions, could be our current focus.

Metroareas Expand Our Capacity for Delight

The order of the metroarea should be an unfolding one, a pattern that is grasped progressively. From it, we could draw a greater potential for delight. We are all supposed to pursue happiness, and we can if we are internally secure and thus free to delight in ambiguity, mystery, and surprise contained within a basic orderly pattern. This can result from a confident mind weaving and experiencing the new within the intricate imagery of the existing metroarea. Unfortunately, in the twentieth century we have yet to develop perceptual models for inner-city schoolchildren who are growing there. We need to help suburban high school students who are circulating about the area to unfold and understand the order of their metroarea. Now it is learned outside the experience they gain through the curricula of their public schools.

True modern metroarea design, committed to neo-Enlightenment principles, would deal directly with the ongoing sensory environment of the entire metroarea. It would be a collaboration with the people who will sense it and experience it. Such a process hardly exists today. Decisionmakers—professionals both public and private—find the technique of consulting the people and finding out what they want discomforting. My experiences as an urban renewal director showed that often local inhabitants had given a great deal of thought to the way their metroarea worked and how it might work better in fulfilling important aspirations of the humans who live there. All one needs to do is to provide a forum, ask, and make a record of the discussions. It could result in significant improvement over elitist policy. Also, it will usually result in a stronger commitment of the population to support the resulting plan.

The United States has an "anti-city" attitude. It is time for its demise. In 1962 Morton and Luchia White, in their influential study *The Intellectual vs. the City*, represented American leadership as anti-city. From Thomas Jefferson to Frank Lloyd Wright to Gerald Ford, some leaders have made extremely biased remarks about our metroareas. They have provided a rallying point for anti-urban motives in American thought and expression throughout our history. This American anti-city attitude is out of step with the rest of our good earth's inhabitants. Globally, the perceived wisdom is that there is an ancient and almost timeless affinity between city life and the life of the mind. Cities, after all, are the places where scholars, artists, and writers naturally congregate. They do so because most of the vital institutions of mental production—universities, libraries, theaters, museums, galleries, publishers and printers, are almost invariably located in cities.

Truly, we are a nation of metroarea builders. When the republic was founded roughly nine out of ten Americans lived in a rural environment. Today, the fraction is less then three out of ten. To some, "anti-city" attitudes are spiritual, the mind inveighing against the humdrum reality of our prosaic human condition. As Thoreau said about his ardent cultivation of the bean field, these repeated moves away from "society" or "the city" are undertaken chiefly for the sake of thoughts and expression. To call *Walden* a viable anti-urbanism, as the Whites do, is to one commentator, Leo Marx, a grand impertinence. Thus, again, my main theme comes to the fore. If we see democratic capitalism as a mere draught horse for our constitutional culture, then making our cities a better place in which to live becomes a categorical imperative. This is evident when we consider, for example, the mass exodus of the white middle class from our central cities to the suburbs. Why did they leave? The usual explanation has to do with flight from poverty, race, and violence, and the decline in the quality of services. But the reality may be that they were simply seeking the proverbial American dream—a patch of land of their own and a home over which they had control. Still, they want to be close enough to the benefits of the metroarea and the urban villages of the suburbs, and also to avoid any responsibility for the dire problems of the city from which they have escaped. In effect, instead of facing the challenge to grow and mature, they pick up their toys and leave. Perhaps it was the flight of emotionally immature human beings. The years after World War II saw massive, chaotic building on our urban fringes. It has created great problems that our nation has yet to face. When will we begin to deal with the suburban problems that were set out in detail by Charles Haar in his summary report on the President's Commission on Suburban Problems?[1] The Nixon and Reagan administrations deliberately suppressed distribution of the report by budgetary gamesmanship. It is conscious avoidance of unpleasant truths. In 1974 Sen. Edward Kennedy stated,

> Amazingly the Haar Report is as timely today as it was when it was first prepared in 1968. Amazingly, up to this day, few of the recommendations made by the task force have been adopted. Since few have been implemented, we have lost hundreds of thousands of opportunities to improve the lives of millions of Americans. The report set forth in clear terms that suburbias are aching with social, physical, and economic strains caused by their incredible changes over time. They need planning and organized help at the federal, state, and local level if a good quality of life in the suburbs is to be maintained. The suburban conditions are an indivisible part of the quality of life of our entire metropolitan areas. They do not stand alone. Help to the troubled central cities and the suburbs should move in tandem. Without the improvement of both, all metro-politan area citizens will suffer. Pollution, crime, and decay are no respecters of municipal boundaries; the economic productivity of the urban region is crippled; and the quality and diversity of life have eroded. The suburbs need help. The kind of help that is part of a wide and comprehensive program for the entire metropolitan area and its parts. We are struck again by the wisdom of Judge Learned Hand, who reminded us of "a satisfaction in the sense that we are all engaged in a common venture."

Consider, for example, that the price of land in suburbs is inflating faster than most consumer goods and the unspoiled countryside is rampantly becoming spoiled through pollution of air and water. Also, low density and dispersal of population has an adverse impact on transportation costs in both time and energy, not to mention our failure to accept manufactured housing for low- and moderate-income people. All these factors together have forced up the ratio of housing expenses for the average American family. The list goes on:

- High interest costs for mortgages and rising housing constructions costs have greatly increased the fraction of household budgets devoted to shelter costs.
- The suburbs have caused a socially disorganizing effect on our society by way of economic segregation.
- The idea of the "good life" seems changed to an endless pursuit of consumer goods. The only saving grace seems to be church organizations, which are also often aimless in their goals.
- The price of growth without planning and orderly development forces many higher costs on capital improvements program.
- The suburbs fortunately are increasingly dedicated to education. Still, the effort is on the physical product—school and stadium construction—rather than the quality of the curriculum. Suburban schools act now as day-care centers for the affluent because they do not place high demands on the students.
- Faced with rising land costs and tight budgets, suburban communities have generally neglected or delayed decisions on public land acquisition votes. In such cases we will have inadequate municipal infrastructure committed for many decades still to come. Although one so-called attraction of suburban land is parks and play spaces, few suburbs have acquired, or otherwise provided,

anywhere near the ratio of open-space requirements that is already present in many of our central cities.

- There is clear evidence that local capital expenditures for water and sewage facilities and other public works are on a decline in proportion to total expenditures. The federal government has withdrawn aid in this important area.
- Crime in the suburbs has been increasing—in many metroareas it is higher in the suburbs than in the central cities.

The problems of suburbia do not add up to a clamorous, visible crisis, such as poverty pockets and crime rates. These are quiet decaying places. Our cities throughout the nation are young compared to other parts of the world. Thereby we fail to perceive that the way we use the land in suburban rings around our maturing metropolitan cities is a commitment of that land for generations to come. Sometimes it is committed to the wrong use, in the sense of what would be good for the people at large. We can build good suburban communities instead of sterile suburbs that simply provide people a dormitory and trading areas to consume goods.

The reason for the exit from the central city, according to some commentators, has little or nothing to do with the intrinsic character of cities. Instead, it is due to the postwar way of development of our national economy and the nature and scope of a defense-dominated market economy. Also a factor were the oligopolistic corporations, who were not subject to home-rule local controls. According to this idea, these same large organizations have more power in the state legislatures and national government than do our metroareas and their inhabitants. The result is that many Americans have simply "given up" and tried to "move away" to a self-contained world of their own. They are a lonely crowd of couch potatoes.

Poverty and Myths of the Suburbs

It is likely that democratic capitalism creates slums or poverty ghettos out of need. If democratic capitalism is to work efficiently for the greatest numbers to efficiently distribute income, encourage vertical social mobility, and be a relative meritocracy, then it is a necessary concomitant that those who will not or cannot work within such a political economy will find themselves living in poverty, unless their extended families, charity, or the state support them.

Poverty may be necessary to support the work ethic. Still, there is a serious problem when our society uses the market-oriented economy and couples it with condoning the inhumane treatment of certain citizens who are poor because of race, color, creed, national origin, sex, mental health, handicap, debilitating disease, or old age. Poverty is no indication that such humans being are, as such, unwilling to work.

But it is nasty for us to prevent able-bodied people from rising from poverty. It is nasty for us to destroy youths because they live in poverty. On the other hand, for alcoholics, drug addicts, criminals, and others who are unwilling to accept rehabilitation, poverty may be necessary for the rest of the system to work. To the poor of post–World War II America, the psychic experience is almost a total reversal of the ingredients listed in descriptions of the nineteenth-century symbols of the slums. Where the slum had been crowded with people, now it is a place of empty lots, fires and housing abandonment. Where scrimping, saving, and patching enforced a discipline to overcome the deprivation of the noble poor in the old slums, now in the new slums essentials are sufficiently supplied. Much worse: today's ghettos have become the graveyard of broken appliances, abandoned cars, discarded furniture, and much local and citywide trash. There is moral and sexual degradation in slums. The old slum was a place of orphaned and malnourished children, child abuse, prostitution, liquor, and theft.

Today, the higher skills of the United States's modern, more educated poor, with television providing exciting ideas, has created a different urban poverty district. It has become a place of fighting gangs of "children" who terrorize poor adults. Today, with the lethal threat of AIDS, and gonorrhea resistant to antibiotics, it is also a place where dirty needles and promiscuity have added the threat of spreading disease throughout the metroareas. This is because the visiting "Johns" come from the suburbs with their money. It is home for teenagers who have become welfare mothers without concern about their employability. It is a place where hard drugs replaced liquor and crime has become so widespread that it defies the older rules of combat between police and criminal groups.

The old slum had been immigrant and white, now it is immigrant, Hispanic, black, and brown. It is made up of both native-born blacks and in-migrant whites. It is especially the brown and black poverty enclaves that challenge the symbol of the nineteenth-century slum. It was a symbol formed without any precondition of race. The principle reason for discarding the semantics of the word "slum" and starting to use the newer term "ghetto" was to fit urban poverty into the American ideology of race persecution. Because of the rise to prominence in our constitutional culture of the idea of social mobility after World War II, it was an important ideological change. But the result has not strengthened our culture. This is because of the conflict resulting from the sense of guilt and embarrassment of those who have a Judeo-Christian conscience. Humanitarianism is frustrated due to inability to solve the problem.

Complex social, economic, and political factors are creating a vast new class of poor Americans who are much younger, less educated, and likely to give birth sooner than recent generations of the poor. Sen. Daniel Moynihan has stated that the United States today may be the first society in history where children are much worse off than adults. Its time we realized we have a problem of significant social change unlike anything we have experienced in the past yet we are almost ignoring it. The reasons are many and are tied to certain government policies or nonpolicies and deep social changes. Some facts that show up in the 1990 poverty statistics:

- About 14 million, or 22 percent, of Americans under the age of eighteen live in poverty, up from 14.3 percent in 1969. Worse, 48 percent of black children live in poverty, up from 39.6 percent in 1969. The federal government defines the poverty level based on a market basket of goods for a family of four and an income of about $12,300 per year in 1990.
- A third of all black children are poor, despite the fact that black children are only a sixth of all children.
- Children living with a mother in a single-parent home were four times more likely to be poor than those in two-parent homes. Recently, child poverty

rates actually grew much more rapidly in two-parent homes. Of the 790,000 families who fell into poverty in the early 1980s, 430,000 lived in households with two parents.

- One-sixth of children below the official government poverty level, about 2.5 million, are living in poverty despite the fact that at least one adult in the family holds a full-time job. His or her pay is inadequate to raise them above the poverty threshold.

- Government programs and considerable other spending have reduced poverty among elderly Americans. On the other hand, the number of poor American children has increased by more than 3 million since 1968. Since 1968 real government expenditures on the problems of youthful poor have declined, while taxes paid by many poor people have increased. This trend has been somewhat relieved by the tax reform legislation of 1986.

- One-third of the nation's poor families manage to climb above the poverty level each year. This is an unrecognized success because they are quickly replaced by other financially stricken newcomers. There is very significant cycling of poverty for the nation. This is to be expected within democratic capitalism.

- A little less than a quarter of American children live in families headed by women, but more than half the poor children live in such households. This is twice the rate of 1959.

- Parents' marital status may be a key determinant of a child's poverty. The number and rate of births to unmarried teenagers has been increasing. For example, in Washington, D.C., 68 percent of teenage mothers were unwed. Virtually 100 percent of them were below the poverty threshold, almost guaranteeing that both mother and child will have a long experience with the effects of poverty.

The statistics are frightening: U.S. adolescent girls get pregnant at twice the rate of teenage girls in England and Canada, three times the rate of girls in Sweden, and seven times that of girls in the Netherlands. Nearly 20 percent of white American females get pregnant by the time they are twenty years old, while 41 percent of black females do. One-sixth of births in this country are to adolescent girls, four out of five of whom are unmarried. As Ann Landers once put it, "Every indicator of social pathology (drug addiction, child abuse, mental retardation) is strongly associated with being born to a teenage mother."

If we can stave off teenage pregnancy, we may ameliorate the effects on children reared in poverty, drastically reducing the number of our nation's youth lost to drug addiction, delinquency, illiteracy, and a legion of other social woes. The Alan Guttmacher Institute has conducted studies that show the big difference between the United States and Western nations where the teen pregnancy rate is lower is that those nations teach sex education and make contraceptives easily available for teens. The United States deliberately does so ineffectively or not at all.

Day-Care Centers

It appears certain that efforts must be made to make it possible for the female heads of households to work by means of subsidized day-care centers. We also need the further reduction in large families that account for a disproportionate share of children who are in poverty. Children also would benefit from more public support of education, child-health clinics, and the like. Unfortunately, such support depends on the willingness of adults, most of whom who do not live with children, to pay for them.

Mickey Kaus has a plan to get and enable single mothers to work.[2] Single mothers would no longer qualify for cash welfare payments. They would have to work like anyone else. Perhaps the prospect of juggling motherhood and a not-very-lucrative job would make them think twice about having additional children. The provision of extremely low-cost, if not free, day-care centers would be absolutely imperative. The objective would be to get children out of the poverty subculture of the underclass families and into schools at an early age. Day-care centers should not be as expensive as some neoconservatives argue.

Barbara Goldman states that free day care, when offered to mothers on welfare, has never been used to the extent people thought it would be. The availability of a workable alternative enables the mothers to make other arrangements through their network in the community or relatives. In any event, the day-care center is an essential link because it makes the "other" familial arrangement "possible." It provides care for those days when the "friend" is not available. Day-care centers are appropriate tenants for neighborhood churches, often vacant during the work week. I found the plan worked during my service as an urban renewal director. Well-baby clinics and adequate nutrition and medical care for the mothers and the children would be essential.

Mothers with children two years old and younger present a special problem for the Judeo-Christian ethic. Much early brain development necessary for verbal and analytical skills occurs in the first few years or not at all. One way to encourage responsible mothering would be to allow cash welfare for the first two years of the first child's life with a three-year limit to avoid the "having another child" problem. There should be no "free ride," for even a pregnant mother, except for nutritional aid and well-baby clinics during pregnancy and immediately after delivery. This could avoid disastrous health problems. By requiring work, society could defuse the teenage attitude that having a child is a way to get up and out of the ghetto community. This would force young mothers into the world of work without letting them grow accustomed to dependency. The compassionate will ask, What if a mother refuses to work? In my experience in urban renewal this happened only with retarded or mentally ill mothers.

Still, some mothers will turn down the state's offer of a job to support her children. The result would be that her children live in squalor and filth. In such a woeful case, we should face reality that the woman is neglecting a basic duty of parenthood. Such a woeful mother is subject to the laws of delinquent motherhood that provide for removal of a child from such an unfit home. It may be a brutal answer, but this is much better for the baby than what we are doing today. The American electorate is unwilling to spend money on child poverty. The child poverty rate has grown apace, while the main welfare program for them—Aid to Families with Dependent Children—has been reduced by a third. A complete prenatal treatment package throughout the gestation period would be about $600, while it costs about $1,000 *a day* for the intensive care of an underweight infant.

Experts know too well that the official notion held by the Reagan/Bush Administration that social spending has created a dependent class is conscious fiction. It is the counterfeit currency of a conventional wisdom that has been purveyed by the editorialist and the complacent conversationalists in America's country clubs. There was no explosion of handouts to the poor during the war on poverty. Another war—Vietnam—saw to that.

From 1965 to 1968 the Office of Economic Opportunity received a total of less than $6 billion. In no year did it absorb even 1 percent of the federal budget. On the other hand, spending for the non-poor rose from $29.4 billion to $197.8 billion in the period from 1960 to 1976. This was primarily due to the increase in Social Security benefits and Medicare. The incidence of poverty among the elderly is relatively low, 15 percent. The United States spent only about 14 percent of its gross national product on all social programs in the late 1970s. West Germany spent more than twice that and still had lower rates of unemployment and inflation and a higher rate of industrial investment. This is weighty counter-evidence to the conservative argument that the United States has fallen behind in productivity and competitiveness because it has starved private investment in favor of vast social-spending programs.

Is the Underclass Black?

Charles Murray, author of *Losing Ground*, says he found a town in Ohio where white mothers are producing illegitimate babies at the same level as blacks. Still, it is simply foolish to pretend that the culture of poverty is not largely a black culture. In a 1986 issue of the *Atlantic*, Lemann debunks the idea that one can treat the underclass as a colorblind phenomenon. Lemann stresses a fairly direct connection between those blacks who have worked in the sharecropping system in the South and those who formed the lower class of the ghettos after the great migration to Chicago, Detroit, New York, and other cities of the North. When desegregation allowed middle- and upper-class blacks to escape the ghetto, Lemann argues, they left behind that part of the black lower class that has always been there. The difference is that this isolated lower-class culture is now free from the restraints of the black middle class, whose dignified presence imposed better conduct on those with lower status.

Ghetto teenagers do not have children trying to get on welfare. They have babies to increase their self-esteem, to give themselves "something to love" in a world where delayed gratification (say, to get an education) seems pointless due to the high unemployment rate of their peers. This is entirely in keeping with what we know to date about the maturation of human personality and from the work of Erik Erikson and others. The men seek to prove their masculinity. Girls in inner-city high schools and poverty enclaves are often ridiculed by other girls if they remain virgins too long into their teens.

Workfare

One extreme is Massachusetts' touted employment and training choices program, known as "ET." ET is not workfare replacing welfare, for there is nothing mandatory about it. Welfare mothers are offered a variety of services designed to help them find work, job appraisal, career planning, workshops on remedial education, job training placement services and more. Those who find jobs get transportation allowances and free day care for a year after they start work, plus Medicaid for up to fifteen months, if their employers do not provide health insurance. One group of liberal thinkers feels that if you try to force somebody to do something you will not accomplish it. Yet the Works Project Administration of the Depression years did produce many fine post offices and other public buildings and well-built parks and highway projects. Also, the military draft has not produced the effects of slavery. With workfare, most welfare recipients get off the rolls within two years without any supplementary social programs. It is a core of 10 to 25 percent (perhaps, 10 to 15 percent) of female welfare recipients who stay on welfare for extended periods. They are the most serious problem—people who won't climb the ladder of opportunity even when the economy, or the government, dangles opportunity in front of them. Slavery, bondage of the indentured servant, and rural peonage are used as hot rhetoric in the workfare debate. But no one, including the Reagan/Bush administrations and Murray, talks about throwing indigents in jail if they do not work. Nor do I. A mandatory program can be carried out without such anti-democratic measures.

Workfare should be mandatory for those ready, willing, and able to work, and who want the welfare benefits. This merely says if you want the state monies to subsidize your living, the state has a right to ask that you do something of value in return. There is much good work that needs to be done in our metroareas. It is not being done now because "we can't afford it." Maybe we should ask the military to do some of it; soldiers and officers might even feel better about themselves and their role in society. Workfare should not be a short-term program to help existing welfare clients, but a long-term program designed to destroy the culture of poverty within people. To be effective, in order for the single teenager, who may have an illegitimate child, or three, to increase her welfare benefits, they must see the prospect of sweeping streets, cleaning buildings, or whatever, to work off her welfare grant. She should know a chain of illegitimate children will place her in permanent poverty if she does not "work" her way out of it.

Those who oppose soft workfare tend to use client-centered criteria. They note evidence that participants with work experience feel they aren't learning any new skills by sweeping streets or cleaning buildings. The same comment could be made about many unskilled tasks required of mass-production lines and fast-food restaurant jobs. Mandatory workfare advocates, on the other hand, think it is good when someone works off his or her grants, whether or not it increases their income. For by doing so, she or he is learning the all-important skill of "industrial discipline." He or she is also getting out of a dreary home environment and mixing with city life. The sense of responsibility, showing up for work, maintaining low-level absenteeism, and being productive are important in democratic capitalism. It also produces valuable feelings of social justice for those with jobs at the lower rungs of the ladder of social mobility.

There is little evidence that a truly mandatory work requirement for the entire caseload of a large state such as Illinois or California could be administered effectively without "gold bricking" and other capricious forms of work avoidance. Of course, anyone who has ever observed the army at the field level is well aware that this is a problem with all large organizations. The "gold bricking" I observed among midlevel Westinghouse executives of the 1960s was appalling. Lee Iaccoca's program to bring it to an end at Chrysler was essential to that company's successful turnaround.

The welfare system does have a "get job training" mentality. But welfare recipients are not required to participate in the program if they are "seriously dependent upon alcohol or drugs," if they have "an emotional or mental problem," a "medically verified illness," "legal difficulties," or "a severe family crisis." To many all this may seem like softheaded liberalism. Nonetheless, the unpleasant truth is that most of the jobs available for long-term welfare mothers will be menial, deadend jobs that do not really pay enough to enable them to work off their grant. Furthermore, we are dealing with humans who have very low levels of self-esteem as we seek to get them up the learning curve. We need to provide them with self-respecting decisionmaking power.

A National Service Corps

I for one join with those who find it hard to accept the idea that the government cannot be the employer of last resort at this time. Why should we be providing human aid for "nothing" while our roads are crumbling? Playgrounds and schools are falling into disrepair. Streets are increasingly filthy and littered. The elderly need home care. The need to recondition many of our parks and to establish new parks and recreational areas is clear. Therefore, why can't these welfare recipients improve their self-esteem and self-identity by doing useful work that serves the commonweal and help to produce domestic tranquility? The reason? There is strong opposition by organized labor.

At the Washington headquarters of American Federation of State, County, and Municipal Employees, the nation's largest public employee union, there is an office occupied by Al Russo. His job is to fight against any attempt to employ the destitute in public service jobs. Perhaps we should authorize the payment of initiation fees to the AFSCME as a part of the welfare recipients' dole. AFSCME has worked hard for state legislation that bars the use of welfare workers to do work customarily performed by union members unless the work done by the welfare recipients does not deprive current state employees of overtime. That's right, overtime.

Mickey Kaus in a classic *New Republic* article, "The Work Ethic State," believes, as I do, that the only program that has a real chance of improving the dismal outlook of the underclass is a program that enforces the work ethic. Kaus's program deserves a detailed review by policymakers. First, it would be a program that expects women to work even when they have young children. I tried this with the cooperative leadership of churches, project area residents, and my relocation director, Paul Owczykowski, in my tenure as an urban renewal director. We agreed that a critically important element of the plan needed to be provision of high-quality, low-cost day-care centers. Our program worked. Second, Kaus's program would offer work to ghetto men and single women. In effect, if you were ready willing and able to work, you would not be given a welfare check. Instead, you would receive a pay check for working at one of several government job sites that would be offered to you. If you didn't show up for work, you would not be paid. I believe the low but subsistence-level wage would itself "ration" the jobs to those who needed them most. It would preserve the incentive to look for better work in the private sector. Workers in these jobs would be earning their own money.

There is an advantage to this program—supervision to learn work discipline. Those who performed well would achieve something most underemployed underclass members desperately need, a supervisor who could give a job reference to other employers in the private sector. It would not be necessary to "require" work. Work would be all that was offered. Those who showed up drunk or on drugs would be discharged. Those who picked a fight with the supervisor would be fired. This is similar to the Roosevelt administration's Work Projects Administration jobs, though the WPA was available primarily to veteran workers who were out of work due to the Depression.

Will there be enough jobs for underclass people? The answer is our concern for the crumbling municipal infrastructure. It has preoccupied knowledgeable people at the state, federal, and municipal level for several years. Are we really going to have teenage girls repairing potholes and painting bridges? Women can fill potholes, and paint bridges, and water lawns, and pick up garbage, as women can be telephone repair workers and sailors. Our current experience has correctly destroyed the sex stereotypes that used to surround much physical work. There is no reason men could not also fill jobs such as nurse's aides, photocopy operators, receptionists, clerks, police assistants, coat checkers, cooks, cleaners, and day-care workers, as many women already do. There will be those who will object that these substitute public workers will not be competent. The response is that realistically, many beginning-level workers in jobs of all kinds are not competent. Supervisors in control could direct workers to a skill level they can handle. If leaf raking is all they can do, that is better than staying home and raising children at an increasing cost to taxpayers who are themselves expected to conform to the work ethic.

Another objection that Kaus calls to mind is the argument that such a program could quickly degenerate into a mere "make work" game. The problem is the bad experience the nation had with the Comprehensive Employment and Training Act of the 1970s. Construction unions, AFSCME, and others opposed meaningful work for the youths who entered the program. Pragmatism and fairness requires that no current government workers be laid off to introduce this program. As workers leave through natural attrition, resignation, death, and retirement, the government could replace them with guaranteed job holders. Guaranteed-job projects could then be chosen based on how useful they are, not on whether some union objects to them. Doing work such as street and park maintenance not being done because of budgetary difficulties should not be opposed by union workers. Why can unions and the public not accept the idea that some public works jobs might be somewhat inefficient compared to those in the private sector? We readily accepted the idea that an army has millions of people who are unproductively involved in calisthenics and military exercises, which have little meaning in the way of work productivity. There is a need for a workforce of utility workers to merely stand by to service the high labor demand costs of disasters. The result is, we have long ago accepted a low level of productivity among our utility companies. Also, our experience with the WPA's public-works buildings is that we did get something for our money. There is no reason to think that we would not find these modern-day workers reasonably productive.

The program would cost money. A reasonable estimate based on previous programs is about $10,000 per job. This is because of the need to pay social workers and others to help these workers in getting into the industrial-discipline mainstream. Thus every million jobs would cost $10 billion. Long term, savings would occur. Many in the welfare culture would be absorbed into the taxpaying work-ethic culture. The idea of the work-ethic state proclaims the equal dignity of those who work. A very recent poll shows that cash for the disabled and jobs for the able-bodied are what the public supports. These types of work programs are likely to emerge soon.

The problem we face is that conservatives who are in power are ideologically incapable of solving the underclass problem. This is because it does involve the use of more government than they can stomach. Like most humans they tend to reason from their own experience. Work for many middle-class teenagers is not working out well for their families. After years of encouraging young middle-class people to go to work, many authorities are concluding that the jobs do not advance the work ethic. The jobs may foster bad grades and a poor attitude toward education among middle- and upper-middle-class children. Commentators say low-level jobs at fast-food franchises, supermarkets and the like detract from studies. Worse, they provide money for consumer goods that teenagers hardly need, such as drugs, alcohol, and muscle cars. An eighteen-year-old Evanston, Illinois, high school senior works thirty hours a week as a grocery clerk for $5.30 an hour. He has bought a stereo, a bicycle, a camera, and joined with his mother in purchasing a 1980 BMW. Meanwhile, he is failing physics and math. He forthrightly responds, "I'd rather have money than pass a class." Fast-food restaurants and grocery stores often call in workers at the last minute. It makes it difficult to complete studying. The students have little choice but to play down the importance of school.

The Institute for Social Research at the University of Michigan has suggested too much discretionary income distorts teenagers' priorities. In effect, there is an appropriate worry that such "premature affluence," while living off the food, clothing and shelter of their parents, will lead to disillusionment in later years when most income will go to pay rent and food bills. This has already produced a crop of "yuffies"—"young urban failures." Some schools in Georgia require students who receive academic credit for working to save 10 percent of their wages. It is a real way to discourage profligate attitudes. Supermarkets, fast food chains, drugstores, and the like, ought to consider not only recognizing the employee of the month, but also awarding significant bonuses to those working students who also are performing with excellence in school.

The work ethic culture we need to set up would be a national program, not state and local. It would increase the role of the federal government, which is an anathema to the ideological leaders of the conservative right. The costs could be met by enacting a value-added tax at the federal level. It could then be redistributed to local metropolitan districts that had been chartered and reorganized pursuant to a properly drafted metropolitan reorganization enabling act. This could result in reducing local real estate tax.

We know current welfare doesn't work. Work "incentives" do not work. Training doesn't work. Work "requirements" do not work. "Work experience" doesn't work and even workfare doesn't quite work. As Kaus says, only work works.

12. Metroareas and the Law

The law, as an institution, has been misused by the power elite to prevent metroareas from having power. American metroareas as centers of power are a great disappointment to those who believe that citizens should exercise their rights in order for them to continue to have power. For those who maximize profits in the short run, without any sense of a communitarian spirit, the "city powerless" is a desirable feature of modern life and of democratic capitalism. To them, the idea of real local power conjures a fearful picture. Some see the strangulation of nationwide business by a maze of conflicting local regulations and the frustration of national political objectives by local selfishness and protectionism. They see no advantage to reenergizing political choice. The rejection of local power is implied by the needs of modern, large-scale organizations both public and private. This kind of thinking is also a product of our blurred vision. We must learn to make a clear distinction between the needs of our constitutional culture and the needs of democratic capitalism.

The Early Modern Town

A bit of history will help to see the problem that arises out of a human quest for power and the abuse of it. It should be known that the king, the church, the university, and the medieval town were the principal examples of medieval corporate bodies. Many of these institutions, together with the feudal manor, were the principal citadels of power subjected to liberal attack. To early liberal thinkers, the attack on the autonomy of medieval corporations, including the medieval towns, was necessary to protect what they considered the vital interests of individual liberty. This was the emergence of the Hobbesian nation-state against the power of the church. This perspective, then, was the predecessor of our own. The liberals of this time sought to end the domination of the town oligarchy. They sought to establish the rule of law, the social contract, over all centers of power.

In its day, the medieval town was the agency of power that unduly restricted individual activity. Therefore, it was critically important to restrict the town's control of individual activity and irresponsible local protectionism. The mistake, seen in hindsight, was that the increase in the power of the nation-state seemed benign. There is a paradox in defending the power of the town, though it is itself based on the notion of freedom. Protection of the separate power of the town, an entity at an intermediate stratum between the state and the individual, could at some time in the future threaten the way of life, the freedom, of those who had been protected by the town's autonomy from the state. We are living at that historic moment, the end of the twentieth century, when, for the sake of the viability of our constitutional culture, we must work out that paradox. By creating new chartered metropolitan governments of limited sovereignty, we would create an intermediate level between the various states and the federal governments. It would be designed to empower local individuals so they will again become involved in their constitutional culture.

The English king of the 1600s remained suspicious of the independent power wielded by the members of the economic oligarchy of cities such as London. He persistently sought to bring them under the sovereign's control. Thus the issues of limiting the king's power with respect to Parliament as well as the cities, were two aspects of protecting the same interest, that of the commercial class. It is important to emphasize that the craftsmen and the yeoman and the common sort, were almost without power of any kind. The suspicions of the king, his desire to expand his independent power, his uneasy relationship with Parliament, resulted in an historic dispute with the cities. He attacked their corporate charters.

This noteworthy suit was brought because the city charter defined both the power of the corporate elite over ordinary citizens and their relationship to the king. The question of the status of corporate charters became the focus of what has been called the most important case in English history, the Quo Warranto, brought in 1682 by Charles II. The king challenged the legitimacy of the corporate status of the City of London. The vested rights acquired by the corporate city franchise were rights of property. Many, taking a Lockeian view, felt those rights must be protected to assure the liberty of all Englishmen. The king, taking a Hobbesian view, believed the issue to be one related to the need for central control, to prevent societal conflict. Therefore he asserted the right to revoke the charter of cities. By that the wrongdoing of an individual could be treated as though it were that of the city corporation. This could result in the forfeiture of the city's charter. The vested rights on which the members of the corporation relied would become valueless, or, at best, under direct monarchial control. Hobbes, having just died in 1679, must have danced a jig in his grave at this prospective increase in the sovereign's power.

The king was victorious in the London case. It was a victory for the Hobbesian positivist's position establishing the legal principle of royal control over cities. But an immediate major social upheaval of 1688, the "Glorious Revolution," ended the Stewart reign. The London charter case was reversed by revolution. The surrender of other city charters was undone, and the immunity of corporate charters from royal review and control was reestablished. Blood was shed to limit the sovereign's power over the natural rights of individuals. Although the revolution protected corporate charters from the only source thought to threaten them at the time, the king, it did not resolve the extent of Parliament's power over those charters. Although English Parliament considered corporate charters inviolate, Anglo-American law evolved a legal fiction to get itself out of this uncomfortable corner. It divided the question: What is a corporation?

The confrontation of sovereign legislative power and corporate rights produced in the United States a legal distinction between public and private corporations, one similar to the role of the individual in society and the other similar to the role of the state. Pressure mounted on the legislatures to expand the opportunities for private corporations. The courts gave birth to the powers of a juridical personality, the private corporation. It was to be an individual rights holder. Late in the nineteenth century an astonishing decision was made by the Supreme Court in *Santa Clara County v. Southern Pacific Railroad Co.* It made this momentous decision *per curiam* ("in secret"), without briefs or argument! The court decided that business corporations, already enlivened with perpetual life, would be placed on a coequal plane with natural persons. The court granted immortal corporations almost the same rights accorded to individuals under a free market economic interpretation of the Constitution.

About the middle of the twentieth century, U.S. law began to recognize "contracts of adhesion." This resulted from the disparity of bargaining power between consumers and large private corporations, and the need for class actions to protect small claim litigants. This continued as an effort to restore to individuals some of the power lost by emasculating the chartered municipalities.

The time has come to fashion something new—chartered metroareas. The modern understanding of federal commerce power leaves very little to "local" regulation. Because of the modern expansive interpretation of the commerce clause, business activities are under the federal government's purview. Any activities affecting interstate commerce are subject to the commerce power.

But this was not to be the case for municipal corporations. They also carved out the public (municipal) corporation, an entity to be labeled a mere instrumentality of the state. The privileges and immunities and powers of business or private corporations regularly expanded. The municipal corporation as an entity that was simultaneously a rights holder and a power wielder thus disappeared from the minds of the judges. Municipalities now found themselves captured within a controlled orbit by their home state. They were subordinated to the state legislature and lost most of their rights and powers because the U.S. Constitution resisted the dangerous principle of divisible sovereignty. The challenge therefore was to find a way out of this dilemma and to empower the cities so they could meet the problems of urbanization. As it stands today, there is only one choice available under the legal system for our metroareas, that of centralized legislative authority at the state level or decentralized administrative authority to the bureaucracies of a crazy quilt of cities, counties, townships, villages, school districts, and municipal authorities. These satraps are the metropolitan Balkans. The result is the worst case for an administrator (e.g., mayor): responsibility and accountability without enough power and authority. Because of states' supremacy in U.S. law, it is not surprising that real political power in states gravitates to the state legislatures. The cities are forced to become increasingly active as mere agents of a more active state government. Their authority is superficial and of little consequence in the scheme of things. We need to break out of the idea—in the constitutional sense—that cities are of merely administrative character.

The impotence of American metroareas is expressed in their legal status. In many states, under current law, metropolitan areas and the cities within have no "natural" or "inherent" power to do anything. They do not even have direct power to do that which should be done in an emergency. Cities have only those powers delegated to them by the state government and sometimes the state constitution. Some state constitutions have been amended to grant cities "home rule." Even in those jurisdictions local self-determination free of state control is still quite limited. Such powers usually relate to "purely local" matters. These limitations sharply lower the prestige of the local officials in the minds of their constituencies.

Limited as the powers of cities appear to be, the metroareas have fewer still. This is because generally the metroareas, the true urban economies, do not exist in law. The existing political cities are usually only "islands"—urban villages—within the larger metroarea. Today, the idea of what is "purely local" is very narrowly interpreted by state legislatures and the courts on judicial review. The result is that cities, as distinct from metroareas, are seen as mere "creatures of the states." Because of the current balkanization of our metroareas, we are limiting the powers of mere cities that cause more friction. Therefore, currently, such limits are probably acts of wisdom by courts. Recall the example of the Four Seasons Hotel on the Beverly Hills city line. The political cities do not usually cooperate. They often act in disconcerting ways to stab each other in their backs while shooting themselves in the feet. To make matters worse, the U.S. Constitution reinforces this lack of power by federal restrictions on our cities' power.

The importance of federal grants-in-aid illustrates a source of powerlessness in the metroareas' declining ability to generate income. City revenues are largely dependent on something cities cannot control, such as the state sales tax or grants-in-aid from the federal government. Although real estate taxes are about 70 percent of their local taxing power, such taxes produce only about 40 percent of the monies necessary for the typical local annual budget. The increasing exodus of wealthier taxpayers away from the central cities, and now even from other city centers of the metroarea satellite cities, has been joined by business exodus to the suburbs. This has made the problems of America's major central cities and the major satellite cities both dire and notorious. The U.S. Constitution, particularly through the commerce clause, restricts the kind of taxes that cities can impose. Court decisions restrain parking permits on out-of-city commuters or city income taxes on nonresident wage earners. Every city decision to change taxes must be expressly approved by the states. Some states may even impose a constitutional limitation on the amount of taxing permitted. Because of the limits on cities' taxing and borrowing ability, metroarea dependence on state and federal aid is almost enslaving. City officials must go to the "good old boys" in the legislatures and obsequiously ask for help even though the area's productivity produces a large part of the state budget.

City power is limited in other ways as well. For example, cities are dependent on a specific enabling act for whatever proper power they use. Their ability to regulate private activity is more like that of an administrative agency than that of a lawmaking, sovereign principality. Besides, state constitutions have generally been interpreted by the courts to authorize cities to do only "welfare-improving regulatory service." Decisions deny them "a general authority to define rights" or the power to "alter the basic legal structure of their local civil society." Not only are cities unable to exercise general governmental political power, they cannot exercise the economic power of private corporations. Municipalities are usually barred from engaging in "business activity" unless it is a "public utility function" and is not for profit. The result is that public and private city functions are largely reduced to the provision of certain, specified, or traditional municipal services. Today, many of these highly valued services, such as education, transportation, housing, health care, and mental health care, are provided not by the cities but by legislative contrivances. Examples are the special districts and authorities organized to cut across city boundaries, and over which the cities have little control or influence.

These limits on city power are traditional, natural, and uncontroversial to many Americans. Still, they sap the strength of our constitutional culture in a day when transnational corporations have gross sales that exceed that of many of our large nations. The "people" are forced to act through their small-area municipal corporations. They do not have parity of bargaining power with the large corporations that take up a residence within the municipal boundaries. In the sense of maintaining the vital flow of commerce, without hampering local discrimination, it is all to the good. In the sense of the people exercising their group political and civil constitutional rights in the "public interest," parity of bargaining power is sorely lacking. The serious unresolved problem is that the legal concept—the city—does not coincide with the boundaries of the metroarea as a viable political economy.

The problem raised by the feeble status of our cities is not one of simply deciding how much power we want to allocate to minor political subdivisions. Instead, it raises the fundamental question: Is any diffusion of power possible or desirable in a large, modern, democratic, representative republic system? *I hold that the evolution of the human brain has reached the point that such decentralization is now necessary for mature personalities to reach full flower. Otherwise, they will "tune out" because consumer hedonism is better than frustrated alienation.* One should expect a vigorous neoconservative counterattack against such empowerment. Independent corporate power of any kind threatens individuals whether public or private, natural or corporate. We should choose to have strong, intermediate bodies governing our metroareas. It is not a choice between vulnerability and protection. The exercise of state power infringes upon individual rights that are somewhat protected by the economic power of independent corporations. Yet, the modern exercise of transnational corporate power infringes individual rights that are seldom protected by the state. Our real option is to choose which danger to liberty seems more tolerable, more controllable, or more worth defending.[3]

The dilemma is how to empower local chartered municipal corporate activities without trampling on the free flow of interstate commerce. Aristotle described the human being as a political animal. The ancient, now archaic, power of cities depended, as does the current power of business corporations, on their actual place in social life. Any form of group power ought to be power that is generally acceptable as a matter of human experience and inner thought. It should be something we can integrate into our lives. Madison, and other planter personalities, saw small units of government as a great danger to individual liberty.

Chartered metroareas—metropolitan cities—could have the kind of power we are willing to diffuse in the United States's constitutional culture. Consider the great power wielded by large business corporations. They exercise genuine decentralized power. Berle and Means argued with success that the separation of ownership and control in the modern, "publicly held" corporation placed the control of corporate assets in the hands of a relatively small number of corporate managers. By the control of proxies the managers are beyond the control of the shareholders, and, to a large extent, the public as well. Since the Berle and Means study was made in the 1930s, one must observe that it was accepted as not very disturbing to most people. Therefore, creating large metropolitan corporations, with new power in the hands of local officials elected under rules of proportional representation, is less threatening than the existing power of self-perpetuating corporate managers who have control over stockholder proxies.

We could have creative fusion of some federal and state constitutional powers. Enabling legislation could be enacted by cooperation of the sovereign federal and state governments. This cooperative granting of metroarea charters could create renovated metropolitan district governments for the geographical areas defined as the metropolitan statistical areas.

Our nation has much previous experience with that kind of legislation by way of our workmen's compensation laws, federal-state unemployment compensation laws, welfare laws, water quality controls, and air-shed regulations. Metroarea power would not insure the success of these new human associations. They would be new forms of city entities. Still, a metropolitan reorganization act could be an act of conception that would move the United States toward maturing and developing such networking. Voting must be mandatory to make it work. To work out a legal concept for chartered metropolitan districts, we would confront a question the courts have wrestled with for centuries, one that has long perplexed liberal theorists. Are cities an exercise of freedom by individuals or a threat to such freedom analogous to that posed by the state? In 1978, in *City of Lafayette* v. *Louisiana Power*,[4] the Supreme Court considered whether federal antitrust laws could be applied to cities, as they are to individual and private corporations, or whether cities should be exempt from these laws, as are state governments. In deciding the case, four justices associated the city as an instrumentality within the state. Four associated it with individuals. The final, the swing (deciding) justice, said that sometimes the city acts like an individual and sometimes like the state. As Gerald Frug states, it appears the failure of liberal theory to classify the city neither produces a legislative solution nor enables the judicial branch of the government to use its imagination to find ways for the city to be more useful as a legal concept. The current legal status of cities in American metroareas ought to be an archaic artifact. It is a remnant of a historical process that has run its course in our metroareas and the nation.

There is a positive side to empowering chartered metroarea corporations as a center of group action by its citizens. It would be a balance against the power of these huge private corporations in their cooperative activities with the state and the power elite. Why not? Otherwise, we are moving rapidly toward plantation management and the centralization of power in the hands of a few. A shift of power to the chartered metroareas would mean a shift of emphasis from hierarchical or authoritarian associations to a more democratic form. Further, the change would be a healthy demotion of our current reliance on business corporations for maintenance of democratic capitalism. Also, it would strengthen the place for natural persons in the scheme of our constitutional culture.

"Black-Run" City Administrations May Be the Catalyst

The ascendancy of black leadership in local politics is breaking down the color barrier to investment banking and municipal-bond financing. Atlanta Mayor Maynard Jackson was a partner with the law firm of Chapman and Cutler between mayoral terms. He was organizing blacks in the securities industry to form a black professional organization and promote black investment banking to serve the central cities. New York black-owned firms have opened in the 1980s and the nation's first investment banking concern owned by a Mexican-American has opened its doors in San Antonio, Texas. Also, major firms are recruiting significant numbers of minorities to appeal to the new leadership of large municipalities. I believe we may see a very independent national coalition of big city mayors, led by the black mayors. They provide enough clout to cause change at both the federal and state level through a metropolitan reorganization act. During the past decade, the number of black elected officials has nearly doubled to 5,700. The officials run cities such as New York, Chicago, Detroit, Philadelphia, and Atlanta. In the meantime, we drift toward a chaos that could result in an ugly fascistic solution—consider the following paradigm.

Models of Free-Market Metroareas

Metroarea "A" is a metropolitan district that has a mature attitude toward social responsibility. Most of the people are competitive, cooperative, compassionate, and rights-conscious. In this metroarea a Judeo-Christian ethic prevails. Democratic capitalism is promoted by aiding all to be productive and to have the wherewithal to decide to do good and aid the lower classes as well as themselves.

On the other hand, nearby, within the effective travel area, is Metroarea "B." It is dominated by people who are fascistic. They believe that the power elite should take care of themselves first and only, except for budgeted charity and voluntary good works. There is no taxpayers' concern at all for the lower classes. The result is that work and sustenance trickles down only as the unwanted surplus of the rich to those less able. The needy get the crumbs. Thus, the power elite lets others fend for themselves. As the quality of life of those at the top improves, to a lesser extent, in the very long run, so does the quality of life of those at the bottom. There will be cycles of prosperity and depression. Occasionally some people will really suffer. Still, this system will automatically improve, over the long run, without effort or active concern of those at the top, except for charity.

Metroarea B has a free press and, of course, its lower class is therefore informed about metroarea A. The poor exercise their right of travel to A to take advantage of the less stressful, healthier atmosphere provided there. The result is that metroarea A becomes temporarily overburdened and metroarea B has a larger surplus for the power elite to divide among themselves. (Poor Texans moved to New York and California for just that reason for decades. Now the laissez-faire elite of the "black hole" of Texas want the rest of the United States to help them!)

Any metroarea is a community. It needs communitarian responsibility from its citizens, both natural and corporate. By working within the constitutional culture and democratic capitalism they can improve the quality of life and emerge at a higher level. On the other hand, anarchy is grounded on a social psychological hypothesis that is sociopathic. We have learned from history that energetic, graceful, intelligent behavior occurs only when there are identifiable goals. It is a direct response to a positive world view. In the United States we believe one can pursue happiness. Lewis Mumford has stated in *The Mission of the City* that,

We must now conceive the city, accordingly not primarily as a place of business or government, but as an essential organism for expressing and actualizing the new human personality, that of "one world man." . . . We must restore to the city the maternal, life-nurturing functions, the autonomous activities, the symbiotic associations that have long been neglected or suppressed. For the city should be an organ of love; and the best economy of cities is the care and culture of men and women.[5]

The Netherlands may be the nation that provides us with a microcosm of our problems. In a *National Geographic* article entitled "The Dutch Touch,"[6] we find that the Netherlands is a land of ethnic minorities. Historically, the Netherlands has always been a haven for refugees: Jews fleeing the Iberian inquisitions, Huguenots forced out of France, the English Pilgrims, before they sailed on the Mayflower, the Moluccans, who turned to the Netherlands at the time of the independence of Indonesia. This small kingdom, about half the size of Maine, is home to 14.5 million people, making it one of the most densely populated nations in the world. At least 10 percent of the Dutch population comes from exotic stock, not impressive by U.S. standards, but a new demographic experience for modern Europe. This unmelted pot now bubbles with a high national unemployment rate, although generous health insurance diminishes the hardship. A quarter of the population of Amsterdam is on some form of welfare or social security. The national government stoutly opposes ghettos. Old Dutch families in working-class neighborhoods do smell the strange food of other ethnic groups and hear the high-decibel sounds of alien music. Native-born Dutchmen must compete for jobs with the outlanders and pay high taxes for services the strangers receive. Despite the new Dutch diversity, many people still follow traditional pursuits. They make cheese, balance accounts, tend tulips, paint canvasses, fish for herring, and wear wooden shoes in muddy gardens.

Their standard of living remains among the highest in the world. Dutch banknotes, for example, are embossed with Braillelike numbers to help the blind make change. For the ethnics, slogans and debates sometimes obscure progress. Still, it is there. A grade school teacher said, "First I had to teach Dutch children not to hit Turks, then the Turks not to hit the Moroccans, now I must teach Moroccan children not to hit little Surinamers." Progress. The Dutch see the electronic age as bringing increases in service industries, information, international specialization, and worldwide travel. Working time will be organized less strictly than in the past. Still, the Dutch are fully aware that people will need places for human contact. There will be more opportunity for religion and social life then in the earlier part of the twentieth century. The Netherlands has a much more flexible capacity to handle ethnic and cultural diversity and to demonstrate a much higher respect for hard work, education, religious devotion, and multilingual language skills.

In American families, our churches, our schools, we need to study the nature of our constitutional culture and its workhorse assistant, the political economy of democratic capitalism. We must learn to live together as Americans. Earlier chapters on the world cities and American metroareas brought home the vast complexity of our urban economies known as metroareas. They also contain large areas of rural land at the outer fringes of the metropolitan statistical areas. Thus metroareas start from the central cities with the problems of an aging infrastructure, old housing, and the parasitic relationship of the suburbs. There are problems of crime control, sewage management, and water quality. They all seem to cry out for a reorganization of our metroareas into districts that are synchronous with the true urban economy. We should redefine our city boundaries to coincide with the metroarea within which residents work, play, attend church, recreate, and pursue happiness in their own way. We need a national colloquy directed at starting acceptable forms of chartered metropolitan reorganization with adequate tax bases of their own.

Part V: Democratic Capitalism

Preface

The best political economy to bring less stressful and workable forms of change for humans is democratic capitalism. This is true only so long as democratic capitalism is controlled by a constitutional culture that takes rights seriously. This section concentrates on clarifying the separate and distinctly different nature of our economic system as chosen and defined by the cumulative wisdom of the U.S. Congress. The United States has discovered what much of the rest of the world does not know. Regulated democratic capitalism can be very productive, so long as human rights are protected and even enhanced. Recognizing that human rights are paramount is the only way to control the tendency toward the concentration of economic power, a natural tendency of unregulated capitalism. Economists either do not know this or they ignore it. Power is neglected in their intellectual models. This is misleading. The United States is happy about some destabilizing changes in the former Soviet Union and Eastern Europe. But we do not know what kind of capitalism or market economy these nations might choose, if, ultimately, any at all. They may elect some forms of democratic socialism such as exist in Sweden and France. They may abandon Communism for a form of fascistic capitalism such as exists in Latin America or South Africa. Will they take rights seriously?

Today we have some very able scholars who are falsely portraying laissez-faire, free-market capitalism, as acceptable to America's constitutional culture. The free marketeers view the criminal acts of Michael Milken, Drexel Burnham, Dennis Levine, Ivan Boesky, Boyd Jefferies, Salomon Brothers managers, and others, as anomalous. They say ignore it. The long run will always restore equilibrium, they say. Meanwhile, ethical and fair-dealing competitors are bested in the competitive marketplace by the deceit of criminals.

The United States now has in its midst transnational, immortal, American corporations that are huge beyond the comprehension of the average mind. Some *Fortune* 500 corporations have gross revenues that exceed the gross national products of sovereign nations as high as eighth in the world ranking of economic size. Exxon's gross sales exceed the GNP of Iran, Sweden, Mexico, or Venezuela. Ordinary American citizens, if not our free marketeers, recognize that such concentration of wealth and capital flows must compete in a socially responsible manner. They are expected to act fairly, not deceptively, and to be under the watchful eye of antitrust compliance actions.

Pure (not democratic) capitalism is compatible with fascism, far more so than even democratic socialism, as in Sweden or France. I use Latin America as an arena of discussion to prove this sad truth.

Part V is an optimistic statement that offers a better, active, aggressive foreign policy, instead of one that is merely responsive to fascist and Communist regimes. Our constitutional culture and its draft horse, democratic capitalism, are something to promote aggressively. I propose some international cooperation in building and rebuilding our burgeoning world cities. This could be a substitute for the arms race.

13. The Spirit of Democratic Capitalism

Our overall concern is the quality of life for human personalities, where they live, work, and recreate. Our focus on democratic capitalism is to consider its nature, today, and how it effects the environments of Americans. It has served us well as our economic system of choice. A historic transformation is happening. "Laissez faire" corporate capitalism of the industrial state quietly battles against being replaced by a renewed "democratic capitalism" more appropriate to the global economy and the Information Age. The outcome is in doubt. Globally, democratic capitalism is not a response to a benign and peaceful world, but to the severe crisis of ecospasm in our LDC world cities. Our dedication to human rights is becoming the center of world attention as we work out a competitive/cooperative environment. The massive increase in technological complexity demands more entrepreneurial freedom to make flexible responses to volatile uncertainty. We are engaged in an ordeal of choices. In the 1990s, the issue is in doubt because the power elite is afraid of this change.

There is a threatening, alternative scenario. It is the dominance of the United States by "corporate America," led by those who think that business is the most capable institution and it should run the country. This variation of supply-side economics' "trickle down" theory encourages amassing of wealth among the power elite in the naive hope that those at the bottom might benefit. Lurking in the wings is a fascistic America. It would be a highly regulated America—a "big government"—arising out of the disillusionment of workers, farmers, women, the poor, and the elderly, who would turn to the taxing power for the general welfare. The voters would be responding to some charismatic leaders who would use government regulation to promote security and a more equitable distribution of wealth. They would do so out of fear.

Between the extremes pictured lies a more competitive democratic capitalism, a political economy that recognizes we will all be happier in a system that recognizes our Judeo-Christian conscience. Americans have a religious sense of social responsibility whenever harmful market failures occur. The success of free enterprise over the past two centuries was made possible not only by a combination of political, social, and environmental factors, but because the American people were given access to a large portion of the world's resources. The laissez-faire free marketeers of the nineteenth century provided a multitude of ways to use these resources to raise the so-called standard of living in the United States. However, in the process they reduced most of our natural resources to a problematical waste. As long as the private economy worked well, we accepted the economists' view that the water, the air, and the land were "free goods"—having no value. We saw no need to make national economic plans, so none were made. In the 1990s, we face a different future. The United States is a debtor nation with sharply diminished natural resources, except for forests, water, agricultural productivity, and coal. We are in a state of conflict with the past. We want to maintain the old, established lifestyle, but we know that we must develop new technologies to exploit substitute resources. Unfortunately, the past shows that venture capital dries up quickly when entrepreneurs must risk the uncertainty of new kinds of productivity. The issue is whether American goods and services can be made and delivered at prices that are productive for us when competing against other nations' goods and services. Here, expert opinions divides between the free marketeers and the would-be national policy planners. In this treatise, we follow neither.

This part of the book takes a direction which divides our domestic economy from foreign markets. In our domestic economy we need the political economy of democratic capitalism because it is so compatible with our constitutional culture. Over time we have developed a form of capitalism that is market-oriented, a democratic, political economy. It provides a free rein to business entrepreneurs, and end users of goods and services within the "rules of the game" that require fair play and the prohibition of deceptive trade practices. We also maintain a national policy of intervening to overcome proven market failures that do occur in such a system. This system is threatened today by those who would eliminate regulation of business and return us to the rampant capitalism that once ran roughshod over the nation. The United States takes pride in having developed a marvelous machine that seems to run on its own. The political economy we have is, unfortunately, not duplicated in other parts of the world, except for Canada. Furthermore, our scholars have done a poor job of explaining it to the world. A major reason for the confusion is that we have failed to make an intellectual separation of capitalism from democracy. The cold and too-often brutal truth is that capitalism, "free enterprise of the power elite," can thrive under fascism. Political scientists do not always understand this important point. The result has been that for many years our wrongheaded foreign policies have supported fascistic governments. This is because the juntas have tolerated a market economy rather than some form of centrally planned economy.

To our sorrow we have rejected nascent democratic socialism in developing countries while at the same time supporting it in Great Britain and Sweden. Our foreign policy posture has been muddle-headed as to which had the highest priority, capitalism or human rights. We have too often opted for capitalism and looked the other way as thousands of supporters of human rights literally disappeared in the lands of dictators. The result is we have devalued, even debased human rights. Fortunately, our new policies toward China occasionally demonstrate a more mature understanding of the high priority we give to, first, human rights, and then business pragmatism. The lack of focus on rights in American foreign policy has led to substantial confusion in other parts of the world as to just what political economy we have. Cynics suggest it is because to many Americans "the business of America is business," even if it requires the sacrifice of human rights to increase profits.

In his lyrical book *The Spirit of Democratic Capitalism,* Michael Novak offers a valuable critique of the different systems we have developed in the United States.[1] He contrasted them with the expectations held by other nations, especially those in Latin America. As Novak states, of all the systems of political economy that have shaped our history, none has so revolutionized ordinary expectations of human life, lengthened the life span, made the elimination of poverty and famine a possible dream, enlarged the range of human choice, as democratic capitalism. In democratic capitalism three dynamic and converging systems function as one: a democratic polity, an economy based on markets and incentives, and a moral-cultural milieu that is pluralistic and, in the largest sense, liberal.

It is also true that modern marketing techniques, designed to promote the sale of goods and services, have confused the American polity. The seductive goods and services have blurred Americans' vision of their purpose in life. Shoppers' behavior has become a major driving force for the economy and has made shopping, arguably, the nation's favorite pastime next to television. Adults, both men and women, average about six hours weekly on shopping for everything. It is not possible to tell what is drudgery or what is pleasure, but the time spent shopping is much more than time spent gardening, reading books, or with the children.

According to Robert Cialdini, a psychologist at Arizona State University, there is a mindless character to American shopping. Purchases are linked less and less closely to need. Six years ago about 75 percent of household purchases were for replacements. Today less than 50 percent are replacements. Recent studies show only 25 percent of shoppers interviewed had gone to the shopping center for a specific item. Why then do so many people spend so much time shopping? The reasons are many and varied. Analysis is beyond the scope of this treatise. However, here are a few of the reasons given by American shoppers: relieving loneliness, dispelling boredom, finding the spoils of a hunt for bargains, relieving depression, and fantasy fulfillment.[2] It is difficult for the arts and good works to compete. Mindless consumers have given up on the constitutional culture except as a myth. The power shoppers have turned into consumer idiot savants of the corporate state.

This is not the system that Michael Novak and I praise. We praise the beaux ideal of democratic capitalism. It was capitalism that gave birth to modern European cities, whose first citizens took as their battle cry "City air makes men free."[3] The market encourages a "consumer sovereignty" that intellectuals all too often think is bad for ordinary mortals. Democratic capitalism appears to the orderly intellectual a morass of cultural contradictions. Not many poets, philosophers, artists, or theologians have smiled kindly upon it. It seethes with competitive, adversarial, spirit.

The Market's Function

When millions of human individuals become economic activists, it appears as if their activities might be anarchic. Alternatively, in human endeavors, do we gain efficiency in the allocation of goods and services from central command economy planning? Central planners have a record of building up wasteful surpluses in some areas and causing unplanned-for shortages in others. Moreover, open-market economic activity is less anarchic in practice, even when freer, than intuition expects. Urban centers grow and prosper because wherever economic activism flourishes, people work together. Markets are created. Lines of transport and communication multiply.

Under the overall conditions of scarcity that persist, human beings need each other. Proponents of the market system do not argue that the system is utopian and flawless, only that it is economically the most productive, intellectually the most inventive and dynamic, and politically the only system compatible with liberty. The usual objections of socialists and the like might simply be taken as the price that must be paid for the benefits gained in a system run by humans. Economic inequalities are inevitable and necessary in technically advanced metroareas. They provide incentive to innovate and they promote the work ethic.

Market societies often produce many nouveau riche. They diminish the role and power of landed aristocracies, create a broad middle class, and raise standards of health, literacy, and mobility among the poor. There is a difference between a defense of the free market and a defense of democratic capitalism. Supporters of democratic capitalism remain committed to its social-welfare aspects. They may be as critical of governmental abuse and corruption as socialists are of abuses and corruption in the large corporations. The free market coupled with a liberal polity follow from the exercise of liberty of conscience. On the other hand, fascism is compatible with the market, too, theologically speaking. Those religious persons who prefer public enforcement of virtue find attractive either an elitist fascism or a centrally controlled socialism. What censorship is to free speech, the command economy is to the free market. What an established religion is to a traditional society, a publicly imposed, collective moral vision is to a socialist society. The pornographic allure of power is such that there will always be an abundance of Christian, Jewish, Islamic, Buddhist, and secular socialists. To them a socialist society promises ways to suffuse their own views into every activity. Democratic capitalism is incompatible with such world views. A free economic market promotes and nurtures a free marketplace of ideas. Defense of the free market can be, first, a defense of efficiency, productivity, inventiveness, and material prosperity. It can also be a defense of the free conscience— free not only in the realm of the spirit, and not only in politics, but also in the economic decisions of everyday life.

Critics of the market usually mock the fabled "invisible hand" mentioned by Adam Smith in *An Inquiry into the Nature and the Cause of the Wealth of Nations*.[4]

> As every individual, therefore, endeavors as much as he can both to employ his capital in the support of domestic industry, every individual necessarily labors to render the annual revenue of the society as great as he can. He generally, indeed, neither intends to promote the public interest, nor knows how much he is promoting it. He intends only his own gain, and he is in this, as in many other cases, led by an invisible hand to promote an end which was no part of his intention. By pursuing his own interest he frequently promotes that of the society more effectually than when he really intends to promote it.

The intelligible order is not commanded by anyone's hand, nor consciously intended by anyone's intellect. It is a product of multiple decisionmaking by millions of individuals with the right and power of independent choice. Still, commerce is not without its own moral structure. The inventors of enlightened capitalism—Montesquieu, John Adams, Adam Smith, Benjamin Franklin, Benjamin Rush, Robert Morris, James Madison, Thomas Jefferson, John Locke, and others—were not, themselves, primarily men of commerce or manufacturing. In any case, they expected tradesmen and merchants to deal fairly—to make a square deal. The founding fathers rejected aristocratic morals in favor of the common, the useful, the mundane.

The law of merchants is a system of fair play. It uses the self-determination of the individual as the main source of social energy. In any event, competitive markets are not sustained by magic but by the eternal public vigilance of competitors, and the state. The rapacity of some merchants leads them to try to corner open markets through monopolistic practices. The success of democratic capitalism in producing prosperity and liberty is its own greatest danger. This is because a new social aristocracy is born, not through inherited status, but through professional interests and ambitions. As "the new class" of commerce took center stage in 1776, so later a "new class" of intellectuals—as Joseph Schumpeter saw[5]—would try to dominate the commercial class by seizing the power of the state. The commercial virtues are not, by themselves, sufficient to their own defense. A commercial system needs taming and correction by a moral-cultural system independent of commerce. It is a mistake to base one's hopes for happiness upon the enforcement of security and equality. In principle, both desires are insatiable. Therefore, democratic capitalism diffuses power.

The structure of democratic capitalism—even its impersonal economic system—is aimed at community. This is not in the nostalgic sense of *Gemeinschaft,* but one of free persons in voluntary association. With the birth of the U.S. Constitution, an international dream of justice entered the world. With the birth of its workhorse, democratic capitalism, every nation was called to develop its own wealth. No longer are the world's people to conceive of justice as resignation to an implacable fate. Most ennobling ideals now influential in the world are ideals that first emerged through the Enlightenment and democratic capitalism in the West: development, modernization, social justice, national liberation, independence, self-reliance, and much more. Between individualism and collectivism, there is a third way: a rich network of associations.

The United States has discovered a new direction, beyond capitalism and "beyond socialism . . . personalist and community-minded, at the same time." Problems of community are acute among Americans. In our sentimental age, however, there is a tendency to desire a different sort of community, less a community of spirit and the inner life than a community of sentiment, emotional support, and oft-expressed intimacy. These are new forms of networking. We desperately need teachers, models, guides—not those who steal our freedom from us, but those who teach us to grasp it surehandedly. The life of the spirit is far from stifled by democratic capitalism, but without strong moral guidance it is often squandered. It is said that capitalism introduces a "competitive" system, a "rat race," "dog eat dog." Yet, athletes from socialist nations are not less competitive than those from democratic capitalist lands. Nor is the competition for political power in socialist states any less fearsome than the competition for power in democratic capitalist societies.

Michael Novak, with a strong Eastern European cultural heritage, expresses strong ties to Anglo-Saxon culture. Novak declares, and I strongly agree, that Anglo-Saxon customs and traditions nourish remarkable social orderliness and a splendid cooperative spirit. One sees it in British common law and in that peculiarly British love of liberty combined with respect for law. It is not at all "every man for himself."

The British may not be as socially disciplined as the Germans—they value their eccentricities too much. Nonetheless, it is a grievous mistake to underestimate their capacities for organizing a good society. A rereading of Adam Smith brings out clearly the important role he asserted for sympathy, benevolence, the good opinion of others, ethical conduct, and other social determinants of virtue. In *The Theory of Moral Sentiments,* Smith pointed out that every self is both individual and social, and has both selfish and benevolent interests. As to which represents the higher virtue, it is absolutely clear to him that, "To feel much for others, and little for ourselves, to restrain our selfishness, and to indulge our benevolent affections, constitutes the perfection of human nature."[6]

Smith found such virtues common among Englishmen. He cited the example of "every thoroughly good soldier" who would willingly "throw away his life when the good of the service required it." Perhaps, it is that which impressed us about Ollie North's bravura theatrical performance before the television cameras, even though we knew the record of his actual conduct did not live up to his soliloquy. In effect, like the British, we said, "Good show."

Adam Smith believed such real virtues to be only common sense. John Poindexter's and Ollie North's instincts for self-preservation in the face of the lack of visible support from their superiors were strong. Unlike North and Poindexter, Smith did not stop at self-reliance, and obedience to superiors. He required fair play within the cultural traditions: "If he would act so as that the impartial spectator may enter into the principles of his conduct, which is what of all things he has the greatest desire to do, he must upon this, as upon all other occasions, humble the arrogance of his self-love, and bring it down to something that other men can go along with."[7]

Smith avoided a mistake many of our contemporary free marketeers make. He regarded "the economy" not as a system of aggregates or mere averages studied by economists. Unlike most economists, Smith saw capitalism as a system of individual acts by individual purchasers and suppliers. Businessmen, not economists with their trends of aggregates, lie at the center of his imagination. In Novak's words, "He does not think to stimulate 'the economy,' but to stimulate 'individuals.' "[8] Adam Smith's dream was that individual self-love of the communitarian personality would, through participation in a good society, come to include all. Adam Smith's hope was that the self-love of human beings might be transformed into a social system that benefitted all as no other system had ever done. Each individual would then participate in a good society, in such a way that his self-love would come to include the whole. The individual of the democratic-capitalist's ideal recognizes allegiance to moral values that transcend historical eras or cultural boundaries. These are ideals like personal dignity, liberty, justice for all, and human rights. Amitai Etzioni, professor at George Washington University, is struggling to reinvigorate communitarian rights with responsibilities and a commitment to community without puritanism or authoritarianism.

Americans lead a life that is thick with activism, voluntarism, and mutual association. The ideal of the middle-class man or woman is not to be a rugged individual, isolated and alone. We are encouraged to be independent, yes, and also self-reliant, but also to be active members of many communities. Americans are open to appeals from the needy, to be informed about the world at large, and to care about its problems. In previous chapters we have emphasized the need to provide day-care centers and other familial support to those below the middle class in the poverty enclaves of our metroareas. The United States has some real problems with our cross-cultural contradictions. Substantial sectors of our society do not join in the communitarian consensus for common bonds and common goals. Now that monolithic Communism is dying, the coming threat may well be from the power elite, who would prefer fascist states.

Latin-American Capitalism—A Market Failure

I now embark on a discussion of Catholic, in particular, Latin American Catholic, attitudes toward capitalism and its effects on our good neighbors. My aims are twofold. First, it is critically important that U.S. citizens understand that Latin American "republics" do not operate under a form of capitalism that is similar to ours. Second, by making this contrast, the reader will see how important our peculiar constitutional culture, with its Anglo-American heritage, is to the past success and future success of our chosen form of political economy—democratic capitalism. Finally, this discussion should demonstrate that we ought to radically modify our foreign policy to foster the growth of democratic capitalism in Latin America (including Mexico, Central America, and the Caribbean) as an act of enlightened self-interest.

These Latin-American nations are class-conscious. Still, the church is confronting the regional states. They work against the state, as Christian socialists, demanding that the government do something about their societies' abuses of the law, due process, and the inalienable rights of individuals. Some Catholic bishops in South America argue that, for capitalism, "Life is power and the will to power." Actually, the will to power is embodied in every human culture, and among baboons and other primates and many other mammals. Under democratic capitalism, it is directed toward competing, which can be a mutually restraining system. Under socialism, the will to power is channeled into politics while grasping for control also of production and other social institutions. These leaders of South American Catholicism have little understanding of the spirit of fair play and stewardship that are within the United States's peculiar capitalism. This is because, too often, democracy's overseas representatives, business corporations and the U.S. State Department, have failed to attack juntas and oligarchies.

The adverse result is, according to one commentator, "In the political dimension, the vicious circle of domination through coercion, the use of force, is produced in various Latin societies, by the domination of dictatorships and the upper classes or those with privileges." To remedy such defects within their nations, many Latin American Catholics, Filipinos, Puerto Ricans, and others appeal for the use of democratic socialism. There is the element of democracy within their socialistic ideology set forth as "the recognition of human rights and the basic rights of the citizen in a state."

The problem is that socialism has not delivered. During May 1991, Pope John Paul issued a papal encyclical that will cause much dialogue among Catholic leaders and rethinking about their attitude toward profits and entrepreneurship. John Paul's text gave a qualified endorsement to the free market while urging just wages, strong unions, even the right to a job. He spoke out against the heedless pursuit of material goods and pleasures. The encyclical focuses on creativity and the risk-taking entrepreneur as generators of wealth. The encyclical is a plea to Eastern Europe, South America, and elsewhere, to open the doors to free-market economies with social justice.

Many Americans have a feeling that it is their constitutional culture, with its protection of individual rights, which is equally crucial to the dynamic success of democratic capitalism. However, very little effort has been made to represent the United States as standing for such principles abroad. Nevertheless, we ought to consider what might have been. Suppose that Latin America had developed industries and manufacturing before the United States did. Clearly, the resources were available. Latin America is rich in oil, tin, and bauxite, among many other important minerals. Its farmlands and tropical gardens are luxuriant. The answer lies in the different nature of the Latin American political, economic, and moral-cultural systems. The last is probably decisive. Yet, its Catholic bishops do not blame the Catholic Church nor the systems of political economy they long supported, or the past values and choices of its peoples. They blame the United States. Psychoanalysts and psychologists would recognize scapegoating in such attitudes.

Novak's analysis places specific emphasis upon indigenous practices of trade and investment. During the nineteenth century, trade between Latin America and the United States was minimal. Between 1900 and 1950, trade began to grow, but by 1950 the total historical investment of U.S. companies in Latin America totaled only $4.6 billion. After World War II, Western Europe lay in rubble, its economies broken, and Japan lay economically prostrate. After the war, trade between the United States and Latin America grew. Still, by 1965, the total value of U.S. investments in Latin America was $11 billion. By 1965, investment by Western European nations and Japan, which were just beginning to revive after World War II, were not of great significance. It is preposterous to believe that such small sums are responsible for the poverty or the dependence of Latin America. They are neither a high proportion of the wealth of the investing nations nor a high proportion of Latin America's internally generated wealth. The total U.S. investment of $11 billion averages out to $44 per capita for the 250 million Latin Americans of 1965.[9] By a relative comparison, Novak points out, U.S. investments in Western Europe and Japan during that same period were many times higher, but did not produce similar "dependence."

Hugh Trevor-Roper discovered that many of the great entrepreneurs of the sixteenth and seventeenth centuries are distinguished less by the fact that many were Calvinists than by the fact that nearly all were immigrants to "free" cities. The entrepreneurs sought out North American cities. They sought self-governing cities of a republican character, no longer under the control of princes and bishops. A sharp contrast arose between such North American cities and the religio-economic shortsightedness of the Spanish Empire that dominated South America. Made rich by silver from South America, the Spaniards, who represented the dominant Catholic state, misperceived the basis of their new economic strength. In Spain and Latin America officials of church and state grew ever more numerous. They produced little, being parasitic upon the producers, whom they gouged and regulated until the latter emigrated. "The Calvinist and for that matter the Jewish entrepreneurs, of northern Europe were not a new native growth: they were an old growth transplanted." Max Weber, in seeing the "spirit of capitalism" as something new and whose origins must be sought in the sixteenth century, had inverted the problem.

The novelty lay not in the entrepreneurs themselves, but in the circumstances that drove them to emigrate, according to Trevor-Roper.[10] Latin Catholic theology bears its due proportion of the blame. "We are the victims," the bishops say. They accept no responsibility for three centuries of hostility to trade, commerce, industry, or individual political and civil rights.

The poor record of Latin American leadership compelled the United States to develop its own policies, such as the Good Neighbor Policy and the AID program. It is certain that we need a very clearly defined national economic policy of cooperation with Latin America. Today, however, we have none. Even Dr. Henry Kissinger, no student of economics, proposed an economic policy for the Caribbean Basin as a first step toward cooperation and autonomy for that area in its relations to the United States. Even when Latin Catholic nations imitate the institutional forms of Protestant lands—constitutional government, industrial development—such institutions work out differently. Patterns of "self-control" are different. Emotional constraints and cultural ideals are different. Patterns of cultural development tend to oscillate between "anarchy and hierarchy," with less moderation and order than is typical of northern European cultures. There are also economic losses involved in a lack of punctuality, in reluctance to compromise. There is a failure to see worldly life as a spiritual vocation.

Consider the assertion of Archbishop Dom Helder Camara of Brazil before the World Council of Churches in 1970: "It is a sad fact that 80 percent of the world's resources are at the disposal of 20 percent of the world's inhabitants."[11] Dumb material remains inert until its secrets are discovered. A technology for bending it to human purposes must be invented. The word "resources," therefore, includes within its meaning the factor of human attitudes and cultural heritage, of which discovery and invention are expressions. Protestant European culture, in particular, has been exceedingly fertile in the discovery of such resources and in the invention of such technologies. Among Nobel Prize winners in science, Protestants have been conspicuously prominent. Why, after 1850, did the progress of North America and Latin America dramatically diverge? For over one hundred years Latin America remained almost static. During this period, the United States and Canada steadily but ever more rapidly developed. Brazil is blessed with extraordinary resources and an energetic population. It has been poised on the edge of takeoff for almost two generations. What holds this huge country back? Is it cultural? Surely, Brazil will be a great world power when it finds its way to the communitarian spirit that dominates democratic capitalism and breaks the yoke of patriarchal military dependency and the purchase of government power through corruption.

Latin Moral Values

The two cultures see the world differently. Latin Americans seem to feel inferior to North Americans in practical matters, but superior in spiritual ones. The Catholic aristocratic ethic of Latin America places more emphasis on luck, heroism, status, and the conquistador image than the relatively Protestant ethic of North America— hard work, thrift, diligence, fair and honest dealings, and the responsible seizure of opportunity. Between two such different ways of looking at the world, intense love-hate relations are bound to develop. Looking at North America, Latins are likely to attribute the United States's more advanced status to luck—and also to a kind of aristocratic power. In their experience, wealth is somewhat static and what is given to one is taken from another. By contrast, looking at Latin America, a North American is likely to attribute its backwardness to an ethos better suited to aristocrats, military juntas, bishops, monks, and peasants, people who lack respect for commerce and industrial life and the moral virtues on which these depend. As Latin Americans do not admire northern virtues, North Americans do not entirely approve of Latin virtues. Thus most North Americans are likely to feel not a shred of guilt for the relative economic position of the two continents. It is for this reason that any policy of economic aid and cooperation North Americans propose should include social auditing, accountability, and the fixing of responsibility to carry out mutually agreed upon goals when carried out by the Latinos. The future of the United States is very dependent upon a harmonious and productive relationship with the southern part of the Western hemisphere. We cannot ignore its problems.

A good example of Latin American fascistic capitalism that serves primarily to accumulate wealth and power for a family while doing little if anything to serve the public interest appeared in a *Wall Street Journal* article about Burger King's search for a franchisee in Venezuela.[12] The company turned to the Cisneros family. It was a logical move. The family owns nearly everything a respectable hamburger place needs. "You take the bread—they own the bakery," says Al Feria, Burger King's general manager for Latin America. They also own the companies that supply the mustard, hamburger, soda pop, cash registers, coffee and shake mixes, as well as real estate in the choicest shopping centers. They own the country's largest television and radio networks, where Burger King advertises. Their powerful political connections enable them to cut through the red tape that plagues other businesses. Here, as in most of Latin America, capitalism differs from our 1990s U.S. version, where most big business is competitive and widely owned. The Cisneros capitalism is more like the rampant capitalism of the robber barons of the United States's Gilded Age. In South America, powerful families with close ties to government often control whole industries. Even in Venezuela, a democracy that boasts the third-largest economy in South America, antitrust enforcement and public capital markets scarcely exist, making it hard for outsiders to break in.

The Cisneros organization is Venezuela's biggest example of elitist capitalism. The family holding company owns Venezuela's largest supermarket chain, its only chain of department stores, its largest record company, its biggest chain of computer stores, 90 percent of its soft drink sales, its second-largest ice cream maker, its second-largest bakery and second-largest coffee producer, baby care, sporting goods and shoe polish firms, and the rights to the popular Miss Venezuela contests. Besides Burger King, Cisneros in Venezuela is Pepsi-Cola and Sears Roebuck, Digital Equipment Corporation, Apple Computer, NCR, Helene Curtis cosmetics, and French's mustard. The heart of the Cisneros empire is Venevision and Radiovision, the broadcasting companies that promote all the rest.

Within Venezuela, the head of the family, Gustavo Cisneros, is a "very important person" in a country where all the VIPs, if not related to one another, at the very least have more than a nodding acquaintance. Cisneros's wife, Patricia, is the niece of the owner of the rival television network. The co-owner of the Coca-Cola bottler in Caracas, in theory the rival of Cisneros's Pepsi plants, is Pedro Tinoco, Cisneros's banker, attorney, and friend. "It wouldn't do to print too much on Cisneros," a Caracas newspaper publisher concedes, "because we look out for each other."

Latin Monopolies

Polar Beer, owned by another big family, so dominates its industry that it helps out its competitor, Nacional, with distribution to keep the competitor in business and technically avoid being a monopoly. "Anti-monopoly laws are proposed in every session of Congress," notes John Pate, a Caracas lawyer. "They never get anywhere because of who supports the congressmen." Gustavo Cisneros finances both of the major political parties. He has helped many politicians, including Venezuelan President Jaime Lusinchi, with television air time, the use of company aircraft, and other favors. Nonetheless, the government is intricately involved in the economy. Companies need permits to raise prices, import products, or do almost anything. "A businessman in Venezuela needs to be close to politicians." Although many are wowed by Cisneros's charm, he lacks an easy style. A local Pepsi bottler says, "When Gustavo visits, his bodyguards get here ten minutes ahead of him." This description of rampant capitalism in Venezuela fits the robber-baron capitalism that was rampant in the late nineteenth century in the United States, before we discovered that capitalism needs rules of the game for it to be fair to the public. The Gilded Age in the United States after the Civil War was a historical period when Goulds, Fiskes, Flaglers, Rockefellers, Morgans, and many others, according to William Jennings Bryan, forced a crown of thorns upon the brow of labor and took from ordinary citizens great power by way of rapacious action. By the time of Teddy Roosevelt, Congress had had enough of it. We began on the road to democratic capitalism by way of the Sherman Act of 1890. Latin America has yet to discover democratic capitalism.

Michael Novak provides us with one of the most eloquent statements that has arisen out of our Anglo-American constitutional culture as he defines the ethos of America's peculiar form of democratic capitalism. Building a humane social order is not a task for merely one generation. It is a journey of a thousand years. For democratic capitalism, barely two hundred have been traversed. Novak does not claim that democratic capitalism is the practice of which Christianity and Judaism are the religions. Nor is that my view. Both Christianity and Judaism have flourished, or at least survived, in every sort of social system known to humankind. Judaism and Christianity do not require democratic capitalism. Still, without it they would be spiritually constrained and less free. Among political economies, there may someday be conceived something better than self-correcting democratic capitalism. If so, it is not yet in sight. Novak judges six such doctrines most important and addresses them in Christian form.

The Trinity: The one God of Christians is also plural; appropriately, then, the human mind becomes accustomed to seeing pluralism in unity throughout creation, even in social systems. No one sees God or comprehends what can be intended in speaking of God as three in one. Yet it is least clear that God is more to be conceived as a kind of community than as a solitary individual.

The Incarnation: "God stooped low to enter human history, as a man, in one underdeveloped country, in one particular location in the world's geography. Thus,

God did not overpower history but respected its constraints. One of the most poignant lessons of the Incarnation is the difficult teaching that one must learn to be humble, think concretely, face facts, train oneself to realism. The point of the Incarnation is to respect the world as it is, to acknowledge its limits, to recognize its weaknesses, irrationalities, and evil forces, and to disbelieve any promises that the world is now or ever will be transformed into the City of God. . . . Although the Founding Fathers, too, were tempted by perfectionism, they strove manfully to design institutions proportionate not to angels or to saints but to sinners. They did not try to construct utopia. They tried to check and limit vice, tyranny most of all, even tyranny in the name of morality and religion."

Competition: "The will to power must be made creative, not destroyed. Judaism and Christianity, in other words, envisage human life as a contest. The ultimate competition resides in the depths of one's own heart. Much is to be gained, much lost. 'What does it profit a man if he gain the whole world and suffer the loss of his soul?' (Mark 8:36). The stakes are real; there are winners and losers. 'Many are called, few are chosen' (Mt. 20:16). The Jewish and Christian view is that God is not committed to equality of results."

Original Sin: "Human liberty is subject to evil expression as well as to good. The system of democratic capitalism, believing itself to be the natural system of liberty and the system that, so far in history, is best designed to meet the premises of original sin, is designed against tyranny. Its chief aim is to fragment and to check power, but not to repress sin. You name the sin, democratic capitalism tolerates it and someone makes a living from it. Such exploitation is tolerated not as a blessing but as a concession to the evil within the ambivalent human condition. . . . A free society can tolerate the public display of vice because it has confidence in the basic decency of human beings, even under the burden of sin. Under an appropriate set of checks and balances, the vast majority of human beings will respond to daily challenges with decency, generosity, common sense, and even, on occasion, moral heroism."

Separation of Realms: "We have already explored the importance of structural pluralism to democratic capitalism. This pluralism renders the mission of Christianity uniquely difficult. Some traditional societies imposed Christianity upon their citizens. Some socialist societies could conceivably do so. Under pluralism, no democratic capitalist society has a right to do so. This means that the political system of democratic capitalism cannot, in principle, be a Christian system. For one thing, a market system must be open to all regardless of religious faith. Economic liberty means that all must be permitted to establish their own values and priorities. A free economy can-not—for all these reasons—be a Christian economy. Liberty is a critical good in the economic sphere as well as in the sphere of conscience. Yet the guardians of the moral-cultural system are typically less concerned about liberty in the economic system than about their own liberty."

Caritas: "The highest theological symbols for Judaism and Christianity are the ones closest to the personality of God: compassion, sacrificial love, *caritas.* The distinguishing feature of Jewish and Christian conceptions of love is that love is realistic. This means that the lover must not be possessive, reducing the loved one to an adjunct of the self. The loved one is other—an autonomous person. True friends give each other correction, lead each other beyond their own infantile fantasies, and grow together in wisdom and friendship. In English, the word "love" is used in so many vulgar ways, to express so many self-centered sentiments, that one instinctively feels a better word is needed: the Latin *caritas*. To look upon human history as love-infused by a Creator who values others as others . . . is to glimpse a world in which the political economy of democratic capitalism makes sense."

Although the individual is an originating source of insight and choice, the fulfillment of the individual lies in a beloved community. But any community worthy of such love values the singularity and inviolability of each person. Without true individualism, there is no true community. In the economic sphere, creation is to be fulfilled through human imitation of the Creator. Creation is no morality play. Nor is it a panglossian perfect harmony. The problem for a system of political economy is how to unleash human creativity and productivity while coping realistically with the human desire for power, domination, control, and sinfulness. Others hold that the common good is better served through allowing each individual to work as each judges best and to keep the rewards of such labor. A system of political economy imitates the demands of caritas by reaching out, creating, inventing, producing, and distributing, raising the material base of the common good. It is based on realism. It respects individuals, as individuals. It makes communal life more active, intense, voluntary, and multiple. An economic system that makes individuals dependent is no more an example of caritas than is a lover whose love encourages dependency. A collectivist system that does not respect individuals as originating sources of insight and choice is no more an example of caritas than is a beehive or a herd of cattle.

It is a tragedy that at the beginning of the 1990s, the dismal science of economics has failed to lead us to an understanding of how love, hate, and power, all of which economists term "irrational behavior," are to fit into a science of efficient allocation of resources in a productive economy. The distorted vision of economic behavior that arises out of the economist's world view has been a driving force behind the "bottom-line," profit-centered, unethical behavior of the paper entrepreneurs who have so badly served our economy since World War II.

We sorely need to regenerate positive ethical attitudes, the sense of being a steward—a fiduciary—who deserves trust and gives integrity, loyalty, fidelity, and honorable accounting in business. We need high personal standards among the players as well as what our free marketeers call a "level playing field."

Capital and Power

Power is an aspect of the relationships between the factors of production that has been seldom examined. How could ordinary citizens have power without the use of force and without continually threatening the vastly outnumbered power elite? The study of power has been neglected by scholars. George Washington, Thomas Jefferson, and James Madison seemed far more appropriate to exercise positions of public power than Collis P. Huntington, J. P. Morgan, or Andrew Mellon. The political statesmen were credited with a capacity for action apart from their interests, while capitalists seem to act in their self-interest. Economists' discussions of the point of central tendency of power has centered on the tools of production, as befits economists. But the power of dominance and control over other human personalities is sought for many reasons other than for control of the tools of production. Freud,

Jung, Meninger, Rubinoff, and many others have understood that a more holistic view of power-seeking must be carried out to understand what motivates human personalities.

We have serious problems with the quality of entrenched management of many American business corporations today. Thus, the manufacturing, banking, utilities, and financial services sectors of the modern American economy are an ossification of what ought to be a creative force for growth and productivity. There has been a failure of the mechanism of creative destruction. In his landmark study, *Capitalism, Socialism and Democracy,* Joseph Schumpeter discounted the significance of the monopoly problem in capitalist society. Monopoly power, Schumpeter felt, would be dissipated, not by the static competition described in economic texts, but by the dynamic competition that comes from the new commodity, the new technology, the new source of supply, the new type of organization. "This kind of competition is as much more effective than the other as a bombardment is in comparison with forcing a door." This kind of competition, in short, unleashes what Schumpeter called the gales of creative destruction that control monopoly and neutralize the exercise of monopoly power. The very large corporations that constitute such giant power agglomerations subject to the gales of creative destruction do not willingly submit to such a devastating force. They refuse to accept creative destruction as a socially beneficent mechanism for the good and sufficient reason that they themselves would be the victims on the altar of the public interest. Today, the giant corporations are led by managers who often share elitist values that place wealth-accumulation objectives above the public interest. The unprecedented executive salaries, golden parachute ripoffs, are examples of abuses of power. We need to restore competitiveness as a prime objective. Stockholders have rights that are not taken seriously.

14. Diversity in Democratic Capitalism

John Kenneth Galbraith says we have a bimodal economy. About half of the economy's productivity comes from large corporations, oligarchies involved in controlling pricing, highly concentrated industries with interdependent traditional market shares. The other half comes from small businesses, which are involved in vigorous competition of an entrepreneurial nature. This entrepreneurship is heretical to equilibrium economics and stable society. Entrepreneurial theory sees change as normal and as healthy. The entrepreneur's major task in society—and especially the economy— is doing something different, not doing something more efficiently than it is already being done. The entrepreneurial personality upsets and deorganizes. The entrepreneur's task is to be an agent of what Joseph Schumpeter called "creative destruction." The trouble for academicians is that entrepreneurship is independent of classical economics, indeed, incompatible with it. Classical economics optimizes; it focuses on getting the most out of existing resources and aims at establishing equilibrium. It consigns the entrepreneur to the shadowy rim of "external forces," together with climate and weather, government and politics, pestilence and war, and also technology. The traditional economist, regardless of school or ideology, does not deny that these external forces exist or that they matter, but they are not usually a part of the general discussion. In effect, in the economists' models, these forces are not usually accounted for. Recently, chaologists, using principles derived from a chaotic view of nature, have been trying to get economists to change their mindset, to consider that economic activity may not be rational but more like nature.

Schumpeter broke with traditional economics. He particularly emphasized that the dynamic disequilibrium brought on by the innovative entrepreneur, not equilibrium and optimization, is the "norm" of a healthy economy. It is a central reality for economics theory and economics practice. This is not a happy thought for those who like a comfortable, laid-back existence. Although businessmen say they prefer competition, they seldom find that it makes life easier. It is much harder to compete than to agree to a price-fixing conspiracy, split up the market in agreeable shares, and go play golf. Due to our transition to the global economy during the next few decades, Americans are forced to operate in a working environment of competition for exports and against imports in domestic markets. Conditions of uncertainty, not easily estimated risks, will prevail. Many of the normal quantitative tools of analysis that are an essential part of business-school training will have limited application. Use of these tools will often result in poor decisionmaking in the uncertain global business environment—unless one agrees to conspire to make market shares predictable. Entrepreneurs are humans who enjoy risk more than most humans.

Usually, entrepreneurs do not bring about change themselves. The entrepreneur always searches for change and responds to it, and exploits it, as an opportunity. We are highly dependent on entrepreneurs for new job formation. Consider that the number of Americans in paid jobs grew by half, from 75 million to 106 million, from 1965 to 1985. That growth did not occur in the old, oligarchic, controlled-pricing sector of our economy, the so-called "smokestack" industries, or insurance, in traditional banking, in utilities. Instead, as Peter Drucker points out, since the late 1960s job creation and job growth have shifted to a new sector. The old job creators, the mature corporations in the oligopolistic "industrial" side of our economy lost jobs in the last few years. It may be a permanent job loss. The *Fortune* 1000 lost 4 million to 6 million jobs. Governments in America, too, now hire fewer people than they did ten or fifteen years ago. Public universities, which grew until the 1980s, are now seeing their employment on the decline.

Where did all the new employment occur? According to the *Economist,* 600,000 new businesses were started in the United States in 1986. That is about seven times as many as started in any of the boom years of the 1950s and 1960s. It is the small- and medium-sized business sector of our bimodal economy that provides the growth. Wider acceptance of innovation and entrepreneurship are needed by American business as it is dragged screaming and kicking into the global economy.

Group action can positively affect the behavior of recalcitrant, wrong-doing corporate managers. Employee stock ownership plans and employee voting of shares held by their vested pension rights could also be a way of making managers more responsive to both quality-of-life and profit-making objectives of responsible stockholders. In the name of stability, under the guise of strategic financial planning, two generations of corporate managers have been trained by finance professors to be sophisticated, overcome the instability of the market arising from the uncertainties of competition, ignore the ethics of the antitrust laws, and avoid getting caught. Modern economics and finance faculty usually urge that profit maximization is the only proper goal of management. According to the leaders of the Chicago school of economics, profit maximization is "the strongest, the most universal, and the most persistent of the forces governing entrepreneurial behavior."[1] Further, "Few trends could so thoroughly undermine the very foundation of our free society . . . (than for managers) to have responsibility other than to make as much money for their stockholders as possible."[2] American managers, instead of acting as fiduciaries, have tended to serve their self-perpetuating self-interests. This has continued and worsened to the point that corporate raiders such as T. Boone Pickens and Carl Icahn, who are speculative traders, not investors, are looked upon as folk heros by the average helpless stockholder—because they feel that at least Pickens, Icahn, and the like, get corporate managements' attention.

We need mature personalities with generally accepted virtues, in effect, fiduciary values, acting as our leaders. We need people who are inner-directed, who will refuse to go along with the corporate behavior that produced the famous Ford Motor Company memo of the early 1970s, in which a group of engineers agreed that it would be cheaper to pay court-awarded damages for burning some Ford Pinto passengers alive than to change production methods to prevent rear-end collisions from igniting vulnerable Pinto gas tanks.

A more recent example is that of Exxon's chairman Rawl, who became the darling of Wall Street by sharply boosting the profits of Exxon in the short-term by laying off about eighty thousand people in 1988, among whom were the entire oil spill crew! When the *Exxon Valdez* ran aground in Alaska, spilling millions of gallons of oil, the profit-maximizing Rawl was overwhelmed. No one at Exxon knew what to do about this ecological disaster caused by Exxon's gross, wanton, and culpable negligence. Rawl, the socially irresponsible leader, has stated that he can't understand why Americans are angry, because he has apologized. A Republican congressman quite appropriately asked him to resign. Rawl's conduct is in keeping with the Chicago School of free-marketeering. The correction we need is profit-maximizing decisions that are also socially responsible. Otherwise our constitutional culture and democratic capitalism will not be compatible. The avaricious power elite will join with Hannah Arendt's mob in forming the state of happy fascism. We have been slow to change the way businesses are organized. However, this need not be a road to serfdom, because of the rights protected by our constitutional culture. We must take rights seriously. Chartering our metroareas for more citizen participation could be a way to protect our rights.

As humans, on the one hand, we need an ambience for those who are most comfortable as entrepreneurial, autonomous individuals. On the other hand, we need a different ambience for those who need the comfort of the more authoritarian group-think of large corporate organizations. The bimodal economy described by Galbraith may well be an intelligent response to the needs of differing kinds of human personalities. Therefore, our constitutional culture needs the kind of economy in which large and small businesses compete fairly with each other. This requires that the power that comes from large size not be abused. The discovery by the United States that capitalism had to be modified by antitrust laws and other fair-trade business regulations may well have been a major human achievement. It provided a way for the Hobbesian world view of fear-dominated persons to work in harmony with those "autonomous others" who seek to increase freedom. This works so long as the power elite does not abuse its immense economic power and crush the small businesses. A main thesis of this book is that those who were important opinion makers in our "old," currently out-of-style constitutional culture have been neutered, or at least neutralized, by use of the large-corporation marketing techniques within the political process. Arendt's greatest fears are, at this time, being realized, because the power elite of democratic capitalism has not heeded Novak's theological doctrines to be socially responsible.

Walter Adams and James Brock have made a compelling and masterful presentation of the high value our society should place on the objective of the dispersal of economic power. Their book, *The Bigness Complex*, confronts head-on the most effective "false idol" of America's corporate culture: that industrial giantism and organizational bigness are the handmaidens of economic efficiency.[3] Brock and Adams reveal how American's obsession with bigness is weakening our economic productivity and endangering our democratic freedoms. I join with them in urging that we need to promote structural decentralization in order to diffuse power and to limit the vast discretionary power of big business, big labor, and big government. When a constitutional culture permits large concentrations of economic power to occur, heavy social costs will be paid later. Where society tolerates the creation of great power concentrations, it may eventually face an intractable dilemma. Shall government be a bailout agency of last resort for the malfunctioning power aggregates, thereby undermining the essence of market discipline for mismanagement? Or, alternatively, should government do nothing while large businesses pay the price for self-inflicted injury? (By doing nothing, we ignore the suffering of hundreds of thousands of people adversely affected by the incompetence of top management.)

As Galbraith has made painfully clear, unlike the natural sciences, economics has no readymade testing ground for the scientific validation and verification of its theories. The difficulty may be, in part, methodological. I laud Adams and Brock for saying that the overemphasis on the mathematical-econometrics approach has resulted in a formidable misallocation of intellectual resources. Economists have tended to ask themselves questions that can be analyzed with their new techniques rather than finding techniques to deal with the questions they ought to ask. As Kenneth Boulding points out:

> We have been obsessed with macroeconomics, with piddling refinements in mathematical models, and with the monumentally unsuccessful exercise in welfare economics that has preoccupied a whole generation with a dead end, to the almost total neglect of some of the major problems of our day. . . . The whole economics profession, indeed, is an example of that monumental misallocation of intellectual resources that is one of the most striking phenomena of our times.[4]

Haberler argued that government toleration, protection, and promotion of private monopolies, combined with the restrictionist pressures of organized vested-interest groups in the private sector created what the Germans call *Anspruchs Inflation*— a pernicious type of cost-push or "entitlements" inflation. We may be experiencing it. Habereler's conclusion is noteworthy:

> I am afraid that our monetarist friends—Karl Brunner, Milton Friedman, Harry Johnson, and Alan Meltzer, to name only a few of the most prominent experts— delude themselves if they believe that things can be straightened out by monetary policy alone. I agree with William Fellner, Friedrich A. von Hayek, and Friedrich Lutz, who are of the opinion that a tight monetary and fiscal policy must be supplemented by measures designed to make the economy more competitive. If we do not succeed in strengthening competition and freeing the market economy from its most crippling hobbles, the fight against inflation will generate so much unemployment that it will be terminated prematurely.[5]

Adams and Brock are adherents, as I am, to the reality of a bimodal economy that recognizes the dominant role of the giant corporation in the social decisionmaking process that John Kenneth Galbraith called the "new industrial state." This approach also calls for revising the traditional view of the giant trade union. In a larger sense, trade unions represent not countervailing but coalescing power. They defend the parochial, short-run interests of their industries. In their Washington lobbying, their demands are indistinguishable from those of their corporate counterparts: "The hand is the hand of Esau, but the voice is the voice of Jacob." What this means is that we must dispense with paradigms that analyze the economic order in terms of individual actions and individual decisions. Corporations are not individuals, nor are they networks. They are big, perpetual organizations involved in group action.

A thorough reorientation of public policy is in order. We need to acknowledge that corporate giantism is more often a liability than an asset to the efficient organization and operation of American industry. It is time to accept that lagging productivity, diminishing international competitiveness, and burgeoning imports may, at least in part, be attributable to structural infirmities in large economic organizations. The failure of American auto manufacturers to compete intelligently with Japanese-American auto factories is a case in point. In 1990, American companies closed seven auto manufacturing plants while the Japanese managers opened six such facilities. Once it is grasped that corporate size and concentrated power have a decidedly adverse impact on economic performance, then, at last, the government might embrace a radically different approach to the seemingly intransigent economic problems of our day. Although the marketplace is ordinarily a good solution, today the global economy (with foreign governments giving aid to their domestic producers) requires that our national government have a national strategy to aid our exporters so they can succeed in the face of the subsidized competition from abroad. Peculiar as it may seem, by way of the Webb-Pomerene Act, as amended to date, and other subsequent statutes, the U.S. Congress has by positive actions already acted to aid American companies joining together for foreign trading.

It appears that the government, in this case, is ahead of American producers. It is the American companies, not the government, that have failed to take advantage of the fact that they are already authorized to cooperate in carrying out foreign trade in ways that are prohibited within the United States. In 1982 the U.S. Congress prodded American managers, again, with the passage of the Export Trading Company Act, which authorized American companies to form trading companies similar to Yamaha and Mitsubishi. There has been very little response. American managers have not learned to be flexible and to wear different hats for different markets. Any Dutch businessman will attest that this is the mark of those who succeed in foreign global markets. A change in tax impact to the value-added tax with border tax refunds would also make a big difference.

It is essential for our national security that American businessmen act in our national interest from time to time. This is well-documented by Clyde Prestowitz in his *Trading Places: How We Allowed Japan to Take the Lead*.[6] Japan abused free-trade principles and used deceitful practices as it gained American trade secrets in fiber optics and space satellites. These are examples of how blind faith in "free-trade ideology" can destroy long-run opportunities when the competitive adversary is not following Adam Smith and Michael Novak's principles of fair-play democratic capitalism. The global economy is a jungle when compared with our domestic economy.

First, perhaps fundamentally, the character traits most serviceable to large organizations are incongruent with those conducive to technical creativity and human inventiveness. To function, a giant bureaucracy must command a considerable degree of conformity, adherence to rules and authority, respect for the status quo, and a measure of human homogeneity. In contrast, the persistent characteristics of a creative scientist or an inventor are rejection of "accepted routine and convention, rebellion against classical modes of thought, repudiation of the tried and true, and of expert authority, insistence on going 'where angels fear to tread.' "[7] Invention is a rebellious act consciously committed by incorrigible nonconformists. The layers of bureaucracy of the giant corporations often paralyze the freewheeling style typical of the high-technology world. One former head of an office-equipment company controlled by Exxon recalls: "Their MBA's came in and said, 'Give us your five-year plan.' Our long-range plan was where we'd have lunch tomorrow."[8]

In 1971, two independent researchers for a company called Stimtech succeeded in designing a solid-state, non-implanted electronic nerve stimulator, called TENS for short, as a drug-free means for relieving and controlling pain.[9] By utilizing electrical impulses transmitted through pads attached to the patient's skin, TENS blocked the transmission of pain sensations along nerve fibers, thereby ameliorating pain. Johnson & Johnson, in 1974, acquired control of Stimtech. The Johnson & Johnson's objective was something other than to unleash technical gales of creative destruction— at the expense of its profitable Tylenol trade—as later became clear. Johnson & Johnson delayed the introduction of new products by Stimtech. It refused to provide Stimtech with funds for research and development. It imposed an internal-pricing system on Stimtech products, transferred funds to other Johnson & Johnson divisions that weakened Stimtech's cash position, and forbade the display of Stimtech products at annual meetings. It refused to permit Stimtech to use the Johnson & Johnson name, imposed a hiring freeze on the company, and turned down at least $200,000 of orders. Johnson & Johnson prohibited the planning and construction of factories abroad, refused to promote the concept of "pain clinics" as centers where doctors could refer patients for instruction in the use of TENS devices, and prohibited Stimtech from entering international markets. "In this case," U.S. District Court Judge Lord observed, "Johnson & Johnson's actions resulted in countless individuals having to suffer the debilitating side effects of painkilling drugs because a product that can afford them the relief they seek without such adverse effects was withheld from competition. . . . The evidence is such that had TENS not been suppressed, it could have benefitted millions of people throughout the world." Lord ruled that Johnson & Johnson had unlawfully restrained innovation.

Urban Transportation

An important component of social efficiency, in urban areas, concerns the particular mix and combination of the alternative transport modes. They are railways, trolleys, gasoline buses, private passenger cars, bicycles, pedestrian walkways, etc. Does the current structural form of American metroareas optimize the combinatorial connections to move many people quickly, comfortably, at low cost, and with the least use of scarce land and space? The answer is a decided no. In reality, urban transportation systems are overwhelmingly dominated by the private automobile. We have a transport mix that in many respects represents the least socially efficient system. As urban expert Wilfred Owen pointed out, the preeminence of the private car results in congestion, pollution, and a growing sense of stressful frustration. Even where all-out efforts are made to accommodate the car, the streets are still congested and commuting remains increasingly difficult. Urban aesthetics have suffered with parking lots and ramps, and the quality of life has been eroded. In an automotive age, cities have become the negation of communities—a setting for machines instead of people. The automobile has taken over, motorists and nonmotorist alike are caught in the congestion. Everyone is a victim of the damaging side effects of the conflict between the car and the community. According to the findings of a federal court, sustaining a conviction of General Motors for criminal conspiracy to violate the nation's antitrust laws, G.M. was instrumental in organizing National City Lines, an operating company that proceeded to engineer the demise of forty-six electric mass-transit systems in forty-five cities in sixteen states.

Automotive fuel economy is crucial to the nation's industrial health and economic security. The Big Three for many decades considered neither the fuel efficiency of their products nor the finite nature of petroleum supplies. The domestic oligopoly was disinterested in engine innovations (including alternative power plants) capable of enhancing fuel economy. A parade of inventors, scientists, and engineers testified to the companies' indifference during congressional hearings conducted in 1973.[10] As early as the 1940s, the United Auto Workers urged Detroit to build a small, fuel-efficient car. It cited an opinion survey conducted by the Society of Automotive Engineers that revealed that 60 percent of the public favored this type of automobile.[11] The academy observed that this long-term evolution in demand toward small cars would not occur overnight; instead, it "reflected fundamental demographic trends (increased suburbanization, shifts in the age structure, changes in female participation in the labor force) and the growth of multi-car families."[12] The Big Three refused to respond to the market forces. They did not seriously undertake to manufacture and market small, fuel-efficient cars until forced to do so by foreign competition and government edict. In fact, for many years they resisted the trend by intentionally discontinuing production of small, fuel-efficient models, such as the Chevrolet Nova, very early in each model year.

Meanwhile, abroad, the foreign subsidiaries of the Big Three were in the forefront of the change to smaller, fuel-efficient models. They were not innovative within the American market until the 1970s.[13] In 1962, for example, Ford canceled the planned introduction of its Cardinal, which was to have featured a front-mounted, four-cylinder engine with front-wheel drive—a compact car quite similar to the X-cars, Escort, and Omni of the 1980s.[14] The Big Three, reinforced by the concentrated structure of the industry and their oligopolistic efforts to protect group profits, imposed on the market large cars that, pound-for-pound, produced greater profits. These cars were thrust upon the captive public by marketing practices that appealed to "muscle car" macho images. (It was the success of this kind of practice that convinced political consultants that we had a captive public ready for political manipulation.)

Energy

The energy field, while less concentrated than the automobile sector, is dominated by a handful of the nation's—indeed, the world's—largest corporations. Six of them rank among the fifteen largest industrial concerns in the world.[15]

They are integrally intertwined with one another through an extensive network of intercorporate relationships. These include joint production ventures, joint bidding arrangements, joint ownership and operation of pipelines, exchange agreements, intercorporate stock holdings, and interlocking directorships.[16] Obviously, public policy incurs a major risk in permitting the petroleum giants to play a significant role in deciding what energy substitutes shall be brought on stream, at what rate, at what cost, and at whose expense. The petroleum giants have heavy investments in conventional fuels. The point is not academic or conjectural. The name of the game has not been the development of energy alternatives but their suppression. The killing of the Synfuels Corporation in the 1980s was the murder of innovative alternative sources of fossil-fuel energy and other alternatives.[17] Like any quintessential cartel, pervasively protected and generously subsidized by a compliant government, Big Oil has seldom confused its self-interest with the public interest. They are joined by the sycophants of power.

Richard Posner says that social efficiency is

> determined by the willingness to pay, and the only way in which willingness to pay can be determined with certainty is by actually observing a voluntary transaction. Where resources are shifted pursuant to a voluntary transaction, we can be reasonably confident the shift involves a net increase in efficiency. The transaction would not have occurred if both parties had not expected it to make them better off. In short, as long as individuals and corporations are free to do as they please, private interests and public welfare will automatically be harmonized.

Thus spake the don of the free marketeers. The statement is a flight from reality, based on underlying assumptions that markets are efficient and that managers seek only profits and never power. It ignores the cozy relationships of shared monopolies, of economically concentrated industries administering prices and territories so as not to disturb relative market shares. It ignores that some managers will willfully violate the law and business ethics to advance their careers, confident they can move on before being discovered.

Planning the use of society's resources—determining how resources shall be allocated—is at the core of social efficiency. Planning by whom? By the competitive marketplace or by lethargic oligopolists and swashbuckling conglomerates? What kind of planning? Planning that enhances national security and promotes productivity or planning that stifles innovation and change? Planning with what consequences? Planning that promotes investment in new plants and equipment or that diverts resources into unproductive financial razzle-dazzle and paper entrepreneurship? Alas, the Chicago apologists ignore these pivotal questions. Their message—"What is, is right"—provides no answers. *The contemporary dilemma is that our founding fathers did not foresee great concentrations of private power that could captivate the public and purchase political action.* The founding fathers predicated the American political system on the assumption that government—the public power—was the principal enemy of individual freedom and equality. The founders did not foresee that society would generate very big concentrations of private power that are as potent a threat as government to individual freedom and equality.[18] Alexander Hamilton had hinted at the existence of this dilemma. "As too much power leads to despotism, too little leads to anarchy, and both, eventually, to the ruin of the people." But, understandably, given the economic setting of his time, Hamilton did not see this problem in economic terms.[19] It took Sen. John Sherman and his fellow members of Congress to realize that the U.S. Constitution had to be supplemented by the necessary antitrust laws if our constitutional culture was to survive the age of capitalism run amok. *In the 1990s our central challenge is to restore democratic capitalism to the dynamic political economy it can be to nurture human rights.* The basic structural challenge to the United States, assuming it is intent on preserving democratic institutions, is well stated by Adams and Brock: "How to prevent private concentrations of power, organized into powerful political pressure groups, from achieving dominance over the economy and, eventually, over the state; and to do so without creating an omnipotent government, strong enough not only to control private oligarchies but also to become an instrument of oppression beyond public control."[20]

The most viable response to this challenge should be the diffusion of power to autonomous individuals, with rights coupled to new powers of group conflict resolutions, such as class actions. Further, we need the creation of a third-level of semisovereignty—American metroareas chartered by federal and state enabling legislation. These metroareas would be centers of local autonomy and networking between individuals. These principalities would provide local power to the citizenry of metroareas who would have the rights to actively participate in shaping their destiny during their lives.

"I think that the free-enterprise system is absolutely too important to be left to the voluntary action of the marketplace." So said Rep. Richard Kelly (R-Florida) in 1979. Every society designing a structure for its political economy must face a fundamental policy question: who shall make what decisions, on whose behalf, at whose cost, and for whose benefit? In the United States, we believe that we should give first priority to our constitutional culture. Our U.S. Congress has chosen to use the American free-enterprise political economy as the basic system for organizing our economic activities. Congress has chosen the competitive market as the system for allocating goods and services. Competition is, in this context, first and foremost a system for decentralizing economic power. It requires, as Corwin D. Edwards observed, that,

> All persons engaged in business dealings with one another are basically equal in status and are not hopelessly unequal in bargaining power. None is favored by a preferential position at law nor by avoidable special privilege. None is exposed to ganging-up, that is, to coercion or exploitation growing out of concerted action by others. Although single concerns are likely to differ in size, wealth, and power, there must be some limit, even though an ill-defined one, to the bargaining advantages that grow out of such differences. . . . Economic freedom for the individual cannot be allowed to undermine or subvert the freedom of the system. It must be viewed as an instrument for doing the work of a free society. . . . As long as the market functions effectively in controlling private power, there is no need for massive government intervention to protect society from economic exploitation.[21]

Maintaining competition by law is the basic rationale of U.S. antitrust laws. It uses the market as the surrogate for direct control. Neoconservatives would agree with Ayn Rand that, "The concept of free competition enforced by law is a grotesque contradiction in terms. . . . The only factor required for the existence of free competition is the unhampered, unobstructed operation of the mechanism of a free market. The only action which a government can take to protect free competition is laissez-faire!"[22] Rand's perception of our antitrust laws represents a profound misreading of Adam Smith's *The Wealth of Nations*. On the other hand, the economic classicists, unlike Ayn Rand, understood the difference between government intervention to protect competition and government intervention to create privilege and promote monopoly. They regarded the former as a virtue, the latter as a vice.

Antitrust Laws

As the regulatory framework of a free economy, antitrust is built on a foundation of four basic competitive prohibitions.

- A prohibition of every contract, combination, or conspiracy that is in undue restraint of trade. (Section 1 of the Sherman Act)
- A prohibition of all monopolizing or attempts to monopolize. (Section 2 of the Sherman Act)
- A prohibition of all mergers and acquisitions that may substantially lessen competition or tend to create a monopoly. (Section 7 of the Clayton Act)
- A prohibition of all unfair methods of competition. This general prohibition is supplemented by the Clayton Act's prohibitions of specific unfair practices such as price discrimination, and prohibition, under the Robinson-Patman Act amendments, of favoritism for preferred buyers or sellers.

All the foregoing are supplemented by important powers of the Federal Trade Commission to prohibit unfair and deceptive business practices and to foster competitive business behavior. For the past ten years the White House has sought to weaken the FTC.

The basic objective of antitrust is not—as the Chicago School insists and as the scholar-lecturer (and, of course, former judge) Robert Bork urged in his magnum opus—to promote "efficiency" and "consumer welfare."[23] These are important parallel benefits that are expected to flow from economic freedom. The primary goal of antitrust is to perpetuate and preserve, in spite of possible cost, a system of governance for diffusion of power in a competitive, free-enterprise economy. Congress perceives the antitrust laws as an attempt to disperse "economic power," to preserve the right of the entrepreneur, "to compete on the merits," to ensure consumer satisfaction, and to maintain the viability of the "competition process." They are also to preserve opportunities for business initiative.

Unfortunately Judges Bork and Posner have caused considerable confusion by promoting their inaccurate, simplistic view of our antitrust law, ignoring the primary objective of Congress, which was to bring an end to, and in the future prevent, the undue concentration of "economic power." In 1890, when the Sherman Act was passed, the robber barons' "oil trust," "sugar trust," "steel trust," to name only a few, were strangling competition. These trusts had succeeded in creating amazing concentrations of wealth. There is no doubt that Congress knew our constitutional culture was threatened by these extraordinary denizens of wealth of the Gilded Age. Perhaps we should require fledgling American economists and new federal judges to take a tour of Newport, Rhode Island, to see the mind-dazzling mansions of the nouveau riche of that day. For God's sake! The children's houses were outbuildings with forty rooms exceeding in their majestic proportions the castles of many of the royalty of Europe! It is certain that the U.S. Congress was engaged in "trust-busting." It took decades.

First, antitrust deals with matters that are economic in substance. But, it must deal with them through a complex legal process of judicial review with the extraordinary powers of the equitable jurisdiction. Second, the effectiveness of antitrust depends on vigorous enforcement. If the enforcement authorities are looking the other way—as under the Reagan and Bush administrations—it is inevitable that the anti-merger statutes will fall victim to neglect and that merger mania will continue unabated. Third, the effectiveness of antitrust also depends on sympathetic interpretation by the courts. This requires an understanding of our democratic capitalism and its place in our constitutional culture. It is very hard work. The judiciary, as Justice Benjamin Cardozo once observed, does not operate in a vacuum; the "great tides and currents that engulf the rest of men, do not turn aside their course and pass the judges by."[24] The ethos of the times inevitably affects judicial outcomes. Antitrust laws are not immune from trendy ideas that are in fashion for a time before their flaws are discovered. A fundamental flaw in the free-market system is the ease of conspiracy. As Adam Smith said, "People of the same trade seldom meet together, even for merriment and diversion, but the conversations ends in a conspiracy against the public or some contrivance to raise prices." The statement should be chiseled in stone at the U.S. Chamber of Commerce in Washington, D.C., and within the U.S. Justice Department buildings.

How to counteract this apparently irresistible temptation to engage in conspiracy poses a fundamental public policy problem. Consider that we prohibit collusive agreements per se, without examining their intent or effect. That policy is based on the presumption that unfettered competition is the basic organizing principle and regulatory mechanism of a free-enterprise economy. It presumes that any unreasonable restraint of trade interferes with the effectiveness of competition. It also assumes that the purpose of almost any collusive action is to restrain, moderate, or eliminate competition. Therefore, if competition is restrained by private action, some other regulatory system, such as governmental supervision over prices and output, would be needed. Justice William Douglas emphasized that monopoly power, control of the market, is not a necessary precondition for condemning conspiratorial action. The thrust of the *per se* rule, he said, "is deeper and reaches more than monopoly power. Any combination that tampers with price structures is engaged in an unlawful activity. Congress has not left us the determination of whether or not particular price-fixing schemes are wise or unwise, healthy or destructive." In short, Justice Douglas concluded, all forms of collective action among competitors are banned, "because of their actual or potential threat to the central nervous system of the economy."

Section 1 of the Sherman Act applies not only to price-fixing agreements but to other types of collusive action as well. These include agreements to deprive others of access to necessary facilities for doing business (such as credit, materials, labor, or transportation); agreements to restrict production or sales; agreements to limit research; and agreements to allocate territories or customers.[25] If competition is to perform its social role of protecting the community from the actual or potential abuses of private interests, then competitors must compete, not cooperate. They must strive for an ever-larger share of the market without being allowed to dominate it.

There is a corollary rule of antitrust law of great value that requires human judgement—the antitrust rule of reason. Applying the rule requires an understanding of its place in our constitutional culture. The rule of reason is not intended to take the place of *per se* analysis. *Per se* analysis reflects the position of Congress, and the courts, that some kinds of competition are so wrong it is obvious without further investigation. A *per se* finding enables the court to turn to working out remedies such as divestitures, injunctions, imprisonment, and fines without the delay of expensive, unnecessary, prolonged litigation. The rule of reason was revived in Judge Learned Hand's celebrated *Alcoa* decision.[26] In this decision, which injected renewed force and vigor into antimonopoly prosecutions, Judge Hand, in unmistakable terms, interred and reversed the old dictum that size is not an offense under the Sherman Act. Size, meaning the power of market control, was what anticompetition and monopoly were about. The Aluminum Company of America, many years after its patents had expired, made and then sold over 90 percent of the virgin aluminum used in the United States. After defining the relevant market and noting that Alcoa controlled 90 percent of it, Judge Hand set forth the underlying purposes of the Sherman Act. Concentrated economic power, he said, was undesirable even if not used extortionately:

> Many people believe that possession of unchallenged economic power deadens initiative, discourages thrift and depresses energy; that immunity from competition is a narcotic, and rivalry is a stimulant, to industrial progress; that the spur of constant stress is necessary to counteract an inevitable disposition to let well enough alone. Such people believe that competitors, versed in the craft as no consumer can be, will be quick to detect opportunities for saving and new shifts in production, and be eager to profit by them.

In the most important part of this statement Judge Hand urged that the Sherman Act's proscriptions against monopolization were

> not necessarily actuated by economic motives alone. It is possible, because of its indirect social or moral effect, to prefer a system of small producers, each dependent for his success upon his own skill and character, to one in which the great mass of those engaged must accept the direction of a few. . . . Throughout the history of these [antitrust] statutes it has been constantly assumed that one of their purposes was to perpetuate and preserve, for its own sake and in spite of possible cost, an organization of industry in small units that can effectively compete with each other.

The rule of reason and the *per se* rule should be vigorously enforced to prevent competition by the powerful few that is not healthy for our political economy. The courts are not the appropriate forum for considering such protestations as "ruinous competition," "financial distress," or "the evils of price-cutting" as justifications for price-fixing. The courts are not—nor should they become—regulatory commissions overseeing hundreds of separate industries. The courts' role is to enforce the rules of competition, not to provide day-to-day regulatory surveillance. Straying from this role defeats the philosophical thrust of antitrust. Unfortunately, Congress has been too responsive to pleas for exemptions from the Sherman Act. Be it baseball, carbonated beverages, auto franchises, or local newspapers, all have used their clout to gain special favor. On the other hand, it is true that Congress, not the courts, is the proper agency for granting exemptions from the antitrust laws—but only when proper cause for such action exists.

Forty years ago Walton Hamilton pondered the impact of American antitrust policy. Surveying the gulf between the ideal of antitrust as a "charter of liberty" on the one hand, and economic reality on the other, Hamilton asked:

> Why has [antitrust] not been a success? Can the basic issues of industrial government be transmuted into causes of action? Can a series of suits be depended upon to hold the national economy true to the competitive ideal? Are the sanctions of the statute of a character to induce compliance? In a word, can antitrust be made the answer?[27]

Unfortunately, the divergence between antitrust rhetoric and the competitive ideal is as real today—and as troublesome—as it was four decades ago. To implement its prohibitions, the Sherman Act empowers the Justice Department to bring criminal charges against transgressors. Specifically, it provides that the violator "shall be deemed guilty of a felony, and, on conviction thereof, shall be punished by fine not exceeding $1 million of a corporation, or, if any other person, $100,000, or by imprisonment not exceeding three years, or by both said punishments, in the discretion of the court, per offense." Criminal penalties—in antitrust as elsewhere—are designed to punish past transgressions in the hope of preventing future ones. In theory, criminal penalties are particularly appropriate in the antitrust field, because, unlike crimes committed in a fit of passion, antitrust violators are rational. They commit premeditated acts often based on cunning cost-benefit calculations. But, in too many instances, the punishment does not fit the crime. Antitrust fines are almost never anywhere near the profits derived from the violation. The fear of imprisonment is an equally ineffective deterrent. Prison sentences are rarely imposed, are typically suspended, and in any event are usually less than six months long. Prison terms in antitrust cases involving millions, even billions of dollars of ill-gotten gains have been incomparably less severe than those handed down for far milder offenses. As Mark Green found,

> A year after seven electrical manufacturers were sent to jail for thirty days apiece, a man in Asbury Park, New Jersey, stole a $2.98 pair of sunglasses and a $1.00 box of soap and was sent to jail for four months. A George Jackson was sent to prison for ten years to life for stealing $70 from a gas station . . . and in Dallas one Joseph Sills received a 1,000-year sentence for robbing $73.10. Many states send young students, who are marijuana first offenders, to jail for five to ten years. The total amount of time spent in jail by all businessmen who have violated the antitrust laws [up to 1960] is a little under two years. Yet the electrical conspiracy alone robbed the public of more than all other robberies and thefts in 1961, combined.[28]

The government largely precludes the filing of private triple-damage actions due to their high costs. This is because a *nolo contendere* plea becomes a protective device enabling the antitrust violator to short-circuit the threat of treble damages for the victims of his or her malfeasance.[29] The sentencing problem may have deeper roots. The government's failure to demand meaningful penalties reflects a proclivity to regard antitrust infractions as a harmless species of "civilized," "victimless," "white-collar" crime. What may be needed most, therefore, is a recognition that antitrust crimes are not inconsequential. As Edward A. Ross argued long ago, in the classic *Sin and Society,*

> The villain most in need of curbing is the respectable, exemplary, trusted per-
> sonage who, strategically placed at the focus of a spider web of fiduciary relations,
> is able from his office chair to pick a thousand pockets, poison a thousand
> sick, pollute a thousand minds, or imperil a thousand lives. It is the great scale
> of the high-voltage sinner that needs the shackle.[30]

The government has since 1890 attacked and defeated monopolies in courtrooms across the country. Yet despite some notable successes, American antimonopoly policy in practice has fallen short of its promise. Substantive structural relief is rarely obtained. Those claiming virtuous monopolies should have the burden of proof that there is adequate competition or face divestiture strategies designed to give competition a fresh start. Upon such showing, the people would be spared the further obligation of proving that this power was obtained or maintained through predatory, exclusionary, or other forms of anticompetitive conduct. Instead, the proceedings would immediately turn to fashioning the structural remedies necessary to dissipate monopoly power. The goal is to create as many economically viable competitors as possible. The U.S. economy's experience with the forced divestiture of Clorox from Proctor & Gamble and the resulting growth of a healthy competitor (i.e., Clorox Industries) in an otherwise overconcentrated industry is a heartening example. There are others, for example the Ford Autolite divestiture. Also, there was the imaginative case of divestiture cum capitalization remedies in the brewing industry concerning Hieleman Brewing Companies. The tiny La Cross, Wisconsin, brewing company, Hieleman, was capitalized at the direction of the federal judge who ordered the divestiture of Blatz, which had been destroyed by Pabst, a national brewer. August Busch of Anheuser-Busch, the brewing industry's giant, reportedly said, "Looks like we've got a new kid on the block." A little more than ten years later, when Hieleman had achieved the status of the seventh-largest brewer and offered to buy out troubled Schlitz, Auggie Busch supposedly remarked, "Looks like we've got the toughest kid on the block." Surely that kind of vigorous competition is what we want and need.

As a contrast, consider ITT, the twenty-first-largest industrial corporation in the nation. ITT boasts that it is "constantly working around the clock—in sixty-seven nations on six continents, in activities extending from the Arctic to the Antarctic and quite literally from the bottom of the sea to the moon."[31] ITT is a firm whose officers and directors have included a former secretary general of the United Nations, a former premier of Belgium, two members of the British House of Lords, a member of the French National Assembly, a former president of the World Bank, and a former director of the CIA. Here is the firm that over a four-day period placed its aircraft at the disposal of two members of President Nixon's cabinet, three senators, five representatives, and two presidential candidates.³² The kaleidoscopic power of a giant conglomerate like ITT—virtually a state unto itself—cannot be seen in a narrow "relevant market." ITT's involvement in trying to change the government of Chile is generally known. Prohibiting mergers where they "may substantially lessen competition" fails to come to grips with the essence of this "power" problem. These phrases, "relevant market" and "substantially lessen competition," were designed by Congress to enlarge the powers of enforcement so as to slow the tendency toward economic concentration. We need to strengthen our antitrust laws to keep our domestic markets competitive.

Nevertheless, some "libertarians" are still reluctant to concede the need for regulation. They see hope in "voluntary" arrangements between cooperative business firms intent on doing the right thing. They want a nonadversarial, nonconfrontational government willing to accomplish the goals of regulation without saddling business with the burdens of regulation. They should find this text's chapters on the nature of the human brain convincing evidence that there is little reason, today, to believe that ordinary humans are capable of channeling their aggressive, atavistic impulses into such altruistic behavior. The benefits of regulation are not without costs; the two must be balanced. Obviously zero-risk society is unattainable. It is economically unaffordable. The free marketeers reason that the victims of pollution or hazardous products can obtain redress by suing offenders for damages. It is an impractical solution due to the inefficiency of the courts. As Mark Green and Beverly Moore have pointed out,

> The victim's ability to collect is persistently undermined by the difficulty of calculating damages, imperfect substantive liability rules, restrictions on class actions, dilatory practices of defendant corporations, ethical prohibitions against lawyers informing consumers of their right to sue, similar rules against lawyers' financing and purchasing consumer causes of action, and most important the generally high (prohibitive) cost of legal representation for the individual victim unless class action is available and appropriate.³³

Antitrust Myth

Some claim that antitrust laws have had a crippling effect on American industry, that enforcement of these laws has put the United States at a distinct disadvantage in international competition with countries not burdened by antitrust inhibitions. Lester C. Thurow, a neoliberal economist, states the proposition in its bluntest form:

> America should abolish its antitrust laws. The time has come to recognize that the techniques of the nineteenth century are not applicable in getting ready for the twenty-first. An economy where growth is stopped and living standards are falling behind those of its competitors cannot afford a legal system that cripples its industrial future. The United States is no longer richer and more technologically advanced than its competitors. It cannot afford to waste billions of dollars in lengthy court battles. Those resources should be going into investment. It cannot afford to force American companies to independently invent the same wheel when they should be engaging in cooperative research and develop-

ment projects. It cannot hope to compete in world markets if Americans are unable to respond to Japanese trading companies with American trading companies.[34]

Thurow's attention-getting remark is not supported by the facts, except in its last sentence. Our economy is growing. We remain one of the most productive nations in the world. We do need to revise, or refashion, our antitrust policies to enable think-tank patent pooling and licensing and other ways previously discussed. Certainly American companies need to learn how to compete vigorously at home, while co-operating with each other where lawful, in foreign markets through trading companies. Congress has already empowered them to do so. All that is needed is a change in the ethos or attitude of American businessmen, who obviously must become more sophisticated. Thurow's claim that antitrust is a costly and counterproductive anachronism is stale wine in old bottles, an assertion almost totally devoid of empirical support. The mere increase of firm size does not guarantee greater efficiency, promote technological progress, or improve the social allocation of resources. Moreover, there is no evidence that tolerating interfirm conspiracies—overt or tacit—improves industrial performance or serves the national interest. More importantly, can anyone seriously suggest that overzealous antitrust enforcement is in any way responsible for the recent malaise of our basic industries? Ironically, the one time antitrust did block a major merger, between the second and sixth largest steel companies, the result was the construction of a new, modern, integrated steel plant by a major steel company.[35] In oil, the record is replete with inaction by the antitrust authorities. In automobiles, did the antitrust authorities stand in the way of the joint venture between General Motors and Toyota—the world's largest and third-largest auto producers?

The Japanese experience is enlightening. The *Wall Street Journal* notes that in almost every industry where Japanese companies have done well in export markets, they have honed their teeth on fierce domestic competition. The fields include cameras, color televisions, audio equipment, copying machines, automobiles, and steel.[36] The United States is sorely lacking in the good sense to use the government as a producer of information while eschewing a role as producer of goods and services or intruding directly into the marketplace. In recent years, the Reagan and Bush administration has starved the agencies that produce statistics, thereby decreasing market efficiency. Gathering data and making it available to the public appears to be a natural function for government in a modern economy.

Opportunity Society: The Neo-Darwinist Vision

The neo-Darwinist vision, like its neoliberal counterpart, is fatally flawed as a guide to public policy. It, too, is based on mythical assumptions. The free marketeers are ignorant of twentieth-century advances in the theory of evolution. The now obsolete Darwinian idea that evolution is "tooth and claw" survival of the fittest is used as a convenient myth for Hobbesian economists. They use natural selection to explain why they toady to those tooth-and-claw wealthy elitists in the hope some grant will trickle down to them. As Helena Cronin has explained in *The Ant and the Peacock,* modern evolutionists understand that animals are driven by things other than rationality, selfishness, and acquisitiveness. Cronin's book sets forth that natural selection is driven by beauty (aesthetics), altruism, intelligence, etc., as well as selection of the strong, the swift, and the best coordinated. Today, no evolutionist would disagree that the male peacock's tail is the product of arbitrary selection by peahens who prefer gaudy, seductive tails on their menfolk. Aesthetic fashion drives natural selection.

For a different example, because apes live in small groups, doing a good turn can bring a reward of help from the beneficiary later. Human society is also built on reciprocity, which is why humans require laws when their settlements get larger and more anonymous. Still, news travels slowly across the divide between evolutionary scientists and social scientists such as economists. All behavior is not explained by a nineteenth-century idea of survival of the fittest. Perhaps the biggest insight from evolution is that in a reciprocating society of any kind—apes, humans, baboons, wolves—it is essential to detect cheats and enforce social contracts. Most modern evolutionists now agree that human intelligence developed because it was needed for amateur psychologizing to detect deception, manipulation, and the general attempt of humans to use their wiles by "hook or crook" to outmaneuver one another. Evolutionists say that this opportunistic game is what humans are good at—not rational behavior. Logic is a mere tool of the clever. Slavish loyalty to the tenents of the free markets is either ignorant or naive.[37]

It is an exercise in the naive belief that no one seeks power, nor would anyone abuse it. The "opportunity society" is more an ideological belief than a policy guidepost. It is a slogan—a code word for primitive, uncontrolled laissez-faire. The claim is that free markets—defined as markets free from government intervention—will solve society's most important problems. Free markets, the neo-Darwinists assure us, will create unbounded opportunity and unleash a now-dormant reservoir of entrepreneurial talent. This vision is not without appeal. In an age of chaotic complexity, its message is comforting and reassuring: do not meddle, do not interfere with the natural order of things—but *caveat emptor!* Forget about industrial and market imperfections, about pollution of air and water, about the safety of foods and medicines! The market will provide all the protection that is necessary! This message is simple enough to attract Hannah Arendt's masses. It can be elaborated and projected to suit the academic taste for sophistication and sophistry. Most important, it promises relief and serenity to all weary of the struggle, the lotus eaters, tired of striving. It grants us respite from the need to act, to face the urgency of making hard choices. The neo-Darwinist vision contains no structural mechanism for compelling good performance. It holds out no reliable system of durable checks and balances that can ensure that the discretionary power of corporate giantism will be directed toward socially desirable ends, using socially beneficial means.

Finally, the neo-Darwinist vision is based on the supremely naive assumption that bigness and economic power have no political consequences. To the neo-Darwinists, the economic sphere and the political arena are hermetically sealed off from one another. Neo-Darwinists presume that all economic giantism that flourishes in their laissez-faire regime would dutifully respect the boundary between "economics" and "politics." The evidence of history from Hammurabi through Machiavelli and the Medicis, John Stuart Mill to C. Wright Mills, is to the contrary. The reality, as opposed to ideology, is that bigness begets its own power elite. The most glaring defect of the neo-Darwinist vision is that it ignores power as a prized good in the political economy. No matter how strong a society's commitment to free enterprise and competition, only ideological zealots would do away with the government's police powers to protect the health and safety of its citizens.

Public Bailouts

Public bailouts of collapsing bigness complexes have become the order of the day: Penn-Central, Lockheed, Chrysler, Continental Illinois, the thrifts, and soon, possibly, the entire farm credit system. Bailouts of bigness when the troubles result from misfeasance and malfeasance are profoundly unwise. Instead of bailouts, bankruptcy is a competitive market society's preferred method for dealing with financial insolvency. Bankruptcy proceedings do not in any way destroy physical plant and equipment. Bankruptcy works to realign the financing of those assets, to replace the management of them, and change the uses to which they are put. Above all, bankruptcy policies, anchored in the principle of diffusion of power, represent a reorientation of current thought that is now taking place. As Henry C. Simons, the great libertarian of yesteryear, wisely observed:

> The great enemy of democracy is monopoly, in all its forms: gigantic corpora-
> tions, trade associations and other agencies for price control, trade-unions—
> or, in general, organization and concentration of power within classes. The
> existence of competition within such groups, on the other hand, serves to protect
> the community as a whole and to give an essential flexibility to the economy. . . .
> If the organized economic groups were left to exercise their monopoly powers
> without political restraint, the result would be usurpation of sovereignty by these
> groups. . . . On the other hand, if the state undertakes to tolerate (instead of
> destroying) such organizations and to regulate their regulations, it will have
> assumed tasks and responsibilities incompatible with its enduring in a democratic
> form. . . . Thus, for one who prizes political liberty, there can be no sanguine
> view as to where the proliferation of organization leads.[38]

After nearly a century of antitrust enforcement, the purposes of antitrust law in general remain shrouded in economic and political uncertainty. The antitrust laws have proven elastic, expanding and contracting to reflect the social, political, and economic conditions of a given time. They acquire temporary identity through the interpretive guides of those in policymaking positions. The opposition to the elevation of Judge Bork was led by some astute scholars of antitrust law who are well aware that Bork's antitrust analysis ignores power and economic concentration.

In a perfect demonstration of the shortsightedness of such purely economic analysis, the *American Lawyer's* Connie Bruck, reported on what she termed, "The Hartz Mountain Corporate Officer's Guide to Committing Perjury, Obstructing Justice, Locking up The Market, and Paying a $20,000 Fine."[39] The case is an example of how vicious competition can be and how difficult it is for ethical competitors who stay within the law to counter it successfully. The need for the intervention of the state on the side of fair-playing competitors is so obvious it hurts. Leonard Stern, Hartz Mountain's chief operating officer and major stockholder, continues to make a pornographic use of his power as he wheels and deals over Hartz Mountain land on the New Jersey side of New York City. He is undisputed champion of a no-holds-barred form of vicious competition about which the Chicago School of economics, Milton Friedman, and judges such as Posner and Bork are nonchalant.

Since the early 1970s, distributors and competitors have brought about a dozen suits against the Hartz Mountain of Harrison, New Jersey, which controls between 75 and 90 percent of the pet-supplies market, depending upon the product. The company has been charged with such violations of antitrust law as strongarming distributors and offering retailers special deals to induce them to handle only Hartz Mountain products. Nearly all the cases have been settled out of court—with, as usual, all records sealed as part of the settlement. On March 29, 1984, lawyers for the government and for the Hartz Mountain Corporation appeared before U.S. District Judge Robert Merhige, Jr., to announce a plea agreement: Hartz Mountain Corporation, an artificial person, would plead guilty to perjury, subordination of perjury, and obstruction of justice. No humans were named. Judge Merhige said, "I'm almost embarrassed to ask the question. Has anyone made any promises to the corporation to induce them to plead guilty?" A Hartz attorney answered in the negative. The judge fined the corporation the maximum: $20,000.

Leonard Stern has avoided the press for the last decade. He is described by some who know him as short (about 5'2"), intense, and arrogant. His friends say his extraordinary business acumen is matched only by his avarice, and that he is notoriously profane. The sign that Stern hung on his office wall—given to him by President Lovitz, General Counsel Andersen, and Senior Vice President Proud— has become legendary: "Once you've got them by the balls, their hearts and minds will follow." Today, Stern's wealth is estimated in excess of $1 billion.

By the early 1970s, Hartz's dominance in the pet-supplies market was unchallenged. Robins was number two, but its total sales were approximately equal to Hartz's profits. Hartz's critics acknowledge that its success was due in large part to positive factors—excellent products and creative merchandising and packaging, many of them attributable to Stern, whose direct involvement was extraordinary for a top executive. By the 1960s, some of the methods by which Hartz attempted to have it all began attracting government attention. In 1973 the Federal Trade Commission launched an investigation. That inquiry culminated in a consent decree, negotiated in 1977 and finalized in 1979. Hartz promised to cease using refusals to deal or threats of termination to force any distributor or retailer to trade only in Hartz products; stop giving discounts to persuade dealers or retailers to boycott Hartz Mountain rivals; and stop disparaging the financial status of competitors or disfavored distributors.

Consent decrees amount to little more than a governmental tap on the corporate wrist, except among honorable businessmen. Indeed, according to one person who left Hartz recently, the company interpreted the decree as requiring no change of practices. "What they have always done, and still do, is to give away free merchandise to get exclusives, on the condition that it's to be kept quiet," he said. "Whole truckloads of cat litter just disappear into the twilight zone." The Hartz agenda was to go on violating the antitrust laws, then settle the record with an agreement to seal the record. The distributors who alleged that Hartz had tried to force "exclusive dealing" on them filed about a dozen suits in the middle and late 1970s. Nearly all have been settled. None has yet gone to trial. In each case, the record was sealed as part of the settlement. Some litigants did succeed in subpoenaing documents gotten by discovery in prior cases.

U.S. District Judge Carl Rubin of the Southern District of Ohio stated that, "Defendant, the Hartz Mountain Corporation, demonstrated a repeated reluctance to produce documents. The task of plaintiff's counsel was made immeasurably more difficult, and intervention by the court was required before appropriate discovery was concluded."

In late September, A. H. Robins, Inc., petitioned the court to extend discovery and postpone the February 1980 trial date. According to the company's lawyers, a massive deposition program had "uncovered evidence of bribery, prostitution, intimidation, destruction of documents, falsification of records, perjury, and a corporate record-keeping system artfully designed to conceal violation of the antitrust laws." Robin's attorneys said that, "This evidence is not confined to a few people or to a single geographic area, but implicates the Hartz organization from top to bottom, and nationwide." Then, in early October—the day Stern was scheduled to be deposed—settlement negotiations started. On October 19, 1979, the parties settled for $42.5 million, then the largest settlement in a head-to-head antitrust suit not preceded by a government indictment. Part of the settlement, as usual, was that the record be sealed.[40] Hartz is still on top with 75 to 90 percent of the pet specialty markets.

The Future of Antitrust

Several alternative approaches have been proposed to reform current antitrust law. For example, an outright ban could be imposed on mergers and acquisitions to *Fortune* 1000 firms unless the company could show—and the burden of proof would be on the firm, not the government—that the merger: 1) would not substantially lessen competition or tend to create a monopoly in any line of commerce; 2) would enhance the operating efficiency of the acquiring and acquired firms; and 3) would promote technological progress not otherwise obtainable. Under this approach, firms larger than a specified size would be prohibited from making any acquisition unless the acquiring firm spun off competitively viable assets equal in value to those that it sought to acquire. A key advantage of this option is that it would put an upper limit on the ability of corporate giants, through artificial, merger-based growth, to short-circuit the market test for success. At the very least acquisitive industrial giants could be barred from floating bank loans or issuing "junk bonds" to finance their megamergers. We must recognize that none of these suggestions limit in any way the freedom of firms to expand through internal growth derived from better products and services, lower operating costs, or greater efficiency in innovation. Unfortunately, antitrust enforcement does not have a powerful political constituency. Therefore, the budgets allocated to the antitrust division of the Justice Department and to the Federal Trade Commission will continue to be inadequate for the job of policing the U.S. economy. Should enforcers crush colluding producers of wood screws and wax crayons while according benign neglect to mergers involving the nation's largest petroleum firms? Should they ruthlessly attack mergers among condom companies while encouraging joint ventures among the world's largest automobile firms?

In 1980, a coalition of cereal lobbyists, the AFL-CIO, and the Michigan legislature convinced candidate Ronald Reagan that continued prosecution of the FTC's shared-monopoly suit against the purveyors of breakfast cereals would have a "chilling effect on American industry." These institutional roadblocks are firmly embedded in our political economy. A consensus among the American people that the antitrust laws are a part of our stewardship of democratic capitalism, that violators should be treated as having violated social norms, would add an effective deterrent.

In evaluating antitrust it is well to maintain a sense of perspective. In the words of Walton Hamilton, "Antitrust is a symbol of democracy. Quite apart from its operation, it keeps alive within law and public policy a value that must not be sacrificed or abridged. It asserts the firm, the trade, the economy, to be the instrument of the general welfare. If the fact falls short of the deal, the call is to amend the fact rather than abandon the ideal."[41]

Government's role can be restricted to making the rules of the game and to enforcing them, serving as an arbiter and referee rather than a participant. In short, government's primary role is to uphold the market's authority as a governance system. In any case, even in a free-enterprise economy there is clearly a place for government regulation. The market cannot have unlimited sway as a decisionmaking mechanism. Only government can provide society with such "collective" goods as pure food and drug administration and the armed forces. Only government can exercise the traditional police powers of the state—protecting the health, safety, welfare, and morals of the citizenry. The government, not the market, should make decisions about clean air, pure water, safe drugs, genetic engineering, and the disposal of toxic wastes.

The United States has not stopped growing economically, but the decades of breakneck expansion after World War II conditioned Americans to expect more than they are getting today. The early-1990s economic slowdown has opened a hugh chasm between expectations and reality. According to a 1987 study by the congressional Joint Economic Committee, measured in 1986 dollars, a thirty-year-old male earned about $25,300 in 1973 but only $18,763 in 1983—one-fourth less. Increased work outside the home by women has made up the difference for families—America's married couples have maintained their standard of living by putting the wife to work. Latch-key children and the disintegration of family stability is the result.

Another economic problem is an aging capital stock. The average age of a manufacturing plant was about fifteen years at the end of 1986. It was 13.8 years in 1980. For equipment, the average age is up by half a year. But the greatest drag on the growth of U.S. productivity has come from the ever-expanding service sector. Since 1979, output per hour in service-related industries has risen less than half a percent a year. Many economists warn that broader efficiency gains will be hard to come by unless workers have the levels of education and skill required to handle advanced technologies. This means that the United States will have to make greater investments in its "human capital." The economy may not be able to abide a 13 percent illiteracy rate—and as much as a 50 percent "functional" illiteracy rate—much longer.

A startling concept is taking hold in the workplace: capital and labor are no longer seen as competing inputs in production. In the new industrial revolution now under way, capital consists of information technologies that require workers' mental commitment and responsibility. Barriers must be broken to make the work climate hospitable to innovation. The most comprehensive outline of a "strategy of permanent innovation" appears in *The Second Industrial Divide,* by Michael Piore and Charles Sabel. Under their concept of "flexible specialization," manufacturing would be performed by small companies, or decentralized units of large ones, based on an organization of work along craft lines. Skilled workers using automated machinery could change quickly from one product line to another without the restrictions of union shop rules. Warren Bennis, an expert on organizational behavior, explained years ago why worker involvement is essential in an innovative plant. "Democracy," he wrote, "is the only system of organization that is compatible with perpetual change."

James Taylor and Ronald Paul decided to seek out companies that were performing "excellently."[42] Future business historians may decide to call the 1990s the decade of excellence. The four objective, quantifiable criteria Taylor and Paul believe make up the American definition of excellence in business is that it 1) create jobs, 2) create wealth, 3) increase productivity, and 4) increase efficiency. Taylor and Paul examined detailed performance records of more than six thousand publicly held companies. They discovered 542 companies operating in the United States that have created jobs, increased productivity, increased shareholder wealth, and improved the use of invested capital. Their work to date represents good news for the United States. Companies in every segment of industry produce results that are truly excellent. There are big companies in the group. Many smaller companies equal the performance of the bigger ones. High-technology companies exist in rapidly growing markets, it is true, but the heart-warming surprise is that virtually every low-technology industry has at least one representative that has displayed excellent performance. Although it is in serious trouble due to the lack of enforcement of antitrust laws and the erosion of the ethos of the communitarian persona so essential to its success, democratic capitalism remains alive in the United States.

15. The Ethics of Pollution and the Quality of the Human Environment

The United States of America has a constitutional culture that divides its sovereignty among the federal and the state governments and the people. Its people have significant personal rights. The U.S. Congress, using some of its constitutionally enumerated powers, has chosen democratic capitalism as the nation's political economy. Democratic capitalism allocates goods and services through a market-oriented, relatively independent economy. But there is much inefficiency in that it systematically imposes very large external costs on American citizens and other inhabitants of the planet earth by way of pollution. This nonchalant dependence on a malfunctioning market economy to manage our environment is a gross, life-endangering market failure. Opening the cloak of secrecy in Eastern Europe has revealed that some of the command economies have a worse record, but that is no excuse for the contemptuous way we degrade the biosphere.

The United States' degradation of the earth's air quality, its water pollution, and its poisoning of the earth's crust by way of stealthy disposal of solid and toxic wastes are examples of market failure. These problems are efflorescing exponentially in the effluent of our metroareas. Rural areas are also suffering. These problems have no simple solutions in a free society that promotes individual choice.

The United States has neither a national energy policy nor a conservation ethic. Our pioneer spirit conquered both the wilderness and the American Indians. It used unbridled capitalism to exploit the forests and extract the minerals of this abundant continent. Least-cost exploitation is no longer an appropriate lifestyle. For decades we foolishly accepted the attitude that "to have a high standard of living we must accept a low-quality environment." We have made some progress in certain sectors, while pollution has worsened in others. The worst change has been in the human minds of too many Americans; they are accepting degradation of their environment, feeling they can do nothing about it. There are countervailing attitudes at work as we drift toward the "greening of America." We can learn from the American Indians an attitude that is more compatible with our beautiful land:

The Great Chief in Washington sends word that he wishes to buy our land. If we do not own the freshness of the air and the sparkle of the water, how can you buy them? Every part of this earth is sacred to my people. Every

"The way I look at it, there's a price tag
on everything. You want a high standard of living,
you settle for a low quality of life."

LOOK 10-5-71

A 1971 cartoon from *Look* magazine. The ethics of pollution haven't improved in twenty years! We need a change of attitude.

shining pine needle, every sandy shore, every mist in the dark woods is holy in the memory and experience of my people. The white man's dead forget the country of their birth when they go to walk among the stars. Our dead never forget this beautiful earth, for it is the mother of the red man. The water's murmur is the voice of my father's father. . . . The red man has always retreated before the advancing white man, as the mist of the mountain runs before the morning sun. But the ashes of our fathers are sacred; this portion of the earth is consecrated to us. We know that the white men does not understand our ways. One portion of land is the same to him as the next, for he is a stranger who comes in the night and takes from the land whatever he needs. The earth is not his brother, and when he has conquered it, he moves on. His father's graves and his children's birthright are forgotten. He treats his mother, the earth, and his brother, the sky, as things to be bought, plundered, and sold like sheep or bright beads. His appetite will devour the earth and leave behind only a desert. . . . This we know. The earth does not belong to men; man belongs to the earth. This we know. All things are connected like the blood that unites one family. Whatever befalls the earth, befalls the sons of the earth. Man did not weave the web of life; he is merely a strand in it. Whatever he does to the web, he does to himself. . . . One thing we know. Our God is the same God. This earth is precious to Him. Even the white man cannot be exempt from the common destiny.

These words were said to be from a 1854 speech by Chief Seattle, leader of the Squamish tribe in Washington Territory, at the moment he turned over his tribe's land to save the lives of his tribesmen from the white man's superior firepower. In truth, this powerful essay was composed by Ted Perry, a staff writer for an ABC documentary in 1971. Many believe the comforting myth that the American Indians had a better understanding of our relationship to our earth. I say it is even more comforting to know that these heartfelt words were written by a latter-day white American.

The basic life materials are the chemical elements. The human organism is 99 percent composed of hydrogen, oxygen, carbon, nitrogen, calcium, and phosphorous. Various other trace elements are found in the body in small, fractional amounts. The mass of the human body is about 60 percent water. Energy, and the materials that are us, are in constant and complexly regenerative flows between, and within, organisms and the environment. Matter and energy are simply different aspects of the same reality and in all their manifestations they obey ineluctable cosmic laws. In the last analysis, everything is energy in space. In the final analysis, we are all energy fields in a temporary state of equilibrium. The perturbations of the unities of the dynamic balance we call ecosystems can be disturbed, even irreversibly. Although our citizens now prefer the political economy of democratic capitalism, their patience may be running out. Our constitutional culture empowers them with the right to change. As citizens they want the market economy operated with a sense of responsibility. There are too many examples of market failure.

Sen. Albert Gore, Jr., is seeking such a balance through technology assessment and future planning. Gore and his colleagues, Vary Coates, Joe Coates, and Liza Heinze, have provided us with a valuable list of indicators of common sources of environmental problems: new technologies, new materials, new processes; increased use or larger scale of technologies or facilities; new uses of familiar materials and technologies; advancing knowledge of health effects via improved detection and monitoring; increased exposure; iatrogenic factors; obsolete, deteriorating, or over-saturated control mechanisms; disappearance of natural control mechanisms; end-of-life-cycle management; unexpected synergism between natural systems; alteration of geophysical structures; transfer of species from natural habitats to new habitats; development in fragile environments; intrusion into pristine environments; cyclic, episodic or severe events; and changing social values.[1]

We need to recognize the value of voluntarism and citizen involvement in the bureaucratic process. We need to use the state's power through incentives, coercion, and persuasion. This can change ethical values and attitudes toward a conservation ethic. U.S. history shows we can make rapid progress, as we did with civil rights, using the powers of government. Our other option is to let the market operate as we have been doing with drugs over the past few decades. The result will be the opposite—slow progress.

Cocaine

Both the supply of and the demand for cocaine are running amok. Heroin is waiting in the wings. We cannot expect the high moral standards of the conservation ethic from minds polluted by chemicals such as cocaine and heroin. Learning from history, we see that at the time of Chief Seattle, inhalable cocaine was easily purchased at the corner drugstore, without a prescription. Parke, Davis & Co., produced "coca cheroots," and Coca-Cola at first contained cocaine. Drugs enjoyed an open market. Sigmund Freud popularized cocaine in Europe by quoting accounts of its miraculous properties from American medical journals. In the early twentieth century cocaine was the official remedy of the Hay Fever Association. After about seventy years of heavy use, by the 1920s the public demanded regulation of the drug. The market was beginning to have its effect, at the leisurely, very long-run pace recommended by the Chicago school of free-market economics. When restrictive laws were finally enacted they reflected fearful attitudes toward narcotics. Cocaine's disfavor grew not only from direct observation of its effects but as an outgrowth of a health movement. Society by the early 1900s was concerned about alcohol, fearful of food additives, and outraged over industrial carelessness in meat packing.

Consider the quandary of Judge Douglas Ginsburg, an avid supporter of Chicago School of Economics "legal" principles. He was recently appointed judge to the U.S. Circuit Court of Appeals. He admitted to the use of marijuana, a currently illegal drug in most states. He stated that he regretted using the drug. I am not sure his regrets related to the illegality or the social impropriety. Blithe spirits that they are, free marketeers generally avoid discussing the reality that they want certain markets to be regulated (murder for hire, and heroin sales, I would hope!) while looking the other way at the lack of regulation of toxic pollutants and dangerous workplaces.

The latest complication in the current cocaine epidemic is "crack," an invention that was a market response to high price. Tragically it made cocaine available to the lower classes. It is a cheap way of inhaling this invidious drug. Can we act responsibly? Compare what we are doing today with the nation's actions in the early twentieth century. In 1914 the government intervened against cocaine because the market failed to act fast enough. Congress passed the Food and Drug Act in 1906 and the Harrison Anti-Narcotic Act in 1914. In the words of Dr. David Musto, "It would be far better if a public consensus against cocaine and other seductive drugs did not have to be relearned every few generations."[2] Our repetition of the cocaine experience in the 1980s is a classic example of market failure to minimize brain pollution. Our environment needs regulation for the good of our health!

We must find a balance of interests because we want to minimize regulation. We are aware that the multifaceted decisionmaking process of the marketplace of goods, services, and ideas gives us more opportunity to participate. Our experience with the cocaine epidemics, with cigarettes, chlordane, dioxin, and other substances shows that we do not always make good decisions. But we do make some progress as time goes by. We need to learn to find a way to balance power in the marketplace for the common weal. We need a consensus by the majority that it is natural for powerful economic organizations to oppose changes that are beneficial to society as a whole.

Housewife and Househusband Leadership

Why not tote our own grocery bags instead of using "disposable" paper and plastic bags? We have a problem of effluent affluence. Americans should be carrying their own sturdy, reusable bags to and from the grocery stores. Swiss citizens of all classes do it as a matter of routine to save the environment from excessive waste and to save money. It is natural and appropriate in a market economy that the plastic bag and the paper companies would fight such a change "tooth and claw," that is, unless the changeover was phased in such a way to enable them to adapt to the serious economic dislocation that would result. Why should we represent them as villains for such survival tactics? Conflict can be healthy; citizens can oppose the powerful for the common good. We could then devote millions of acres of our tree farms to producing other products that would give us greater independence in the global economy.

We are experiencing many such expensive market failures. Yet we refuse to accept the idea of planned, phased-in changes for our market economy. We aren't comfortable with the reality that conflict is inevitable in a constitutional culture that uses democratic capitalism as its political economy. Elementary school curricula should teach personal ecology and appropriate technology. We must adopt intermediate technology for use in the next few decades as we prepare the way for a solar-energy-oriented world in which the conservation ethic will prevail. We need to adopt the idea of "each one teach one." We need more utility company and university "open houses" to teach "good cents" energy conservation. We sorely need a massive educational effort on what both government and the market can do, acting both independently and together. We can do it without destroying our constitutional culture or democratic capitalism through too-elaborate controls. We need a new social ethic about energy use.

Acts 8 says, "They went through the country preaching the word." Christian missionary Frank Laubach found a special vocation in fighting illiteracy in the Philippines and other parts of Asia. The miracle of his mission was implicit in the method he used, summed up in the slogan "Each one, teach one." Laubach realized that if he could get the attitude "each one, teach one" moving, he would have the law of geometric progression working for spreading knowledge to simple peasants. We can try it. Americans are among the cutting edge of another technological evolution of man.Cybernetics is here, and with it the extension of the control capacities of the human nervous system on into electronic-mechanical devices. Yet as we enter this new age for the world the American population is afflicted with some serious forms of functional illiteracy. One is the lack of understanding by most Americans of our intimate relationship to energy in the production of goods and services, in our lifestyle, and in our polluting ways.

All of these occur wherever our population lives. Less than a quarter of the available land space on the continents is usable. The remainder is desert, jungle, icecap mountain peaks, and other uninhabitable areas. One critical present limitation is both biological and terrestrial. Human society is still almost wholly dependent on the chain of the plant-animal food yield from a relatively fixed area of arable land. Recent calculations have shown that the present maintenance of approximately 5 billion humans in our biosphere requires a plant yield sufficient to accommodate 24 billion other animals that are crop-consumers. These other creatures are an essential element in maintaining humans by acting as intermediate processors for many products otherwise indigestible by humans. Pigs, for example, consume as much as 2.25 billion people when measured on a global scale. The pork products provide energy for man. The supply and demand equation of the economist is a specialized view of the world that fails to acknowledge that energy is not a mere commodity, whatever form it may take. *In the face of an inevitable quantum leap of the world's population to 7 billion within the next twenty to thirty-five years, humans will require the concomitant increase of other animals to approximately 35 billion!* Only a functional illiterate would suggest that all we need to do is raise the price to adjust long-run supply to the shifts in demand. The short-run social and political degradations could be catastrophic to human culture.

Speaking in geological eons of time, the human being is a somewhat new force brought to play on the earth. This force has been different in kind from other natural forces. The impact of the human race has been and is especially heavy within the last few hundred years. This creature, the human animal, who arose within the natural system, became capable of envisioning his own dominant place. The human then even entertained the illusion that he could manipulate, command, and conquer nature wholly for his own designs. However, to the contrary, from the original emergence of plant and animal down to the present day the design of the energy chain of food-giving and food-getting has not changed in its essentials. A typical chain in a climax forest comprises a multitude of nuts fallen from the trees feeding a smaller multitude of squirrels who are eaten by a much smaller number of foxes. At the head of the chain, the human shoots the fox for mere entertainment. He once ate it. He will again, as food shortages occur.

Although we must sing our praises to the modern technology of pig, chicken, duck, and catfish agricultures, the fundamental gene pools and crop-conversion processes remain the same and are few in number. Forests can handle a great variety of changes. In a mature forest, which is a so-called "climax ecosystem," all the various food chains are self-sustaining. In theory, the climax ecosystem can live its life of gently rapacious vitality for millennia. But we are now experiencing deforestation of our rain forests because of overcropping by humans. The situation is emergent.[3] These energy-matter chains connect with each other to form webs that include the widest variety of plants and animals. Some chains even extend across continents from or through migratory birds. There is still some uncertainty as to the mode of transport of DDT, but it is a striking manifestation of the interrelatedness of things. On a global scale this insecticide, used in temperate and tropical countries, has turned up in the fatty tissues of penguins in Antarctica.

In September 1987, thirty-one industrial nations out of the over 180 sovereign states on the planet earth met to agree on a protocol to regulate chemical emissions depleting the ozone in the earth's upper atmosphere. Ozone absorbs much but not all the damaging ultraviolet radiation from the sun. To prevent extensive ozone depletion, substitutes must be developed for products that have relied on the chlorofluorocarbon (CFC) chemical family. Immediate substitutes are critical. It is of the utmost importance that all countries significantly reduce the amount of CFCs they are, or could be, releasing into the atmosphere. Even if all CFC use were to stop today, ozone breakdown would continue for at least another century. The compounds persist for many decades in our atmosphere. These particular compounds are not affected by common removal processes such as rain, oxidation, and decomposition by visible light. This issue is no longer disputed. A "hole" the size of the continental United States has developed over Antarctica. Another is forming over the Arctic. This is no longer a hypothesis. As CFC molecules diffuse in the troposphere they contribute significantly to the "greenhouse effect." We are learning that the carbon dioxide released by coal burning is but one of the culprits in this dance of the molecules. Several other compounds from human activities also are contributing to the "warming" or greenhouse effect. These include methane released from flooded rice paddies, stomachs of cattle, and swamps, nitrous oxides released from both fossil fuel use and bacterial processes, and fluorocarbons, aluminum-processing byproducts. Fortunately, substitute materials can probably be developed for almost all major uses of ozone-depleting CFCs. Some alternatives already exist. Manufacturers could act immediately. Other substitutes could take five to ten years to come into full use because factories may have to be retooled or products redesigned. The United States, Canada, Sweden, and Norway banned CFC use in aerosol cans in the latter 1970s. Aerosol manufacturers in other countries could easily follow suit, but they have not. Regulations in the United States to compel automobile dealers to install CFC recycling units for processing car air-conditioning CFCs are an example of a way to overcome market failure. Still, this is not widely done. A major problem with global regulation is the old problem of the "runaway shop" or the "free rider." Developing countries such as Taiwan, South Korea, and India could refuse to join with the rest of the world on many issues that require economic sacrifice. Rapid growth is projected for the CFC refrigerant freon, especially in LDCs. In 1992 the planet Earth called its human inhabitants to a conference in Rio de Janeiro to cooperate in protecting the environment. It is tragic to relate that the rest of the world had to coax and cajole the United States' president to attend. We have failed to lead.

Julian Simon, an optimistic economist, tell us to fear not, future technology will solve this conundrum. In the meanwhile, skin cancer and rashes are on the rise. Lotion manufacturers find this all to the good. Grave dancers are looking forward to an increase in business, too. Keep in mind that CFCs are only one of many substances that cause worldwide problems.[4]

The trembling envelope of air, water, and soil within which life can survive, the biosphere, extends vertically into the air only a little more than six miles, downward to the known depths of the ocean, around seven miles, and into the first few thousand feet of the earth's surface. In this "life space" is a unitary complex of organic relationships contained within three main layers, the atmosphere (or air envelope), the hydrosphere (the oceans, lakes, and rivers), and the lithosphere (the soil). Within this layered system the balance of life conditions for each of the various organic creatures forms a highly specific "ecological niche"—the conditions of temperature, pressure, humidity, electrolytic potential, exchanges of liquid, solid, and gas that constitute the life-giving ambience of a particular life form. The focus of our concern is the creature known as human, the one who tampers with the system. The overall system is, in turn, conditioned by energy radiation from the sun, providing "power" for all the life exchanges within the biosphere. To this major source of life's sustaining force—solar radiation—may be added the kinetic and potential energy of the gravitational system of the earth mass itself, and the geothermal energies radiating to the surface from the earth's core.

This process is a flow—those who see television weather reports would say a "swirl"—of activity. It is not always to the good. Our current problem with global acid rain is an example. The Great Lakes, U.S. rivers, the Bavarian Black Forest, the Blue Ridge mountains of Tennessee, the great forests of Canada, all are suffering severe degradation from the byproducts of human settlements and production processes.[5] Accepting that man is a part of ecology could be a force for world peace. Our children ought to be taught that the scientists' vision of orderly law, the philosophers dream of overarching unity, the sages' sense of a single cooperative order, are not baseless imaginings. These are facts, not dreams.

All citizens need a basic knowledge of the creative and destructive relationship between the nuclear fusion at our sun's core and the emergence and preservation of life on earth. Most of us are capable of understanding the inventory of chemical elements in the universe. Between thirty and forty are known to be essential to life forms. Some are required in large quantities—carbon, hydrogen, oxygen, and nitrogen—others in minute or trace quantities. All are in more or less constant circulation within the biosphere. Thus, local "shortages" may occur, as in the loss of critical soil components. All elements are theoretically and potentially inexhaustible. They recirculate in the ecocycles or are "in reserve" in the great reservoirs of the ocean, air, and earth crust. In this world view man is unique in his use of the elements. He employs in his internal metabolism a range of approximately forty elements essential to biophysical maintenance. But in his external metabolism of extractive, productive, and redistributive processes of agricultural and industrial activities, he employs all the other naturally occurring elements, as well as their isotopes, in the universal inventory.

The psychosocial extensions of man throughout the biosphere have added another layer. This post-industrial "knowledge society," in effect, the idea of organizing human thought, networking it over the globe, and extending it through the atmosphere, as a functional part of the overall ecological system, is in a sense an evolution of man. It is physically demonstrated by our present global communications satellite networks. It can also be seen in the enormously accelerated growth of human knowledge, with its parallel increase in the number of messages, meetings, journals, and so forth, ceaselessly circulating around the earth.

The Global Urbanized Human

Early tribal man became disoriented when separated from his locality and early city or state. Man of the Middle Ages could barely conceptualize his external surrounding environment beyond these limits. We are now in a period when many men and women think easily and casually about the whole planet earth. Such emerging world-humans are not confused by the explosion of information about the earth and its peoples. On the other hand, most humans are now barely able to deal with this expanded horizon as easily as man and his family once conceived of neighborhood, hometown, and surrounding country. This is a major part of the epochal change that is occurring. In the United States of America, we have one of the few population bases that is intimately intertwined with the electronic devices, the tools of the cybernetic revolution. Man's affairs have reached the scale of potential disruption of the global ecosystem.

Ancient man provided his own transportation and communication. He walked to fulfill his needs (food, water, fuel), to socialize and recreate, and to get to work. This transportation/communication system required an input of water and food to energize the transport mechanism, legs. It produced human waste that had to be disposed of in some convenient but inoffensive place. Modern man, in the 1990s, uses today's technology to achieve the same goals. He uses an automobile, bus, train, or other short-haul means of transportation to get his shopping and shipping done, get to work, and meet friends. These transportation modes now require the use of fossil fuels. These fuels produce byproducts of substantial waste that are emitted into our atmosphere and into our waterways. Sometimes they are captured by anti-pollution systems such as sanitary sewage treatment districts and pollution abatement devices.

Consider a gross symbol of modern pollution in America, the power plant in the Four Corners region, where Utah, New Mexico, Arizona, and Colorado meet. This power plant puts forth more smokey soot in the way of fly ash particulates and other smoke residues than all the sources of such pollution in New York City. The Four Corners plant pumps out a total of 250 tons of particulate matter per day, 236 tons of sulfur dioxide, and 240 tons of nitrogen oxide, despite the fact that it burns low-sulfur coal and uses modern pollution abatement techniques. The pollutants disperse through a scenic region where six national parks, twenty-eight national monuments, and three national recreation areas attracted 18 million tourists last year. The building, somewhere, of the power plant was caused by the growth of the Los Angeles megalopolis. Many residents near the plant are galled that pollution emissions far exceed levels permitted in Los Angeles. Although Los Angeles is importing the energy produced, it has exported its pollution—hardly a good solution to the problem.

Pollution is not solely an American problem, nor one found only in market-oriented societies. A review of old Soviet newspapers indicated a deep concern by ordinary citizens for the quality of their environment because of the failure of the state planners to exercise adequate pollution control. According to "K. Iosifov," quoted in an April 1965 article in the Soviet newspaper *Izvestia,*

> The Vokhna was a merry little forest river. Then misfortune befell the Vokhna. The frogs were the first to feel that something was amiss. For several days they overstrained their voices discussing the warning signals, and then began jumping onto the shore. There, under the scorching rays of the sun, they died a painful death. Some of them tried to return to their native river, but there death awaited them; the water burned them unbearably. Next came the turn of the fish. Some of the fish swam to the surface, others scurried to and fro, surface to bottom; still others, following the frogs' example, threw themselves on the shore. And they all suffered silently, as is the custom with fish.
>
> One day a house in a hamlet situated on the bank of the Vokhna caught fire. Firemen arrived instantly in their showy red engines. They said, "Look— a fire. That is nothing! We'll put this one out in a second. It's only hard to put out fires when the river is far away." They dropped their hose into the river and turned on the pumps. But no matter how hard they pumped, no water came from the hoses. While they were cleaning the hoses, the house burned to the ground and a second one caught fire. They lowered their hoses deeper, where the water was not so thick. Water came out but, to everyone's surprise, it only made the fire burn faster. So what has happened to the Vokhna?
>
> The city of Electrostol began dumping industrial wastes into its upper reaches. Upon learning this, and deciding that the Vohkna river was already lost in any case, big and little plants and factories situated up river stopped watching over the purification of their waste water. When this happened, people decided it was shameful to call this putrid little river the Vokhna—"Let's call it the *pereplyuika!* ("over spill")."
>
> The Vokhna flows into the Klyazma. That's an interesting river—the Klyazma! Long-time residents assert that recently a craftsman opened a dyeing shop on its banks. He used a simple technique. In the morning he dropped a fabric in one spot on the river, in the afternoon in a second spot, and at night in a third, and thus he obtained unexpected abstract color patterns that fashionable women flocked to get from his fabrics. The shop soon was forced to close. Not because the financial agencies took an interest in it—it was simply that so many textile factories began dumping their dyes into the river that all the color patterns came out the same: grey, maroon, violet!
>
> The Klyazma flows into the Oka. The Oka is also an interesting river. If you go to a restaurant situated on its bank not far from a perfume factory you will be served a royal dish; carp with a rose aroma, perhaps, or a pike with a magnolia scent. You can have still tastier dishes: perch cooked in benzene, brim in kerosene, or turbot in first class lubricating oil!

These conditions have not improved in the intervening decades. This sad description of a river abused in Russia should be a lesson to all Americans who blame the degradation of our environment on rampant, uncontrolled capitalism. Russia's experience shows we cannot depend on the state to protect the quality of the environment of man. *In the United States, the difference is that individuals have significant power of their own. Since we cannot depend upon the government to enforce the laws, we are highly dependent on feisty individuals to confront polluters. They protect the rest of us from the ongoing degradation of our environment.*

Americans are emerging from a dark age of almost total environmental ignorance. Only diehard free marketeers are continuing to urge that air and water are free goods without value and therefore not meriting our concern. The market does not internalize the costs of degradation of our air, soil, and water unless society forces responsible conduct on profit-maximizing producers. The socially responsible, with humane concerns for the quality of the environment, will be driven out of business by the lower costs of greedy competitors. In this world of confusion and uncertainty, the United States has the greatest potential to demonstrate more meaningful achievement through wiser conservation of the earth's precious energy resources. This is because the United States can do it without significant personal deprivation.

The United States consumes about 32 percent of the world's energy although it has only 6 percent of the world's population. Some economists and energy analysts contend that although the United States may consume the lion's share of the world's energy, it produces a nearly equal amount of the world's goods and services (about 28 percent). These benighted scholars miss the point. Japan produces twice as much of the world's goods and services per unit of energy. By making progress in meaningful energy conservation policies, the United States could be a shining example of socially responsible behavior while at the same time improving our balance of trade and diminishing our foreign policy problems. The United States has a long way to go in developing a conserver's ethic before it achieves the efficiency of Japan in the use of energy supplies.[6]

A quiet revolution is underway. Many companies have discovered through co-operation with utilities that minimizing high economic and environmental energy costs makes them more competitive. They are using energy-efficient equipment and benefiting from regulatory incentives provided by the utility companies. This paradigm shift has resulted in utility companies shifting to conservation of power instead of building more megawattage to meet anticipated peak demand.

There is great room for improvement. Dramatic gains could be made in trans-portation. This means taking on ways to discipline the prodigal consumer of gasoline. We could change lifestyles, while maintaining our high standard of living and a high quality of life! Driving is heavily subsidized. The U.S. gas price does not reflect the full social and environmental costs of the fuel. Americans should go on an energy diet. Amory B. Lovins, a pioneer of energy conservation techniques, said in 1991 that there is such a technological revolution in various aspects of energy efficiency that it is possible to save twice as much electricity at a third of the cost of only five years ago.[7] It is archaic attitudes that are holding us back. Why shouldn't the American people consider substituting sailboats and rowboats for power boats and waterskiing? In what way has the quality of life declined if we give up bun warmers and charcoal starters and increase the use of the bicycle?

There are myriad ways to use wise and moderate regulatory intervention. How-ever, it would be folly to say that either law on the one hand or the marketplace on the other can cause the changes to lifestyles necessary for us to achieve an intel-ligent level of energy consumption per capita as we produce the goods and services for a good-quality life. We sorely need socially responsible conduct on the part of our professional and business leaders as well as our politicians. Our need is to measure the "social performance" of our large institutions such as business corporations, universities, and governmental agencies. A strong case can be made for the prompt adoption of a social-auditing system to supplement the accounting methodology by which we measure profitability of an enterprise. The Committee for Economic Development has strongly urged the adoption of the corporate social audit to measure a business's social performance. Social auditing should be extended to metroarea governments, foundations, universities, hospitals, newspapers, and other major social institutions that are affecting our capacities to deal with the quality of our environment and the quality of life. The state of the art of these audits is that the very selection of the indicators for this monitoring could add zest to the competition between metroareas and institutions without being harmful, carping, or criticizing. The process of carrying out the audit and the reporting on the "accountability and responsibility" of large organizations could do much to reduce stress on ordinary humans. The lack of hard knowledge and information on which to base intelligent decisions concerning energy matters such as pollution and energy conservation show that the sooner we make this social change the better. It is unreasonable to urge that a diverse society such as ours should adopt the Japanese business-by-consensus methods or the other characteristics of Japanese lifestyle to reach Japan's level of a 50 percent reduction in per-capita consumption of energy. We must find ways to achieve the objective of a quality environment within the milieu of our Anglo-American heritage— the constitutional culture and our democratic capitalism that our representative republic has chosen as its political economy.

Bruce Hannan, a professor formerly in charge of the Energy Research Group at the University of Illinois, Champaign Urbana, demonstrated how a society determined to save energy could increase economic stability, employment, and equity in its system. In *Technology Review*, Hannan showed that economic growth is not necessary to ensure steady employment in a culturally and technologically changing and growing population.[8] Under conditions of zero economic growth, the United States could have had full employment in the 1935-70 period by raising the price of energy relative to wages. To the contrary, I believe that the opportunity to work is necessary in the relative short run to support the personal identity of humans, and that our democratic capitalism has the capacity to produce growth while decreasing the per-capita use of energy. Still, Hannan's paradigm is useful because it shows the great value of the conservation ethic. A conserver society would be wise to choose energy, particularly solar energy, as the most valuable commodity.

Labor's productivity can be maintained with renewable energy resources, but capital, at the current state of art and technology, in any significant quantities, requires nonrenewable energy. So capital would be chosen as the next most scarce input. Consumption of material goods would be diminished to reduce the need for an expanding population. The concept of the conserver society is most appropriate to the conversion of the high-technology industrial countries to a more rational use of energy in open recognition of their relation to the soaring world population. It is a transitional concept designed to give us time to learn about the relationship of energy consumption, pollution, and production for a higher quality lifestyle.

At present few individuals in the United States would volunteer a major reduction in energy use for the advantage of society. They would know that reducing the energy used by one person will only depress the cost curve of energy enough to cause the foregone amount to be consumed by others who are less attentive to future needs. Both energy taxation and rationing require broad political support and a large governmental effort. On the other hand, self-control in the consumption of a finite resource is an example of the ability of individuals to act in their own best interests. Why flush the toilet every time you use it to urinate even if the "money" cost is very low, especially if you are alone in the house? Flushing only a few times a day could save literally millions of gallons per day in many large metroareas. Soon the government will force the use of redesigned toilets for all new installations that will use about 1.6 gallons to flush rather than five to seven gallons. However, this will do nothing for older neighborhoods. Why couldn't most clothing be washed in cold water? Why use a seven-watt nightlight when quarter-watt lights are satisfactory and readily available? If not guided by the rules of economics alone, clearly, one might respond to some higher ennobling spirit. In the United States today those who advocate energy conservation are usually painted as advocates of the use of economic coercion. Conservers are those who wish to call a halt to the frivolous race to consume more energy goods without any beneficial purpose, measured by quality-of-life criteria.

Cities, counties, and regional areas in Connecticut, and in at least forty states, are operating, or building, or considering, resource-recovery plants that would separate and burn debris and garbage. Such regional solid waste collection stations could use separators and incineration to both salvage valuable byproducts and conserve energy by burning some kinds of waste. If waste is properly prepared and pollution control devices are run by highly skilled personnel, regional metroarea solid-waste collection stations can act as points of central convergence for wastes. They can be "mined" for valuable waste residuals. There may not be much gold in our garbage but there is aluminum, glass, waste paper, iron, copper, and many other valuable, recoverable elements. We should become a conserving, salvaging society and consider it patriotic.[9]

Major metroareas are running out of places to dump solid waste in acceptable landfill sites. The 1986 tax reform has sharply diminished interest by private industry in construction of resource-recovery plants, despite the critical shortage of landfill sites. Such sites are carefully monitored for contamination because groundwater contamination from a landfill can be a serious toxic waste problem. Resource-recovery plants can be low in cost with fewer technological faults such as uncontrolled bad odors and air pollution. They are the appropriate technology in states that are running out of landfill the most quickly—Massachusetts, Connecticut, and Rhode Island. In some states, such as New York and New Jersey, the industry's pace has hastened because of court orders shutting down existing dumps for environmental reasons.

It won't be easy. A recent Swedish government report asserts that garbage-burning plants may be responsible for abnormally high levels of dioxin found in samples of fish, milk, and dairy products. Dioxin is a known byproduct of garbage incineration. Sweden now incinerates about half its municipal waste. However, in St. Paul, Minnesota, the solid-waste supervisor for the Metropolitan Council, Michael Ayers, recently studied the "issue rates" of twenty garbage-burning plants in the United States and Europe. He found that "the health risk to Joe Q. Public is minimal." The key is there is risk, but on the continuum of risks we must face in a complex urban society, it is down near the bottom of the list. Refuse-recovery plants are clean compared to, say, the exhaust from an automobile. Fears about toxic gases are stirring alarm in some communities. Unfounded fears are given equal status in the press with the statements of experts. In 1988, less than 5 percent of the municipal landfills had state-of-the-art environmental controls. Some argue that landfills eventually leak no matter what. Roger E. Carrier, spokesman for Chambers Development Company, says that that is a myth. Whatever the case, at the fifty-nine-acre "Southern Alleghenies" dump site run by Chambers near Johnstown, Pa., there is no mountain of uncured garbage, no musty smells, and not much dust. Underneath the landfill is a matrix of pipes buried in a layer of clay that collects seeping water and funnels it into a ten-foot-deep containment pool. From there the water is pumped through "biotowers" to a new treatment system designed by Lancy International, a subsidiary of Alcoa. One of the tall, cylindrical, biotowers contains thousands of black plastic rings seeded with bacteria that literally eat as much of 99 percent of organic waste particles in the water. The water is then transferred to another tower where different bacteria devour up to 98 percent of the toxic ammonia in the water.

Unfortunately, at most landfills the leacheate is not treated at all. The municipalities or contractors are not held responsible without litigation. This leachate is being percolated back into rivers or streams. It is a situation that is probably criminal under federal law. In contrast, the Chambers landfill also uses a photoionizer that is aimed at arriving garbage trucks. It is designed to detect hazardous waste materials aboard. HNU Systems of Newton, Massachusetts, estimates that only one in twenty or thirty municipal landfills is now using the device to detect toxic wastes. Another device, an infiltrameter, measures the rate of soil permeability in the landfill soil. Other techniques are also in use to reduce or eliminate the pollution effects of concentration of solid wastes from human activities within small land areas.[10] This recital about a pollutant—solid wastes—and the sophisticated technology necessary to control its effects on the metroarea, makes clear that pollution today requires a high level of complexity to manage. Metroarea-wide reorganization districts are necessary to cope with such complex problems the most cheaply.

Officials of Machida City, Japan, about forty miles from Tokyo, population 320,000, go door to door explaining why everyone must separate wastes. In third and fourth grade the benefit of recycling is a part of the curriculum. Machida residents comply with the separation of waste into seven separate categories. Over 95 percent of all newspapers, 50 percent of glass bottles, and 70 percent of steel and aluminum cans are recovered. The citizens have a weekly toilet-tissue-for-newspaper exchange program. The town also collects bulky items once a month and sends them to a "recycling cultural center." Yet, Machida City must still burn 34 percent of its waste—in an incinerator that supplies steam and heat for the cultural center, a greenhouse, and a swimming pool. Total recycling is not possible because of the dangerous nature of some materials, such as products containing plastic resins. About 8,000, or 10 percent, of American communities are recycling one or more commodities. The best American programs, in Davis, California, and Camden, New Jersey, have reduced waste levels by no more than 25 to 30 percent. Under our present leadership, the United States has not made recycling a priority. Instead, current landfills are becoming legally unacceptable because of their effects on groundwater and the soil.

According to Allen Herskowitz, director of solid waste research for INFORM, the time is now for us to buy the best technology available and teach people how to run it. Let us hope they do not cheat on the tests![11] We also should provide entrepreneurs with prizes as an incentive to solve difficult pollution problems. At this time Ogden, Utah, suffers from an overabundance of disposed "seconds"—defective disposable diapers that are a waste product of the local factory. No use has been discovered for them yet.[12] A prize might work. Some have suggested that we transport such wastes, on a cost-effective basis, to abandoned deep-shaft mines and compact them there. If West Virginia and other states could accept this, then long-term storage could be designed to await the discovery of an economic use.[13] By using regional solid-waste disposal facilities we would gain much greater control over many dangerous, even lethal, toxic wastes.[14]

What if the United States were to supplement the idea of regional solid-waste collection facilities with household waste separation requirements? For example, the United States could, through a metropolitan reorganization act, require municipalities to distribute to all households a group of pentagonal collection containers. Through their usage we could see a substantial reduction in net energy consumption. Little labor would be imposed on American households if, say, we were to separate our paper, metals, glass, and plastics. This division of waste materials by household labor could result in a sharp increase in the efficiency of collection and recycling of waste materials on a regional basis. Waste Management, Inc., has reported on such a voluntary plan being carried out in Palo Alto, California. Recently, the college-age and older population seems to be moving much faster than the government in adopting a recycling ethic.

Let's reconsider some old and new ideas primarily to start up imaginative, entrepreneurial personalities in these large bureaucratic organizations such as utility companies and our large petroleum companies. The United States has not encouraged innovation in the energy field. Witness our shutdown of the synthetic fuels program just as some innovators were coming forward with some exciting possibilities in oil shale, tar sands, and microexplosive coal particles. As a nation we have no energy policy.

Nuclear Power

On October 5, 1966, the new Fermi atomic breeder reactor outside Detroit was gaining power when something went wrong. The fuel inside the reactor core began to melt. This development could have lead to a rupture in the reactor and the release of lethal radioactive gases over the densely populated Detroit region. The crew quickly shut down the reactor and began to agonize over what to do. Former Atomic Energy Commission engineer Carl J. Hocevar said, "Nuclear power is an unforgiving technology. Perfection must be achieved if accidents that affect the public are to be prevented." Perfection is not human.

In 1961, the most grisly accident of all occurred in Idaho Falls. One of three crewman at a small test reactor pulled a control element too far out of the reactor, causing the reactor to "pop." When rescue teams arrived, they found two of the human bodies emitting lethal radiation doses. The third was impaled on a reactor rod that was imbedded in the ceiling. Three weeks later the radiation count was finally low enough to permit burial of the bodies.

Some of us are also aware that a huge reactor in Alabama lost all its emergency cooling systems in 1975. There, a fire started because a worker had used a candle to check for air leaks near a cable room. Although a rules violation, use of a candle was not uncommon. Pressure in the reactor vessel climbed dangerously high before human ingenuity improvised an untested cooling plan that worked. There were no deaths, no release of radiation. Nevertheless, it was another black eye for the nuclear power process. Recently, Professor Leo Tumerman, at the Weitzmann Institute in Israel, described his eyewitness account of the aftermath of a nuclear accident in the Soviet Union. He stated that the nuclear accident had turned hundreds of square miles into a "vast nothing" that will leave the land barren for "perhaps hundreds of years." The first reports of the disaster reached the West in 1975, when Soviet scientist Zhores Medvedev published an account of a 1958 nuclear explosion in the town of Kyshtin that killed hundreds and resulted in the evacuation of the local population. Tumerman said that only chimneys remained of the towns there. For almost twenty miles on either side of the main road the terrain was wasteland. There were trees and grass, but where there were once villages, herds, and industry, only chimneys remained.

Although it is true that controlled nuclear fission plants (atomic reactors) give off less radiation than a coal-fired, steam-generating electrical plant, we should not ignore the reality that we lack the knowledge to dispose of the nuclear wastes resulting from the process. We do not know a proven, safe way for our present and future environment. The informational fallout from the Chernobyl international disaster is that we must reconsider the use of nuclear power as a way of satisfying a growing population's need for more energy. Recently, Western Europe has been offering large grants to Eastern Europe to construct safety modifications on its water-cooled reactors similar to the one in Chernobyl.[15]

Until we find a way to dispose of nuclear wastes without danger of degradation to our biosphere, either now or in the future, we should cease and desist construction of any more nuclear reactor plants. The truth about the radioactive wastes of our federal nuclear weapons plants is unfolding to be a toxic waste disaster. Cleanup costs may exceed $100 billion—if the plants can be cleaned up at all. Our nation's experience with the nuclear wastes now located at West Valley, New York, show us the quiet terror that lurks in radioactive solid-waste disposal sites. While the nuclear reactor industry is struggling for momentum amidst a welter of delays, criticisms, and uncertainties, a specific job is waiting at West Valley, a result of the current methods of operation of the industry. Over 600 metric tons of fuel were processed at West Valley from 1966 to 1971. This produced 600,000 gallons of liquid high-level radiation waste. A small portion of this, some 12,000 gallons created from reprocessing a single consignment of thorium-based fuel, now resides in a stainless steel tank. It is estimated that 85 percent of all the radioactivity in the tank is contained in about 3,000 gallons of sludge at the bottom.[16] Some permanent accommodation could be found on the site. Whether the main waste inventory must be removed from the site and who will pay for the operation has been a topic of lively debate. No one wants to accept responsibility. The question is, How do humans manage a waste problem with a life exceeding 100,000 years?

The next twenty-five years will be a time of testing of man's capacity to do something he has not done before—to make very rapid change in social and cultural living styles to adapt to the possible coming shortfall of energy in relation to population.

Over the past years, since the first Earth Day in 1970, our understanding of environmental problems has dramatically improved. In 1970 we focused our cleanup efforts on five pollutants: carbon monoxide, sulfur oxides, particulates, hydrocarbons, and nitrogen oxides. The goal was to reduce the level of concentration of these notorious pollutants. This regulatory strategy cut particulate emissions 62 percent, sulfur oxides 26 percent, hydrocarbons 26 percent, and carbon monoxide 31 percent. Only nitrogen oxides increased, by 7 percent. In the process of making these gains, however, we have learned that the source of the problem is not this handful of substances, but scores of them. Some are still unidentified. In spite of our imposition of threshold standards that we imposed on industry, we have learned that there really is no threshold. Instead, a broad continuum exists along which exposure produces increasingly severe health problems ranging from small changes (rashes) to death. We sorely need a crash course in the conservation ethic for all our citizens. We must become infused with the communitarian spirit.

We depend on adversarial justice, which does not work well overall, but does succeed intermittently. In 1977 forty-one families who lived near the American Salt Company, a salt-processing facility in central Kansas, legally proved that the company's brine discharges had made their well water unfit for irrigation or household use. In 1984, Judge Theis awarded the plaintiffs a total of $13 million in damages. The Kansas Department of Health obtained a consent order with the company requiring it to clean up the mess over the next fifty years! We sorely need a public educated to favor the conservation ethic. We must preserve and persevere, for the environment that surrounds humans is the air we breathe and the water we drink.

16. Crime and Insecurity

The United States has experienced a terrifying, disastrous rise in criminal violence over the past twenty years. No one is more aware of it than the good and decent people in ghetto neighborhoods and barrios who suffer as its victims. The "Harper's Index" makes clear where democratic capitalism and the constitutional culture stand: the budget for a single episode of "Miami Vice," a television show, was about $1.5 million. That's showbiz! While the *annual* budget for Miami's real vice squad is $1.1 million. The pornography of this surreal reality is not lost on the average American.

Healthy humans need to know what kind of behavior is criminal so they can draw the line at only fantasizing—not performing—acts of moral turpitude. This is especially true in a culture that supports democratic capitalism with its exploitive, pornographic uses of television, radio, film, and other media to glorify crime.

The issue is personal security. The fear of crime in the community not only affects the mental health of the residents of the area, but it also may lead to isolation of strangers and new residents from those who have lived in the community for longer periods. The feeling of not being safe in the neighborhood leads to deterioration of social cohesion in it because residents may stay indoors rather than walk on the streets and get to know their neighbors. In the last two decades, the number of crimes committed in the United States has quadrupled—from 3.3 million in 1960 to 13 million in 1982. Crime has quadrupled because of one thing: it pays. It pays because those who commit the crimes are not held properly accountable for their actions. The only way to reduce crime is to make its cost prohibitive to those who consider committing it. Another major weakness in our justice system is the overgenerous use of unsupervised probation. The average time served for violent crimes is as follows: murder—4 years 8 months; rape—3 years 6 months; assault— 2 years 2 months. This laxity does not encourage a sense of security among the average victims and other peaceful citizens. Americans no longer believe government can protect them. Private spending on crime protection is rising at a faster rate than public spending on crime protection. Households spent $8.5 billion in 1984 on crime protection and businesses $6.5 billion. There are now twice as many security guards in the United States as policemen. Yet we already account for the highest per-capita rates of policemen in the world.[1]

The poor quality of human knowledge about crime, criminals, and the problems of enforcement of the laws are such that we should consider taking away the constitutional rights of those convicted of multiple felonies. This would separate them, categorically, from our ordinary citizens for the processes of the criminal law. When criminal law concerns previously convicted criminals or fugitives or defective humans such as criminal sociopathic personalities, we sorely need stronger law enforcement powers. There is a qualitative difference in criminals. The wrongdoing of otherwise peaceful citizens who have crossed the line from fantasy to the terrible performance of criminal acts is not the same as that of repeat offenders. For most first-time offenders, once is more than enough. For such wrongdoers remorse and guilt are heavy upon them. We also should separate and treat differently the unlawful acts of those with a bonafide belief that they are exercising their constitutional rights by marching, picketing, protesting, and the like. This is the peaceful exercise of political and civil rights by ordinary citizens. (Of course, those repeat offenders who use "human slime" techniques such as laying like slugs in the street to disrupt peaceful traffic are a special case requiring contempt citations.) For our sake, most such activists need a jury to decide whether they went beyond the line of acceptable protest against police action.

Americans believe they have a right to privacy and to the safety and security of their person and of the property they own, both real estate and personal goods. We have drawn on a rich Anglo-Saxon experience in developing the ideological principles of the right to privacy and the right to be secure in our persons and property. But street conditions today are such that Americans perceive the surrounding area and their neighborhoods as threatening. Within their dwellings there is no psychic sanctuary. Consider this statement made by crime analysts Cronin and Milokovich:

> The past several years have witnessed a dramatic rise in the number of people who say that crime is increasing in their neighborhood. Public support for harsher punishments and the death penalty has reached record high levels. In the early 1980s well over half the American people say that they are afraid to walk home alone at night. Increasingly elderly are prisoners of fear even at high noon. More and more Americans can say they have little or no confidence in the ability of the police to protect them from violent crime.[2]

The stratum of our population that is growing the fastest is the elderly. What worries the elderly the most? Nationally, the old have answered: 1) crime; 2) health; 3) money; and 4) loneliness. Nonetheless, as a population group, the elderly are among those least likely to be victims of violent crimes. The general population experiences thirty-two kinds of violence per thousand persons in a study of victimization done in 1974, but the elderly population experienced only nine such crimes per thousand persons. Law enforcement agencies concede the fear is real, but say it is exaggerated. It may be a product of the way the media handles the dissemination of news, overdramatizing its immediacy. The old people have a rebuttal. Their fear of crime is so stressful that it places them under house arrest, thus the quality of their lives is lessened. This does not show up in crime statistics. Furthermore, the impact of crime, when it occurs, is greater on the elderly. I argue that the removal of convicted felons and fugitives from the class of ordinary citizens, those who do have political and civil rights, will do much to provide the elderly and others with a sense that the police have more power over crime and the capture of the criminals.

For the ordinary citizen this could prove very reassuring and provide sorely needed peace of mind.

A 1981 Harris poll reported that at least 79 percent of Americans feel that our system of law and order does not discourage criminal activity. In 1989, the *National Law Journal* and Lexis, the computerized law library, through Penn/Schoen of New York, conducted a scientific sampling poll, "Crime in America—Perceptions and Reality." They found that 82 percent of Americans think that drug-driven crime is increasing, but that rape, robbery, and assault are the most threatening crimes.[3] The truth is that households touched by such crimes declined from 11 percent to 8 percent from 1981 to 1985. In any event, the news media seem to report constantly rising crime rates. Consider that since 1982 the percentage of people who say they used any illegal substance in the past year fell from 49 percent to 38 percent. Crack use was first tracked in 1986 at 4.1 percent; in 1988 it had declined a quarter, to 3.1 percent. Scholars say that the erroneous perceptions of the public arise from crime news. The experts say that the media—primarily television—have fostered a grossly distorted perception of the reality of crime. According to James Alan Fox, professor of criminal justice at Northeastern University,

> The worst thing that ever happened to the public perception of safety was development of the live minicamera. Now, with twenty minutes to the scene, you get live footage of people wounded, drive-by shootings, families crying, murders—in your bedroom. . . . If we were able to cut the crime rate by 50 percent there would still be enough rape, murder, and mayhem to highlight three major crime stories a night.[4]

In 1987 the FBI reported declines in murder, rape, robbery, and burglary and increases in aggravated assault, theft, and auto theft. The biggest increases in crime from 1978 to 1987 were embezzlement by women under eighteen years old, fraud, and violation of liquor laws. Clearly, the perceptions fostered by the media are out of kilter with reality. The *Law Journal*/Lexis survey revealed that 33 percent of the respondents do not feel safe on public transit. Yet the federal "Report on Crime and Justice" said that a person is thirteen times more likely to be assaulted at home than on public transit.[5] A final comment leads to befuddlement. When experts were asked if the growing rate of imprisonment caused the slowdown in crime, the responsible answers ranged zanily from "absolutely" to "absolutely not."

In the meanwhile, President Bush has proposed the use of federal troops to patrol the streets of Washington, D.C. As Ramsey Clark, former U.S. attorney general has said,

> Fear of crime is at a fever pitch unrivaled for twenty years. Two decades of demagoguery by political leaders who never propose constructive policy have forced the public to accept police-state practices foreign to our ideals. . . . Those who commit most of the crime were not born twenty years ago. They are America's children. We can create a fascist state to stop them . . . or we can eliminate poverty and racism that cause crime, assure health for all, build decent housing to hold families together, provide good schools and growing job and opportunity. . . . If the last twenty years haven't got us there . . . there are no shortcuts to domestic peace, we haven't learned the obvious.

What Can Be Done?

A missing cornerstone on which we could build an effective crime prevention program is knowledge about what does and doesn't work to stop crime. The list of what doesn't reduce crime includes, surprisingly enough, such long-touted police tactics as saturation patrolling, quicker response time, advanced technology, and college education for police. Sociologist Marvin Wolfgang testified in January 1978, "The weight of empirical evidence indicates that no current preventive, deterrent, or rehabilitative intervention scheme has the desired effect of reducing crime." The notion of mandatory minimum sentences has recently gained support for correcting the current disparities in sentencing for similar crimes and to incapacitate repeaters. America already has on the books some of the harshest potential sentences in the Western world. These sentences do not serve as a deterrent because of plea bargaining, which is used to prevent a total collapse of our overcrowded criminal courts and prisons. The result is that only a small fraction of criminals who are apprehended serve a significant sentence.

We have learned that if we want to make sure crime does not pay we have to make punishments swift and certain. Convicted criminals should be required to compensate their victims for economic, mental, and emotional losses. The personal responsibility for crime must be increased. Victims know too well that the state has been largely indifferent to their plight. Thirty-eight states have created victims' compensation programs to repay some of the medical cost and lost income to the victims. In 1982, the federal government passed the Federal Victim and Witness Protection Act. Among other things, that law permitted inclusion of victim-impact statements in presentence reports and made threats of retaliation against victims and witnesses a felony offense. It permits federal trial courts to order criminals to make restitution to their victims. The logical companion to that act, the Victims of Crime Act of 1984, established a treasury fund of up to $100 million annually to provide matching funds for state victims compensation programs and to support local victims' assistance programs. The benefits to society in the reduction of psychic stress for the victims, their families, and friends are large, though immeasurable.[6] Psychic disintegration and alienation of the underclass causes unresolved aggression and crime.

There may be another root cause of crime and the resulting insecurity of peaceful citizens. There is a significant gap between the myth of the rights of citizens to equal opportunity and the reality of our denial of these same rights for citizens concentrated in our ghetto enclaves. Since World War II the chronic unemployment rate of black males has been more than twice the rate of whites of the same age group. If those no longer seeking employment are included, then black teenage (sixteen to nineteen years old) unemployment could well exceed 65 percent. American males and some females are trained to center their self-esteem and sense of identity on their employability. The effect of pervasive joblessness on young black Americans may be very heavy. Tens of thousands of young blacks in our major cities are left to fend for themselves. One result has been a level of juvenile crime that law enforcement officials believe is unprecedented in the United States and probably the entire world. The aggression is mostly directed at other blacks. Homicide is the leading cause of death among black men aged sixteen to twenty-five.

During the summer of 1976 Detroit and New York experienced roaming gangs of black youth who occasionally invaded mostly white sections to rob and assault whomever they might meet. It took huge turnouts of police to beat them back. Police officials in one large midwestern state stated, "What is surprising to me isn't that this sort of thing happens, it is that it happens so seldom." One wonders whether the next L.A. riot will see such an invasion. Perhaps white flight doesn't work. The most obvious factors affecting young blacks in their search for jobs is lack of appropriate skills and poor academic training. Such may be among the least of their problems. Statistically, we are convicting a disproportionately large number of blacks. The incidence of criminal conviction of certain minorities has caused widespread dissatisfaction with the practical application of our concept of justice. This is probably because a high percentage of crimes committed occur in the poverty enclaves of the inner cities of our metroareas. Thus, both the perpetrator and the victim of the crime tend to be from the minority person's home area.

More than half of all serious crimes in the United States are committed by youths ages ten to seventeen. In Detroit, youths commit so much crime that city officials have even tried imposing a 10 p.m. curfew for anyone sixteen or under. This was done in 1976. A search through history shows that in the early-nineteenth-century cities such as Manchester, Liverpool, Glasgow, London, and Bristol, were just as vulnerable to their youthful predators. During the early days of the Industrial Revolution in England, gangs of rapacious children roamed the streets, filling passersby with dread. This was a subject of Dickens's novels. However, the crime of those people had a clear purpose: destitute, they would kill for food. Obviously a relationship still exists between poverty and crime, but today persistent offenders may come from the ghetto yet have more money than the people they rob.

Some of the repeat offenders should be treated as second-class citizens. The police need more power to deal with them. To feel safe giving them such power, we need to, at the same time, both protect and enhance the rights of law-abiding citizens. Today's urban gangs commit roughly 25 percent of the juvenile crime. They are better organized than ever, more heavily armed, and less queasy about the blood that they spill. The peer pressure on youths to enlist in gangs is almost irresistible. The great numbers in a gang suppress the last vestige of conscience engendered by family, church, or school values. In Los Angeles one gang is called the "Cripplers" (with a special auxiliary for girls known as the "Crippettes"). This is because a member is initiated only after furnishing evidence that he has physically injured someone. How can such addicts of sadism, committing behavior that moral philosophers would call sheer evil, be explained satisfactorily by poverty and deprivation? What is it in our society that produces such mindless rage? Was the nineteenth-century French criminologist Jean La Cassagne right when he observed that societies have the criminals they deserve?

Most important is the breakdown in the family. Some kids manage to resist the most earnest efforts at rehabilitation. A Boston youth officer described a typical failure: "We gave him everything—intensive education, group sessions, counseling, forestry, experimental camp, acting in plays. We thought we turned the corner with him so he was given a twelve-hour pass—only to disappear until he was booked for robbing a bank and stealing two cars."

Rather than decreases, projections suggest sizeable increases in the size of "minority gang" population. It is a population which now manifests the highest potential for involvement in violent and predatory crimes. Recidivism among youthful criminals runs high. Recently, nearly one in five persons arrested for felonies in New York City last year was a fugitive from earlier charges. Thousands of crimes could have been prevented if police had the personnel and power to more aggressively enforce bench warrants, capture those who have jumped bail and are escaping detention or are violating parole while on probation. However, the New York Police Department is so badly understaffed and overwhelmed by its workload that it could not effectively carry out this duty.[7]

Recidivism is too high for us to treat repeat offenders as normal humans. They are developing sociopathic personalities. Seventy-four percent of offenders released after serving their prison time with time off for good behavior were rearrested within four years. Of those persons released on parole, 71 percent repeated. Fifty-seven percent of those placed on probation repeated. When criminal repeating is analyzed by type of crime, rearrests range from 28 percent for the embezzler up to 81 percent for burglars. The largest repeater rates for the same crime were for narcotic offenders and gamblers. The most stressful and fearsome offender for peaceful citizens is the repeat offender who has already been convicted of violent crimes. More extreme measures are necessary. It is now technologically possible to implant an electrode signal, connected electronically, to a perimeter monitor. It would provide an unpleasant shock until the probationary criminal returned to the prescribed area. This may sound cruel, inhumane, or a violation of individual rights, but in fact it would just be a condition of parole like any other. Its abuse can be controlled by requiring informed consent as a condition of using the implant or manacle.

Why Are Some Humans Criminals?

Recent books by major authors in the field do not illuminate why some people become criminals and others do not, given the same environment. Still, some conclusions do arise: criminals are overwhelmingly young, overwhelmingly male, on average less intelligent, and more impulsive than noncriminals. Elliot Currie in his book *Confronting Crime* notes that criminal behavior in the United States is much worse than in any other industrial democracy.[8] There is a failure to handle criminal antisocial behavior in a harsh, "no-win" manner for the habitual criminals, among other factors. In Currie's view, what distinguishes us from the more crime-free societies of Western Europe and Japan is the overemphasis in the United States on the importance attributed to success in the economic marketplace. Instead we should strongly support communitarian and family values. In effect, we tell a young, impulsive male with lower intelligence and poor family training that he is not a man if he doesn't have a job, that he must sink or swim on his own. Accordingly, he becomes a street entrepreneur. He finds his employment—in crime. George Gilder, Charles Murray, Milton Friedman, and other free marketeers should understand that this criminal behavior fits their paradigm of rational, free-market behavior. I find it to be a form of market failure that cries out for regulation and governmental intervention.

We are at the edge of history: we are about to rewrite the American creed because we want security from the criminals amongst us. Justices on the Supreme Court intend to diminish the rights of everyone. Those who live in the poverty enclaves tend to be less educated than in higher-income neighborhoods. Thus, their ignorance of the constitutional safeguards causes many of the poor to waive their rights without the foreknowledge of the results of doing so. This "ignorant waiver" and police abuse of it caused the Warren court in the *Escobedo* and *Miranda* cases to require those making arrests or conducting interrogations to formally notify arrestees of their rights; failing to do so, evidence gathered by the resulting confessions should be excluded as wrongfully gained by the state. This nation fears the power of the state. As citizens we feel that the power elite may, in cooperation with the state, begin to use the power of the state to imprison dissenters. The result is that peaceful, law-abiding citizens take great comfort from the constitutional controls on the power of the state to apprehend, arrest, and prosecute ordinary citizens.

We should not diminish these rights for ordinary, law-abiding citizens. Instead, we should set up a new classification of citizens who would no longer have these rights due to conviction by jury for criminal behavior. There is now a palpable psychic threat to the security of the home and person—the constitutional freedom for criminals is nearly coequal with that of law-abiding citizens. We need a second-class citizenship for "reprobates" until we find a way to successfully rehabilitate criminal minds.

Identifying the Sociopathic Personality

Is there such a thing as the criminal personality? The most important work in recent years on this question has been done by Samuel Yochelson and Stanton Samenow. They looked into the question of what causes criminal behavior by interviewing criminals. The criminals skillfully seized upon adversities that occurred in their lives and blamed it for their criminality. No matter what kind of community he lived in, the criminal's siblings and most neighboring children lived within the expectations and rules of society. The criminal was an early social dropout, shunning most of the conventional activities and interests of his peers. He had to do the forbidden. He sought out and associated with other children like himself. His family was never sure where he was or whether he was telling the truth. Lying, fighting, and stealing began early in his life. The criminal as a child rejected his parents, responsible peers, and school. This was before he was ever rejected by them. Every hard-core criminal, no matter how many thousands of crimes he has committed, believes that he is basically decent. To satisfy others, he acknowledges that he has broken the law. He really does not know right from wrong in regard to his own conduct—even though he is knowledgeable about societal norms. All hardcore sociopathic criminals are habitual liars. They fail to put themselves in the place of others.

The task of change is much greater than Yochelson and Samenow ever imagined. Samenow states that we have found that it is possible to help a minority of career criminals become responsible citizens without knowing what causes the crime. However, the criminal must abandon the life-long patterns of thought and action, and learn about a way of life he has heretofore spurned. He must be habilitated, that is, socialized for the first time, not rehabilitated.

For hard-core sociopathic criminals, crime pays. Peaceful citizens must keep in mind that "crime pays" for the dedicated criminal. The chances of being caught are low. As a member of the underground economy he or she pays no taxes on income. The pay is rather good for the work, ranging in 1976 dollars from about $15,000 for a shoplifter to $165,000 for a drug importer, to millions for a Wall Street financial insider. A good house burglar can net about $25,000. An ordinary pickpocket takes in about $20,000 per year. We know what crime is, but we do not know how to change those who do it. This is fearful for those who are law-abiding.[9]

Former U.S. Surgeon General C. Everett Koop, stated, "Violence in American public and private life has indeed assumed the proportions of an epidemic." An epidemic is defined as a condition occurring at a rate exceeding its natural occurrence. At least 80 percent of the countries that report homicide statistics to the United Nations have rates of homicide that are lower than the United States. Poverty alone is not a sufficient condition for high homicide rates. The extreme poverty of Haiti drives desperate citizens to flee the country. It does not, however, cause them to kill each other in great numbers. It is contradictions such as these that underscore how little we know about the causes of criminal violence, pointing to the need for more multivariant analysis such as the Centers for Disease Control are equipped to do.

Death Penalty

The majority of American citizens feel that life imprisonment is too good for some slayers of their fellow man. There is little doubt that the existence of a death penalty is a heavy burden.[10] Retribution, as justification for a death penalty, is abhorrent to intellectuals. They see man as a divine creature. May it always be so. May the day come that we do not need the death penalty. But, its *appropriate* use is a sad declaration that society has failed to "habilitate" a human who is too dangerous to walk about among peaceful citizens, and that it is too expensive for us to maintain him in a decent lifestyle to salve our Judeo-Christian guilt. It does, however, make our society better to have conscientious objectors against the awful act of war, and of the ultimate use of force by a state—the death penalty. *We should restructure the use of the death penalty, to make its use a precise surgical tool of very limited usefulness. Most one-time murderers of a single person perpetrate the act among family members and neighbors. Such guilt-laden homicides should not be classified as homicides subject to the death penalty. On the other hand, regardless of proven deterrent effects, we need the death penalty available to a jury for political assassins, perpetrators of treason, police killers, killers of guards in prison without provocation, the multiple slayers, torturing murderers, and chronic offenders who have committed repeated atrocious felonies.*

The current state of the law is such that this probably requires a constitutional amendment. This would clarify society's position that the body politic is in such a sorry state that it does produce human waste that it must eliminate. These remorseless creatures should be examples that poetic justice is possible in a peaceful society. If we choose to follow this course, statistics from the past would not apply. The change should be toward a highly selective use of the death penalty. Aside from retribution, its other primary objective would be to promote the idea that peaceful citizens live in a just society, one which will not tolerate repetitious violent acts by chronic offenders who endanger the lives of their fellow human beings or the abuse of the marketplace by the intentional addiction of others through hard drugs sold by a narcotics dealer who has repeatedly been convicted of the crime. By this new use of the death penalty we would lower the level and even the ordinary threshold of violence on the streets and in our homes in American society.

Our focus has been on crime's effect on urban stress. With white-collar crime, we start with the criminal elite. The lack of fiduciary values and good business ethics among many of our ordinary citizens is a nurturing climate for crime and its organization into larger networks and even formal organizations. White-collar criminals are very damaging role models. This nation has undervalued the power of public disgrace, the shunning of those who by their daily conduct severely damage our constitutional culture and the spirit of democratic capitalism. These things undermine the essential trust we all must have in the system. As Schumpeter said, for democratic capitalism to continue to work we need "creative destruction." Slaps on the wrist are not enough. No doubt such penalties would cause losses to innocent stockholders. However, stockholders suffer from their companies' blunders, misjudgments, and bad luck of other kinds, so why not from their criminal conduct as well?

Peaceful citizens overreacting to crime will play into the hands of the power elite for fascist rule. Experts who have an interest in civil liberties warn that overreaction is more dangerous than even terrorism. J. Boyer Bell, a researcher at Columbia University's Institute of War and Peace Studies, noted that repressive measures used to crush terrorism often remain in force long after the threat of violence has passed. For example, in Uruguay, in 1973, a military-backed coup overthrew the elected representative government during a crisis precipitated by the Tupamaro guerrillas. For years the military junta remained firmly entrenched. The Tupamaros disappeared, but so did most civil liberties in the new fascist state. Fascism took the place of what had been a vibrant representative republic. Fascism feeds on insecurity in our streets. We propose a radical change to diminish insecurity to protect the constitutional culture. By doing so we can take away one of the most useful fulcrums for fascism—crime. The "reprobates" constitutional amendment may be the most effective way to get criminals under control and restore the peoples' faith in the state's capacity to protect ordinary citizens and their society. It will strength the power of the police, so we can obtain the necessary secure atmosphere we need to pursue happiness. In this way we will protect the average citizens rights to due process, equal protection before the law, privileges and immunities of citizens, yet enabling the state to deal swiftly and effectively with the sociopathic criminal humans amongst us. It is also much more cost effective than our currently chosen solution—more prisons.

Efficacy of Unusual Punishments

Our founding fathers had a deep concern that our peaceful citizens should be protected against the state's abusive power. They knew about the use of torture and cruel, unusual punishments. Recent annals of the shah of Iran's secret police's uses of torture show that man has a peculiar penchant for cruelty. It must be curbed and controlled. Yet we sleepwalk to disaster hobbled by our myths. We hold this myth to be self-evident that all persons have an equal right to criminal justice. Why? First, because the communication media—press, radio, and television—have heightened our consciousness of the subject of crime and violence by their very heavy emphasis on it in the news. Second, we all fear that someday we may be wrongly accused of a crime, for capricious or evil reasons. This causes us to seek safeguards. We know the accused faces an unequal battle for justice against the great power of the state. The agonizing choice we have not faced is whether we should continue to provide these protections to sociopathic persons who have been convicted and sentenced for having committed atrocious felonies.

I propose that, in particular, we end the prearrest and prearraignment protections, and the exclusionary rules, for twice-convicted felons. In any case, we would continue to bar cruel and unusual practices or punishment, and continue to provide adequate legal counsel. This would enable the police to more closely monitor the activities of convicted felons, to pick them up for interrogation, to hold them for suspicion, and to more severely restrict their probationary and parole behavior, such as, more effectively, barring them from consorting with criminals. These felons could earn their way back to full citizenship rights by way of good behavior and exemplary conduct. If we were to adopt such a constitutional amendment the government should also stand ready to be the "employer of last resort." Such convicted felons need help, because they often lack industrial discipline. Furthermore, society will probably treat such "reprobates" with cultural intolerance. Having been classed as "second-class citizens," through their own criminal conduct, then, by their own conduct they should have the chance to work their way out of the predicament over a time proportionate to the atrocious crime.

At the time of the founding of the United States in 1783, during the period of negotiations for the Treaty of Ghent to end the American Revolutionary War, the British crown bargained unsuccessfully with Benjamin Franklin and others for the power to continue to banish undesirables to the former colonies. Those founding fathers refused, knowing that we already had many of these second-class citizens in our midst. The result was that Britain began banishing undesirables to Australia. This judicial sentencing practice continued for many decades in England. Therefore, the United States, from 1783 to 1789, the period of the Continental Congress, had two classes of citizens. The first class, ordinary voting and non-voting citizens such as farmers, planters, merchants, professionals, artisans, in effect ordinary monied persons, and another class—felons, fugitives, indentured servants, and bankrupt debtors. When we started the United States we chose to discontinue this distinction and opted for the ideal that "all men are created equal." It has not worked well. Criminals are not law-abiding. They are undeserving of equal rights with those who are. We need the constitutional creation of an outlaw class—the reprobates—for the protection of ordinary citizens and to promote domestic tranquility.

We could use informed consent for first-time offenders and empower judge and jury to impose the sentence of the "reprobate" classification for repeat offenders. When the accused is arrested, according to the law since the 1960s, he must be notified that he has the right to the assistance of legal counsel. The presumption is that he is not learned in the law and needs advice because the police are acting in an adversarial role by way of the apprehension. If the person apprehended cannot afford to pay for counsel, then one shall be provided. This right to aid of legal counsel continues throughout the trial and until appeals are exhausted. During the course of a trial, it is wrong to compel any accused in such a criminal case to be a witness against himself. Nor may the state comment adversely on the exercise of that right. The ordinary citizen cannot be compelled to incriminate himself, as set forth in the Fifth Amendment. In the event of a conviction, the court is barred from imposing cruel and unusual punishments. Finally, the defendant has under federal law the last hope of the president's right to reprieve or pardon. The Warren Court's interpretation of the Fourteenth Amendment has extended this description of criminal justice to the several states' criminal law procedures. This brings about uniformity of our criminal justice system throughout the United States.

For convicted criminals, we can use informed consent, with an appropriate waiting period for deliberation. During this time, the indicted felonious defendant should have the opportunity of advice and counsel of lawyers, psychiatrists, and social workers. The defendants could deliberate on the effects of being classed a reprobate. They could also be offered alternatives such as volunteering to be a part of medical experimentation involving the sort of research proposed by Richard Berglund in *Fabric of the Human Brain.* Berglund says we need to place catheters into the pituitary region of human brains to study hormonal affects on the human. It is not a painful experience. Other possibilities might be voluntary castration (I reject this idea based on the record of eunuchs), hormonal treatments for repeat rapists, and various other substitutes for life imprisonment. Another alternative, banishment to remote rural areas, could be used. Perhaps Alaska, Idaho, and Montana, only for examples, might be willing to be paid a small annual per-capita stipend to accept prisoners interned to remote rural work camps. There, they could improve the surrounding environment by reforestation, timber harvesting, mining, or cleaning up watersheds, toxic waste sites, and the like. It could be healthy rehabilitation—a way for an outlaw to earn his way back into society through good productive behavior.

Criminal Sociopathic Personalities

In reality we are unable to rehabilitate hard-core criminal sociopathic personalities. Yet if we can identify them, some thought should be given to allowing a jury, after due process, to find that such a sociopathic person shall henceforth be a second-class citizen, a reprobate. Once convicted of an atrocious felony such as murder, rape, arson, armed robbery, and other violent crimes such as aggravated assault and battery, a routine process could be set in motion for the convicted criminal. Thus, if psychological testing would demonstrate that the person had the traits indicated in the Yochelson/Samenow study, then a separate due process hearing could be held to determine whether he or she should be reprobated. Such a jury finding for the criminal sociopathic person would have harsh results. Henceforth he or she be would be denied equal protection of the law in arrest, indictment, and future trial proceedings. It appears that such a convict could be implanted with a homing device that would emit a unique signal and henceforth identify his or her location. Such an outlaw would be barred from consorting with criminals, frequenting places of ill repute, and be required to work at some gainful occupation. The government would act as a standby employer of last resort so such a person could gain self-esteem by doing useful work.

Long-term good conduct could result in a restoration of ordinary citizen's rights after, say, ten years of good conduct and an unblemished record. The rights could be granted after a due process hearing, giving the public the right to hear and be heard. Another possibility would be to make all future income subject to partial garnishment. The outlaw would be provided the minimum necessary for food, clothing, shelter, and minimal entertainment from his net wages. The proceeds of such garnishment could be paid to the victims of the crime. The same cap of ten years, based on good behavior, could be placed on the garnishment powers. If the creation of the reprobate classification did not produce worthwhile results it could be terminated by a "sunset" clause. Instead, today we are building more prisons and closing down more parks. Crack is destroying our constitutional culture. Heroin and fascism are coming.

Crime Control

A federal statute with grants-in-aid designed to implement a few effective crime-prevention policies could cover the geographical areas of chartered metroareas. State compacts could be provided for metroareas that cross state boundaries. This approach is not unfamiliar. Historically, it is the way we solved the unemployment security, elderly security, minimum wage, and, to a lesser extent, wages and hours legislation. In effect, we usually pass a federal omnibus bill. It offers to the state the opportunity to join a federal system of regulation and apply their own taxes collected as a credit against the federal taxes imposed. Usually, local regulations may not conflict with federal standards by setting lower standards. But they may be more rigorous so long as they do not deny equal protection before the law and due process. This time-honored method of combining federal enabling legislation with state cooperative enactments is the technique we should use to deal with our metroarea problems of crime, blighted housing, traffic congestion, air and water pollution, and solid-waste disposal. These problems should be dealt with on a metroarea-wide basis if the problem solving is to be effective. If we are not willing to improve our institutional and personal response, we must live with high levels of crime. Politics will not and should not be separated from crime-control policy.

Handguns

Today, it is easier to buy a handgun in most American cities than it is to obtain a library card. Conservative critics of handgun control laws insist our laws should be directed toward the criminal use of firearms, not toward restricting the ownership of firearms by otherwise law-abiding citizens. However, any urban convenience food store clerk can tell us how regularly they have been held up. Sometimes it is as much as once a week. In Japan, crimes involving handguns are rare. Why? Because under Japanese law, the only persons allowed to carry handguns are law-enforcement officials. In the United States, merely banning Saturday-night specials is not enough. The Brady bill is a first major step in the right direction of slowing down the purchase of handguns. The number of handguns in private use must be reduced to a minimum.

Fifty percent of the murders in the United States are committed with handguns. The rate of intentional homicide in the United States has gone up 61 percent over the last twenty years. By a wise use of tax money, Baltimore police bought fifteen thousand guns from citizens in 1974. Handgun murders promptly fell 24 percent the next year and 35 percent the following year. Some states provide stiff mandatory sentences for illegally carrying guns. Still, studies find handguns are manufactured and exported by other states with no restrictions. Plainly, a serious national policy on firearms control is needed in the United States. Instead we are headed in the other direction. In our fastest growing state, Florida, we have chosen violence. Florida leads the way on handguns! In May 1987 Gov. Bob Martinez signed into law the right of anyone over twenty-one years old, who is not a convicted felon or demonstrably mentally incapacitated, to be licensed to carry concealed weapons. During debate on the law, legislators were undeterred by opponents citing statistics on increased gun violations among teenagers and children. Nor did they heed the recommendations against the bill by police organizations of Miami, Jacksonville, and Orlando. Gerry Arenberg, executive director of the National Association of Chiefs of Police, said that many people will apply for the purchase of a concealed weapon and the required two- to four-hour training simply because it was so easy to qualify. Florida is expecting about 130,000 applicants this year.

In any event, in Florida and across the nation people are increasingly relying on the perceived protection of handguns. Most gun buyers and owners in the United States are frightened by the media's reports of the rising rate of crime. They want to defend themselves! Tragically, their state of mind in the dead of night does not lead to good marksmanship. The prowler they shoot at in the panic of the night frequently turns out to be a member of the family. How many family members live in fear that their spouse may shoot and wound them, by mistake of course, as they return from the toilet to the bed during the night? The psychic stress for peaceful citizens is real and immeasurable.

Have we learned from our battle against tobacco? Are we now ready to act on a public mental-health problem—American's love affair with guns? On tobacco, our constitutional culture has worked slowly. In the spirit of maximizing profits, large companies with powerful political influence have been very resistant to social responsibility. The United States is getting control over tobacco addiction and its effects on smokers and nonsmokers alike. Is gun use a mental health problem in the United States?

Dr. Weiss, an epidemiological researcher in psychiatric criminology, states that death by gunshot is a serious public health problem in the United States. In addition to about 11,000 handgun murders each year, more than 250,000 other crimes— assaults, robberies and rapes—are committed with the assistance of the handgun. The United States ranks first among all industrialized nations in the rates of homicides and suicides by shooting. The United States does not rank first in international homicide death rates (countries such as Columbia, Mexico, Nicaragua, and South Africa have many, relatively, more murders), nor are we first in suicide rates (persons in Czechoslovakia, Germany, other countries in middle Europe, and Japan are much more likely to kill themselves).

Advocates of gun ownership say that statistics are meaningless. They assert that people who kill are going to kill with whatever means is available. Most homicides, however, are not planned, but seem to result from a dispute in which the most readily available weapon is used. When that happens to be a knife—the second most common weapon used in homicides—the victim has a much better chance for survival. The death rate for all victims assaulted with guns is five times that for those assaulted with knives. This statement is an indicator of the higher value we should place on public health research into crime issues. Detroit psychiatrist Emanuel Tennae says impulsive homicide is a result of three circumstances: "A relationship that is creating tension, a sudden explosion that disrupts a person's usual control, and having a suitable tool of destruction available. . . . A baseball bat will do, but if it's a baseball bat, the result probably won't be a homicide. . . . First of all it's difficult to kill someone with a baseball bat, and since the act of lifting the bat discharges some of the aggression, it's possible that the individual using it will return to normal before anyone is terribly hurt. . . . Some guns are much easier to use than other weapons. It is the gun that does the killing. All the assailant does is pull the trigger. The victim dies but the assailant feels a detachment and a blurring of personal responsibility."

Tennae contends that handguns convert homicidal urges—urges that everyone feels—into homicide. He says that, "Murderous wishes, murderous rage, and murderous fantasies occur in every human being." He makes an appropriate analysis of the National Rifle Association's famous bumper sticker that proclaims, "Guns do not kill people, people kill people." Tennae states, "That is absolutely right. Therefore, it leads to the option of eliminating either the people or guns. To change people into creatures incapable of aggressive impulses is like trying to cure prostitution by eliminating the sex drive." Most people who buy guns have no intention of becoming murderers or killers. They buy them to protect themselves and their families. So, as the rate of violent crime goes up, so does the public's fear. The result is more gun sales. Americans own more guns per capita than any other people in the world. It is conservatively estimated that there are between thirty million and fifty million handguns now on the streets (supplemented by many more millions in the homes). About 2.5 million are being manufactured and sold annually. Guns purchased for protection are rarely used for that purpose. Many are stolen in home burglaries and used to kill people elsewhere. Others are used by family members against each other. One study found that accidental firearms deaths are six times as frequent as intentional killings of residential intruders. Federal legislation is the only effective way. Piecemeal handgun control by some states can be overridden by criminals crossing state lines.

Consider this horrifying example. In February 1972 Richard Thrift, a native of South Carolina, made some purchases at Roberts Trading Post, a discount store for guns, ammunition, and fireworks in Greenville, South Carolina. During that day he made six trips from the store to his station wagon while buying 241 handguns. South Carolina is one of forty-two states that places no restrictions on the sale of handguns. The transactions were legal. A few days later, someone used a handgun to put two bullets into a police officer near the Bruckner Expressway in New York City. About the same time, a man was shot and killed in the South Bronx in a dispute over a lovers' triangle. In ten similar police actions in New York during 1973, it was discovered that the weapons involved were among those purchased by Richard Thrift in February 1972. During that year Richard Thrift, an unemployed high school drop out, spent about $40,000 at the Trading Post. He bought 3,600 handguns from Roberts that year. All of them eventually hit the streets of New York City. Thrift was a part of a sophisticated black market network that took the guns from Roberts Trading Post, via Thrift, to two middlemen near Greenville to two other middlemen in North Carolina, onto a truck bound for a factory in Brooklyn, and from the factory to about a dozen street sellers in the Bronx. A study by the New York Police Department revealed that of the handguns seized in the first six months of 1973 from the people arrested for murder, robbery, assault, and other crimes, only forty-nine, 3 percent, of the 1,802 traceable handguns had come from within New York State.[11]

For crying out loud! Our police need the outlawing of handguns! A very high percentage of our local state and federal police killed in the line of duty are killed with guns, usually handguns. With the exception of the assassination of public officials and celebrities, and crimes against friends and loved ones, nothing heightens the ordinary citizen's sense of insecurity more than the shooting of our law-enforcement officers. To the greater shame of Colt Industries and other aggressive supporters of the National Rifle Association, 127, or 98 percent, of the law enforcement officers killed in 1985 were slain with firearms. Handguns were used in ninety-three of the deaths, rifles in twenty-one, and shotguns in thirteen. It is a national shame that police officers and their families must face the real fear that the officer may not return home at the end of the day.

Every public opinion survey indicates that a large majority of adult Americans, including those who own guns, support some form of federal gun control, most often mandatory registration for handguns. The outcry the opposition raises is the nonsense of complete confiscation. Complete confiscation of all guns would not only be extremely expensive, impractical, and possibly an abridgement of our constitutional freedoms, but would be opposed by most Americans.[12] Consider a solemn warning to all citizens that came from Hubert Williams, director of police in crime-plagued Newark, New Jersey: "We can give up our Constitution in return for our safety. If you give police unfettered rights, I assure you that crime will drop. The price will be a garrison state. As a policeman, I think that is a price we cannot afford."[13]

Prison

In the United States the public is ready for major changes in law enforcement. In poll after poll, Americans have asked for more effective crime control. Large majorities have favored gun control. Other majorities have indicated impatience with the delays of justice and the uncertainties of punishment. We see widely publicized stories of some individual's unwillingness to involve himself in witnessed crime. Yet it is notable that when the American Institute of Public Opinion asked a large sample of Americans in 1986 whether they would be "willing to work with local police in a community anti-crime operation, reporting on any suspicious activity" in their neighborhood, 87 percent answered yes. Furthermore, not one educational, income, occupational, or other category fell below a 76-percent affirmative opinion.

Japan and other Asian nations have been infinitely more successful in controlling drugs and crimes of violence in their major cities than has the United States of America. Gabriel Nahas has provided us with some invaluable insight into how other nations have succeeded where we have failed in curbing the abuse of narcotics.[14] The United Nations International Narcotics Control Board states that since there is no medical remedy for drug dependence, the only effective measure is to suppress the drugs as much as possible, just as if they were a public health problem involving infectious agents. In addition, rehabilitation of addicts should come through quarantine until they are able to lead drug-free lives. Over the past twenty years such measures have been successfully implemented in Japan, Taiwan, and Singapore. We must emphasize, however, that in each nation, a national consensus supported a successful social taboo against the illicit use of drugs. That may be of great importance in this success story. Cultural taboos on the use of drugs have also existed in the United States from time to time since the 1920s. This protected millions against the temptations of illicit drug use. These taboos were shattered twenty years ago by the false prophets and social nihilists of the drug culture. In the United States the ethic against the use of addictive drugs and addictive behavior needs to be revived if our society is to better control the supply and demand of dependence-producing drugs.

If we are to be the nation that leads humans into higher consciousness, we must control and sharply diminish crime and criminals. However, while accomplishing that objective peaceful law-abiding citizens should not give up the rights of a trial by a jury of our peers or the benefits of cultural diversity and a multivariate approach to the solution of difficult problems. Also, we should not ignore that for many peaceful citizens access to social justice is a reassuring, stress-reducing modus vivendi only if it is a reality. Our culture of unusual ethnic diversity has made access to Anglo-American law difficult for some due to language barriers and a lack of sophistication about the traditions of that law. The economic barriers to social justice are a heavy burden on the middle and lower classes. We can do better. We should.

17. Militarism, National Security, and a New Foreign Policy

The spirit of nationalism rose as the Berlin Wall fell. Eastern Europeans no longer have a scapegoat. Now they are rediscovering why they hate each other. The former Soviet Union, the Baltic states, and Eastern Europe are groping their way to new directions. Saddam Hussein still hopes to lead Islam to a final resolution of the Israel problem. War breaks out frequently. However, American national defense is a too-expensive charade carried out by using a public relations scam called threats to our national security. Can U.S. voters seize the day and gain control of the nation's military industrial establishment?

The warrior-hunter has always laid honorable claim to human emotions. The warrior-hero has been celebrated by virtually all known cultures for his individual courage and for the collective glory he or she made possible for the nation. The respect and awe that the average man holds for the warrior-hero finds its origin in prehistory with a continuity extending to today. Through the centuries popes, kings, and generals have used the emotions of love and fear to encourage or command allegiance, loyalty, and service. The adrenalin rush of fear is a shock to the human system that can cause superhuman heroic feats or panic and flight. Primitive fear has been diluted by civilizing acculturation. In centuries past, warrior kings such as Charlemagne sallied forth from their castles into the lawless countryside to bring a priceless treasure—peace and order—to their lands. The warrior king battled for every man, his glory arose out of the symbolism that his killing was done in the service of his people, and often it was. That symbolic torch of the warrior-king has been passed down hand-to-hand through history to the modern military of the world. Today, they still strive for veneration and respect. They preserve the myth so they will gain support. They allege they are the defenders of the national security. Moreover, they now bolster this claim by asserting they are a primary provider of jobs. For Americans, this pornographic propaganda has sullied the American creed and misrepresented our national purpose to the rest of the world.

The U.S. Defense Department's budget reputedly produces jobs throughout the country. Little thought is given that those jobs could arise from employment in producing goods and services that would be useful, such as manufactured housing, water and sewerage systems, bridges, and crime prevention. Slowly our good sense may be overcoming our fears. It is an uncomfortable prospect for many of our leaders. In July 1988 McGraw-Hill's *Business Week* trumpeted the most recent defense scandal—saying that nothing seems to change—and called upon the nation to "throw the book at the defense bid riggers." The United States is confronted with a large internal mini-state—the military-industrial complex—that is really just a subsidized economy. Democratic capitalism no longer diffuses the economic power of the arms makers and their sycophants in the Pentagon. That power is centered too much in the form of state-military capitalism at the Pentagon. It has all the power of the robber barons' trusts. It is "state capitalism"—a partnership of the Pentagon and the military contractors, a shared monopoly of the worst kind. According to Ruth Leger Sivard, at present levels of world spending the average individual can expect to give up three to four years of his or her life to support the military. The military of the twentieth century has succeeded in setting up a worldwide shogunate. It is a Bushido Empire for twentieth-century samurai that functions in the same way as in ancient Japan. Gen. Douglas MacArthur, in a speech to the American Legion in 1955, outlined his thoughts about world peace:

> War has become a Frankenstein to destroy both sides. No longer is it the weapon of adventure whereby a short cut to international power and wealth—a place in the sun—can be gained. If you lose you are annihilated. If you win, you stand only to lose. . . . Science has clearly outmoded it as a feasible arbiter. The great question is, Can war be outlawed? If so it would mark the greatest advance since the Sermon on the Mount. It would lift at one stroke the darkest shadow that has engulfed mankind from the beginning. It would not only remove fear and bring security, it would not only create new moral and spiritual values, it would produce an economic wave of prosperity that would raise the world's standard of living beyond anything ever dreamed of by man.

This chapter investigates why we are acting as though this great military general never said those fateful words to our nation's veterans. Why does our constitutional culture use its war-making power in ways that misrepresent us to the world today as a worshiper of Mars, the god of war? We need to return to the original intent of our founding fathers concerning standing armies and making war.

In an early draft of the Constitution, Congress was empowered to "make war." Others suggested that the power should better be vested in the president alone, in the Senate alone, or in the president and the Senate. Finally, the sentiment of the convention was that the "making of war"—the calling up of the army—was to be by the concurrence of the president and both houses of Congress. This was in contrast to the English system. The framers of the Constitution did not want the wealth and blood of the nation committed by the decisions of a single individual. Madison and Elbridge Gerry jointly introduced an amendment as a substitute. The president as commander-in-chief should have the power to repel sudden attacks. The Constitution makers clearly wished for the conduct of war to be vested exclusively in the hands of the president of the United States. The war power was clearly not a power of the various states. The war power resulted from the investment in the federal government of the powers of external sovereignty and did not depend upon the affirmative grants of the Constitution. The power to declare and wage war, to conclude peace, to make treaties, to maintain diplomatic relations with other sovereignties, if they had not been mentioned in the Constitution, would have been vested in the federal government as necessary concomitants of the creation of a nation state.

As noted, the English system endowed its king with the power not only to initiate war, but to raise and maintain armies and navies. These powers had been abused to the detriment of the liberties and well-being of Englishmen. To this end, the English Declaration of Rights of 1688 insisted that the standing armies could be maintained only with the consent of Parliament. Being aware of this, the framers of the Constitution vested these basic powers in Congress.[1] The framers made it unequivocal. The federal government was to be supreme in the sole exercise of the war-making power. No state was permitted without consent of Congress to engage in war unless invaded, or unless such invasion was imminent.[2] On the other hand, a well-regulated militia was perceived as necessary to the security of a free state.[3] No state was permitted to keep troops or ships of war in time of peace. Congress's power to call out the militia, to execute laws, to suppress insurrection, and to repel invasions was not shared with the states.[4] The former USSR's new republics would do well to grasp these separation principles.

The main focus of this study is to consider how we can improve our American cities and the environment of the American people. Therefore, this discussion on the military is without hostility or rancor. Nevertheless, it is my view that the orgy of spending on the military has weakened our constitutional culture. Ronald Reagan's military budgets were so excessive that it would be unfair to the military to use those costs for the basis of discussion. Sadly, the American population has become inured to a complacent acceptance of their defense establishment. The size of the Defense Department expenditures boggles the mind if seriously contemplated. For example, if only five B-2 bombers were canceled, the dollars saved would be an amount far greater than all funds authorized to maintain and manage the U.S. Congress and the federal judiciary. Why does our free press attack sensible pay raises for our Congress and the federal judiciary? Still, the American newspapers give more bold headlines to an attempt of Congress to do a "catchup" of their salaries with inflation, than they do to the waste of money on unnecessary, too elaborate, and, in some cases, inefficient weapons such as the Sgt. York artillery gun.

Atlantic magazine declared, "We waste a third of our weapons budget. Our nuclear strategy no longer makes sense. Our subsidy to NATO is a care package to the rich. And we're about to embark on a build-down that will hollow out the forces we've built up."[5]

The Center for Defense Information has repeatedly emphasized the appalling waste of the taxpayers funds carried out annually by Defense Department procurement officers in sweetheart relationships with defense contractors. The gist of these many reports is that we could spend each year about 20 to 30 percent less on national security. We would still have superior first-strike capabilities, second-strike capabilities, a balance of terror, and the capacity to win a conventional war if we would spend our funds intelligently. The frills and baubles, bells and whistles are an immense waste of resources that could have been used on our metroarea infrastructures. Instead, we have a failure of adequate maintenance throughout our nation.

Thankfully, we have a few whistle blowers who have made us aware of our folly. Adm. Gene La Rocque, A. Earnest Fitzgerald, Sen. Charles Grassley, Sen.

William Proxmire, Dina Rasor, and Ruth Leger Sivard are all public-spirited citizens who have been unwilling to tolerate the astounding waste of the military and the defense contractors. Norman Cousins in his book *The Pathology of Power* provided a detailed factual account of the excellent work done by these leading watchful Americans.[6] I know there are many patriotic military personnel who are opposed to these excessive expenditures, duplications, unnecessary redundancies, and unwise policies. However, as Sen. Grassley found when he tried to interview Franklin C. Spinney, a cost analyst with the Pentagon, the department made every effort to prevent what Spinney knew from becoming known to the public. As Norman Cousins says, these fine, brilliant Americans have shown that curing the ills of the military-industrial establishment is not beyond public reach and correction.

What we need is a public that will pressure its Congress and the Defense Department to get less elaborate, better weapons at the best price. This requires the kind of competition associated with democratic capitalism. By reducing the budget of the CIA and the Defense Department we could move toward fiscal responsibility and a reordering of our priorities in federal expenditures and revenues. The slush fund attributed to wasteful practices is difficult to estimate because of secrecy maintained in the name of national security. It is fair to set it at no less than $20 billion to $30 billion. My personal guess is that we should attribute $40 billion to $80 billion to various kinds of wasteful practices. Another $20 billion to $30 billion a year could go far to lessen some of the serious problems of our large urban centers. It would provide significant funding to ameliorate our pollution of the air and water.

The truth is, defense expenditures are not necessary to our gross national product, or for making jobs. The American Friends Service Committee, a Quaker organization, has determined that defense is a very inefficient producer of jobs.

Jobs per Billion Dollars of Federal Expenditure, 1980

Teachers	52,000
Health, sanitation, and welfare	46,000
Housing	36,000
B-1 bomber at peak production	22,000

The B-1 and B-2 bombers have now been effectively killed in Congress, along with a number of other arms programs. Do we have enough mature autonomous personalities for our constitutional culture and democratic capitalism to win? The fleeting popularity of Ollie North suggests the issue is in doubt. The roar of approval of Gen. Norman Scwhartzkopf suggests we may already have a captive public—Hannah Arendt's mob of happy fascists successfully manipulated by the power elite who abuse our system. Our founding fathers made it unmistakable that this nation was to have no large standing army in peacetime. Military appropriations to the army were to be placed under strict legislative control, limited by review every two years. We have since World War II circumvented that severe limitation in the name of long-term research and development necessary to bring sophisticated weaponry into mass production. We need to return the reins to control appropriations to our U.S. Congress to put a leash on the junkyard dogs we have created. This requires the American people to elect the right kind of representatives. The power is in the

Constitution, waiting to be reasserted.

Since the Cold War is over in Asia, it is time to bring the U.S. troops in Japan home. We spend $9 billion every year supporting our soldiers and dependents in Japan. Japan pays nothing to the U.S. treasury for this service. Japan maintains one of the world's most powerful military forces and is the third-largest military spender. The Center for Defense Information has proposed a new military budget for a new world. Over half of U.S. military spending is devoted to preparing for war in Europe, the prospect of which has essentially disappeared. Desert Storm proved we can make war for profit, but making the world safe for feudalism in Kuwait is a disappointment. After the military control of the press ended, Americans saw that the Sab'ah regime had no respect for due process and individual rights. American citizens must aggressively support their Congress if we are to gain control of the military and its contractors. The United Nations could, if nurtured, provide an attractive alternative to unilateral U.S. intervention. According to the Center for Defense Information, we could reduce military spending from $286 billion to $200 billion in 1995 while still fulfilling all our essential military requirements.[7]

Gen. MacArthur said that war had changed in significant ways. It is archaic. Today the destruction produced by war is such that war can be neither won nor lost. Thus wars for gaining more territory or economic power are nonsensical. Unfortunately, the mass media is far behind modern reality in explaining the nature of modern war to the masses. Success or failure in war today is in the hands of mathematicians and scientists. Civilians will be the powerful ones who end future wars, not generals, admirals, or the fighting man. This is illustrated by the revelations of F. W. Winterbotham, the chief of the British Secret Service in World War II. The seed bed of fascism is nurtured when movies such as *Midway* and *D-Day* reiterate the tale of overrated brilliance of military figures such as Adm. Chester Nimitz in the face of revisionist history. The truth is now provided by the release of classified materials such as Winterbotham's book *The Ultra Secret*.[8]

Nine Reasons War No Longer Works

Currency counterfeiting (including even holographic currency). Today, any large industrial nation could in time of war produce bales of the paper money of the opposing belligerent, "dirty them up a bit," then deliver them to the other nation through clandestine operations or like manna, from the sky. This would create financial chaos in the economy of the enemy through hyperinflation. This was contemplated in World War II and in the Vietnam War but rejected as "unfair" or "sinful" or some such claptrap of the propertied class. They were horrified by the idea.

Cryptography. The microcomputer has enabled computer wizards known as "hackers" to use telecommunications to break through top-secret security and "read" the data retrieval banks of the military. These hackers are often in some upper-class residential bedroom![9] In peacetime the military keeps this under control by preventing the patenting of cryptographic analyzing programs. It is a crime to gain access to such files. In time of war the military would have no successful defense against these electronic guerrilla tactics. The military has also failed to stop the KGB and Israel from buying important military secrets. Consider the cases of Kim Philby, Klaus Fuchs, Anthony Burgess, and the Walker family, people who committed heinous acts of treason by selling our military secrets for money during war and peace. Or worse, consider what our friends Japan and Norway did. They recently destroyed an extremely critical advantage held by U.S. submarines over their Soviet counterparts. They enabled the Soviets to quiet their submarines to similar levels. Toshiba has taken out full-page advertisements in newspapers such as the *Wall Street Journal* apologizing for this extraordinary breach of secret protocols for the sake of profits over ethics. Think of what would happen in time of war![10]

Microwave disabling tactics. Computers and telecommunicating technology are highly dependent on the microprocessing chips, optic fibers, ferrous oxides, and other technologies that transmit and store information. Now add an atomic device—discharged in the lower atmosphere—that would do no surface damage and thus be "humane." It would discharge an "electromagnetic wave shower" that would knock out military, industrial, and civilian capabilities to communicate over a wide area via radiation effects on computers, telephone switching, microprocessor chips, coaxial cables, and the like. Thus modern warfare could not be conducted. The military has already spent over $400 million trying to develop components that would not be affected by radiation.

Occupation costs. Let us suppose that somehow one superpower or the other survives a nuclear holocaust or that we agree to a builddown so we can revert to conventional war without nuclear bombs, nerve gas, poison gas, our other horrors we seldom contemplate. It now appears virtually inconceivable that any superpower could afford the costs of occupying a loser after the conquest. Imagine the size of the former Soviet Union, China, Brazil, and the United States. How many soldiers of occupation would be necessary to keep the conquered people of such countries docile? Twenty million Soviets died trying to rid themselves of the Nazis in their "Great Patriotic War." We have been conned by the military. American families would not tolerate having, say, thirty million of their young men and women acting as occupation soldiers in the former Soviet Union. It would take sixty million men and women to occupy China. A whole generation of hopes and dreams would be lost to playing the part of a cop in a dangerous, hostile environment. It would not be acceptable. Nor do I believe the Russians, Chinese, or Brazilians could persuade their civilian population that this would be a worthwhile use of their lives. War for territorial expansion or subjugation of the conquered people is impractical and politically unacceptable for most peoples.

Fire bombing. Dresden, Yokohama, Hamburg, and Tokyo can attest to the terrible total destruction of this form of "conventional" warfare. The rain of phosphorous bombs causes fires everywhere. Fire is so widespread that it uses up the local oxygen and the population dies in the bomb shelters from asphyxiation. The military must find it strange that those who oppose nuclear warfare apparently do not object to this weapon. It is total war. Ironically, despite the hundreds of thousands of deaths caused by fire bombing, it has had virtually no effect on the war-making capacity of those so attacked. Fire bombing is a clear example of how ineffective war has become in achieving its aims despite its great firepower.

A world power grid. The use of electrical power and the need for building power utility capacity to handle peak demand has made it painfully obvious that we should carry out Buckminster Fuller's dream. We should interconnect the world's electrical utility plants to take advantage of the "day" and "night" phenomena to decrease the capital we must spend to meet the electrical energy needs of an increasing population. Energy could be much lower in cost if we would adopt this worldwide strategy. This is painfully obvious. Why do not we do it? Does the military mind fear it? With such a worldwide power grid in place we could no longer tolerate a nation's willingness to turn to war to solve a problem. War would be such a madness that other forms of conflict resolution would be chosen.

Biological and chemical warfare. The only reason these weapons have not been used is the difficulty of controlling the cloud of death. Some say it is only ethics that has prevented its use (let us now pause and meditate).

Satellite propaganda. Hate grows from disinformation. Our world leaders do not understand this as well as Ted Turner of Cable News Network. True, we witnessed with wonder as the world's leading democracy managed and controlled the news media at the warfront during the war in the Persian Gulf. Yet we are well aware that the news blackout games primarily kept only the American population uninformed. Sovereigns no longer have control over the flow of information or disinformation that can be communicated to their public in time of war. Space station satellites communicate to every nook and cranny of any country. Fax machines are also beyond central control. It would be difficult to maintain regular work days in face of what could be done to telecommunicating facilities.

The cruise missile. A small, pilotless jet with a nuclear warhead capable of traveling 2,500 miles and landing within forty yards of its chosen target—this is a weapon of mass destruction that allows no conceivable means of defense. It is a versatile weapon that the American generals do not want to surrender. The French-built Exocet sank the HMS *Excalibur* warship during the Falklands War, and the Iraqis badly damaged the USS *Stark* with the same device. These are the handwritings on the wall. Aircraft carriers, office buildings, oil refineries, regional shopping centers, our nation's capital, and nuclear power plants are targets that cannot avoid the available technology. The possibilities for sabotage in the next war are mind-boggling. The security precautions taken to prevent such action have been routinely and successfully breached by tests of friendly adversaries. Fortunately, we are using diplomacy to try to remove these weapons from our arsenals. Unfortunately France, Israel, Brazil, and other sophisticated arms makers are unwilling to be a part of these negotiations. They enjoy the obscene profits of arms sales!

I have intentionally eliminated from the list the unthinkable use of hydrogen bombs and plutonium radiation poisoning. Everyone knows that no rational human mind would press the "red" button. Still, we also know it is not beyond imagination that some sociopathic human being would perform that "fantasy" for the powerful thrill of that final night of terror. Arthur Kopit's successful Broadway drama, *End of the World,* has presented that terrible reality very well.

The military industrial establishment is well aware that too much money is being allocated to its ends. The question arises: why does the military state demand more than its share of the pie? Is it to coddle the favored child—happy fascism? We should be involved in multilateral international cooperation projects rather than alliances for armament. Why do we so eagerly, willingly, fearfully support war? Does the human brain have an addictive need for it? It is doubtful. Males seem to be aggressive and some are prone to violence, but on a personal level we seem able to substitute games and competitive behavior for death-dealing aggression. Why not on a social level? Does American fascism corrode our constitutional culture? This question is more fully explored in Wilhelm Reich's *The Mass Psychology of Fascism*. Reich's experiences as a psychiatrist with people of various classes, races, nationalities and religions taught him that,

> "Fascism" is actually the organized political expression of [a] structure [within] the average man's character, a structure that is confined neither to certain races or nations nor to certain parties, but is general and international. Viewed with respect to man's character, "fascism" is the basic emotional attitude of the suppressed man of our authoritarian machine civilizations and mystical conception of life.

Reich found there is not a single individual who does not bear elements of fascist feelings and thinking within his character structure. As a political movement, fascism differs from other reactionary movements inasmuch as it is born and championed by the masses. A sharp distinction must be made between ordinary militarism and fascism. The German Kaiser Wilhelm regime was militaristic, but it was not fascistic. It appears that the Chinese leadership of the 1980s is fascistic. The nature of authoritarian military classes is that fascist personalities are more likely to rise to the top. Persons with compulsive sadistic and self-aggrandizing mannerisms are more compatible with authoritarianism than with cooperation.

Fascism is not the act of a Hitler, Stalin, or Joseph McCarthy, alone. It is an alliance, the expression of the irrational alliances of mass man. The key to fascism is not the leader's personality, but that of the followers. The fascist mentality is keyed to the mentality of the unimportant person, enslaved and at the same time rebellious. He craves adulation of authority. It is natural for the industrial leader and the feudalistic militarist to exploit this social fact for his own power purposes. It evolves within the framework of a general suppression of natural life impulses. The result is that in any society there is always the potential for fascism. It forms as a mass response and creates an authoritarian civilization. The "little man," such as Hitler, succeeds by studying the mannerisms of a noble statesman's behavior and reproducing it in a distorted and grotesque fashion.

The United States has drifted toward the creation of a permanent military class with a large military industrial machine. Is it not ominous—and insane—that we are so quick to identify and point out the external enemy while ignoring the one within? Such behavior was to be expected within fascistic communism, with its oligarchic *nomenklatura*. However, we, too, have found it workable to sustain the "evil" empire—yesterday the former Soviet Union, today Saddam Hussein—and to at the same time support dictatorships of a fascistic nature in South America.

Reich held that love, work, and knowledge are the wellsprings of human life. He believed they should also govern it. Therefore, we should take some comfort that most American military leaders are raised within an environment where traditions of American political ideology contribute to the development of their character. A ripe field for social research would be an investigation of the progeny of the southern military families who have sent successive generations of sons to the nation's various military academies. Pat Conroy's books, *The Great Santini* and *The Lords of Discipline* have served us well in warning of this growing military caste. It is reasonable to guess that these military "brats" were raised in authoritarian, repressive households. Some no doubt escaped and became doctors, lawyers, and other professional people. It is probable that the child who most readily accepted the repressive training became the anointed one, chosen for carrying on the family name at the service academy. We are fortunate Pat Conroy escaped.

In 1990, the military-industrial establishment is like the "robber barons" of the antitrust days of the 1890s. I have used the term "military-industrial complex" as shorthand for one kind of concentration of economic power. It is contrary to the spirit of democratic capitalism and is overwhelming our constitutional culture. In the late nineteenth century this nation saw a wave of merger and consolidation in most industries. One "robber baron" after another sought the businessman's dream of a monopoly over the production or transportation of goods and services. The Harrimans, the Rockefellers, the Goulds, the Morgans, and many others sought to create the steel, oil, railroad, and sugar trusts. Finally the American public had enough of laissez faire economics and the Sherman Antitrust Act began a few decades of trust-busting. The act found its full flower in the 1912 decision by Judge Kennesaw Mountain Landis to break up the Standard Oil monopoly and establish new rules for the game of democratic capitalism.

The rise of militarism in the United States has created an especially dangerous form of oligopoly. The military-industrial establishment does not have to use corruption and bribery to influence legislation. The "fox is in the hen house." The Defense Department cooperates and orchestrates for the oligopoly. It demands first claim on our national resources. It is exempted from the effects of inflation, all in the name of national security, "so we can all sleep at night." An early-1980s report by the *Wall Street Journal* based on internal Pentagon documents is sobering: "Despite more than $600 billion in defense spending during the first three years of the Reagan administration, military-unit combat readiness has declined significantly."[11] We need more spare parts, not more ponderous, gizmo-embellished Tonka toys and Transformers for adults to play with.

Policy Options

Society is suffering from poor economic performance in the defense sector. Keep in mind that independent citizens such as the Boston Study Group have already observed that a sane strategy for military spending is feasible at reasonable costs. They have shown us a complete program for a safer, more efficient defense establishment. What are the public-policy options?

Outright nationalization of major defense contractors is one option. Indeed, this would be a minor step, except for the hypocritical hot rhetoric about interfering with "free enterprise." This is because of the current concentrated structure and absence of competitive conduct in the defense sector.[12] Second, giant defense contractors might be regulated by a kind of public utility commission independent of the Pentagon. However, experience with airlines, trucking companies, and nuclear power utilities teaches us that regulatory agencies are prone to be captured by those they are supposed to oversee. Third, a policy of effective competition can be adopted. Here the overarching principle would be that the government act like any rational buyer by contracting in a manner calculated to secure a maximum number of options and alternative sources of supply at all stages of the weapons acquisition process. Competition would take advantage of the bimodal nature of our economy. For entrepreneurs in the smaller firms the gains could be large. Knowledgeable analysts variously calculate that effective competition could reduce weapons costs by 50 percent or more.[13] This would neutralize monopoly power by setting one private interest against another, channeling them into the more socially beneficial avenues of reducing costs and prices and advancing productivity and innovation.

Competition would prevent society from being dependent upon, and thus susceptible to capture by, a handful of corporate giants. Implementing the competitive approach to weapons procurement would not be easy. Nevertheless, as we are now discovering, the public interest in reducing the costs of defense may permit no other choice. We are "gold plating" defense while starving other public sectors. We are avoiding social responsibilities for market failures such as the homeless while wasting taxpayers funds.

According to *Washington Watch*,[14] a defense production chief with experience extending back to World War II put it this way:

> Why go through the charade that Lockheed, Grumman, Northrop, and all the other major suppliers are "private enterprise" when they are dependent on the government and taxpayers for most of their working capital, most of their plants and equipment and most of their sales? . . . Why go through the padding process of six figure "private enterprise" managers with their unlimited expense accounts, slush funds, hunting lodges, country clubs and other corporate prerequisites? Why go through the risk of foreign bribers and middlemen payoffs to help sales abroad when you could have the full and above-board leverage of the United States government to encourage those sales only when they serve our foreign policy lines? . . . Give me a dozen really patriotic $56,000-a-year government managers, like Ernie Fitzgerald [the C-5A transport plane whistleblower] and I'll show you how effectively and efficiently a military supplier can be run in the interests of both national defense and the taxpayer's pocketbook.

The balance of terror—mutually assured destruction—has prevented a global World War III. There is considerable historical evidence to support this awful deterrent thesis. A nuclear bomb did not prevent Korea and Vietnam, but the threat of nuclear escalation kept both from spreading into world conflict. Any number of lesser conflicts and events such as the Berlin blockade, the Hungarian and Czech uprisings, the *Pueblo* incident, the invasion of Afghanistan, the attack on the *Stark,* the Falklands War, the eternal struggle between Israel, Syria, and Lebanon, and countless outrages against American persons, property, and government installations abroad have been contained to prevent the triggering of a cataclysmic chain reaction.

Is it possible that only the very believable threats of the nuclear bomb and the possible extinction of civilization have prevented the wider employment of such horrible devices? Both Russian and American military strategies contend that nuclear weapons have rendered obsolete extended wars involving massed national armies. It may not seem much of a hope, but this pacifist would prefer that a peaceful nation such as the United States remain resolute in its clear intention to use nuclear warfare. We forbid penetration of our stated and disclosed lines of defense by a belligerent who threatens our continued existence. Israel is doing just that today.

South Africa is said to be following that lead and Pakistan is soon to follow.

We have reached the point in history where the United States should withdraw from the network of military alliances it has with ninety-some nations. We should terminate the dispersal of American troops throughout the world. We need no huge standing army at home. A large, highly skilled, air-capable, Marine-type strike force is probably necessary to protect our naval bases. We should return to the plan of our founding fathers. We need to adopt the Swiss and Swedish models. Provide instead for state militias. We then would have a citizen army ready to defend our homeland. The same state militias could provide valuable public service workforces for public construction, rehabilitation of our cities, and improvement in water quality and air pollution controls. They could be disaster workforces in the event of floods. The Air Force could drop foam bombs on burning tankers to prevent pollution. This shift in policy could restore our belief in the honor of public service in our military.

We need a new foreign policy that promotes the ethos of the U.S. constitutional culture—human rights—and a better understanding of the spirit of democratic capitalism. President Carter sought to promote and maintain a difficult and delicate balance. He sought arms control and nonproliferation of nuclear weapons on the one hand while on the other pressing for human rights for all. President Carter's firm and open stand on human rights may have reflected a too-visionary ideal for some nations, especially where the people are poorly educated. For example, consider Indonesia, where many tribal and primitive people are still dominated by minds that are magical and superstitious. We do not know if they are ready for exercising the attitudes of the Enlightenment that have long inspired the American people's respect for individual liberty. Ayatollah Khomeini raised a whole generation of religious zealots with twelfth-century minds. Nonetheless, promotion of human rights and the mind space in which human personalities grow and thrive in an atmosphere of freedom and liberty is certainly less dangerous for the world than the sorry illusion of Marxist-Leninist and Islamic dreams that can never come true.

Congress and the executive branch should proceed to debate openly, in a bipartisan way, the human rights issues in our foreign policy. We should not shy away from the idea of human rights standards, nor can we forget to apply them everywhere, including in the United States. We shouldn't forget what we have fought for, and what we live for.

National Security and a National Service Corps

We need to wind down the global war machine. The United States needs an aggressive foreign policy that promotes a global understanding of America's constitutional culture and the spirit of democratic capitalism. We should become an armed fortress domestically. We should change our foreign policy to adopt a very aggressive economic-aid program to foreign nations to replace our eighteenth-century diplomacy and arms merchandising. In its place we need to hard-sell the world on democratic capitalism and human rights. We should change the role of the United Nations, not abandon it. George Bush has done much to foster a peace-keeping role. The United States should propose adoption of our National Institute for Peace's program for teaching conflict resolution using futurist tools such as those proposed by the

World Future Society, Buckminster Fuller, and others. This is not neoisolationism; it is active involvement in the planet earth in a different way.

To convince our military of our sincere support of goals they cherish, we should enlist (or draft) youthful state militias. They would work in their home areas for a quality environment while training in military discipline and service. This service corps would be based on the work ethic and responsible personal conduct. It would be a domestic Peace Corps under the aegis of the military as a part of our state militias.

We should make a vast change. *We would seek a new era of multilateral co-operation on mega-engineering work projects of global significance.* It would be a tradeoff. New great "international cooperation peace projects" would be substituted for military aid and some foreign aid. We could sharply reduce loans for arms sales and military aid, increasing foreign aid to, say, 3 percent of U.S. gross national product in five years and more in later years. We would need large increases in foreign aid and loans by Japan, West Germany, and other hard-currency countries because of our own debt status.

We need to make a paradigm shift. It is the only way to break away from our failed bipartisan policies and find new direction. We need new world leadership that is more appropriate to ecological man on Spaceship Earth. This proposed national policy is proactive and coupled with a new foreign policy. It is based on the idea of mutually cooperative action. The wary nations in the jungle of foreign relations are aware of the high value that ought to be placed on peaceful coexistence. The sovereign nations are fearful of each other and have conflicting ideologies.

All the goals described could be done to celebrate the year 2000. The millennium could be a threshold to a new world peace. The earth's autonomous sovereign nations could be promoting local cultural heritage. Our world's cities could be centers of friendly competitive cooperation toward building mature humans who can cope with their problems of personal growth. American metroareas can be good models of how cities can work toward good physical and mental health while reducing stress on our fellow humans. However, we cannot get there without facing the overarching problem of our woefully ineffective and inappropriate foreign policies. They dominate our lives today.

According to Ruth Slivard's famous annual reports, "World Military and Social Expenditures," the world's military expenditures grew from $344 billion in 1960 to over $770 billion in 1985 (measured in constant dollars). Desert Storm did not reduce this. The real burden on the world economy has grown by 37 percent.[15] Arms sales to the impoverished LDCs is big business. It has increased faster than the ability of their economies to support it.

Consider the French arms trade. The archbishop of Paris, Francois Cardinal Marty, has said that the French arms export is a "commerce of death." He said the arms industry should be converted to the manufacture of other goods. He called the French arms-selling policy a "collective hypocrisy." In a nationwide television program, the courageous cardinal said, "France justly defends peace. She has no enemies, but through an economic necessity that is poorly understood, France allows herself to fix her balance of payments by developing this commerce in deadly weapons. In view of our present social problems, there are only a few who raise their voices against this." Prime Minister Jacques Chirac replied for the government, "The sales provide jobs for many workers, which is particularly helpful in the present period of unemployment." France is the second-largest arms merchant in the world, after the United States. Brazil and China are close behind.

Armed to the Teeth for Peace

In a speech to the Chicago World Affairs Council made during his drive for the 1976 nomination, President Carter may have said it best:

> Every time we have made a serious mistake in recent years in our dealings with other nations, the American people have been excluded from the process of evolving and consummating our foreign policy. Unnecessary secrecy surrounds the inner workings of government and we have sometimes been deliberately misled by our leaders. . . . Every successful foreign policy we have had—whether it was the Good Neighborhood Policy of Franklin Roosevelt, the Four-Point Plan of President Truman, or the Peace Corps and Trade Reform of President Kennedy—was successful because it reflected the best that was in us.

Americans take pride in the great open covenants of the post–World War II era such as the NATO treaty and the Marshall Plan. Could it be they are still a matter of national pride, in part, because of the open public and congressional dialogue at the time of adoption?

A Different Foreign Policy

The U.S. State Department's foreign policy is based on aping European diplomatic traditions. State simply does not trust the judgment of the American people. Under the brilliant leadership of Henry Kissinger, a great nineteenth-century diplomat, the department preferred to conduct foreign policy in a secret and personal fashion. Kissinger was current secretary James Baker's tutor. Both Baker and Bush truly believe in the nineteenth-century ideals of diplomacy, hegemony, and balance of power. These stratagems continue to be useful and viable as the self-fulfilling action of the world's lonely superpower.

Somehow Americans must come to realize that America's greatness is based not on the power of its physical resources and technological prowess alone, but on the attitudes and ideals of its citizens. America made its place in history not by Scott's march on Mexico City, but by the Monroe Doctrine; not by the Crusade for Europe, but by the new government we helped establish in Western Germany, the common-sense generosity of the Marshall Plan, and our moral stance in imposing the antitrust laws on Japan's and Germany's famous cartels. Secret action is at the root of one failure after another: Vietnam, Cambodia, Laos, Chile, Iran, Angola, Nicaragua, and, earlier, the Bay of Pigs disaster and the invasion of the Dominican Republic. Throughout this time we have engaged in stealthy, expensive violence and "disinformation" (translation: lies), desecrations of our creed.

There is a critical but limited role for State Department–style diplomacy in the modern world. Intelligent fear of totalitarian governments is part of the price of eternal vigilance. It may be, as Robert Heilbroner suggests, in the light of increasing scarcities of energy and materials and the pressures of rising conflict, that the wave of the future is tyrannical, centrally planned societies. As the world's developing countries face soaring population and pyramiding urban densities, many will opt for the thralldom of highly centralized bureaucratic power, even if they choose market-oriented economies.

First question: Can America prevent the next war? Second question: Can America win the next war? Preventing the war would make the question of winning it moot. Preventing the next war may be the last chance for mankind. I am ignoring for now the use of war as diplomacy, a la Desert Storm, the war to make the world safe for feudalism in Kuwait. Preventing the next war means much more than maintaining military strength, important as that may be. It means excelling politically, socially, and economically. It is time to realize that war with Russia was not the real danger Americans faced in the very long run. In August 1985, Javier Perez de Cuellar, then the United Nations secretary general, warned the United States and other nations that the additional billion in population expected within the next twelve years faced the world with a food crisis worse than anything before. In the capital city of de Cuellar's home country, Lima, Peru, over nine million in population, millions of them homeless squatters, have become a symbol of a world descending into degradation. "The developed countries were asked to put aside 1 percent of their gross national products," to solve the problems of underdevelopment, de Cuellar said. "But the average has been 0.3 percent." The U.N. leader added that, by contrast, the oil-producing nations are giving an average of 2.6 percent of their GNPs. The short-term outlook for food is encouraging. The long-term trends in the food production in developing countries remain alarmingly inadequate.

The citizens of the United States of America did not share in many of the fundamental experiences that predominated the formative years of the foreign affairs of most Western nations. Our foreign policy arises from a constitutional culture, not the imperialism of royal families. The United States never experienced feudalism and the rise of the city states. The centuries of struggle in Europe over the birth of nationhood, the dilution of ecclesiastical power, and the growth of the merchant class, were not part of our political history. We are lacking a sense of proportionality, a balanced world view. It has taken the "cold war," nuclear fusion, and long-range air-delivery systems of the twentieth century to make us feel danger. Neither Canada or Mexico pose a credible threat even to the most paranoid. The American in-experience with danger has given us a lack of sense of proportion. In the words of Bayless Manning:

> When a hawk does fly over, or is reported to fly over, the American henhouse goes wild. A nation oversecure will banish to concentration camps thousands of its best citizens at the rumor of a Japanese submarine off the California coast. Europeans who have lived for millennia with a clear view of the armor glinting in the campfires of the enemy just across the border have never understood the American reaction to Russians in Cuba; Khrushchev also misestimated it and nearly precipitated World War III.

Another basic difference between U.S. and European traditions is the generalized humanitarian impulse that has been an integral part of our foreign relations. There is little to be found in the foreign affairs history of European countries of this impulse. It would be in our national interest to agree to the "Five Principles of Peaceful Coexistence" derived from Zhou Enlai's life work. These principles guide China's foreign diplomacy to this day, even though its takeover of Tibet and the massacre at Tiananmen Square in June 1989 cannot be reconciled with them. Still, the principles seem better than a new world order based on unilateral assertion of American interests and values for the world. The principles of Bush's "New World Order" are peaceful settlement of disputes, solidarity against aggression, reduced and controlled arsenals, and just treatment of all peoples. This a reactive role for the United States. The list omits the values of self-determination (Wilson), freedom (FDR, Truman, Kennedy), human rights (Carter), and democracy and democratic revolution (Reagan). Bush did invoke justice in his decision to retake Kuwait, but last and least. As Charles Krauthammer states, "For Bush, the new world order is principally about order."[16]

Five Principles of Peaceful Coexistence

The five principles of peaceful coexistence form an inseparable whole. The first four are: mutual respect for sovereignty and territorial integrity, nonaggression, noninterference in others' internal affairs, and equality and mutual benefit in actions. Together, they all yield the fifth principle—peaceful coexistence.

China wrote these principles into its constitution. China, as it sees itself, has not stationed a single soldier abroad, nor occupied a single inch of foreign land. It has not infringed on the sovereignty of another country or imposed an unequal relationship. We should argue whether Tibet belies this position. Recent arms sales by China are a covert conflict with these principles. Nonetheless, the United States would ennoble itself by following this pragmatic set of principles. The CIA would no longer interfere with Ecuador, Uruguay, Cuba, Chile, Iran, Mexico, and other countries. It would have less to do. Peaceful coexistence does not mean merely staying off one another's lawns. Every country adhering to these principles would not only refrain from invading another or interfering with each other's internal affairs; they should also actively promote mutual exchanges in various fields of arts, crafts, science and engineering, and growing economic cooperation on the basis of equality and mutual benefit. Until now, international economic cooperation has been seriously impeded by the irrationality of world geopolitics. The world is faced with two outstanding tasks—the safeguarding of world peace and the encouragement of development. As Han Nianlong of China's Institute of Foreign Affairs said in 1985, "To facilitate peaceful coexistence between all nations, China hopes to see the superpowers stop their arms race and to take steps to ease their relations. When two elephants fight, the grassland suffers."[17] The United States and what was the USSR are now taking a new stance. It is a an opportunity for innovative policymaking.

The spirit of humanitarianism dominates the world view of the average American's idea of a good foreign policy. Americans have a tradition of helping others. Herbert Hoover became a national celebrity when he headed a program to provide food to the starving new communist state in the early 1920s. This impulse, together with the tradition of voluntarism in American life, has over time poured billions of dollars and the energies of hundreds of thousands of Americans into every imaginable form of relief work. We have benefitted peoples in all regions of the world.

Our foreign policy ought to be an affirmation of our American creed. Every man and woman deserves to be his own master, has a right to express his or her attitudes, and should be able to develop his or her talents in competition with others.

Food Diplomacy

Lester R. Brown, director of World Watch Institute, reported that the world food trade pattern has been altered profoundly in recent decades. A generation ago, Western Europe was the most urbanized region. It was also the only importing region. The other continents were exporting grain in at least some quantity. Recently, that situation has changed beyond recognition. Virtually the entire world has come to depend on North American food exports. Asia, Africa, Latin America, Western Europe, and Eastern Europe, including the Soviet Union, are net grain importers. A great amount of the food imported into these regions is used to feed the cities. Much progress has been made in India, China, and Thailand. Argentina is showing great promise once again, but the immediate future is bleak. Analysis on a country-by-country basis shows that most of the world today consists of food-deficit countries. The remaining important food exporters can be numbered on the fingers of one hand. We are entering, again, a time of grave responsibility for nations such as the United States, Canada, Australia, New Zealand, and, hopefully, Argentina and Ukraine. The Soviet Union and Poland tried to anticipate future difficulty by gaining access to surplus food supplies. They negotiated long-term agreements that tend to ensure their access to North American grain supplies. We should trade, that is, barter, on a "needed commodity for needed commodity" basis only until the world has solved its competition of ideologies. The emerging situation creates an opportunity we should not miss—the politics of food—a type of food diplomacy.

The fossil fuels exploitation of the past hundred years has been an extraordinary social breakthrough that changed foreign relations. In 1847 we started the petroleum boom. The energy breakthrough permitted larger populations, even majorities, to be sustained in city life. It was the discovery of fossil fuels, initially coal and later oil and natural gas, that allowed this. Today, the cities of the LDCs are growing at an exceedingly rapid rate. By 1985, ten cities had surpassed New York's present ten million inhabitants. The results of this unprecedented, very rapid urbanization may be so horrendous that the urbanization trend may be slowed or reversed by pandemic epidemics from malnutrition and poor sanitation. Lester Brown believes that growth will slow because of the increasing scarcity of food, a shortage of energy for life-support services, and the lack of jobs. Government support, through international cooperation for rural development, could pay large dividends by helping farmers to produce more food instead of migrating to the overcrowded cities. Rapid urbanization characterized much of the world during the early twentieth century, but it occurred during an era of cheap energy. Now oil production has peaked in many major producing countries. Production declines in other countries will certainly follow. The end of the petroleum age is in sight.

The world must turn to other forms of energy. Until recently, many assumed the world would transit from the fossil-fuel era into the nuclear-power age. Twenty-five years of experience with nuclear power cause the earth's people to have very serious reservations. Failure to devise a satisfactory technique of waste disposal, unsolved problems of decommissioning the worn-out facilities, and the proliferation of nuclear weapons along with nuclear power (coupled with the terrible prospect of terrorist groups), have raised doubts in even the most sanguine of minds. Urban planners need to consider the possibility of a world that must move from a fossil-fuel era right through the so-called nuclear-power era and on towards growing reliance on solar energy. This would require a major change in foreign policy. The solar age will require international cooperation. As the world moves toward a solar age, international cooperation may become a necessity. It would free up capital to support the population because of the daily alternation of darkness and light. It calls forth Buckminster Fuller's dream of a worldwide power grid to take advantage of the availability of sunlight where it occurs, night and day. The potential of solar energy, and its related wind and ocean power, is great. We need to start a strong conservation-of-power ethic, now.

Fish protein is a resource that must be conserved and cropped, not exploited. It is another example of the greater need for multilateral, global cooperation. Japan harvests an estimated 15 percent or more of its catch within the two-hundred-mile zone off the United States's shores. It has an obvious need. The technology has been so improved that highly efficient foreign frozen fish fleets and whalers are exhausting some of the fish stocks off the United States coast as well as that of nations such as Mexico and Canada. Continued world negotiations—world cooperation, not threatening behavior—have paid off in reducing the whale killings. Hopefully, earth is slowly heading toward fish "cropping," instead of exploitation. It is the only way we can save this extremely critical protein source. In effect, the State Department's diplomatic skill will be essential to the world's peace. There is a need to spread international multilateral control that restricts national sovereignty.

There is a growing list of global-scale potential hazards to the environment and human health. They require an international role for every nation to control human conduct. Many nations have come to understand that control of chlorofluorocarbons to stop the degradation of ozone is essential. However, every nation must cooperate without exception for a ban to work. Americans would prefer the cooperation of ordinary business and social institutions for the solution of global regulatory problems. Who wouldn't? But, is there a choice? To preserve democratic capitalism we must be realistic in acknowledging that "market failures" do occur. Former President Handler of the National Academy of Science stated, "If you had a really adequate world monitoring system you wouldn't need to worry about an international environmental protection agency." The monitoring system would raise the warning flag when it saw problems. Then, let national government do the regulating? "What else can you do?" Mr. Handler asked, "Unless you are willing to have a worldwide military force, there is nothing to do but exert moral suasion."

A National Peace Institute

We should give the National Peace Institute cabinet status—embark on a proactive program of international cooperation on causes that ennoble the American spirit. The

State department can work on military alliances and for the business corporations, while the Peace Department would work on cooperative projects. There would be obvious turf problems, but much could be done to clarify our image by this clear separation of function. In the battle for the minds of humans, as we try to preserve a constitutional culture in the face of the drift toward fascism, cabinet status for the National Institute for Peace would be a major change in direction for the United States.

In September 1987, the board of the Institute for Peace demonstrated a cooperative spirit with the State Department by the appointment of former ambassador to Israel Samuel W. Lewis as its new executive director. Lewis believes that diplomats are not well-trained in negotiating techniques. The United States Institute for Peace arises out of a new culture of modern communications. It sees new techniques of conflict resolution as key elements in developing a peace-making orientation in international negotiations. Nonetheless, some congressional opposition tried to zero out the modest $5.3 million budget of the infant organization. The Peace Institute hopes that, in time, anyone running for office or serving in government will have to say that they have taken a course in peacemaking and peaceful conflict resolution.

Going beyond the present stance of the Institute for Peace, I propose an entirely new posture for our foreign relations, exciting possible projects for international cooperation. They call the world together on the year 2000 (Gregorian calendar) as a time for international cooperation. The examples are intentionally visionary, though hardly impractical.

The Brahmaputra-Tsangpo Hydro Project

The best potential hydroelectric power site in the world is at the border within Chinese Tibet, near Nepal on the Brahmaputra-Tsangpo River. It is at a hairpin turn in the Himalayas. Its potential exceeds the Grand Coolee and Hoover dams and a few others all put together. Hans Thirring has estimated that the hydroelectric power generated by the project could reach an annual 330 *billion* kilowatt hours! How? By carving a tunnel through the rock of the mountains! The thundering waters could drop about eight thousand feet in the course of only ten miles. The site is accessible only by constructing a railroad over the Himalayas, or, perhaps over land from the Szechwan area of China. The possibility of large helicopter transport of earthmoving equipment has not been investigated. At the time Richie Calder[18] proposed this dam, in the late 1950s, it seemed too arduous to most people. Today, we are drilling oil on the North Slope of Alaska and in the stormy North Sea for the same objective, new energy sources. The location calls for some super-international agency and multinational personnel staffing. Estimated costs for the Brhamaputra project are in the range of $65 billion to $80 billion.

The Nicaragua Trans-Ocean Sea Level Canal

This sea-level canal would produce immense energy savings. The Panama Canal would still be useful for smaller ships. It would enable the United States to maintain a smaller navy. Nicaragua was always the best location for the canal, but we didn't have the earthmoving equipment of today in 1900. Now is the time to build it to bind the wounds of Nicaragua and the United States. Japan wants to finance it.

Super Computer and Human Brain Parks

In 1967, Buckminster Fuller proposed that the United States build a "great logistics game" played by world leaders, researchers, students, and the public. His award-winning 250-foot-diameter geodesic dome was to house the game. A computer would store an inventory of the world's resources, human trends, needs, problems, and opportunities. The "Big Map" in the "Peace Room" would display these vital statistics in various ways for the public to see. Different teams of individuals from around the world would then use this database to develop and evaluate alternative strategies for solving world problems. What an opportunity for Japanese landscape planners, Brazilian architects, and Disney World people to join with the leaders of the computer world in turning out a "breakthrough" permanent world's fair. In Fuller's vision the first week might focus on food. The first team of individuals who showed how humanity might eliminate starvation and malnutrition using only known resources and existing technology would be declared the "winner" of round one. The next week the "World Game," as it might be called, would focus on energy. Illiteracy, health care, and housing would follow, and eventually food would come back for another round. Each round would seek a better way to solve the food problem given the positive and negative feedback of what had been learned from earlier rounds.

Traditional war games are based on assumptions of scarcity, the need to control scarce resources, and defeating the enemy. Conversely, the World Game is based on the pursuit of happiness—an economy of potential abundance, the possibility of solutions where everyone wins. In 1967, the U.S. Information Agency rejected the idea as too expensive. How many "War Rooms" have we built in the Hobbesian world of the military that are considerably more expensive?

Solar Energy From the Ocean

This project could be started promptly and achieved within the next ten years: the conversion of some of earth's ocean surface into a solar power source.[19] International cooperation on such a project would also work toward developing staff personnel who could work on the development of a twenty-four-hour worldwide power grid. Humans would take advantage of peak capacity in power-generating capacity of our utilities throughout the day—which always exists somewhere on earth—instead of the "night" and "day" limitations we have now. As Buckminister Fuller pointed out, this would make it very difficult for regional demagogues to rouse national enmity because of our global interdependence on each other. Dire predictions have been made of the effect of withdrawing heat from the ocean's waters on overall ocean and atmospheric climatics. We do not know if this project would affect plankton or change the migratory patterns of fish. The rights of passage of submarines under the project platforms and ships near them would have to be fleshed out. This visionary idea of the 1970s was shelved when oil prices dropped. We should go forward now with a test to find out if we can work out the engineering and ecological problems. A working alternative is a project for solar farms at desert locations. Luz International has a profitable, working solar farm in the Mojave Desert in California. Luz creates enough energy to provide power for 250,000 homes. Saudi Arabia is in the forefront of solar farm development.[20]

* * *

The planning, construction, administration, and maintenance of such extraterritorial projects is beyond the special competence of the State Department. A federal United States corporation such as the Tennessee Valley Authority or the Federal National Mortgage Association (FNMA) would be the appropriate organization to work with the Peace Department. With good humor, one might suggest the name "Great International Projects for Peace, Energy, and Renewal" (GIPPER). The United States must protect its national interests because the base of energy production and food production is shifting in the world. It would be unwise to continue depending upon the loyalty of such entities as the transnational corporations.

Recently a new organization called New Directions was conceived as an international counterpart of Common Cause, the public affairs lobby that has been active in election reform and numerous other domestic causes. Executive Director Russell W. Peterson explained,

> Our existing governmental machinery is so preoccupied with crisis of the moment that it is difficult for anyone to take a long view. Conversely, a lot of people outside of government are looking far ahead, but generally on an academic level that does not get any further than that. What we intend to do is provide a missing link between these two elements and get long-range thinking translated into political action now. . . . When you look ahead now, the unresolved problems are frightening. Energy resources, nuclear development, the population bomb, the arms race, the confrontation between the have and have not nations all are inexplicably tied to national policies. They are both national problems as well as international.

Problems do not stop at the waters edge of the United States. Food prices and energy prices are all tied directly to the ways in which these difficulties are handled. We can no longer separate our problems into "domestic" and "foreign."

Harland Cleveland has proposed some internationally accepted norms for a nation to use to adopt the "peace ethics." Using these ethics, each nation would be obligated to:

- Refrain from annexing its neighbor's territory.
- Protect the premises and person of diplomats accredited to it.
- Protect civilian air traffic, foreign or domestic, in its air space.
- Join with other nations for disaster relief and survival aid for refugees.
- Refrain from subjugating other peoples.
- Cooperate in protecting and enhancing the human environment.
- Treat its own people as human beings with rights.
- Recognizing international "common spaces" such as regional seas, deep ocean and seabeds, Antarctica, and outer space.

Furthermore, each nation would understand that the above are only the beginnings of international cooperation. A "Working Global Political Economy for Ecological Man" would include working toward:

- Better weather forecasting, control of infectious diseases, an international civil aviation regulatory body, radio wave frequency allocation, better use of outer space . . .
- Controlling multinational corporations both private and state-operated so they are beneficial to humanity in the long term.
- Improving efficient information flows through international utility networks for money exchanges, commodity markets, airlines reservations, and the coverage of news and sports.[21]

The floundering of the Law of the Sea Conference shows that greed and nationalism brings out the worst in people. The challenge to the State Department's diplomatic corps in handling the problems of negotiation are now and will continue to be exceptionally demanding. The potential for greed and corruption, in effect, the pornographic effects of power, call for an ethic of peaceful coexistence. The Hubert H. Humphrey Institute of Public Affairs has been and is a center for promoting such thinking.

Like the nouveau riche, the United States and Americans neither know what to do with our wealth or with ourselves. For example, in fiscal 1985 $1 billion of tax money could pay for say fourteen F-16 fighters, one attack sub, and one fleet oiler for the United States Navy.[22] It is sad to relate that $1 billion would also build 350 elementary schools, 100 playgrounds, 1,000 swimming pools, and 12,000 units of multifamily dwellings. All these good, long-lasting, useful things—for a total of $1 billion! But since 55 percent of the defense budget is devoted to personnel costs, we have a very serious political problem reducing it. Military staff has a vested interest in their salary, fringe benefit, and pension fund entitlements. It is an obvious conflict of interest. Who among the military and civil service has the courage and patriotism to admit that adjusting these future rights to fit reality is absolutely necessary?[23]

Our naive try for the Pax Americana must end. The Pax Britannica of the nineteenth century died with Britain's death struggle to prevent the spread of Nazism over the world. The United States then sought to bring a good-natured Pax Americana to the world. But the social turmoil of competing ideologies has proved to be beyond the capacity of an American "military policeman." A Pax Americana is a dangerous fantasy. We need a radically new global policy that is a response to the ecospasm and the rapid pace of change. Russia's military machine has discovered domestic problems that cannot be ignored. In the United States, the riots in our cities, housing shortages, poverty, crime, intense external urban stress, and other critical domestic problems have made glaringly clear that we have been guilty of maldistribution of our own resources. Priority must be granted to certain problems and, unfortunately, others must be deferred. The purpose here is to now set forth a possible workable plan for, say, the next ten to twenty years.

First, the United States should declare an end to our existing foreign policy. We should simultaneously offer a substitute that would require a separation of function and specialization of task for the State Department and a newly created Peace Department. It should be an obvious and dramatic change. We should develop a multilateral treaty of nations for peaceful cooperative development of the economic resources of all treaty nations that would be an alternative to military aid and military intervention. All this would be based on the five principles of peaceful coexistence and the ethics of peace. We must maintain a strong military posture. However, it would radically change. We would warn all nations that during the transition period war-making across national boundaries is absolutely unacceptable. It would result in the threat of an appropriate kind and level of nuclear retaliation on the part of the United States. The balance of terror shall be maintained as long as it is needed for the transition to a mutually beneficial policy of peaceful coexistence. Some of the details of such a military program are set forth below.

Second, the Congress would establish the Peace Department, which would develop, initiate, and administer programs for cooperation with friendly nations. We would substitute economic aid for the present military aid and sale of arms to any nation capable of maintaining peace and order. The economic aid would bear fruits of progress for that nation's people.

Third, all military alliance treaties would be honored only to the extent of providing materials and equipment for a transitional, five-year period. During this time, we would vigorously prosecute any American citizen involved directly or indirectly in arms sales.

Fourth, twelve months from the promulgation (or sooner by mutual agreement), we would phase out the presence of American troops on foreign soil, over a three-year period. There would be exceptions, such as our embassies, our military enclaves, and bases necessary for tracking stations, weather stations, strategic air command, and those bases necessary to provide naval material and fuel support.

Fifth, during and by the end of the five years, the member nations who participate in existing military alliances would either take over material and equipment responsibilities or meet with us for some mutually accepted alternative.

Sixth, the United States would declare its intent to continue and expand our Navy and the Marine Corps. This has already been accomplished to a large extent by the Reagan-Bush administrations.

Seventh, as long as the United Nations fails to maintain a peace-keeping force, the United States would make its military presence known throughout the world by way of friendly visitations. Our aircraft carriers, troop ships, and submarines would ply the open seas everywhere. On the invitation of friendly nations, these forces would circulate on liberty as goodwill ambassadors in their sea ports.

Eighth, the United States would temporarily make strike forces available in time of emergency—Marines and airlifted troops from the continental United States—to members of the United Nations. Such forces would be used whenever the General Assembly and Security Council of the United Nations officially acted to direct such a peace-keeping force to quell belligerent crossings of national boundaries.

Ninth, the United States would maintain airborne troop bases within its continental limits and on its island possessions. Antimissile surveillance system would be maintained for the security of the nation. During this dangerous transition period, we would maintain the highest first-strike and second-strike nuclear delivery capacity.

Tenth, the United States would offer to join all other nations in multilateral research. It would be an open architecture offer, as with IBM's microcomputer. This would result in annual expenditures for research and development to get the highest level of capability in electronic, computer hardware and software, laser, satellite, missile, and other sophisticated war instruments. They could be delivered from the continental limits of the nations of the world to anywhere else. I would prefer not to include this alternative. However, France and other countries force such an offer of cooperation to other nations. I find it terrorizing. Yet, I feel it should result in more pressure for the multilateral adoption of a "build-down" of weaponry. It could, over time, result in all nations seeing the need for a supersovereign "conventional warfare" U.N. peacekeeping force.

Eleventh, finally, in what is the keystone of this radical change, the government would call on the American people to form under the Second and Fourth Amendments to the Constitution "citizens' state militias" in every state and territory. Our solemn intent never to be invaded or conquered would be clear to the world. This would be universal military training along the lines of the Swiss army model, and extended to the Army, Air Force, Navy, Marines, and Coast Guard. This proposal is costly, but it is necessary. The source of funds would be the peace dividend resulting from the great change in direction of our foreign policy, for example, by way of reductions in the CIA's budget from, say, a current $24 billion to $12 billion, and the reduction in weapons development and military staff personnel costs, together resulting in budgetary discretion of about $40 billion. To achieve it, we will need to stabilize the dollar as the world currency of choice. Japan, West Germany, Great Britain, France, and others would need to cooperate. In this manner, the fiscal burden could be managed. Furthermore, the United States must adopt the value-added tax and renovate our federal-state taxing system to shift taxing to production and consumption. We should avoid taxes on capital formation and artificial capital growth (inflation-generated capital gains). These actions would produce the funds to deal with crime control, air quality, water quality, solid waste management, unsafe and unsanitary housing, worn-out municipal infrastructures, traffic congestion, and other problems of stress and its management in our metropolitan and rural areas.

Some commentators argue that the Reagan-Bush deficits have so changed us from a creditor to a debtor nation as to have made any "peace dividend" an illusion. Certainly it has reduced the size of the benefits resulting from a shift to peaceful pursuits rather than nonproductive arms production. Nevertheless, economic analysis indicates much increased productivity, with very strong multiplier effects, arising from embarking on an active program of building and rebuilding the world's cities. Such cannot be said for arms production. Armaments actually have negative effects of withdrawing resources from the productive process. I assert without proof that there would be immense, nonquantifiable psychic benefits resulting from the change in mental attitudes of Americans and other world citizens. These new positive attitudes would boost productivity.

Foreign Aid Conditions

For this planned changeover from a "wartime" to a "peaceful coexistence" foreign policy we would need the help of all other major net-exporting industrialized countries, and OPEC nations as well. Europe and Japan, for example, must share the costs. In view of world conditions, we should be willing to go hat in hand to beg them to join with us in a multinational foreign aid program, so long as they supported human rights and the spirit of democratic capitalism. In effect, an IMF/World Bank-type "Peaceful Cooperation Fund" would be created by promises of credits from the nations capable of granting them. If rejected by other nations the United States should be prepared to go it alone. We did with the Marshall Plan. This would be a much more modest undertaking, given our current debtor status.

This program is a hybrid of the Marshall Plan and some of the United States's community renewal programs. Under this proposal credit would be made available to those nations that offer a workable plan for national economic development. Each nation's plans for cooperative economic development would be required to proactively address the economic problems faced by that particular nation. It would be critically important for each country to develop its own indigenous plan. Examples of priority aims would be: agricultural land reform; a balanced economy, rational phased development of an industrial base, elimination of illiteracy, increased agricultural productivity, vocational training, railway and highway construction, sanitation, water quality and health measures, decent housing, communications systems, increased energy resources, development of power grids and electric generation stations, increases in per-capita income, equitable distribution of national income, newspapers and other communication media, private communication systems, banking and currency stabilization, the development of savings and loan and other thrift institutions and banks, and international trade facilities and export/import agencies.

All of the above are of lesser importance than rational family planning and stabilization of our global population growth, as Japan has done and as India is trying desperately to do. The *Futurist,* the World Bank, the Rockefeller Foundation, and leaders such as C. P. Snow have all joined in showing that the gains of all economic plans, no matter how well-conceived or well-executed, will be wiped out by the continuing rise of population in the LDCs. Each nation would be asked to propose methods to balance population and economic growth.

More general aims of this proposed program would be to 1) assure that some benefits of the program flow bilaterally between the donor and recipient nation, 2) set up techniques to prevent corruption, such as generally accepted accounting principles, and 3) avoid aiding dictatorships and oligarchies who are seeking to promote totalitarianism rather than diffusion of power. The donor nations would have first opportunity to show that it is cost-effective to purchase goods from the donor country. The goods and services originating from the United States could be shipped in American airplanes or ships, or those of favored nations, so that American workers would share in the fruits of growth by producing goods and services for the cooperating countries, until they develop their own capabilities to do so.

Second, if the foreign nations participating in the program need technical personnel not available domestically, then the donor nation would be given preference to supply them. All donor nation personnel so employed by the development plan would work under the supervision and control of the native administrators of the participating nations. Thus, American personnel would be no more than assistants, there to provide technical advice and skills. This would prove frustrating at times, but it would be the only way to develop adequate local administrators. This could prove stimulating to the growth of the educational plant in the United States, particularly in languages, arts, science, history, business, engineering, and anthropology. Great Britain is far ahead of the United States in this regard.

Finally, to assure continued congressional and public support, it would be imperative that any cooperation agreement between the United States and another nation provide for uniform accounting procedures coupled with periodic team audits from the recipient nation, the Peace Department, and the congressional General Accounting Office.

Countries unwilling to come up with comprehensive, workable economic plans, or unwilling to provide for thorough auditing, would simply be ineligible for the development programs. This could set up a healthy competition for development funds.

The plan proposed for national defense preparedness—the citizens' militias—would drastically change the current form of federal service. Instead, we should follow the lead of William James, the philosopher, and the proposals of Sen. Sam Nunn, (D-Georgia). I proposes that we offer to provide every high school (of all kinds) with the opportunity to have an armed forces education station within it, Army, Navy, Air Force, Marine, or Coast Guard, or a combination, depending on the size of the school system. During the junior and senior year of high school, every able-bodied person could be trained in defense security preparedness. The nation's youth would no longer be forced to go away from homes to be trained, nor would we maintain a draft. Instead, youth would get their national guard training under the auspices of the state government. In effect, the federal training officers would simply introduce them to military discipline. Their actual service would be with local state militia units.

In metroareas youth would be taught concepts of riot control and maintenance of law and order. In more rural areas the concepts of counter-guerilla warfare would be part of the training. Along the seacoast youth may prefer service at a Coast Guard or Navy station. It could be possible for seniors to volunteer in advance for "exchange service," on a bid basis. They might serve in the various branches of the military at distant places, thus gaining additional personal life experience. We should repeal and rewrite the 1914 law in which we "nationalized" our state militias into the National Guard. It would be necessary for the president to continue to have the power to call up the state militias in times of "national emergencies," with the consent of the U.S. Congress. Recently that power was abused. The various branches of the federal military service have called up units for "training" in foreign lands almost at will or caprice. State militias' time would be better spent repairing our municipal infrastructure and planting tree seedlings.

There is a movement in the United States to break the hold of the imperial presidency over our state militias. These reserve forces, known collectively as the National Guard, are an armed service that the president shares with the governors of our fifty states. The state militias are part-time soldiers, serving on the weekends or during emergencies at state direction. The president has the right to call them to active duty. There is a case pending on appeal that raises a constitutional issue: what powers do governors have over their state troops? The Constitution gives the states the right to maintain their militias, and, in particular, the right to control their training. The Second Amendment enshrines the notorious "right of the people to keep and bear arms." It is premised on the need for a "well-regulated militia." After some of these local forces refused to serve overseas in the Spanish-American War, Congress created the National Guard, an umbrella reserve force composed of state militias. Guardsmen have traditionally been thought of by the professional military as second-class soldiers. However, they are the ones who win the wars.

In the past, enlistment and service in the state militia has often enabled individuals to avoid being called up for wars such as those in Korea and Vietnam. There were perhaps as many federal conscription-avoiders among the Ohio National Guard units at Kent State University in 1970 as among the students they fired upon. At present, state National Guard units routinely train throughout the world during their annual two-week tours of duty. This is a way the professional military has of cementing their relationship and emphasizing that they are troops subject to call-up. In January 1985, the Republican governor of California, George Deukmejian, refused to allow 450 guardsmen to take part in combat training missions in Honduras. Other state governors have followed suit. The result was that President Reagan inspired Rep. Sonny Montgomery of Mississippi to attach an amendment to an appropriations bill that stripped governors of any right to veto overseas National Guard missions on policy grounds. The governor of Minnesota, Rudy Perpich, challenged the Montgomery amendment in January 1987, when the Minnesota Air Guard was ordered to fly units to Honduras. Joined by ten states, Minnesota has asserted that the Second Amendment makes unconstitutional the call-up of National Guard for foreign service not based on valid foreign policy.

The states' lawyers assert that, "If certain states and their citizens should balk at overseas training of the militia in peacetime, it does not show a conflict with any federal power, but reflects precisely the type of local reaction that the framers intended to protect." The federal government argued that to resist a call-up for any reason is an invasion of foreign policy by the governors. But what if the governors are supporting their own senators and representatives who have already passed statutes or even resolutions opposing such a use of the troops that the president is violating? A federal judge in St. Paul has sided with the central government, citing the evolution of the autonomous state militias into one armed force under national control.[24] Minnesota appealed immediately.

Assuming we work out this problem of dual supremacy over our state militias, one can envision some of this militia or Navy personnel serving as assistants on the solar sea-energy platforms discussed earlier. However, the primary objective is to create a locally oriented military force. It would be a home-defense force, knowledgeable in the local terrain. After school graduation, local youths would be sent to a training camp in the local area for training and military discipline on a short-term, full-time basis. They would be inculcated with the idea that it is their duty to defend their country from invaders and armed insurrection. It is likely a number of these youths would volunteer for a term of service in the federal armed forces. The quality of those forces would be improved.

A spillover benefit of using our high schools for citizens' militia training by our states is that private schools that volunteer to participate could be eligible for constitutionally proper allocation of funds. This could be on a "no strings attached" basis, for improving the quality of education of the children in the school system so they would be better citizen soldiers. Most critics agree that we must find a way to provide federal aid to all schools. Those jealous of maintaining separation between church and state are opposed to payments to parochial schools and other nonpublic schools. In all cases, except that of pacifists, this plan would enable the federal government to advance its legitimate constitutional duty of providing for the common defense without the necessity of categorical grants and special-aid systems that constrain the independent function of the local educational plant. Another significant spillover benefit could result from extending this citizens' militia concept to require that each graduate maintain complete military equipment in a readiness state, in their homes, as in Switzerland. This idea fulfills the Second Amendment aims in the true sense. Each citizen with his rifle in his home was what our founding fathers considered as the possible objective of our state militias. The National Rifle Association and other gun-loving folks would have less reason to oppose hand-gun controls if every home had a rifle for the constitutional purpose.

The United States would maintain this nationwide military force, locally oriented, as long as the United Nations failed to provide a peacekeeping force. There would be no selective service system or universal military training in the usual sense of the word. Youths would be required to participate only in those programs that related to their state's local military education center, subject to conscientious objection. The aim is a withdrawal and demobilization of a large part of our present federal military forces and ancillary civilian personnel. Military equipment and material no longer used could be placed in mothballs.

Under this plan, the United States would continue a research and development program for sophisticated defensive weaponry. We would continue to show our preparedness. First- and second-strike nuclear capabilities must be the ever-present deterrent to the destructive use of force by any "cross-boundary" belligerent nation. All must know that the United States would continue as a superpower with nuclear-powered Trident submarines deployed throughout the world. During this transition period it would be imperative that we maintain the posture of continually urging the United Nations to meet and consider questions of staged disarmament of member nations.

Those who are guided by a Hobbesian world view still have a place. Some military minds are better equipped for fighting war than waging peace. For them, a United Nations peacekeeping force could well be a noble vocation. We do parent and develop some very aggressive males (and females) whose capacity for preventive violence exceeds their love for peace. They would be hardhearted and unrelenting in their pacification duties. Therefore, the military and naval professionals who see no place for themselves in the new approach to national defense should promote the idea of United Nations peacekeeping. Sad to say, they would probably see plenty of violent action in the foreseeable future.

America can be a military power of a defensive nature that is second to none. We can still pursue the goals of social justice while maintaining the vitality of our constitutional culture. Thereby we could restore the competitiveness of our political economy and start to work on regenerating the nation's metroareas.

Part VI: Overcoming Yesterday in Order to Start on Tomorrow

Preface

We must overcome old roadblocks to open the way to tomorrow. This section urges that we diminish stress by promptly resolving conflicts. We can use class actions and small-claims systems such as arbitration, mediation, and neighborhood justice centers. This section proposes that Committees of 1000 be empowered to act in the public interest using class actions against wrongdoers, be they the government, large corporations, trusts, the church, or individuals. The ordinary person would have power when his cause of action was meritorious. This section promotes the idea of a national colloquium on the rights and powers of the people. It would be a way of celebrating the ratification, in 1791, of our Constitution's Bill of Rights.

Legal scholars have raised doubts that the right to privacy in our phones, telecommunications, mails, and homes exists in law. Is privacy really protected by the U.S. Constitution? What are those vague, penumbrous rights referred to in the Ninth Amendment to the U.S. Constitution? I call for a constitutional convention to enumerate more of our civil and political rights. We need to get out of the gridlock between the executive and legislative branches brought about by the Supreme Court's *Chadha* decision. Some constitutional reforms are necessary to reenergize the people.

Our nation may be a "machine that runs of itself," but it is more likely a dissipative structure that is running down. Why not risk a constitutional convention under the rules of the Ervin-Helms bill? Over forty years ago Franklin Delano Roosevelt proposed a new list of rights to be added to our existing Bill of Rights. The United Nations has sought to set forth rights that every human ought to have. I do not go that far. However, if we do not have a constitutional convention to enumerate more of our valuable political and civil rights, then we appear to be drifting toward a happy fascism based on the power elite pleasing the mob with more consumerist toys, as they pursue not happiness but nihilism. This section is a call for individual action, to networking, as a living sequel to this book, having investigated what so proudly we should hail, having provided some answers. I call upon everyone to take action for a better, happier world, with social justice for the possible humans of the coming century. Let the year 2000 be a celebration of our new directions.

18. Private Class Actions and Other Forms of Conflict Resolution

We need to multiply and expand effective ways to resolve conflicts. *American urban society's critical problems declare that much of the street anger, the deepening frustration and alienation, or worse—depression and despair—of the American people are due to the internalization of stress caused by the inaccessibility of low-cost conflict resolution systems. Promised social justice is a main mythological promise of our constitutional culture.* Social, political, economic, even religious and family institutions have abused their power. In a representative republic, conflicts arising from such abuses can be channeled by society to be less harmful, even healthier, for a pluralistic and thoughtful people. This requires that the people have the power to force confrontation and resolution by positive dialogue and change. As humans subordinate to these powerful institutions, we must seek a better balance of power for more equitable results. We should do this within our constitutional culture with its democratic marketplace of ideas. I propose a way to give much greater, albeit court-supervised, power to the people through class actions and combination suits. There are other, lower-cost techniques of conflict resolution available—arbitration, mediation, and neighborhood justice centers are a way of balancing the scales of justice. They lessen the impact of the often prohibitive cost of litigation by preventing the need for it. Class action suits spread the cost of litigation out over a number of people, increasing access to the courts for every citizen.

The law permeates our personal as well as governmental relations. It has become a social cathartic for many issues that were, at one time, handled well by family, church, and craft union or guild. The American people hate lawyers but they certainly want to use them.

"Why can't we at least discuss going to court, counselor? I have my rights, don't I?" is the way many clients present themselves to attorneys. They do this instead of seeking legal advice and counsel. As soon as a human wound, mental or physical, oozes forth from a bit of legal tangle or personal anguish, in rushes another lawyer. Derek Bok, president of Harvard University, charges that our American legal process is the most expensive in the world. "The blunt, inexcusable fact is that this nation, which prides itself on efficiency and justice, has developed a legal system that is the most expensive in the world." Richard D. Lamm, former governor of Colorado and now professor and director of the Center for Public Policy at the University of Denver, states,

The legal system is imposing staggering transactional costs on American business and industry. . . . The United States has two and a half times as many lawyers as Great Britain, five times as many as West Germany, and twenty-five as many as Japan. . . . Litigation is taking an increasing percentage of our national assets. . . . Litigation in the United States is increasing five to seven times faster than our population.[1]

There is considerable animosity toward the legal profession. We cannot deny the overall total of lawyers in the United States has doubled in the last fifteen years. Why? It seems to arise from Americans' sense of how to resolve conflicts. There is a carryover from frontier rugged-individualism. The U.S. Constitution creates conflict between the three branches of the federal government, between the federal government and its many instrumentalities as well as the fifty states.

Lawyers are used, too often, for cathartic, role-playing, mental therapy. Clients often want litigation to work out their pain and anger over what has occurred. Today the scales are heavily weighted in favor of those who have the resources to bear the costs. No one ever said life is fair. Only the naive expect the law to be fair. Yet all lawyers know that the mythic phrases, "to act in good faith" and "fair dealing" are supposedly meaningful fundaments for our system of adversarial justice. Recently, class actions have been successful in bringing us more safety in products and more competitiveness in our economy. We need to empower more private attorneys general to act for the people in order for law to more nearly achieve justice.

The Economics of Litigation

Most international comparative-law lawyers agree that throughout the world the recent growth of private actions started by private parties to protect the public interest is one of the most significant developments in contemporary civil procedure. This type of litigation is characterized by plaintiffs' civil attempts not only to vindicate their own rights, which may be minor, but also to redress injuries of a broad, diffused class of persons similarly situated. In such actions, the subject matter of the lawsuit is no longer merely a dispute between private individuals' private rights. The issue is acknowledged to be a grievance about the operation of our society. This change in societal attitude is ably stated by Cappeletti:

More and more frequently the complexity of modern society generates situations in which a single human action can be beneficial or prejudicial towards the larger numbers of people . . . making inadequate the traditional scheme of litigation, it being merely a two-party affair. . . . For examples, false information divulged by large corporations may cause injury to all who buy shares in that corporation; and an antitrust violation may damage all who are affected by the unfair competition; . . . infringement by an employer of a collective labor agreement violates the rights of all his employees; the imposition of an unconstitutional tax, or, the illegal discontinuance of a social benefit maybe detrimental to large communities of citizens; the discharge of waste into a lake or river affects all who want to enjoy its clean waters; defective or unhealthy packaging may cause damage to all consumers of these goods. . . . The possibility of such mass injury represents a characteristic problem of present times.[2]

All legal systems have rules concerning *standing* that limit access to the court to persons who have some stake in the outcome of the controversy. These standing requirements were once aimed at insulating the court from officious intermeddlers and to ration scarce judicial resources. In modern times, standing has been used by sycophants of the status quo who sit on the bench. They represent it as judicial restraint. Standing enables judges to cleverly avoid important questions of broad societal import that have reached their forum. The legislative response has been to broaden the standing requirements in specified statutes. The class-action device may also effectively expand the right to standing in a properly worded statute. Standing requirements favoring class actions have the effect of forcing the court to face issues that are larger than the individual interest of the appearing litigant. This is all to the good.

The traditional law of standing is based on a built-in bias. It unduly favors economic interests of individuals or organizations who have discriminated against "fragmented and diffuse" interests of the public. Furthermore, under traditional rules of standing, some cases and individuals who have standing for a suit may be unwilling (say, for fear of economic reprisal), to consent to litigation conducted in his or her name. In other cases, there may be no individual who would qualify as a plaintiff under the traditional law of standing, even though there is a diffuse wrong. A classic example would be to suppose that a governmental agency erroneously refuses to grant a company permission to emit certain allegedly harmful vapors into the air, or to use certain allegedly noxious substances for dyeing food. In such a case the company obviously has standing to challenge the agency's decision, but may choose to do nothing. Thus, even if the agency's ruling is challengeable on scientific evidence available, nothing would be done because of the business firm's indifference. Result? American society could lose the use of a beneficial substance, or, we would experience an uncalled delay of its introduction to the economy. The saccharin/aspartame situation comes to mind as an example. Pharmaceuticals acceptable for years in foreign nations but not in the United States are another.

The tendency to lower barriers to standing will come to its logical conclusion when the common-law concept of standing is abolished altogether for causes of actions based on diffused wrongs, and a substituted kind of standing is provided. The limited case of diffused standing could be called citizens suits. For example, what I label Committees of 1000 could champion the public interest. So far, only the United States has explicitly sanctioned citizens' suits. This is done by way of remedial legislation in our state and federal statutes. For example, the Michigan environmental protection act of 1970 permits private individuals to bring polluters to court without showing that they personally have in any way been adversely affected by the defendant's conduct. Considering that Michigan is virtually surrounded by the Great Lakes, we can all be thankful for that broad power. Other states, including Minnesota and Florida, have followed the idea. At the federal level the Air Quality Control Act, the Water Quality Control Act, and the Noise Control Act, as amended to date, have by congressional action, in response to opposition by the Supreme Court, authorized citizens' suits against individuals and governmental agencies. President Reagan and his Chicago school free marketeers have vigorously opposed this citizens' countervailing power. No showing of direct personal harm is now required for standing before some agencies, or for actions against the industries subject to the regulatory power. However, the persons damaged by the wrongdoers are fragmented and diffuse. The lack of knowledge of their new powers, as a class, is a case of "market ignorance" belying the assumption of "perfect knowledge" so dear to the free marketeers. There is a need to use modern communication techniques to inform and encourage public-interest litigation in the United States.

The class action is viewed by European lawyers as a distinctive achievement of American legal genius. To the European, exposure to American contemporary class-action law provides a breath of oxygen-enriched air. The ever-increasing powers of the legislative and executive branches of the government, along with the growth of transnational corporations, justify, even necessitate, by way of class actions, a countervailing power. It could offset the obvious influence of special interest groups in our political processes. The public interest must be permitted to litigate; no one else is able or likely to do so. I do not encourage the idea of increasingly rigorous enforcement of the public interest through criminal prosecution. Instead, effective protection of any interest means more guarantees of rights to the average citizen, plus the economic power to effectively enforce those rights. Group access would provide civil or civic justice through enhanced participation. On the other hand, serious problems might arise if a democracy enabled full-scale control of the political branches of the government by a nonrepresentative judiciary.

Committees of 1000

The idea of public-interest law is to ensure participation for those not represented by organized, well-funded, private groups. Public interest law therefore reflects an aspiration for civic justice. I call for the formation, if necessary, of ad hoc Committees of 1000, at least one thousand citizens who would contribute, say, a minimum of $100 each. This may appear to be a large aggregation, but it is presumed they would contract with a chosen attorney who would then have the authority to act as their champion. The group must be large enough to produce a war chest to achieve certification of the class to act. Remedial law would empower the committee to have standing in meritorious suits, to act as the enforcer of various diffuse rights.

As with any social problems, there are possible problems. The threat of multiplicity of suits and overburdening of the courts is real. The creation and use of this extraordinary power—the public interest lawsuit—should be well-balanced and used in a socially responsible manner. We do not want mob rule by a thousand Committees of 1000. Nevertheless, this is a valuable, albeit sleeping, countervailing power that should be awakened. It would be critical that we prevent a multiplicity of public-interest lawsuits. It could damage democratic capitalism. In a market-oriented national economy where a national name brand may cause diffuse harm over all fifty states, one can see the possible "horrible of horribles"—the name brand as class opponent facing a large number of class actions representing plaintiffs throughout the nation, as many as fifty separate combination suits by each of the attorneys general claiming to represent plaintiffs who have opted out in those fifty states. Such an occurrence would obviously be unduly burdensome on the national name-brand company. Unfortunately, it is unlikely to be opposed by the yuppies of the defendants' bar, who would enjoy running up their timesheets. I argue that the public interest class action (such as the Committees of 1000) should be treated as a special case. This could prevent its abuse by self-seeking people who otherwise could use it as a strike-suit to intimidate governmental and private organizations. We must prevent abuse by such selfish actions. Being a nuisance to get payment from the powerful so they can rid themselves of a lawsuit is not social justice. But, we need these new forms of action to press people to follow the law and support the basically communitarian and moral spirit of democratic capitalism. A balancing of interests is a healthy objective.

Public officials who try to ignore the duty to act within the law of our constitutional culture should fear *Bivens* v. *6 Unknown Named U.S. Bureau of Narcotics Agents* and *Westfall* v. *Erwin*[3] and whatever future course these cases might take. The need for congressional action at this time is obvious. The federal jurisdiction should take over—"occupy the field"—based on a comprehensive statute that preempts the field for these large interstate cases. The Supreme Court should constitutionally require "pretrial opt-in" of all the nonresident class members who have minimum contacts with the forum. Our modern communications media, with targeted direct mail, enable a trial court to localize a mandatory class. The Court could thereby impose the requirement of the parties to "opt out" or "in." Thus, the Court could reach a goal of unitary binding adjudication. If some party had an extraordinary or unusual right not to be counted as a member of the class, the judge could allow such a suit.

When a Committee of 1000, or a group of such committees, start their action, the federal jurisdiction should be enabled to reduce multiplicity of damage claims. To reinforce the committee's power, the judge's common-law power of *remittur* of damages in the courts should be weakened. The state of Missouri has seen the right path in bringing to an end this invasion of the juries' decisionmaking powers. The nation should sharply diminish the power of *remittur* if not abolish it. Today, it stifles the disciplining effect of public-interest class action suits. It diminishes the juries' attempts to impose really effective economic penalties, as in the case of the Ford Pinto gasoline tank defects. Furthermore, we should limit the use of *res judicata* and collateral estoppel on future class actions by Committees of 1000. Consolidation should be encouraged. We need Committees of 1000 that would exercise: writs of *mandamus, quo warranto, qui tam* suits, and *amicus curiae* briefs, in effect, a new "nonviolent," peaceful *posse comitatus*—power to vent the citizens' outrage and effectively redress their grievances.

These committees would use the adversarial law forums, which are much healthier than going to the streets. Public-interest injunctions would be allowed. This would enable judges to promptly hear complaints of Committees of 1000. By this process the committees would serve as adversarial champions to empower claims against various social institutions abusing their power, for example, the National Collegiate Athletic Association's control of college football.

Here's an idea that's a bit unconventional: Committees of 1000 could be available to military personnel *in times of peace only,* especially to conscripts against their military superiors when (by secret hearing) a federal court is satisfied that the aggrieved have been refused access to a military judicial inspector general. Thereby, the federal citizens' rights would be called into play for a hearing under federal jurisdiction.

Judgment in favor of a Committee of 1000 could result in another new idea for social justice in our society—a "Covenant Enforceable by Others." Violation of economic, political, or civil rights could result in personal damages being levied against the wrongdoing party. Such damages could be paid out of the wrongdoing parties' net worths. Furthermore, the victims could have a right to reparations from the government when it subsequently failed to enforce the law against the wrongdoing party. This right could arise when the wrongdoer continued to violate a judgment issued in favor of a Committee of 1000. Our constitutional law—*Bivens* and *Westfall*—supports this idea.

There are barriers to effective use of Committees of 1000. Be forewarned. The propertied class has several old tools to oppose and delay these group actions. Remedial legislation should take away these powers of judicial restraint in public-interest lawsuits. One is *de minimis non curat lex*. By this motion a court is called to treat the matter before it as too trivial for a judicial forum. Diffuse damages, such as hotels' overcharging for phone calls, are susceptible to this under present law. We also should expand stockholders' derivative suits to include enforcement of the public interest when it is adverse to the corporate business interest, corporate assets, and corporate legal rights. Class actions should be promptly tried on the merits. *Supersedeas* ought to be used to avoid the dilatory practices of the "big purse" corporations, large institutions, and government. There is also the problem of a preemptory directed verdict—or judgement on the pleadings. These procedures are often wrongfully used as a tactic by a wily judge to throw out a meritorious case. This could happen before the Committee of 1000 had the opportunity to present the merits of its cause, or before it had available "discovery" to find the necessary evidence.

Diversity of citizenship jurisdiction should be available to the defendant. This would provide a presumptive right of removal to the federal jurisdiction, avoiding local and regional bias. Burke and Hobbes were wrong. Those who hold the power of the sovereign have failed to demonstrate the capacity to lead wisely and effectively. By restoring the power to the people to act collectively, we can tap the wisdom of the populace in open forums of adversarial justice.

A plaintiff in a class action is a member of a class of persons who are in a similar position. Suit is brought by the plaintiff, not only on his or her own behalf, but also on behalf of all the class members similarly situated. The court is required to pass upon the propriety of maintaining the action as a class action, define the class, direct that the best notice practicable be given to the class members, and supervise and control the process by making other appropriate orders. Developments in recent years have shown that the primary purpose of the class action has been, "even at the expense of increasing litigation," to provide means of vindicating the rights of persons who individually would be without effective strength to bring their opponents into court at all.[4] This purpose is less apparent in class actions brought for declaratory or injunctive relief because the United States requires an actual case or controversy.

We could use class actions to relieve urban stress. For an example, suppose a class action was brought on behalf of all black parents who wanted to participate with a defendant school board in planning for integrating a guilty segregated school system. A single class action could show the court, the press, and the public the wrongs that need correcting. This would provide power in negotiations for not only those black parents instituting the class action, but to all black parents and children similarly affected. More important, such a class action case could provide all other black parents in the district with the right to demand compliance henceforth on the basis of an extended definition of *res judicata*. Since the matter had already been tried by one group, the existing precedents could provide other parents with the power of the court to obtain desegregation. This should be without forcing then a "new frustrating beginning" of expensive litigation with their own school district. Why should they have to prove the fact situation was similar to the existing precedents when there had already been a class action?

The same type of group action could be used by many stockholders when misled by false statements, especially by management, which might promote a so-called "white knight" tender offer with lucrative golden-parachute contracts for the greedy managers. In some cases, the white knight is operating only to favor management, and at the expense of the stockholder-owners of the enterprise. A class action could be an effective sanction against management when used by a group of injured small stockholders who would otherwise not have the means to enforce the law. For another example, in August 1986 the *New York Times* reported that the Environmental Protection Agency repeatedly and intentionally violated the Endangered Species Act by failing to protect certain animals and plants from pesticides. The source was an EPA report. The report said that the agency often took no action to restrict the use of pesticides, even when the Interior Department's Wildlife Service presented a formal opinion that wildlife on its list of endangered species was in jeopardy from specific insecticides or herbicides. The report was prepared by the Center for Environmental Education, a private nonprofit group in Washington, under a contract with the federal agency. John Moore, assistant administrator of the EPA, stated, "There is no question about it, we didn't comply with the requirements of the law."

Those who are opposed to direct, violent, political action and disorder, which fuel revolutionary action, ought to support class actions and combination suits. The aim here is to enhance direct involvement. It would be a gross oversimplification to attribute the "access to law movement" in the United States to urban problems such as immigration and pollution. The underrepresentation of diffused and dispersed interests, the chronic social problems of a largely middle class population, result from a society that does not take rights seriously. It reaches far beyond our large metroareas. In any case, it is our metroareas that have the masses of citizens who could champion the essential changes. They could feel better about themselves if they were empowered to work for the common good and to promote the general welfare.

A Primer on Class Actions

Congress made a start with Rule 23 of Federal Civil Procedure. Will class actions continue to grow and develop within our body politic? There is sophisticated hostility among the power elite. And, as expected, the 1966 revision of Rule 23 had a dramatic effect on federal civil litigation. Some say the provision did more to change the face of federal practice than any other procedural development of the twentieth century. Some class action adherents call it a panacea for myriad socials ills because of its deterrent effect on unlawful conduct. Compensating those wronged, at the expense of the wrongdoers, would be healthy.[5] Its opponents have rallied around characterizations of the procedure as a form of "legalized blackmail" or as a "Frankenstein monster." The opponents charge widespread abuse of class-action rules by litigants on both sides—unprofessional practices relating to attorney's fees and sweetheart settlement of disputes. The naysayers also assert that many Rule 23 cases are in practice unmanageable and inordinately delayed by opposing counsel, creating a millstone of monstrous character to the litigation that diverts federal judges from matters more worthy. Whatever the case, the Supreme Court chose to amend Rule 23, restricting a rule that had remained unchanged for thirty years. It is time to expand it again.

This time, Congressional action by remedial statute will be necessary. The Supreme Court's decision in *Eisen* v. *Carlisle & Jacquelin*[6] now requires that a preliminary hearing on the merits for apportioning the cost of notice is improper under Rule 23. Congressional inaction has made it well-nigh impossible to properly define and certify a large class, so we are limited to small or self-defining classes in most cases. The powerful opponents from the "defendants" bar have been hard at work to weaken Rule 23 class actions. Recently, very capable plaintiffs' attorneys have quit class-action practice in the face of recently developed constraints. The United States should consider revival of such old common law forms of procedure as writs of *coram nobis* and writs of prohibition and *qui tam* suits. These ancient common law writs ought to be available to Committees of 1000. We have found ways to limit abuse of judicial power in the past. For example, in 1932 we expanded laborers' rights to strike and peacefully picket. At the same time, Congress limited the power of federal judges to issue injunctions in labor disputes. It worked. We prevented the arbitrary and capricious abuse of the injunction and entered a period of healthy confrontation between management and labor. The process healed the wounds of a democratic republic that might have veered to communism, but for the healthy powers of change within our laws.

Congress should raise the status of the class action. The current Supreme Court erected major barriers to the class action's potential to add consumer power to both the marketplace of democratic capitalism and to the marketplace of ideas for political and civil rights enforcement. Justices Rehnquist, Kennedy, O'Connor, Scalia, and a few others have cleverly manipulated the barriers of standing, prudential abstention, *forum nonconveniens,* and exhaustion of remedies to weaken group action. They use these ancient common law canons of judicial restraint to bar access to the federal jurisdiction, or to make the costs of litigation prohibitive for the common man. Justices Brennan, Stevens, Blackmun, and Marshall have spoken out against this arrogant and offhanded use of judicial restraint. In any event, we need accessibility to the grievances of small-claim litigants.

The public interest Committees of 1000 would need the possibility of punitive damages and the recovery of attorneys fees and court costs and fees. Of course, the problem of multiplicity of damages must be avoided. These class actions would serve to discourage the abuse of economic and political power. *The goal would be to force stewardship on those who operate on the low road known as "situational ethics." This healthy change would require them to know that the "situation" may well include personal liability for consciously violating the law and abridging the rights of others. Federal Rule 23 is a workable tool for populist action. Still, most judges have a personal class bias against populist ideas such as mass actions in the public interest.* As expected, there is much resistance to its development on the part of the defendants' bar. One problem is its novelty. Traditional ideas of social justice derive from contemplating and reacting to single, bipolar transactions with adversarial justice, A versus B. However, the world today is one of many A's who can ill-afford litigation against well-entrenched and well-financed B's.

It is a truism that there is no typical model for class certification. Every class action is different. This is in part due to the inexperience of many judges with the nature of a class action. The propriety of a class action certification is a serious threshold question, because it opens up discovery. The court has the capability to later redefine the class for manageability, notice requirements, and the like. There should be minimal requirements for certification of class suits. Class suits create a formidable and powerful plaintiff adversary. *The most basic requirement for class suit, therefore, is to test the real existence of a class of parties in interest too numerous for joinder in a suit under ordinary bipolar, adversarial practice.* Traditionally, "too numerous" has been a concept given content on a case-by-case basis. Numerosity does not appear to be susceptible to doctrinal analysis, so it will not be discussed in detail here. *Numerosity* means there must be enough potential members of the class to make it otherwise impracticable to require them to be joined as individual parties represented by many separate counsels in one suit. The great technological advances made in database management and direct-mail solicitation indicates that the idea of "too numerous" is more of a convenience for opponents to class actions than a practical reality. Adequately budgeted courts could, of a certainty, handle mammoth classes. Keep in mind that the current budget of our entire federal judiciary does not equal the development and production costs of one typical Defense Department war-making weapon. The other requirements are that there be common questions and commonality, typicality of the parties in interest, and an actual case or controversy.

Common Questions. The common question has not been defined under Rule 23. In adjudicating the class action, the judge must search the complaint to see if the question states a common element of the claim for the group that will be affected by adjudication of the complaint.

Commonality requires only the existence of a common question of law or fact. Generally, courts have held that in employment discrimination lawsuits the common question of whether a group has been discriminated against on the basis of a common characteristic such as sex or race is enough.[7]

Typicality. This is a criterion often analyzed when the court considers the commonality question. Consideration of the typicality criterion is often subsumed under the court's consideration of the commonality and the adequacy issues. Is the class in fact described by the class allegations in the complaint?[8]

Adequacy of Representation. The adequacy criterion is usually satisfied by showing that plaintiffs' attorney is qualified and able to conduct the litigation, and that there are no antagonistic interests between the plaintiff and the other members of the potential class. Inevitably the trial judge will depend upon representatives of the class to identify themselves and make assertions as their interests appear. The ability of the trial judge to accommodate someone within a class is severely tested when members of the class align themselves with the class opponent. Usually they claim their differences would be better served if the class opponent was not found liable in the particular case. The better remedy in such a situation is for such a second class to "opt out." Failing to do so, they should be barred from suit under the doctrine of *res judicata* in lawsuits.[9] The broad impact of class actions calls for congressional action to force such cases into the federal jurisdiction or to require that they be treated as federal questions to avoid diversity of opinion and forum-shopping. Almost all contemporary class actions are predicated on a statute or the Constitution.

This is not to say intrastate class actions are impossible. Lawsuits based on such public laws inevitably affect the rights and interests of individuals not actually represented before court. Such people have a choice—to "opt in" or "opt out." Federal and state courts have a difficult time with this issue. Courts are required to determine which of the two positions (community of the class, or consent of the individuals) they are going to follow. Perhaps Congress will act by way of a comprehensive codification to resolve the direction we should take. There is no clearly correct direction. The "community of interest" philosophy is more compatible with the reality of urban life than the idea of some rugged individual deciding whether or not to join suit. The Supreme Court's holding in *Eisen* v. *Carlisle & Jacquelin*[10] is more defensible if one assumes that for a proper case under class action theory an action should be granted on a unity idea of community of interest. Such a policy bias would require the consent of the individual class members. It is possible that class actions may be a much more credible weapon than a threatened invocation of other legislation or administrative action, because once a claim is filed both the court and the defendant are forced to respond. The class action that allows absentee-class members who have not opted out to be bound without their consent at least puts inertia on the side of settlement.

By requiring absentees to opt out, we provide a mechanism to ease a negotiated outcome. This is partly because of procedural obligations triggered by *certification*. For example, the responsibility to pay for and give notice may significantly increase the cost of litigation. Therefore the bothersome question to the judges is the sufficiency and propriety of the notice and the opportunity to "opt in" or "opt out" (that is, to make a choice about the exercise of one's individual right). The ideal is that this issue be judged in the light of the facts of a particular case. Nevertheless, in a huge country, over three hundred metroareas and fifty states, such stringent controls are out of synchronization with our modern telecommunication media. Congress and the states should authorize judges to find practical ways to fund "adequate notice" in meritorious cases. On the other hand, some autonomous individuals may see valuable "noneconomic, nonpolitical, moral, and ethical imperatives" that would urge them in a particular case to want to "opt out" or "in," depending on the factual situation.

The importance of *notice* in class suits flows from its cost. The function of notice is to bring a class suit to the attention of absentees who may well be the customers, creditors, or potential shareholders of the defendant company. A defendant may well fear that such publicity will interfere with his or her day-to-day operations.[11] On the other hand, class action notice gives a means of creating adverse publicity about defendants. The courts could adopt modern, cost-efficient forms of notice that are adequate. Publicity using forms of publication other than the mail has been effective in several cases. In *Elliot* v. *Weinberger,* a class of claims under the old age provision of Social Security Act, the Court ordered posters placed in every local social security office, advertisements of a nonlegal nature in two papers of general circulation, and a mention of the suit in every communication from the Social Security Administration to class members. This was an efficient and satisfactory solution for both parties in terms of cost-benefit analysis. Others have used media press releases and the like. Alternatively, potential members of a class could be notified by a mailing to a random sample of the class, or through cable television or over public television and radio channels. Of course, more traditional publication notice could be used. The media likely to reach class members could be identified.

Discovery

To argue the merits of their class complaint, litigants to class actions need the traditional access to discovery tools that are available in single-party suits. The power of discovery in civil cases compels the opposing parties to produce documents, witnesses, and exhibits before the trial. This results in the litigants and the judges being able to see the issues and the probable outcome of the case more clearly before the trial. It minimizes surprises, encourages settlement, and speeds the presentation of evidence during a trial. The potential for unfair exploitation of discovery by either the champion of the class or the class opponents to the detriment of absent class members can be controlled through increased judicial control over the timing and content of discovery requests. As a basic principle, discovery of absentees should be discouraged because of the potential for abuse. Discovery can also be a bargaining weapon. Class actions tend to be big cases. They cover complex factual patterns and many more documents and exhibits may be relevant than in a simple lawsuit. The class may demand more information than could possibly be sifted at trial. Unfortunately, this may be an effort to interrupt corporate activity, probe for embarrassing secrets, or impose other costs. The defendants' bar calls private bargaining while using class action procedures "blackmail." Cases are further strained during the certification process by motions for summary judgement made by the defendants' bar.

   In the usual case, class attorneys receive a fee only if they benefit the class. Thus they have economic incentives to screen out meritless cases. Proper class action procedures should include other mechanisms by which litigants may obtain official determinations of the substantive claims. At present, the trial itself provides the necessary means of determination. Other, less drawn out, more economical alternatives ought to be available. Mediation or mini-trials are possibilities. In the pretrial stage of a class action, mediation undertaken by the judge hearing the case raises a number of ethical difficulties. To be perceived as fair by the parties, mediation requires the judge to be aware of the merits of the case. If the judge makes a concerted effort to make a fair evaluation of the case, that evaluation may color his subsequent ruling if the case should go to trial. Many of the problems raised by mediation in the context of class actions could be avoided if a judge appointed someone else to act as mediator. This eliminates the problem of prejudgment bias. Of course, mediators must be paid. Congress and the state legislatures could consider legislating mediation and conciliation services as they have done in the past in the national labor relations and railroad regulatory statutes.

   The class action, because of manageability problems, can be abused. There is a need to protect absentees. The court should use its administrative powers and skills, for example, in its appointment of masters and experts, implementation of committees, subclassing, determination of adequacy of representation, and oversight of communications with the absentees. New federal judges should be required to attend judicial training centers if we are going to call upon them to administer such complex class actions. Database management and the use of computer software ought to be mandatory.[12] Certainly the judiciary is often called upon to be artful and find out if there really is a class action that can be structured by the court. Our courts are archaic in their administrative procedures. They ought to have statisticians, systems analysts, economists, and business administrators on staff, or available per diem on a budgetary basis.

Assessment of damages against wrongdoers may sometimes be necessary to relieve generalized psychic stress. Dreadful occasions may arise where there is a deep concern for deterrence and a need to command public disgorgement in order to assuage anxiety and depression resulting from generalized knowledge of a wrong done. This calls for something akin to retribution. An example might be the Kansas City skywalk cases, or, the Dalkon shield cases,[13] or the Bhopal, India, toxic release case. The Kansas City skywalk collapse and the line of Dalkon shield decisions present more than enough policy reasons why federal court ought to have the power to group plaintiffs scattered throughout the nation, even the world, because of a product liability calamity. These occurrences ought to result in mandatory class actions at a single jurisdictional location with a very limited right to "opt out." A judge might permit special "opt in" or "opt out" privileges for, say, family members who witnessed the horror of a loved one being killed by the calamity. The need for redress, in the psychic sense, extends to everyone in our telecommunicating age of on-the-scene network news coverage of a shocking spectacle that may call for retribution if fault is found.

Procedural battles over certification of a class and its composition are a favorite delaying tactic of the defendants' bar. These delays are a classic example of how the sycophants of the power elite jealously guard the power of their friends at the clubs. They use their deep-pocket economic power to fight class litigation, which they know to be in the public interest, by erecting sophisticated technical roadblocks, unknown to intelligent layman. These delays prevent plaintiffs from getting to the merits of the case. The power elite does this because they fear the populist power of the class action. The judges have Rule 11 of the federal rules of civil procedure. In theory, it can be used to discipline attorneys who repeatedly file insincere, vexatious, and harassing procedural delays. However, American judges have a very poor record of using this power of disciplinary action. Congress should recodify the class action for broader use in the public interest.

Having worked our way through this primer on class actions, let us consider some recent cases.

Beverly Hills Supper Club

The second-worst nightclub fire in U.S. history occurred in 1977 in the Beverly Hills Supper Club, located in a Cincinnati, Ohio, suburb. The blaze killed 165 people and injured 81 seriously. Immediately after the blaze, few legal observers saw any hope of large recoveries. The United States District Court judge, Carl B. Ruben, had said he saw the litigation as a $3 million to $5 million case.

Stanley Chesley, lead counsel for the plaintiffs, acted as the champion of the cause of the class of fire victims and their families. He recalled valuing the case at $40 million based on the present value of the lives lost, the pain and suffering, and the medical and other expenses. Chesley led the various plaintiff lawyers in a move to include the makers of products used in the club that could have extended the fire and the resulting injury to the dead and injured parties. Ultimately, the case involved more than 1,100 defendants, including aluminum wiring manufacturers, utilities, and a consortium of hundreds of insurance companies. Through 1982, the plaintiffs' lawyers won a number of settlements. The Union Light Heat and Power Company had to come up with $5.75 million because it negligently failed to inspect the wiring before the club was opened. About $2 million was paid by the manufacturer of the polyvinyl chloride wiring insulation that produced fumes that killed many of the victims. About $4.7 million came from a consortium of nine hundred insurance carriers accused of negligently inspecting the club before approving it as insurable and accepting premiums. The final group of settlements came from fourteen manufacturers of aluminum wiring and outlets who sold products in the vicinity of the club. The plaintiffs could not identify the specific manufacturer of the aluminum wiring used at the club, but argued that the industry acted in concert in using a technology they knew to be dangerous. The attorneys argued they should be liable based on their shares of the wiring market. There is case precedent for such market-share allocation of damages. In the thirty-eight-day trial, thirteen of the fourteen aluminum manufacturers agreed to out-of-court settlements, leaving General Electric as the lone remaining defendant. The jury decided that aluminum wiring caused the fire. It was about to begin deliberations on the plaintiffs' damage claim as a class when General Electric agreed to a $10 million accord in August 1985.

The total amount awarded was about $49 million to 282 plaintiffs. Attorneys fees were 6 to 7 percent. The judge's original perceptions were wrong. But for this class action, justice would not have been done. No doubt safer technology, wiring, and insulation has been adopted in the Cincinnati area and throughout the United States in part because of this class action lawsuit.

Attorneys fees appeared to be in the neighborhood of $3.2 million for the Beverly Hills Supper Club fire. Consider the complexity of the case and the difficulties of proving the truth against such highly skilled and well-financed defendants. Consider the many hours of research and training required to learn about the dangers of the technology and their proximate causation of the injuries. To a reasonable person, a contingent fee representing less than 20 percent of the total damages is quite reasonable after eight years total immersion in difficult and complex litigation.[14] The mere resistance to paying millions of dollars in damages is understandable. However, tactics often used by defendants and their attorneys to avoid responsibility for compensable acts of negligence are sometimes harassing and vexatious. Delays by defendant counsel are sometimes even criminal because of their deceitful lack of good faith. Frivolous defenses are made, primarily, to wear down low-budget plaintiffs.

Asbestos

The asbestos litigation concerning many corporations, such as Johns-Manville, is an example of how ordinary newspapers present more myth than fact and thus consciously bias reports in favor of business defendants. The news media have raised great cries about the legal fees charged the plaintiff victims while saying nothing about the legal fees of the defendants' counsel, which totaled nearly three times that of the plaintiffs' lawyers. Lawyers for asbestos victims argue that few of their clients would have gotten any compensation had it not been for the costly pretrial preparation carried out at the expense of the attorneys. The attorneys combed through voluminous asbestos industry documents. If their clients had lost, these plaintiffs' lawyers would have gotten nothing for all their time and expenses. Furthermore, there can be important spillover benefits for society as a result of discovery by plaintiffs' counsel. The foreknowledge that discovery may expose nefarious actions can shore up business ethics for democratic capitalism. Consider the shocking conduct described below.

The plaintiffs' attorney, Carl A. Shick, uncovered in 1977 correspondence between the president of Raybestos and Manhattan, Sumner, Simpson, and Vandiver Brown, general counsel of Johns-Manville. This correspondence discussed British studies concerning the hazards of asbestos. These letters were written in 1935! The *Atlantic* in 1984 brought to public attention one of Sumner's letters, in which he wrote, "I think the less said about asbestos the better off we are." Brown replied, "I quite agree with you that our interests are best served by having asbestosis (a scarring of the lungs) receive the minimum of publicity."

The attorneys for Johns-Manville successfully fought the introduction of these letters as trial evidence. They argued that Brown was dead and therefore his signature could not be authenticated. Fortunately, for our society, the plaintiffs' lawyers were aggressive in championing the cause of the diseased parties. At their own expense, they found that Brown was actually alive and well in Scotland! What a classic example of "market failure."

Industry awareness of the dangers of asbestosis as far back as 1935 became known to the general public in 1967. This was the year Dr. Irvin J. Selikoff released an epochal study that documented a shockingly high incidence of lung disease and cancer among 1,700 workers exposed to asbestos.

Worse, these stealthy tactics continue to be a stressful threat to the American psyche. For a 1992 example, consider Dow Corning's concealment of its knowledge of the danger of silicon gel breast implants. The lid is coming off on the truth, slowly but surely, on the implants that have been leaking death into the bodies of millions of American women. One lonely, autonomous human has lead the battle against this serious health risk. Former Dow Corning engineer Thomas Talcott warned the company before 1976 that its chosen silicon gel was too dangerous. Talcott put his reputation on the line to reveal the lethal truth: when ruptured, the implants damage the women's immune systems. Dow Corning poohpoohs his expert testimony as that of a disgruntled employee. Soon we will see another massive class action suit.

Gas Utility Monopoly

In 1984, 300,000 gas utility customers in New Mexico were awarded as much as $700 each in refunds. The award was due to a successful class action. The customers were also to receive small monthly credits over a twenty-seven-month period. The state's gas prices may be further reduced. The six teachers who started the suit were angered when a promised pay raise was withdrawn by their school district because monies were being eaten up by rising school gas bills. In July 1979 the teachers decided to challenge the state's gas utility company, Gas Company of New Mexico, for overcharging. They didn't have the foggiest idea on what grounds. Ramon Huerta, the high school Spanish teacher in Albuquerque, stated, "We knew we were taking on a giant, but we didn't know what else to do." The New Mexico chapter of the National Education Association put up $25,000, saying, "We figured that a few bake sales and raffles would take care of the rest of the legal costs." They found a champion for their cause—J. E. "Gene" Gallegos from Santa Fe.[15] Gallegos formed a three-member team of attorneys. They faced a host of lawyers from law firms Fulbright and Jaworski and Vincent & Elkins, among the best in the United States. "I remember the first court hearing," Gallegos said. "I think they had close to thirty attorneys, all with their yuppie three-piece suits and *Wall Street Journals* tucked under their arms. It was rather intimidating." Gallegos had never worn a three-piece suit.

Early in the pretrial proceedings one of the high-priced gas-company attorneys tossed a $20 bill on the table and said, "The plaintiffs ought to take this, it's the best they'll ever get." To save costs, Gallegos enlisted help from college professors, students, and housewives. They pored over company records, studied the fine print on some gas contracts and reread depositions. Gallegos set out to prove that collusion had driven up the utility's gas costs. Underlying the scheme, he alleged, was some feigned litigation. Some utilities who were buying gas pretended actual controversy and then settled out of court agreeing to higher gas prices. Next, the elevated prices were passed along to consumers whose gas utility rates tripled in a short time. Using the powerful tool of discovery provided by class actions, Gallegos was able to find a Conoco memo stating, "There was some speculation, and with good reason, that Southern Union wants us to sue them." He showed that Conoco's revenue from Southern Union and other New Mexico corporations jumped from $600,000 a year to $9.8 million five years later. This was an average increase of 75 percent per year. After building a case based on this circumstantial evidence, Gallegos was able to persuade the state attorney general to join the suit. A six-person jury ruled against the gas companies. The verdict was eventually thrown out on a technicality, another delay. Nonetheless Gallegos gained some impressive settlements negotiated separately over a two-year period. The total of these antitrust settlements were $121 million. The last company settled in April 1984. Conoco agreed to pay $50 million.

Gallegos asked the court for $12 million for his legal work. Surprisingly, few consumers have complained. The teachers wholeheartedly support the fee. Gallegos could be compared to the champions of the days of chivalry such as El Cid. Gallegos brought power to the people, without the sword of violence, and more effectively than any knight of old!

Cases taken from product liability, utility rate cases, and securities fraud show the class action can balance the scales of justice by diminishing the effect of the crushing weight of the "deep pocket" litigant. More importantly, it provides nonpecuniary psychic satisfaction and turns the myth of justice into reality, on occasion. The economics of litigation currently bar most small investors from even considering a meritorious lawsuit against deep-pocket wrongdoers. Yet, the free marketeers are seeking repeal of the Supreme Court's decision that implies causes of action for stockholders arising out of SEC Rule 10(b)-5 on the grounds that Congress never authorized such an extension of the law by the courts. Vested interests fear the class action because it increases access to the court and provides leverage for those shareholders with small claims.

Anyone who saw the spate of mergers and acquisitions in the 1980s is aware that we have a dormant Justice Department. It has little interest in enforcing the many provisions of our antitrust laws. Staffing has been reduced by over 50 percent since 1980.[16] Fortunately, Congress and the Supreme Court entrusted to private litigants some of the enforcement of our antitrust laws.[17] The class action device could be used in the place of a somnolent Justice Department and an inactive, underbudgeted Federal Trade Commission. Committees of 1000 and other class actions could be used with increasing frequency. Congress chose to permit all persons to sue to recover three times their actual damages for every time they were injured in their business or property by an antitrust violation. By offering potential litigants the prospects of a recovery treble the amount of their damages, Congress sought to encourage these persons to serve as "private attorneys general."[18] The consumers pay a higher price for goods purchased for personal use as a result of antitrust violations. They sustain an injury in their "business or property" within the meaning of the Clayton Act. They should be empowered to sue as a class against the producer of the goods or services.[19]

Congress should act in the public interest and rescind limitations on fluid-recovery funds. It is more likely that a fluid recovery bulk fund, under court direction, would be used for general welfare purposes. Today, fluid recovery is not an available remedy under the antitrust laws. The "private attorneys general" are denied a proper function in the forum. The legislative mandate to favor democratic capitalism and competition in ideas, goods, and services should not manifest itself in such limited ways. For actual examples, we have hotels who overcharged on long-distance and local calls made by guests and taxi-cab companies who colluded to overcharge on fares. There is corrective power in the fluid distribution of a fund that resulted from classwide calculation of damages when the damages are so diffused. Publicizing the wrong, by payment to the state, then distribution of the benefit to the public, is a strong market discipline. Likely, it would discourage such deceitful and unfair trade practices.

Sometimes it may be practical to establish a damage fund to be distributed through a proof of claim procedure. Today this can often be done through computer management of the massive mailing required. However, the dispersal of small awards to many members of the class would not result in maximizing deterrence. It would be a more effective deterrent to future action by insensitive class opponents such as multinational corporations. Punitive damages may be necessary where there is such great disparity in market power. Fluid recovery might also be used to avoid the problem of penalty damages and multiplicity of suits. For example, tobacco companies might be class opponents on the grounds of liability for a class of emphysema or throat-cancer victims. In such a case the fluid recovery funds could, in bulk, be allocated to the American Cancer Society to broadly publicize the dangers of, say, snuff and chewing tobacco. This would act as a more powerful deterrent than distributing small amounts of money to the victims. Again, it is our independent judiciary, with the unique qualities of a human being, that is needed here. They can administer the remedies as we seek social justice. Congressional support of the use of the courts to enforce market activity ought not to be so concerned about the relative merits of government versus private action. Legislative intent ought to seek market compliance with the policy against unfair and deceptive trade practices. Unfortunately, the Supreme Court's decision in the 1976 *Illinois Brick Co.* case, made it very difficult for ultimate consumers to institute a suit. They are dependent upon finding a public-spirited retailer, because *Illinois Brick* barred suits by consumers against violations done by "remote parties" in the channel of distribution, such as the manufacturer or the wholesaler. Congress should broaden the standing of class plaintiffs acting in the public interest. Recently, Congress did authorize consumer suits to partially overturn the Supreme Court's restrictive interpretations.

Employment Discrimination

The American system of justice in employment is peculiar. At the state level, the employers generally have a unilateral right to discharge with or without cause. This may be a good general rule in support of the work ethic, but surely we should not permit outrageous abuse of such a power. Georgia's Supreme Court has upheld the unilateral discharge of a "whistle blower" who turned in an employer who was flagrantly violating the law. The Court thought the employee's action was praiseworthy, but held that the employer still had a right to discharge him for that reason or any other.

On the other hand, we offer the same person, as a federal citizen, a set of laws enabling the least powerful among us to invoke the machinery of federal jurisdiction in a trial of claims of employment discrimination. In 1989, in *Wards Cove Packing Co.* v. *Antonio,* the Supreme Court imposed the heavy economic burden of litigation on any employee in a discrimination case.[20] Employers could have avoided responding to complaints unless the employees already have the proof of bias. They could have refused to disclose employment criteria and rules of work practices. Rather than make such rights a myth via economic barriers to litigation, the class action could allow ordinary working people to share costs of otherwise too expensive litigation on a relatively even basis against the corporate giants. In 1991 President Bush finally signed a bill that overturns this decision.

Class Action Attorney's Fees

The American Bar Association's "Code of Professional Responsibility" reflects the traditional understanding of the role of the lawyer in individual plaintiff litigation. In the class suit, especially one aggregating otherwise nonrecoverable claims, these traditional assumptions are not valid. The disparities between the theory and practice of professional ethics in the class action setting have not gone unnoticed. The opponent attorneys aggressively joust over this as a controversial aspect of class actions. They have centered media attacks on the nature of the plaintiffs' attorneys' role in amassing an adequate class. At least one federal judge has cited solicitation of class representatives as justification for refusal to certify a class, in *Carlisle* v. *LTV Electric Systems, Inc.*[21]

A comparison of advertising and solicitation indicates that a rule banning solicitation but allowing advertising would screen out the worst aspects of lawyer-initiated client contact. Solicitation presents greater opportunity for abuse than does advertising. There is a greater danger of misrepresentation by the attorneys during direct solicitation. Unlike advertising, solicitation is not readily subject to scrutiny by the legally informed. Furthermore, individuals who agreed to become class representatives after responding to an advertisement have demonstrated at least some interest in pressing a claim. On a cost-per-unit basis, advertising maybe just as effective as solicitation in furthering class action objectives.[22] Advertising by class action attorneys plainly falls within the compass of rules established in *Bigelow* and its successors concerning commercial advertising's rights to First Amendment protection.

In *Bates* v. *Arizona,* in a 5-4 decision of far-reaching implications, the Supreme Court ruled in favor of lawyers' right to advertise. In 1978 only 3 percent of lawyers polled by the American Bar Association advertised. By 1985 24 percent were using advertising to promote the use of their professional services. A 1983 study by the Federal Trade Commission concluded that fees for wills, uncontested divorces, and uncomplicated accident cases were 5 to 15 percent lower in the cities that had the fewest restrictions on advertising. According to one major law firm, advertising has forced lawyers to become more efficient.[23] However, it is certain that the power elite of the propertied class will try to bar such advertising. We are dependent on an independent judiciary to reject the idea of imposing a prohibition on advertising by class action attorneys whose advertising could withstand the exacting scrutiny of *Bigelow* and *Bates.* Signs are that the courts are accepting television and cable advertising by attorneys soliciting clients. Cases by class opponents against advertising are very likely to diminish.[24]

Recently, courts have been making increasing efforts to control plaintiffs' fees awarded in class actions. It is a crass example of the elitist bias of our courts. They have little interest in protecting the stockholders of large corporations from the size of the fees paid by corporate management to the defendants' private firms who act as defense counsel for class action opponents. The courts do not act in the best interest of the stockholders, as demonstrated during the asbestos litigation. The various court efforts to control the plaintiffs' fee awards focus on the hours an attorney has worked. Worse, they have simply reduced the size of fee awards. This is, in part, a laudable effort to reduce the temptation that settlement negotiations pose for attorneys to sacrifice class interest to self-interest. Certainly the courts should not permit the class attorneys or the class opponent to fix the amount of the class attorney's fee as part of a settlement agreement. Court supervision is necessary to protect the public from sweetheart deals and self-serving. The courts have developed their own criteria to control fees. In *Lindy Bros. Builders Inc.,* the Third Circuit developed a formula for fee calculation requiring the court to consider only four variables: hours worked, attorney's hourly rate, risk born by the attorney, and quality of the attorney's work.[25] The *Lindy* approach appeared to be replacing the percentage-fee method as the principle basis for fee calculations in these common-fund situations. However, this method appears to be fading. Percentage fees based on the class fund awarded are more and more common. In 1984 the Supreme Court approved the percentage method as the better method in common-fund cases.[26]

A survey of lawyers and judges by Harvard law professor Arthur Miller showed that 63 percent of the judges thought lawyers, on both sides, too often worked more hours than necessary. The courts' concern is appropriate. There are more than a hundred federal statutes that provide for awarding attorney's fees in public interest situations. Some recommend that attorneys be required to negotiate their fees at the outset of such cases. One must keep in mind that in the contingent fee class action contract there is no incentive for lawyers to file losing cases. They get paid only if they win. In contrast, there is economic incentive for defending attorneys to create elaborate defense maneuvers that will consume many hours of work at the expense of their clients. It is difficult to see how a contingency fee creates any sort of conflict between attorneys and their clients. Subject of course to fraud and deceit in billing excessive hours and doing work unnecessary to the case, the *Lindy* rules probably act to penalize the plaintiffs' bar.

It would also be wise to reduce the public subsidy for litigation. Today, most courts charge only nominal fees for their services. This shields litigants from the real costs of their action and leaves the taxpayers with the bill. At minimum the losing parties should be required to pay the other party's attorneys fees in those cases where it was proven the litigant had a meritless claim after discovery was available. Realistic costs should also be assessed upon those who use frivolous, harassing, and vexatious defenses. All courts should be called upon to vigorously enforce Rule 11 of the federal rules of civil procedure.[27] State legislatures ought to adopt the same rules for all other courts.

Another real barrier to successful use of class actions to promote the public interest is that the code of professional responsibility does not allow attorneys to advance or guarantee the other costs of litigation. In effect, "the client remains ultimately liable for such expenses." This should be changed. The risk of frivolous suits being financed is too low to warrant enforcement of such an ethical ban. Vigorous enforcement of Rule 11 of the code of civil procedure is the more appropriate avenue to control such abuse.

Entrepreneurial Partners for Social Justice?

Because of the diffused nature of the claims in a class action, it would be proper for Congress and the judiciary to permit attorneys forming the class to also form a business entity (say, a limited partnership) to assume some of the risks. It would be capitalized to provide front-end costs similar to venture capital seed money. The partners would agree to risk the invested funds for a share of the attorney fees at the outcome of the case. Such worthy ventures would introduce a sorely needed form of market discipline into democratic capitalism. A court may refuse to certify a class even though the underlying claims have merit. It would further peaceful conflict resolution to permit party restructuring and class realignments.

Richardson v. *Ramirez,* with its challenges to the legality of acts performed by each of a class of local governmental officials, is an example.[28] Note that in *Richardson* the plaintiffs' class, ex-felons in California, challenged the constitutionality of the state constitution and statutory provisions designed to bar plaintiffs from voting. They brought a suit for declaratory and injunctive relief against a class of county clerks and voter registrars. During the course of the suit, the three county officials named as representative defendants decided not to contest the action. They agreed to register the ex-felons, including the named plaintiffs. This was a sophisticated and clever maneuver, for it could have mooted the suit of the class action. Fortunately, the Supreme Court held in a finding that the case was not mooted and proceeded to the merits.

American society needs to acknowledge the burden of the economics of litigation, the ignorance of class members, and the lack of knowledge of the rights of similarly situated parties. The broad sweep of public interest class litigation argues for going forward with certifying a class action where it is obvious that the interests of large numbers of absentee plaintiffs are implicit in the case. The class can be realigned and reassembled as litigation proceeds.

Future Class Actions

Provision for scientific sampling of notice in conjunction with new, liberalized intervention rules will permit significantly affected private parties to join in filing briefs. This could effectively enlarge the power of the people both directly and through their representatives. It would further the public interest against those who are abusing it for their private ends. Class actions seeking injunctive and monetary relief affect a wide range of interests beyond the actual participants of the suits. Statutory revisions could empower the court to compel agencies with relevant expertise to join the suit. Legislation could enable the litigants to call upon the courts to call for *amicus* briefs or full intervention of other parties. This would broaden the courts' perspective. Such a broader process would assist the court in evaluating settlements and formulating relief.[29]

The Federal Trade Commission Improvements Act created class action against unlawful trade practices about consumer product warranties. The old FTC Act provided *only* for "agency action" to seek damages and other legal and equitable relief. This was a paternalistic approach toward consumers injured by unlawful trade practices. A relatively new provision appears to authorize calculation of damages on a classwide basis as well as distribution of unclaimed funds through a fluid recovery mechanism. The FTC Improvement Act's private class suits, under this provision, cannot be recognized unless each individual claim is greater than $25. Furthermore, the aggregate value of all claims in the action should exceed $50,000. In addition, to bring a class action there must be at least one hundred named plaintiffs. These changes break new ground. Private actions in the public interest are now possible.

Derivative Suits

Corporations have increasingly become the dominant private "actors" in our society. This is in part because they were granted immortality, as a person, in *Santa Clara*. An unwary Supreme Court created in this artificial person a wealth accumulator with the power to use deep pockets as well as to indenture natural persons through employment contracts. Thereby it caused many of these employees to turn their working lives over to the corporation with the correlative duty of undivided loyalty.

Legal techniques designed to encourage the use of private litigation to vindicate significant public interest rights urge the use of class actions by way of the shareholders' derivative suits. The shareholders' derivative suit permits a shareholder to represent the corporation. The stockholders maintain an action when the regularly elected or appointed corporate functionaires do not act either because they are wrongdoers or because the majority in control of the corporation does not want them to act. It provides an action against a management that has acted in malfeasance, misfeasance, or nonfeasance of office. The rights being litigated in a derivative suit are those of the corporation. If the action is successful, and damages are assessed, they are paid to the corporation's treasury. This restores value to the stockholders' general benefit. Recent cases indicate the courts may be moving in the direction of using their powers of judicial review to protect the stockholders from management activities that are self-serving and clearly against the interest of the corporation. By holding corporate officers and directors accountable as fiduciaries for their conduct, society has an effective means of enforcing the "public's interest." Dean Stone of the University of Chicago Law School has argued for more social control of corporate behavior in *Where the Law Ends.*

Lawyers and the Public

Distrust of lawyers is hardly new. Shakespeare's Dick the butcher spoke for the ages with his famous blunt suggestion, "First, let's kill all lawyers." Any American who loves our constitutional culture with its rule by law and its peaceful resolution of disputes cannot be indifferent about this current public attitude. Many people believe lawyers recommend more work than needed. People believe they send more disputes to court than necessary. Dan Quayle believes it. In 1986, the *National Law Journal* polled average Americans about what they thought of lawyers and what lawyers ought to do about it.[30]

- Almost 75 percent of the respondents said the lower level of the federal judiciary ought to be popularly elected, not appointed by the president subject to congressional approval. The respondents said federal judges should serve for a fixed term, not for life, as is constitutionally mandated. I strongly disagree. Life tenure protects independence of judgment and minimizes conflicts of interest, although Alzheimer's disease and the like require monitoring of the bench.
- The principles behind the First Amendment are not supported by much of the population: 37 percent of those questioned said they would not favor Congress passing a bill stating, "There should be no law abridging the freedom of speech or freedom of the press." This is the First Amendment, in part.
- The respondents believe that *pro bono* work should be mandatory for lawyers; 55 percent said lawyers should be required by law to devote time to public or community service.
- The nation is split over the cause of the so-called American "litigation crisis." About equally blamed are lawyers, insurance companies, and consumers. A mere 6 percent said that the lawsuit volume is the fault of manufacturers.
- Blame for the medical malpractice crisis was spread around: 32 percent blame patients, 25 percent lawyers, 23 percent physicians, and 15 percent insurance companies.
- According to 57 percent of the respondents lawyers should defend a client despite knowing he or she committed the crime.
- A hefty 84 percent said they wouldn't care about the sex of their lawyer,

while 12 percent preferred a man as counsel. Only 4 percent preferred a female lawyer.

- Seventy-three percent of respondents felt that lawyers were average in their honesty, 17 percent felt they were less honest than average, and 7 percent felt they were more honest.
- Fifty-four percent of respondents felt satisfied with their lawyers, 29 percent were somewhat satisfied, and a surprisingly low 8 percent were very dissatisfied.
- Lawyers were near the bottom of the list of professionals in terms of public respect. Only journalists, elected officials, professional athletes, entertainers, and corporate executives rated lower. Strangely enough, the same respondents showed that business was the first profession they would recommend for their children after medicine. Law was a trailing third, but it was far ahead of accounting, teaching, and the clergy.

It appears that the legal profession has bad press. The negative perception of the law is due to public perception of limited access to justice—that neither the law as an institution nor society as a political-economic process takes individual rights seriously.

Due Process—Access to Our Courts Is Not a Right

To the masters of efficiency the independent judiciary looks like a relic of the past, a link to an earlier day when power was more diffuse. Of course, that attitude dominates only when one takes the view of economic efficiency. Good access to justice for the ordinary citizen provides an effective countervailing power against the increasing self-aggrandizement of the modern state and its masters, the power elite.

The right to due process reflects a fundamental value of our American constitutional system. Due process implies common-sense rules of fair play that define the various rights and duties of our society. These rules are binding on its members, enabling them to govern and handle their affairs. They may then definitively settle their differences in an orderly and predictable manner. *United States of America* v. *Boddie* v. *Connecticut*[31] drew upon the broad principles established by due process cases. The Supreme Court concluded that the state's refusal to admit these opponents to its courts, the sole means they had in Connecticut for obtaining a divorce, was equivalent to denying them an opportunity to act upon their plain right to ask the state to dissolve their marriage. The absence of an efficient countervailing justification for the state's action resulted in a denial of due process before the U.S. Constitution.

In concluding *Boddie*, the Supreme Court found the due process clause of the Fourteenth Amendment required that these litigants be afforded an opportunity to get into court. The Supreme Court, however, has not yet decided that access for all individuals to the courts is a right under all those circumstances guaranteed by the due process clause of the Fourteenth Amendment. In this Connecticut case, we have observed only that a state may not, consistent with obligations imposed upon the state by the due-process clause of the Fourteenth Amendment, prevent a citizen from presenting his case for due process in the dissolution of the legal relationship of marriage.

The Supreme Court refused to extend the *Boddie* rationale to other fees. This has effectively prevented low-income litigants from achieving access to the courts on other matters. The poor and the middle-class are still faced with the heavy burden of paying for the costs of litigation to prove that the precedent of *Boddie* applies to their particular cases. A federal legislative solution will be necessary if we are to have even-handed access to justice throughout the United States.

The modern state may be committed to the rule of law, but it is also committed in practice to economic planning by huge, independent private corporations, a huge military establishment, and to social welfare. It is the independent judiciary that those with awesome power bump up against. Programs call for command and central planning, continuity, forecasting, and technical services for greater efficiency. Efficiency becomes an end in itself. When seen in this light, the modern state is an administrative state. It wants freedom from the constraints of individual natural rights.

In 1972, in *Papachristou* v. *the City of Jacksonville,* the defendants challenged a Jacksonville ordinance that lumped together as vagrants "rogues and vagabonds, common gamblers, night walkers, thieves, persons wandering or strolling about from place to place without any lawful purpose or object, habitual loafers or persons able to work but habitually living upon wives or minor children."[32]

The defendants were arrested on such charges as "prowling by automobile." The rule of law, said Justice Douglas, writing for the Court, demanded equality. Vagrancy laws were "useful to the police." They made it easy "to round up so-called undesirables," but the ordinance gave the police too much power. What excuse could there be to arrest people walking or loafing or strolling who merely looked suspicious to the police? The ordinance was so vague it wasn't giving fair notice to the public. It did not explain in simple terms what was right or wrong conduct according to the ordinance. The Court found it plainly unconstitutional. *Papachristou* was decided nearly two centuries after the Bill of Rights, one century after the ratification of the Fourteenth Amendment to the Constitution. This long span of time speaks loudly about how long it takes the law to respond to those who are genuinely poor and unorganized. Not until the "rights consciousness" of the 1970s did the common sort reach the threshold of legal change. Yet, in all this time the courts were, to most Americans, symbols of a national commitment to the mythology of basic rights.

Arbitration, Mediation, and Neighborhood Justice

Americans for Legal Reform, led by Glenn Nishimura and the publishers of ALR-HALT, find themselves fighting against heavy-duty machinations of the professional bar in Texas, Florida, California, and throughout the nation. They seek to reform legal institutions to make legal remedies accessible at reasonable costs to the average American. Their indefatigable battle has resulted in the American Bar Association moving forward in a ponderous way, trying to try. Some pilot projects could provide less expensive alternative forms of dispute resolution that are so sorely needed by most Americans. In 1980 the U.S. Congress passed the Dispute Resolution Act, which assigned the U.S. attorney general the task of setting up a dispute resolution program. Implementation of the act was not undertaken because of a lack of appropriated funds. The period set by the act's sunset provision has passed, so this aspect of government facilitation of dispute resolution is a dead letter.[33] *Much urban stress could be ameliorated if practical, common-sense forums were available at low cost for neighborhood resolution problems in housing, domestic relations, friction with local officials, traffic, and petty crime.* The effete bar has been unwilling to dirty its hands in such grubby, mundane problems. It has not acted nobly.

The framework to analyze the merits of judicial interaction with private ways of ending conflicts can be developed by considering four ideal types of dispute resolution techniques: regulation of private ordering, mediation, privately controlled adjudication, and publicly controlled adjudication. In the first two, public control would be minimal. The ultimate disposition of the dispute is shaped by the values and interests of the disputants. The outcome will depend on their skills and bargaining power, which will reflect, in part, the credibility of their presentation of real claims. In the latter two, the dispute is resolved in a court. Perhaps society will permit the aid of paralegal social agencies or their extensions. Privately controlled adjudication, as public litigation, is always limited to one opportunity. The same is true of submitting the dispute to negotiation or mediation, as the disputants may choose. These four methods are not mutually exclusive. A dispute may be worked out on several levels simultaneously or successively. American society has difficulty enabling simultaneity. We should consider each of these forms of dispute resolution.

Private Ordering

This is the oldest form of dispute resolution. It predates society itself. It is self-help by putting the parties back to fighting it out. Its chief advantage is that it promotes pluralistic decisionmaking. The state does not dictate a solution. Rather, the parties work out a settlement based on their interests, shared expectations, and relative bargaining power. There are two disadvantages to private ordering. First, the solution may result in irreconcilable collective notions of injustice by the disputants, as with the Hatfields and McCoys (or the Montagues and Capulets). Second, conflict between parties can result in violent social disruption. All societies, therefore, regulate self-help to some extent. Japan is more successful with its use.[34] Judges and commentators also acknowledge that, on occasion, U.S. courts often act as a theater in which the parties have a ritualized fight.[35] Private bargaining is ineffective if one side is too disorganized or too weak to protect itself. One party may have no incentive or need to bargain with the other outside an expensive legal forum, due, perhaps, to its superior power (for example, a public employer). The press, television, and other media have promoted private ordering in such circumstances by reporting the failures of businesses and corporations to show respect for small and unorganized consumers.

The corporations and businesses have responded with 1-800 hotlines and other mechanisms through which the aggrieved may organize themselves. Thus, our society knows that disputants can negotiate in good faith without litigation. The consensual aggrieved group holds individually, substantial recoverable, claims. However, reconciliation of the dispute is dependent on the goodwill of the business. It is under no more than a very soft social compulsion to negotiate at all. The crass free market economist's expectation is that the business will settle only when cost-benefit analysis proves the savings in litigation and other costs outweigh the outlays for settlement.

On the other hand, the powerful may be governed by a communitarian spirit and their own sense of good business ethics. Nevertheless, such persons of goodwill are at a disadvantage in the market. Therefore, compulsion is necessary. Some private ordering may be possible without the compulsion of an actual class suit. There is no research to show whether businesses feel more compelled to settle private disputes since the 1966 renovation of Rule 23, which vitalized class actions.

Parties who can afford to litigate may agree to a resolution of their controversy by way of privately controlled adjudication such as Judicate. Society may subsidize private litigation—through provision of attorney's fees and forum costs—to create an opportunity to enunciate general principles, for example, private antitrust cases. Through antitrust law we exercise social control over external conduct. I have proposed public interest lawsuits by private parties through Committees of 1000 as a way for private ordering to resolve conflicts. To the extent society successfully encourages such private adjudication, the bureaucratic distortion of regulatory statutes caused by private bargaining is eliminated.

Mediation

A settlement can be handled by mediating peacemakers. Their conflict resolution methods are different from law-school training. Mediators seek to bring the people together. Their way is to get us to resolve our differences among ourselves. They arrange solutions so both sides can be "satisfied." They are not necessarily optimal solutions. They are the doves of conflict resolution. Mediators are dedicated to the proposition that with proper guidance and help most of us can and will resolve our disputes in a mutually constructive, least-cost way. Some lawyers can learn to become good mediators. However, their propensity is to do combat (a trait that motivated them to choose law school). They prefer "go for the jugular" strategies. Lawyers are mostly opposite from mediators. Mediators seek mutually helpful negotiation based on creative, individualized problem-solving. They are uncontrolled by precedent and legal tenets. Today, in the United States, the personnel best-trained to do successful mediation are labor negotiators, industrial psychologists, psychiatric social workers, psychotherapists, pastoral counselors, and the like. This assumes they have training in group-therapy processes. In view of the content of many of these small disputes, such training ought to be supplemented by training in business negotiations. Certainly those trained in arbitration and labor-management grievance-handling procedures have the skills.

Publicly Controlled Adjudication

When aggrieved parties use publicly controlled adjudication as their method of conflict resolution, society will impose a solution whether or not both parties want it. Public control may be exercised in any one of four areas: investigation, initiation, litigation, or settlement. Official investigation toward initiation of many kinds of lawsuits represents the greatest degree of public intervention in private disputes. There is little room for private bargaining; the victim has very limited power to forgive the offender (principally by withholding testimony). Paradoxically, official control of suit initiation is used to delay private access to the court, to promote negotiated solutions between the government and a private party.

To diminish the level of urban stress, we need a much more cost-effective legal profession with a willingness to redefine its monopoly over the practice of law. The legal profession insists that simple, routine tasks that ought to be performed by paralegals or clerks are "the practice of law." It is an arrogant abuse of power to arrogate to lawyers' coffers excessive charges for legal work that can and should be performed at much lower cost.[36]

Fees and affordability are twin, related problems. The legal profession must face them to improve its cost-effectiveness as a dispute-resolving social institution. At least 50 percent of the legal needs of the poor are unmet. The legal profession has failed to successfully fulfill its duty to the public interest. A required number of hours per year of *pro bono publico* work, or, possibly, a tax or fee paid to bar associations in lieu of pro bono service, could be mandated. Even better is a "peer group expectation" that one must serve the community, as some business executives do, as an expected cost of doing business. There has been positive movement of late. Conditions are improving. The law profession could provide for aggressive and skillful services sorely needed by the poor and middle class. U.S. justice will continue to languish as we await it becoming a normal expectation.

The power elite does not take middle- and lower-class rights seriously. One commentator has suggested value billings and means billings as alternative structures for legal fees to solve the problem of unaffordably high litigation costs for the middle class. A first step would be for business to insist on an itemized breakdown of billings. Law firms should be charging a sliding scale for separated rates: for the senior partners, the lawyer associates, the paralegals, the legal secretaries, the librarians, the clerks, the photocopying machine, the couriers, the subpoena servers, etc. Any business executive knows that this itemized billing should be extended to the other profit centers, such as charges for job and administrative overhead. Society has been too patient with the abysmal failure of liberal arts–trained lawyers to be efficient, organized, and cost-effective. The English have led the way by officially certifying paralegals. Today, in England, simple real estate conveyances and the like will be done at lower cost. There is no reason why such restructuring of fees wouldn't be profitable to the well-organized, computer-assisted, word processing law firm. Honest physicians have learned to use X-ray technicians, medical technicians, practical nurses, and paramedics, and they charge for services accordingly. The law profession must rapidly adapt to these changes.

I hasten to add the following comment. Service in the public interest is the first distinction of law as a profession. Surely the pursuit of learning is a close second value that distinguishes law as a profession from other profit-dominated careers. Lawyers counsel and advise on every aspect of experience and endeavor. The demands on lawyers to understand and appreciate other fields of knowledge are extraordinary. A lawyer's education and learning never end. The best lawyers are searching by nature, and good students by training and experience. They maintain open and flexible minds, attentive to the past and alive to the future. They pursue learning, not primarily for profit, but for knowledge and competency. These are important caveats against those with "bottom line"–oriented mentalities.

Today, there is a clear and present danger. The law may follow the Chicago school of economics and make all personal values and satisfaction subject to cost accounting and net-profit analysis by way of computerized hourly billing and narrow specialization. Our constitutional culture will be the loser, for democratic capitalism will soon be replaced by a society dominated by a neofascist power elite. If the first commandment of the legal profession becomes two thousand billable hours a year, what happens to public service? How will we provide for pro bono participation, community assistance, and awareness of current geopolitical legal developments?

In the old days of this nation's "melting pot" and "frontier justice," we had law-givers who were usually self-educated, simple, but intelligent men. They had rich life experience and meted out justice to people they knew personally. As the waves of migration occurred, legal education was dispersed widely. It was of varying quality and not under the unifying control of the states. As a result all sorts of people from various family backgrounds became lawyers in the late nineteenth and early twentieth century. Those lawyers who were most entwined in the daily political life of their neighborhoods and the local political machine (and often the least learned in law) became the local judges. It was a product of patronage. This disorderly mixture of local politics and local justice produced a court system far more accessible to immigrants than if the judicial corps had been chosen from the elite educational institutions. Competitive entry through career service, as in Europe, would have resulted in the domination of the bar and the judicial branch of the government by the old American Anglo-Saxon upper middle class. This system was operative and handled millions of small claims each year. But, state by state, the nation decided to abandon it after 1945.

Tragically, after World War II there was a disintegration and decay of the justices-of-the-peace system that had been much more responsive to the average citizen. Judicial appointments in the 1970s and 1980s were taken by the more remote, upper-middle-class people. We destroyed common-sense justice based on the life experience of a man trusted by his neighbors and failed to replace it. We need to create new conflict-resolution centers at the local level to restore the myth of justice.

Let us now take a more detailed look at mediation, arbitration, and neighborhood justice centers. Systematic dispute resolution is here to stay. It has a place in the justice system. It will become a field for many practicing attorneys as well as social scientists, psychologists, and professional arbitrators and mediators. Recently, the American Bar Association has nurtured alternative means of dispute resolution. However, it has not done this with the idea that the alternatives are a means of eliminating litigation. Quite appropriately, the ABA believes that litigation—the full-scale adjudicatory process—defines only one end of the continuum of dispute resolution techniques. On the other end is the simple two-party negotiation. In between are all forms of alternatives such as arbitration, mediation, and the use of neighborhood justice centers. Litigation remains important. It is one of the primary forms of dispute resolution. However, litigation can be overused and misused to the detriment of the disputants and the public. Let's first consider mediation.

At present, when it comes to settling disputes—divorces, automobile collisions, minor injuries, neighborhood affrays, family feuds, and the like—American society is doing a poor job of offering choices. This chapter has provided much discussion about the uses of litigation as a way to vent or relieve urban stress. Lawyers, trained to believe in adversarial justice, offer zealous advocacy based on the feudal jousting principle. They champion their clients' causes, jousting with words, evidence, delay tactics, legal tenets, and loopholes. They divide us. Your side against mine. One wins. One loses. There are less aggressive ways to resolve conflicts. Neighborhood justice, mediation, and arbitration must be promoted by business leaders and leaders from other powerful social institutions such as the churches, universities, and foundations. Nationwide, these methods should become a United Way project. The idea would be to get the law to accept practitioners of mediation and neighborhood justice from other scholarly disciplines and vocations. We need here people with common sense, based on a varied life experience.

Mediation

Conventionally, mediation is the intervention of a third party to settle disputes without the use of coercive force. Villages in India conduct dispute resolution negotiations that resemble group therapy sessions. Related disputes are brought up and grievances aired. There is a general talking out of group problems.[37] Mediation differs from adjudication in that the mediator seeks to further the interest of the parties. The adjudicator stipulates the outcome not necessarily pursuant to the desires of the parties. The mediator may foster agreement by articulating compromises that are mutually acceptable to the disputants. The mere presence of a third-party mediator is likely to inhibit negotiation in bad faith since the disputants would generally not want to appear unreasonable. In addition, the outsider may be able to facilitate agreement by clarifying or qualifying the issues. The parties are free to talk out the full range of their grievances, unfettered by legal categories or rules of admissability and relevance. The mediator, through request to the parties, may seek to restate areas of agreement and disagreement through his or her own statement of the issues and through direction of discussion toward the most fruitful areas. Of course, an outsider may be able to break deadlocks and secure a compromise agreement to which each side has contributed. Ideally, there will be no unilateral ascription; all will be partly vindicated and none condemned.

The formality of the courts prevents them from identifying root causes of disputes, and, thus, effecting lasting settlements. Here a number of reforms are being put forward to supplement existing legal processes. This movement for delegalization, simplification, and informality has been directed at a number of activities, ranging from rethinking our antitrust laws and the deregulation of major industries through the development of alternative forms of dispute resolution to handle petty criminal and civil disputes.

The Multidoor Approach

Larry Ray, director of the American Bar Association's Standing Committee on Dispute Resolution, oversees a program called the "Multidoor Approach." Pilot projects are now in place in Houston, Texas, Tulsa, Oklahoma, and Washington, D.C. The aim is to resolve many problems by providing a highly efficient, cost-effective, personalized referral program. The programs compile lists of all consumer agencies and organizations that offer social and legal services. An intake specialist analyzes the problem, checks the lists, and directs the person to the appropriate "door." This is a multidoor approach to using existing agencies that the average person knows little about. The heavy emphasis is on mediation, guidance and counseling, intervention, and other alternatives to litigation. The multidoor approach is working because it is based on common sense. People like it because their options are laid out for them. The help given is to lead them through the process. Besides advising aggrieved persons about other programs to resolve their disputes, all three projects have ongoing small-claims mediation programs. Judges urge those filing suits to first try mediation, scheduling a trial only if mediation fails. In Washington, D.C., consideration is being given to expanding the service to major disputes. Eventually the process ought to be compulsory, with the judicial process as a last resort.[38]

In 1986 the Department of Justice's National Institute of Justice published a report by John Lodge Euler on the ABA-directed comparative study of community-oriented alternative dispute resolution (ADR) programs located in Houston, Tulsa, and Washington, D.C. None of these programs handles particularly serious criminal matters or large civil disputes involving complex issues or large sums of money. Instead, the efforts are directed at resolving everyday disputes between average people. The study indicated that judges, lawyers, arbitrators, and litigants all seem favorably impressed with ADR programs and are generally of the view that time and money had been saved.[39] ADR is here to stay for some forms of government/private party disputes. To broaden its base so it can become a fair and efficient manner of resolving conflicts with real savings in time, money, and resources, we will need good faith accommodation by the private bar to a nonadversarial system in which both sides win in some way.

Neighborhood Dispute Resolution

We need to reestablish the function once performed by the justices of the peace. To some extent the low-level tribunals grew out of the magistrate of Roman times, when the idea of justice was tied to politics. It is foolish to think that some ethnic groups have not brought to this country that same Roman (Latin) cultural bias, summed up in the adage that, "It's not what you know, it's who you know." This attitude was reinforced by the "big city" bosses of a bygone era. One metroarea, Chicago, is particularly afflicted by this malady of democracy.

Consider the relative clarity of the vision of justice in the medieval world as a contrast. Whatever its merits, the ancient Roman solution was not suited to the medieval world. In the Middle Ages, church councils often commanded magistrates to forgive the court fees of poor litigants and to assign a private lawyer to help them gratuitously. In England, the maxim that the poor should not pay for writs was accepted by the time of Henry III. Neither of these solutions should be confused with the modern idea of state aid. Such an idea was not intelligible before the modern state emerged. This spirit is more akin to *pro bono publico* than forcing the cost of services on individuals. In the Middle Ages charitable solutions to problems of the poor were required in a powerful way. The impetus to charity grew from the strongest intellectual forces affecting the mind, brain, and soul of the time—the fear or love of God.

Its spirit was owed to an oft-told story, "The Appeal of Alice." A humble servant, Alice appealed to the magisterial circuit justice for help, saying that, "Alice can get no justice at all, seeing that she is poor and this Thomas is rich." She had no one to plead for her. She prayed, "For God's sake, Sir Justice, think of me, for I have none to help me save God and you."

The story of Alice had great moral force in its day. However, in the twentieth century the human mind has been formed by different affective forces. We must look another way to find universal appeal to do what is right. It will be difficult to find something that is soul-satisfying to the yuppies and the narcissistic "me" generation. The magical, mystical nature of medieval minds and the class divisions of those superstitious times should not cause us to ignore the quality of their answer to the problems of the poor, who were viewed with compassion, a spirit notably absent in the attitude toward the needy held by many of our conservatives, who tend to be the well-to-do.

There is a final major theme, barely perceived, shimmering on the horizon but harkening to a time when ancient society centered all authority—executive, legislative, and judicial—in the single institution of the village elders. In ancient times, the citizen was speaking at one time to the entire government concerning his grievance. The right to due process of his grievance was always guaranteed—he was always able to talk to the people who could make a change, though there was no guarantee they would act. In recent centuries, society has become more complex. Today, private citizens with political fears of reprisal have become distrustful of remote government and its powerful allies.

Neighborhood Justice Centers

Neighborhood justice centers now number well over a hundred in the United States. They vary widely in structure and specific mission, but they share a role as alternatives to courts for handling both criminal and civil grievances and doing so using mediation and compromise rather than compulsory formality and winner-take-all. Some proponents are arguing that by removing the case-load of these minor issues from the dockets, the courts will have the opportunity to more effectively and expeditiously handle the serious and difficult problems that remain.

Neighborhood justice centers have been designed without adequate knowledge. We do not know if the justice system is weak because it does not provide adequate alternatives, or because many people, including those with minor disputes, prefer other means to resolve their problems. Some commentators suggest people are so alienated from society as to be disaffected and apathetic. Generally there is a need for careful empirical research before any single solution is adopted on a grand scale. This is the right time for multifarious solutions and experimentation. Today there is not much evidence of a "market" for the neighborhood justice style of intervention. It appears residents use and strongly prefer an apparently effective set of informal neighborhood-based options for resolving disputes. Most respondents are reluctant to bring in an outsider, preferring to deal directly with their adversaries. When third parties were brought in, it was as advocates and advisers, not as negotiators. Those called upon were most often people seen as a part of the neighborhood. These patterns may reflect an unwillingness to negotiate, or a deep distrust of formal institutions. Perhaps it is just a strong penchant for self-reliance, and, hopefully, a growing sense of mutual dependence among residents of the same neighborhood.

A few years ago, three neighborhood justice centers (NJCs) were created by the United States Department of Justice. They substituted mediation for adjudication as the means for resolving minor disputes between persons with ongoing relationships. The experimental centers were located in Atlanta, Kansas City, and Los Angeles. The Institute for Social Analysis, a private research organization, was asked to conduct an evaluation of these three centers to assess their impact on the disputants, the community, and the court systems. Below are some statements that draw upon that evaluation. They present a healthy diversity of sponsorship, board involvement, and management style. Thus, while one can speak of the neighborhood justice mode, we must recognize that the different programs possess distinct purposes and processes. *The central concern was whether NJCs could provide relatively inexpensive, fast, and fair resolution of disputes, while enhancing the quality of justice delivered to the community.* A second major concern was whether the centers could attract civil and criminal dispute cases from a variety of sources within the community and the criminal system. Specifically, program sponsors wanted to know whether NJCs could handle various types of interpersonal disputes, such as landlord-tenant disputes and consumer complaints, as well as disputes both begun by citizens referred by the justice system and social service agencies.

Atlanta's NJC is a private, unaffiliated program operating under the guidance of a board of directors composed of court officials, attorneys, and representatives from the police department and community agencies. It is chaired by a popular local judge. Primarily because of many referrals from the civil warrants division of the state court, over half of the NJC cases were disputes between landlords and tenants, consumers and merchants, and employees and employers. Interpersonal disputes between persons with a prior relationship (families, couples, neighbors, friends) made up approximately 40 percent of the cases. Through a conciliation process, the Atlanta NJC was able to foster an agreement in about half the cases. The Atlanta center did not use arbitration, but it did occasionally refer cases to other agencies for assistance.

Kansas City's NJC program was officially formulated by officials of the City Manager's Office and the city's Communities Services Department. The center continued to focus on an area developed by an antecedent dispute program operated by the Kansas City police department. In sharp contrast to Atlanta, two-thirds of the cases in Kansas City involved criminal issues referred by prosecutors in the police department. With this work, the police increasingly became a source of referrals. Over 70 percent of the NJC cases involved disputes between couples, relatives, neighbors, and friends. The remainder involved a variety of civil issues, primarily landlord-tenant and consumer merchant disputes.

The Venice/Mar Vista NJC was sponsored by the Los Angeles County Bar Association and directed by a board composed of bar association officers and public relations agency representatives. In contrast to the criminal justice in both Atlanta and Kansas City, the Venice/Mar Vista NJC was oriented to receive voluntary referrals from within the community itself. Toward this end, the staff engaged in an aggressive outreach campaign by making many presentations to local community groups, undertaking an extensive media campaign, and distributing literature in shopping malls, beach areas, and meetings of community groups. Over 50 percent of the cases were individuals there on their own initiative. Other cases came from local communities, legal aid, and government agencies. One-third of the cases were referred by court personnel. Nearly all the Venice/Mar Vista NJC cases were small-claims disputes which involved landlord-tenant or consumer-merchant disputes, even those of a criminal nature. They usually involved disagreements over money, property settlements, and other civil matters. Because the center relied so heavily on self-referral, not surprisingly it ended up referring a large number of disputants to other agencies. In fact, because of its aggressive media outreach, it became something of a referral center for telephone callers.

Mediation is not, nor should it be, expected to be a panacea for all the problems of people in relationships that have deteriorated to the point of criminal acts or other forms of aggression. For those who want to talk things through with each other, mediation is appropriate, especially if followed up by additional services when problems are deep-seated. For people who do not want to reconcile and/or negotiate settlement, mediation is not likely to work. Prosecution or civil litigation may be the more appropriate response. The challenge to the justice system is, of course, to make available a variety of dispute settlement options.

Compulsory Arbitration

Starting in 1925, the U.S. Congress has repeatedly tried to expand the use of arbitration by way of the Federal Arbitration Act. It was most recently reenacted and recodified in 1947. The purpose of the FAA was to reverse the long-standing hostility of the judiciary and the bar to the enforceability of arbitration agreements. Progress was very slow, but during the past few years a half-dozen or so Supreme Court decisions have made it clear that predispute arbitration agreements will be enforced in a wide variety of cases not previously subject to arbitration. *American citizens have a growing opportunity to lower the costs of dispute resolution by adopting extralegal and extrajudicial compulsory arbitration of their disputes.* Hostility of the bar and the judiciary will continue; only independent citizens' action will cause widespread use of low-cost compulsory arbitration.[40]

As used in Pennsylvania and California, compulsory arbitration is a desirable alternative, particularly when the issues are merely fixing the total amount of property damages and there are no personal, political, or social rights or criminal charges involved.

Beyond the idea of neighborhood justice is the reform idea that there should be greater lay participation in the legal system, particularly in dispute resolution and judicial administration. In the 1960s and 1970s we saw a concerted attack on the notion of required professionalism in the legal system. The growth of demand for legal services delivered by nonlawyers, as well as the greater regulation of the activity of lawyers, has been an expression of this supposed flight from professionalized ways of delivering conflict resolution services. The growth of the neighborhood justice system may well be a product of this trend. In effect, it may be a symptom of our national search for alternative solutions as a result of the defects and imperfections of the dominant system.

Taking Rights Seriously

To the economist, if a right cannot be valued in terms of money it is not worthy of discussion. To the economist, a citizen is acting irrationally if he or she pursues a fraudulent merchant by exposing them to the public, if they cannot make a profit doing it. Furthermore, seeking punitive damages for the malicious and deceitful sale of a lower-priced, defectively designed, but highly profitable products (such as a useless and dangerous antiaging cream) is seen as profiteering. This is because the costs of litigation exceed the cost of buying a replacement product. Such rights-conscious conduct does not meet the economist's paradigm of rational, self-interested conduct.

The result is that taking rights seriously is sneered at by many of the yuppie "me" generation. Bringing the fraudulent merchant to justice is, to them, an irrational frittering away of scarce resources on a quixotic pursuit of "rights" that are outside the economist's paradigm. Still, in America, we are highly dependent on those lonely citizens who will fight for their rights in a fair-playing marketplace. We need them because they are willing to go after the profit-taking and deceitful seller who harms the reputation of democratic capitalism. Yet, as we enter the 1990s, because the free marketeers have been in the ascendancy, such "taking rights seriously" is treated contemptuously. It certainly cannot stand the test of cost-benefit analysis.

The public thinks the legal profession is another profit-driven business. Lawyers can change that view. This chapter calls upon the legal profession, and those clients powerful enough to influence the law, to turn lawyers toward public service. They can take positive action in the public interest as a paramount professional responsibility. Even among lawyers, some lead and others follow. Federal administrative law judge Foster Furcolo, former congressman and ex-governor of Massachusetts, makes the law understandable to the average citizen in his book *Practical Law for the Layman.* According to Furcolo, "Law is the vehicle by which society makes it easer for individuals to live together and enjoy the rights and privileges of civilization without interfering with the rights of others who want to exercise their legal rights."[41]

We, the people of the United States, in order to form a more perfect union, should call upon the legal profession to follow the right honorable Foster Furcolo and renovate the institution of the law. Empowerment of the average person is necessary for the maintenance of the vitality of a democratic economy. We need active support of the free market flow, not only of goods and services, but also of ideas. This is essential for the survival of a democratic republic.

Part VII: A National Colloquium

19. Expanding the Ninth Amendment

The enumeration in the Constitution of certain rights shall not be construed to deny or disparage other rights retained by the people.
                                        —The Ninth Amendment, U.S. Constitution

We are heading toward a paradigm shift to assure and secure the rights of the people—liberty—for all Americans in the United States. This could result in reenergizing the spirit of individual action and promote responsible group participation in our constitutional culture. We need a national colloquy in the forum of the telecommunication media on the nature of these "other rights." What are the limits on the powers of the federal and state governments, and large institutions such as the transnational corporations? We may find by way of our dialogue that our perceived rights are not assured by our current U.S. Constitution. If so, we need an amendment adding clauses to the Ninth Amendment. We could use sweeping language to empower the citizens through class actions and individual action to act for social justice in the public interest. We should explicitly set forth rights such as privacy of our mails and phone communications to remove any uncertainty about whether or not these rights exist.

Randy E. Barrett's *The Rights Retained By the People* is a book on the history and meaning of the Ninth Amendment.[1] According to Barrett, the Ninth Amendment is a basic statement of the inherent natural rights of the individual. It is a declaration and recognition of individualism and inherent rights. Its absence elsewhere in the Constitution accounts for its presence as an amendment. The framers of the Constitution and the Bill of Rights carried with them into their work the English concept of individual liberties inherent in the individual irrespective of the form of government. Their theory of the Constitution was that it was only a body of powers that were granted to government and nothing more than that. The individual inherent rights and liberties antedate and are above constitutions, and may be called pre-constitutional rights.

The current Constitution hobbles participatory democracy and stultifies our growth in a telecommunicating age. The history of the Constitution is one of healthy compromises on very important questions. It was expected to be reworked through time. Our founding fathers had the original intent to leave some questions for future discussion and compromise. "Nothing human can be perfect," wrote Governuer Morris, looking back at the work of the Constitutional Convention twenty-eight years after the fact. "Surrounded by difficulties, we did the best we could; leaving it with those who should come after us to take counsel from experience, and exercise prudently the power of amendment, which we had provided." Madison wrote, "I am not one of the number, if there be any such . . . who think the Constitution lately adopted a faultless work."

When Madison wrote, public dissatisfaction centered on the absence of a Bill of Rights. That omission was corrected when the 1st Congress proposed for ratification by the states the ten amendments—our essential Bill of Rights. The states ratified them by 1791. Since then, the Constitution has been amended only sixteen times in nearly two centuries, mostly on substantive matters. We have followed the original intent of our founding fathers in acting to amend the Constitution over time. Expansion of our Bill of Rights is appropriate now. Some insouciant, or simple-minded, persons characterize the U.S. Constitution as a "living document." The truth is that it is defined, revised, and covertly amended by our judiciary, especially the Supreme Court justices. Why not shift some of the amendatory power into the hands of the people?

Some commentators suggest that the first additional amendment ought to be an easier way to amend the Constitution. The founders erected large barriers to the amendatory exercise—obstacles that proved to be greater than they could have expected. Nonetheless, approval of an amendment by two-thirds of both houses of the Congress, followed by its ratification by three-fourths of the states, can on occasion be attained, as the twenty-six successful efforts attest. But with one-third plus one of those voting in either the Senate or the House, or one-fourth plus one of the states, able to block any amendment, and this in a modern nation with well-financed countervailing powers able to mount dissembling resistance, needed amendments will be virtually impossible to achieve. The amendment process in the hands of Congress and state legislatures is a procedural glacier.

It was a stroke of genius, to be venerated, that John Marshall moved into this ineffective process and created the "amendatory" power of *Marbury* v. *Madison* for our highest court. To preserve tranquility, myth has prevailed. The Supreme Court never refers to its decisions as the use of the amendatory power. Euphemism to the contrary, through the years that power has been exercised many times. The result is a great body of law, "constitutional law." The Court has acted slowly, shy and reluctant to use such a power. After all, it is ostensibly in the hands of the legislative bodies. The Court's historical record is not bad, on balance. Otherwise the ideas of the evolving constitutional culture and democratic capitalism would already be dead. But it would be false to say it is constitution-making by the people in the real sense. The myth of the Supreme Court's hidden amendatory power cannot survive much longer. Rising educational levels and the telecommunicating media are destroying the operative power of many of our old myths. If one believed the Supreme Court justices were embodiments of the will of the sovereign people, one could call the Constitution a living document.

We should not fear a reopening of constitution-making. Those who would be constitution-makers at, say, a convention, would realize they are mediators for not only today but also for all who are to come. It is likely they would act with high moral purpose and a very long time horizon. The atmosphere of such a great debate discourages pet solutions to petty problems or quick fixers of current difficulties. The secret convention at Philadelphia in 1787 succeeded because its members were careful in their phraseology. They were general enough to be enduring but specific enough to preserve that which they believed to be good. It is possible that a national debate would result in little change to the Constitution. However, in such an event, it is likely we would see a revival of the power of our withering branch of government, the Congress. A national dialogue on the peoples' rights could reenergize the Congress.

The pressures of a demand for a constitutional convention could send a healthy wind of change through the halls of Congress, even without a convention. It is worth a try. I propose a few changes to the Ninth Amendment in this section. Constitutional amending is an artful exercise in semantics, psycholinguistics, history, law. That is, it is the effective use of the English language. Plain-speaking should be the order of the day. Here I begin the discussion of the difference between social rights and political rights. There is a real question as to whether we want to do more than preserve equalitarian rights. The recitation of egalitarian social rights within a constitution raises serious economic issues.

"We hold these truths to be self-evident, that all men are created equal, that they are endowed by their Creator with certain inalienable rights, that among these are life, liberty, and the pursuit of happiness." This justly celebrated passage is a proud expression of a commonly held belief of some eighteenth-century European philosophers that all men are by nature equally free and independent, and have certain inherent rights. Further, when people enter a state of society, they cannot by any compact deprive or divest their posterity of these rights, namely, the enjoyment of life and liberty, with the means of acquiring and possessing property and pursuing and obtaining happiness. Take note that "happiness" was added to Locke's three rights. We have the eloquence of Jefferson lending wings to the plain thoughts of Locke.

Today, many Americans expect the state to take positive action to protect the rights of ordinary citizens. But such expectations are naive. Our adversary system requires protest and litigation to protect these ostensibly positive rights from infringement by the state, powerful private organizations, and the power elite. We are a people with a blurred vision of our rights.

FDR and the Economic Bill of Rights

On January 11, 1944, during his annual message to Congress, President Roosevelt specifically set forth what these new rights ought to be:

> This republic had its beginning, and grew to its present strength, under the protection of certain inalienable political rights—among them free speech, free press, free worship, trial by jury, freedom from unreasonable searches and seizures. . . . As our nation has grown in size and stature, however . . . these political rights proved inadequate to assure us equality in the pursuit of happiness. We have come to a clear realization of the fact that true individual freedom cannot exist without economic security and independence. . . . In our day these

economic truths have become as self-evident. We have accepted, so to speak, a second Bill of Rights under which a new basis of security and prosperity can be established for all, regardless of station, race, or creed.

Among these are the right to a useful remunerative job in the industries, shops, farms, or mines of the nation; the right to earn enough to provide adequate food and clothing and recreation; the right of every farmer to raise and sell his products at a return that will give him and his family a decent living; the right of any businessman, large and small, to sell in an atmosphere of freedom from unfair competition by domination from monopolies at home and abroad; the right of every family to a decent home; the right of every family to adequate medical care and the opportunity to achieve and enjoy good health; the right to adequate protection from economic fears of old age, sickness, accident and unemployment; the right to a good education.

Roosevelt actually proposed that some new "economic rights" be made a part of the Bill of Rights. This would be a vast change. It is open to real question whether we can even afford to pay for them. *This treatise has taken the position that our Constitution is "equalitarian" as to political and civil rights, but not "egalitarian" as to economic rights to income.* Of course, the Congress does have the power to make our society "egalitarian" by use of its existing powers delegated from the Constitution.

The "Right" to Privacy

We are searching for the meaning of the "other rights," which are not to be denied or disparaged by the federal or state governments because of Ninth Amendment protection. Today, the best we can say is that privacy is subject to definition and redefinition on a case-by-case basis by our judiciary. Telecommunications and wiretapping have made this a major issue of late. Recently, a surreptitious wiretap was illegally placed on the phone lines of Prof. Lawrence Tribe in a closet in the hallowed halls of ivy at Harvard Law School.[2] We expect the state to react to protect us from such foul play. The duties of the modern states are increased by rising expectations on the part of citizens concerning such liberties.

Let us consider the idea of universal "human rights."[3] Is the idea of "human rights" a late-twentieth-century equivalent for the eighteenth-century idea of the "rights of man"? If so, why was the earlier formulation ever abandoned? Is it because the new concept embraces a greater complement of individual and collective "entitlements"? Are there rights that did not figure prominently during the Enlightenment? Human rights may be the rights of man in twentieth-century dress. Can we, with our twentieth-century minds, recapture the resonance and full meaning of those natural rights, once held in the minds of the Minutemen at Valley Forge, or of the men who joined Capt. Daniel Shay in his rebellion against the ineffective Continental Congress before we ratified the Constitution? Human rights may be the single most important neglected subject of both our national and international political agendas. The rights rhetoric of our time is in urgent need of repair. Its revision might serve to inspire confidence in our goals.

In the 1940s Eleanor Roosevelt promoted the use of the expression "human rights." She did it when she discovered, through her work in the United Nations, that the rights of men were not understood in some parts of the world to include any rights of women. Today, we silently shudder at the burnings alive of young wives in India. They are killed by evil families who have claimed the dowry and are now ridding themselves of the woman who brought gifts to the bridal feast.

No one spoke more bitterly against natural rights than philosopher Jeremy Bentham. "Rights are the child of law; from real law come real rights; but from imaginary laws, from laws of nature, come imaginary rights. . . . Natural rights is simple nonsense; natural and imprescriptible rights (an American phrase), rhetorical nonsense, nonsense upon stilts." Bentham's utilitarianism is not to be confused with the American pragmatism of James and Peirce that certainly has ennobling rights within its humane spirit.

Most nineteenth-century champions of the doctrine of the rights of the nation state scorned the rights of the individual. They were in accord with the theorists of rival camps—positivism, empiricism—who regarded natural law and natural rights as nonsense. Rights to those who think in such a way are what the courts allow you to do. If the courts forbade you to do something, it was meaningless to say you had a right to do it. (It is fair to say that Chief Justice Rehnquist appears to think this way.) However, history informs us that there is always self-help in the hands of desperate mortals. A short time before the Constitutional Convention, Capt. Shay and his rabble in western Massachusetts insisted on being heard! They were willing to die for rights denied! The power elite knew it was best not to ignore such violence. Are today's urban riots delivering the same message? We ratified a Constitution, while acknowledging that a bill of rights had to be passed immediately if the Constitution was to have the support of the people. The twentieth century has sorely tested our capacity to have faith in the state's ability to protect human rights. After 1933, when Nazi Germany founded the Third Reich, the Western world realized it was living in a new age of absolutism supported by media propaganda. The age of totalitarian dictatorship was far worse than the worst of the old absolute kings. Such regimes can be seen to be enforcing a "law" that is not the command of a benevolent "sovereign," but of a cruel and genocidal despot.

Law, if it is to deserve the name of law, must respect at least some basic rights to which every human being is entitled, simply because he or she is human. Common sense, once again, was ahead of philosophy. Today, of course, virtually all the most fashionable legal and political philosophers—H. L. A. Hart, John Rawls, Robert Nozick, Ronald Dworkin—are natural rights theorists of one kind or another. Legal positivism (like logical positivism) is effectively dead except in the minds of Rehnquist and Bork and others of their ilk. People feel they do have rights. The United Nations is perhaps responsible for much of the refurbishing of rights imagery. What emerged was the Universal Declaration of Human Rights, "passed and proclaimed" by the General Assembly in 1948.

Universal Declaration of Human Rights

The language of the first group of articles in the United Nations Declaration of Human Rights is that of Locke, Jefferson, and Lafayette.[3] The rights to life, liberty, property, equality, justice, and the pursuit of happiness are spelled out in a readily intelligible form. The U.N. Declaration specifies the rights to freedom of movement, to own property, to marry, to equality before the law and to a fair public trial if accused of any crime, to religious liberty, to free speech and peaceful assembly, and to asylum. Slavery, torture, and arbitrary detention are prohibited.

The U.N. Declaration does not, however, confine itself to the elaboration of these straightforward and compelling assertions. The United Nations, never a body to confine itself to a life that is self-supporting, proceeded like a blithe spirit to assume a world of plentiful, cheap energy, a good, cheap, global transportation system, and an efficiently working agricultural system that could provide adequate food for everyone in the world. The United Nations further theoretically assumed a social organization that could prevent maldistribution so it could adopt a further set of articles. It therefore specified human rights to such things as social security, an adequate standard of living, medical care, rest, leisure, and even "periodic holidays with pay." Who would not pray for that wonderful utopian day! In the meanwhile, we must be more realistic about enforceable rights. Americans have always been more practical with their fantasies.

In the records of the Commission of the United Nations General Assembly, the first set of articles, twenty in all, are called "political and civil rights." The "further rights" are called "economic and social rights." An obvious consequence of including these "economic and social rights" in the 1948 declaration was that it was very difficult to pass from hot rhetoric to deeds.

Americans would be wise to take heed while they consider the enumeration of rights to expand the stated language of the Ninth Amendment. Unfortunately, we cannot all agree with upholding human rights if we try to introduce as human rights claims that we cannot afford and therefore uphold. Nevertheless, I think we can justify the existence of some set of universal human rights. *A human right ought to be defined as something no one, anywhere, may be deprived of without a grave affront to justice.* If a declaration of human rights is what it purports to be, a declaration of universal moral rights, it must be confined to realism. Nothing is more important to an understanding of a right than to acknowledge that it is not an ideal.

Early economists such as Adam Smith argued that, in addition to reducing individual freedom, infringements of property rights tend to reduce economic effort, initiative, efficiency, willingness to take risks, and, ultimately, national prosperity. This perception is the central message of Milton Friedman's *Capitalism and Freedom,* and of the other critics of the welfare state. The core of modern social/economic rights has always been represented by various kinds of income protection and services that make up the modern, multifaceted social security system. "Economic and social rights," however, include also free public education, public housing, publicly financed retraining and rehabilitation, as well as minimum wages and income-oriented production subsidies. The combination of rapidly rising benefits and lagging revenues during the 1970s and early 1980s has led to the present welfare state fiscal crisis. The crisis reflects, first, the revenue/expenditure constraints imposed by current economic conditions. However, there are also long-term problems caused by the rising proportion of elderly persons in society, the maturing of pension programs, and the unabated escalation of medical care costs.[4] The real question is whether the economic and social rights established by the welfare state on balance increase or decrease human freedom. This depends, of course, on how various aspects of freedom of different individuals are weighted. My loss of freedom due to a small tax may be less important than someone else's freedom from starvation. On the other hand, a high tax may not be justifiable if the purpose is to maintain that same person in comfort.

Mancur Olson asks that critical question to those who might demand that a Ninth Amendment convention consider, today, "economic rights." Should we strive for a society that guarantees "freedom from poverty" in the same way it guarantees "freedom of speech?"[5] Such welfare grant transfers, if excessive, may have adverse effects on the incentives to work and save, both for those who receive the transfers and for those who are taxed to provide them. The familiar idea that an excessively generous welfare state weakens the incentive to work and to save is true.

Few citizens had the right to vote at the founding of our republic. Most Americans did not take an active part in the political life of the new republic. Free men contented themselves with voting, if they met the requirements established by state constitutions and laws. All the states maintained some form of property test for voting. Even higher property qualifications were required to hold elective office. How many Americans met these property tests for voting in this period is a matter of vigorous historical dispute. In any event, American society was governed by unspoken assumptions and principles bound up in the shorthand term "deference." There were basically two kinds of Americans, first, "gentlemen," who did not need to worry about earning a livelihood and thus were well-suited to hold office and shape policy, and second, everyone else, often called "the common sort." Still, the distinction was not a rigidly defined class barrier of the type found in Europe. In Denmark, for example, there existed a nine-class system in which it was a crime for members of the upper three classes to interact with members of the lower six.

The United States was innovating—developing a classless society through vertical social mobility. Although social commentators had not discerned the idea, equal opportunity was working for some Americans. Consider, the achievements of the great Dr. Franklin, who became a symbol of the possibilities of America to his admiring compatriots. Similarly, a brilliant illegitimate child could find backing to be educated at King's College (now Columbia University) and become a pillar of the New York legal profession. Such was the climb of Alexander Hamilton, one of the most able and respected proponents of a stronger national government. There was a fluid and evanescent quality to the distinctions between the blue bloods and the common sort in this budding nation. However, since this book has proposed we create a second-class citizenship category for convicted felons, fugitives from the law, and criminal sociopaths, we need to observe that at the founding of the republic there was a subclass, below even the common sort. Several key groups were excluded from rights of citizenship by common consent. They were excluded even from the common sort and had no direct role in shaping American politics.

This subclass was composed of Indians, blacks, women, convicts, fugitives, and the desperately poor or the debtor class. The least obvious group of Americans excluded from political decisionmaking in this period was not the women of the new nation, nor the free and slave blacks, nor even the Indians. It was those thought to be too poor to have a legitimate voice in politics—in a popular phrase of the time, the "desperate debtors." Many people, male and female, came to the British colonies, and later to the United States, as indentured servants, thereby to pay for their passage from Europe. Indentured servants were not treated as property in theory or in practice. They also knew that they were bound only for a finite period. In all other respects, however, they were virtually indistinguishable from chattel slaves. Others not bound for service were not immune from economic collapse. Because there was very little specie, or hard cash, in the United States in this period, the dominant medium of exchange was the promissory note. Unfortunately, thanks to the uncertainties of agriculture and of commerce, many Americans' notes came back to the makers when they could not satisfy the demands. The problems of debt struck most often and most cruelly at the small farmers and tradesmen. For every failure of a Jefferson or a Wilson, there were thousands of failures on a much smaller scale, equally catastrophic for the debtor involved. In some states, those who owed debts sought to induce the state governments to cause inflation by printing new issues of paper money.

Although we do not have the threat of debtors' prisons today, thanks to progress in the humanitarian spirit, we still have debtors who like inflation and abhor garnishment. At the birth of the republic there were many citizens like the indentured servant, who, until he completed the years of service or paid it off in some way, was a second-class citizen. My proposal is that second-time convicted criminals, recidivists, and those convicted of atrocious felonies and treason, could lose their refuge in the Bill of Rights for a period of probation when convicted of another felony. It is not a novel idea, simply prudence. A constitutional amendment would be necessary to separate the second class. This would protect "ordinary citizens" from the power of the state. Peaceful citizens, of course, would still have rights to the exclusionary rules.

It is foolish to think that the power elite that supplied our founding fathers and provisioned the Constitutional Convention did so with elation and alacrity. Most of them preferred the great power they had through deference (that is, the plantation management governance model) within their home states as landed gentry and professionals. They authorized the Constitutional Convention to meet because the Continental Congress established by the Articles of Confederation was "little more than shadow without substance." Daniel Shay, a former captain in the Revolutionary Army fully exposed the deplorable weakness of the federal government in his famed rebellion. Shay was the Boris Yeltsin of his day. Henry Knox, one of Washington's former generals, estimated the rebels could raise 12,000 to 15,000 "desperate and unprincipled men." This was more than Washington had commanded during the Revolution! Under Gen. Benjamin Lincoln the Shaysites were routed. Nevertheless, guerrillas continued to make war through February 1787, looting, burning, and kidnapping merchants and judges. It was this kind of violence that caused the power elite to issue a call for the reform of the federal government and to send delegates to the convention. But, the great majority of our founding fathers had no confidence in popular government. They opposed direct election by the people. Elbridge Gerry stated, "The evils we experience flow from an excess of democracy. The people are dupes of pretended patriots." Fortunately, George Mason, a wealthy planter Jefferson referred to as the wisest man of his generation," shared none of the apprehension of other delegates.[6]

The battle for ratification was a contest of words, arguments, votes, and of parades and bonfires, with an occasional riot thrown in for good measure. The ratification controversy was both a direct, unabashed contest for votes and a complex, impressive argument about politics and constitutional theory. It acted as a catalyst for the creation of a national political community. The dialogue transformed the ways Americans thought of themselves and encouraged the growth and popularity of national loyalties. There were critical issues at the Virginia convention. In Virginia, the Federalists scented victory. Patrick Henry and George Mason showed signs of "despair," as Madison reported. The Federalist delegates then brought forward the idea of recommendatory amendments to accompany a vote for ratification. These recommendations included a solemn commitment from Madison that he would propose the Bill of Rights at the first session of the U.S. Congress. Most states gave little discussion to the essential "natural" humans rights because they were proposing their immediate addition to the Constitution.

Capt. Shay and the rabble-in-arms had their say! George Mason was to have his day. Madison finally introduced Mason's bill of rights before Congress as directed to do so by the Virginia House of Burgesses. The anti-Federalists may well be the unluckiest and most misunderstood losers in our history. Not until this century was their opposition to the Constitution taken seriously and their right to be counted among the framers of the Constitution firmly established. A pamphlet called the "Federal Farmer" put forth their best-reasoned positions. Of paramount importance for all anti-Federalist thought was the Constitution's omission of a bill of rights. Anti-Federalist writers repeatedly invoked the lack of a bill of rights as their most telling argument against the Constitution. George Mason led off with this point in his objections at the convention in Philadelphia. Like the Federalists, the anti-Federalists stressed that the decision to adopt or reject the Constitution was a watershed not only for Americans, but for men and women everywhere who valued freedom.

If the United States has a constitutional convention before the year 2000, Americans must realize the world will be watching, again! I am hopeful we will choose to act because of the reasons set forth. The anti-Federalists forced the Constitution's supporters to engage in a dialogue to explain and justify the new charter, clause by clause. Most important, the anti-Federalists compelled James Madison and other Federalists to pledge themselves to work for the framing and adoption of the Bill of Rights. Madison was swayed by Thomas Jefferson's letters of appeal from France for the adoption of a bill of rights. Jefferson described them as something "the people are entitled to against every government on earth, general or particular, and [that] no government should refuse, or rest on inference." When Congress adopted the Bill of Rights, the dialogue shows that it was in a fluid, dynamic state of the mind. The Ninth Amendment served as valuable assurance that Lockeian natural rights were not to be denied by the rights and powers delegated to the federal and state governments.

There was a significant limiting condition on these rights, however. The Bill of Rights restrained only the federal government. Individuals seeking to vindicate their rights against the actions of state or local governments had only the protection a particular state's constitutional declaration of rights. Nonetheless, the Bill of Rights complemented the creation of a national government by recognizing its citizens' individual liberties. Once the balance between the federal government and the states was radically reshaped by the Civil War and the adoption of the Fourteenth Amendment, most of the rights guaranteed in the first ten amendments were thought to be extended to protect ordinary Americans.

Donald Robinson, editor of the *Bicentennial Papers of the Committee of the Constitutional System,* has provided us with a sensible challenge: we ought to celebrate the bicentenary of this remarkable instrument, but we should not stand completely in awe of it.[7] We should not treat it as immutable, like the Ark of the Covenant. We must remember that while it entrenched the Bill of Rights, it also entrenched slavery, and that only the capacity for amendment enabled us to correct that evil. As Thomas Jefferson wrote,

> I am certainly not an advocate for frequent and untried changes in laws and constitutions. . . . But I know also that laws and institutions must go hand in hand with progress of the human mind. As that becomes more developed, more enlightened, as new discoveries are made, new truths disclosed, and manners and opinions change with the change of circumstances, institutions must advance also and keep pace with the times.

The rarity of constitutional amendments demonstrates how difficult it is to improve on the work of the framers. The same history also shows that when the need is great enough, the required national consensus can be found.

Nowhere in the U.S. Constitution or its amendments do the words "federalism," "county," "city," or "municipality" appear even once. Local government is a total nonbeing in the Constitution. Even in an urban age, Justice William Brennan could write—as he did in the *Boulder* cable television case—"ours is a 'dual system of government' that has no place for sovereign cities."

I consider this a serious defect of the Constitution. We are ignoring the growth of metroareas and their major importance. The size of these dense concentrations of population is extremely significant. Some have proposed we provide an enabling clause in the Constitution that would compel the president, the Congress, states, and local governments to work on pressing problems. An example of such an amendment is set forth below, taken from those bicentennial papers. Its chief author is Benjamin Read, former president of the German Marshall Fund of the United States:

> Section 1. Every decade the president shall convene a convocation to make recommendations to achieve a more cooperative, responsive, equitable, accountable, and efficient federal system.
> Section 2. Such decennial convocations shall consist of citizens knowledgeable about intergovernmental relations and are selected in equal numbers by federal, state, and local governments under procedures established by act of Congress.
> Section 3. When a convocation so requests, its recommendations for legislation shall be considered and voted upon promptly by the Congress and the state legislatures.

Local governments would be constitutionally recognized for the first time in American history. This would be a fitting development, for in matters ranging from foreign trade to technological innovation, the efforts and success or failure of metroareas are of substantive importance to the entire nation. We continue to face the problem of a Tenth Amendment that provides the courts with only the vaguest outlines for the intergovernmental division of powers and responsibilities. A convocation could and should set down guidelines for the benefit of the judiciary. A decennial convocation might also dramatize to the nation oft-hidden issues of federalism. It could publicize the gross inequalities between our rich and poor states, explain the case for a representative tax system, expose our states' neglect of beleaguered inner cities and the dilemmas of governing metroareas that sprawl across state lines, and the proliferation of special districts that undermine budgeting and cause complexities for the states and localities. The essential point would be to write the requirement for the decennial convocations into the Constitution and not settle for mere statute alone. The constitutional path would avoid the various legal challenges that could be raised against a convocation created by statute alone. Of even greater importance, such a constitutional amendment would dignify each level of our intergovernmental system. It would pledge the people of the United States to a regular and far more serious effort, as their history rolls on, to mold their system of governance, from White House to town hall, to the exigencies of the time.

Chadha—The Cause of Legislative-Executive Gridlock

The American press has done a poor job of informing the people of a profound change in our unwritten constitutional structure wrought by the Supreme Court in a case involved the deportation of an alien. The Supreme Court, by a majority vote, declared in *Chadha* that, "It is unconstitutional for Congress to reserve the right to veto an administrative action."[8] Here, from the majority written by Burger,

> The fact that a given law or procedure is efficient, convenient, and useful in facilitating functions of government, standing alone, will not save it if it is contrary to the Constitution.
>
> Convenience and efficiency are not the primary objectives—or the hallmarks—of democratic government, and our inquiry is sharpened rather than blunted by the fact that congressional veto provisions are appearing with increasing frequency in statutes that delegate authority to executive and independent agencies. Since 1932, when the first veto provision was enacted into law, 295 congressional veto-type procedures have been inserted in 196 different statutes, as follows: from 1932 to 1939, five statutes were affected; from 1940-49, nineteen statutes; between 1950-59, thirty-four statutes; and from 1960-69, forty-nine. From the year 1970 through 1975, at least one hundred sixty-three such provisions were included in eighty-nine laws . . .
>
> The Constitution sought to divide the delegated powers of the new federal government into three defined categories. . . . Not every action taken by either house is subject to the bicameralism and presentment requirements of Article I. . . . Examination of the action taken here by one house pursuant to Section 244(c)(2) reveals that it was essentially legislative in purpose and effect . . .
>
> The one-house veto operated in this case to overrule the attorney general and mandate Chadha's deportation; absent the House action, Chadha would remain in the United States. Congress has acted, and its action has altered Chadha's status. . . . The veto authorized by Section 244(c)(2) doubtless has been in many respects a convenient shortcut: the "sharing" with the executive by Congress of its authority over aliens in this manner is, on its face, an appealing compromise . . . but it is crystal clear from the records of the convention,

contemporaneous writings and debates, that the framers ranked other values higher than efficiency. There is no support in the Constitution or decisions of this Court for the proposition that the cumbersomeness and delays often encountered in complying with explicit constitutional standards may be avoided either by the Congress or by the president.

Justice White dissented:

Today the Court not only invalidates Section 244(c)(2) of the Immigration and Nationality Act, but also sounds the death knell for nearly 200 other statutory provisions in which Congress has reserved a "legislative veto." [Emphasis added.] For this reason, the Court's decision is of surpassing importance. . . . The prominence of the legislative veto mechanism in our contemporary political system and its importance to Congress can hardly be overstated. It has become a central means by which Congress secures the accountability of executive and independent agencies. Without the legislative veto, Congress is faced with a Hobson's choice; either to refrain from delegating the necessary authority, leaving itself with a hopeless task of writing laws with the requisite specificity to cover endless special circumstances across the entire policy landscape, or, in the alternative, to abdicate its lawmaking function to the executive branch and independent agencies. To choose the former leaves major national problems unresolved; to opt for the latter risks unaccountable policy-making by those not elected to fill that role. Accordingly, over the past five decades, the legislative veto has been placed in nearly 200 statutes.

The Court heeded this counsel in approving the modern administrative state. The Court's holding today that all legislative-type action must be enacted through the lawmaking process ignores that legislative authority is routinely delegated to the executive branch, to the independent regulatory agencies, and to private individuals and groups. . . . If Congress may delegate lawmaking power to independent and executive agencies, it is most difficult to understand Article I as forbidding Congress from also reserving a check on legislative power for itself.

Absent the veto, the agencies receiving delegations of legislative or quasi-legislative power may issue regulations having the force of law without bicameral approval and without the president's signature. It is thus not apparent why the reservation of a veto over the exercise of that legislative power must be subject to a more exacting test. . . . A legislative check on an inherently executive function, for example, of initiating prosecutions, poses an entirely different question. But the legislative veto device here—and in many other settings— is far from an instance of legislative tyranny over the executive. It is a necessary check on the unavoidably expanding power of the agencies, both executive and independent, as they engage in exercising authority delegated by Congress . . . I regret the destructive scope of the Court's holding. It reflects a profoundly different conception of the Constitution than that held by the courts that sanctioned the modern administrative state. *Today's decision strikes down in one fell swoop provisions in more laws enacted by Congress than the Court has cumulatively invalidated in its history.* [Emphasis added.]

The Congressional response has been legislative/executive gridlock. For instance, having lost its veto over arms sales, would Congress respond by granting a blanket power to the president to sell arms to anybody, including Saudi Arabia or Mexico? Or will it tell the president, when you have a deal worked out, bring it to us? We will authorize it, if we so choose. The latter action is the better bet. The quest for a broad, uniform solution will be unproductive. The range of veto provisions is too broad, the kinds needed too diverse. The many delegations of power now subject to the veto will have to be reviewed one by one, piecemeal. Predictably, the Congress will delegate power to the president in the relatively unimportant areas while retaining control over actions that are significant and controversial. This is gridlock. Bush has become the veto president because of *Chadha,* in part.

Why Not Risk a Constitutional Convention?

It is C. Herman Pritchett's view that, given the political temper of the country, a convention called to draft a budget-balancing amendment might go far afield.[9] Is there any way to guard against this possibility? Former Attorney General Griffin Bell has said that he absolutely believes that Congress can set limits on what kind of amendments a convention can propose. Congress has considered such a limiting bill from time to time.

The Ervin-Helms bills, if adopted, would dispose of many of the concerns about runaway conventions. The principal provisions of the bills are:

1) State legislatures can call for a convention to propose "one or more" amendments to the Constitution;
2) Legislative adoption of resolutions calling for a convention are to follow the regular state legislative rules of procedure, except that the governor's approval is not required;
3) Applications for a convention are to remain effective for seven calendar years. However, rescission would be possible up to the time that two-thirds of the state legislatures presented valid application;
4) When applications from two-thirds of the state legislatures are confirmed, the two houses of Congress must by concurrent resolution designate the time and place of the meeting. Congress then "sets forth the nature of the Amendment or Amendments for the consideration of which the convention is called." The convention must meet within one year;
5) Each state is to have as many delegates as the number of senators and representatives in Congress it is entitled to. Two delegates are to be elected at large and one from each congressional district "in the manner provided by law." Vacancies are to be filled by the governor. Delegates are to have the same immunities as members of Congress, and the concurrent resolution shall provide for their compensation and all other expenses of the convention;
6) The convention is to be convened by the vice president of the United States and would then proceed to elect permanent officers;
7) Each delegate is to have one vote. In Ervin's original bill, the vote was by states as in the convention, each state having one vote;
8) Amendments are to be proposed by a "majority of the total number of delegates to the convention." This is the only real point on which the 1971 Ervin and the 1977 Helms drafts differ. The Ervin bill originally provided

for majority vote. It was amended on the floor of the Senate to require a two-thirds majority. The Helms bill goes back to a simple majority;

9) Three provisions undertake specifically to guarantee against runaway conventions. Section 8(a) requires each delegate to take an oath "to refrain from proposing or casting his vote for any proposed Amendment . . . relating to any subject that is not named or described in the concurrent resolution of the Congress by which the convention was called";

10) Then Section 10(b) provides, "No convention called under this Act may propose any Amendment or Amendments of a nature different from that stated in the concurrent resolution calling the convention." Finally, Section 11(b)(1) permits Congress to disapprove the submission of any proposed Amendment to the states if "such proposed amendment relates to or includes a subject that differs from, or was not included among the subjects named or described in the concurrent resolution . . . by which the convention was called, or because the procedures followed by the convention were not in conformity with this act";

11) As required by the Constitution, ratification is by vote of three-fourths of the states. Congress retains its Article V right to direct whether ratification shall be by state convention or state legislative action. State legislatures shall adopt their own "rules of procedure" in voting on ratification, which must be completed within seven years of submission of the amendment to the states. A state may rescind its ratification before ratification by three-fourths of the states;

12) To avoid the possibility of judicial review of any issues raised by the convening of a convention or the exercise of powers by that body, the bills provide that any questions on adoption of state resolutions calling for a convention shall be determined by Congress. Its decisions thereon shall be binding on all others, including state and federal courts. Likewise, questions on whether proposed amendments are of a nature differing from that stated in the concurrent resolution, "shall be determined solely by the Congress of the United States." Its decisions shall be binding on all others, including state and federal courts.

The intention of the Ervin-Helms bills is to settle, in advance, any question as to the organization and powers of an Article V convention and to guarantee against a runaway body. When the Ervin bill was before the Senate in 1971, it won praise from different ends of the political spectrum. The *New Republic* said, "Ervin's bill is sound insurance against a runaway rewrite job by latter-day founding fathers. Congress should adopt it." Columnist James Kilpatrick wrote, "This is a wise and prudent bill." The American Constitution is, in a sense, the victim of its own success. Veneration of the Constitution has resulted in an "amendment phobia." Peter McGrath's warning in a 1976 *New Republic* article, is eloquent and timely:

Illegitimacy is one thing that a constitution can never risk, for it is the main agent of legitimacy for substantive policy decisions. This is why it is unwise for us to force our Constitution too far into the bitter controversies of the moment, such as those over busing and abortion. Each time we do so, we demystify it a little, which even in this secular age is not necessarily a good thing. The Constitution is an organism, and when you kick it, it kicks back, as Richard Nixon found out to his sorrow and surprise. But like any living thing, it can be worn down, burdened with work it was never made for.

Austin Ranney reviewed proposals to institute policy changes by Americans who want changes in our U.S. Constitution.[10] Neither the polling nor the voting data provide conclusive evidence about what constitutional changes Americans want. However, the survey answers help. For example, survey respondents are considerably more receptive than members of Congress to constitutional change. Ranney reviewed eleven proposed constitutional amendments recently introduced in Congress. Large majorities of the public favored nine of the eleven (ERA, balanced budgets, school prayer, direct election of presidents, regional presidential primaries, a national presidential primary, national initiative, limiting terms of senators and representatives, and presidential line-item veto). Popular majorities rejected only one proposal (outlawing abortions). Respondents were evenly divided on another (a single, six-year presidential term). By contrast, Congress has sent only one of these proposals (ERA) to the states for ratification. It gave two others less than the necessary two-thirds majorities. No action was taken on the others. On this showing, then, there is considerably more resistance to constitutional change in the Congress than among the public.

The earliest systematic criticism of the constitutional system came from Woodrow Wilson.[11] It was trenchant and is pertinent today. In 1879, Wilson proposed the British plan for cabinet members. Wilson said that cabinet members should have seats in the Congress. And they should be chosen from among the legislators and resign when their proposals were rejected. Wilson felt it would clearly fix responsibility and accountability in American national government.

How long should our congressional members and the president be in office? James Sundquist reported that President Lyndon Johnson, an old Washington hand, justified his frenetic attempt to pass a controversial measure in 1965—the first year after his election—on the ground that it was the only chance he would have.[12,13] For a president who is less well prepared, more time is required. He or she must assemble a staff, analyze the issues, and define a program. By the time the organizing and learning period is over, much of the first year may have passed. In the four-eight-four (years) plan, senators would be divided into two classes rather than the present three. One member from each state would be chosen in each presidential election. With half rather than one-third of the Senate at stake in that election, a trend toward either party would have greater impact on the partisan makeup of the Senate. This might give the president's party somewhat more seats and reduce the likelihood of divided government. The shield against despotism—the system of checks and balances—has assuredly served its purpose. As Sundquist points out, it is a truism that the power to prevent bad acts can also be employed to prevent good ones.

Should we change the time horizon of our U.S. representatives to, say, one ten-year term? This could take their minds off electioneering and they could concentrate on lawmaking. Others see "none of the above" (NOTA) as the lesser of two evils. This would empower the voters to disqualify an election by refusing a minimum plurality to any of the candidates. A special election would be required. In the 1991 Edwards vs. Duke runoff in Louisiana a poll indicated that 60 percent of Louisiana voters preferred NOTA.

Should we change the presidency to divide its function into two offices, one ceremonial, the other functional? The ceremonial presidential office could be held by a "statesman of the constitutional culture" with an independent budget but no authority other than moral suasion. He or she would be on standby to take over the presidency only in a crisis where the vice president was unavailable. In that event, his function would be for the purposes of being a caretaker only until a replacement for the "functional" president was elected or selected by constitutional process. Such a moral leader would carry out all ritualistic functions and most of the pomp and circumstance. He or she would be like the British constitutional monarch. Perhaps we would call him or her the premier. On the other hand, the other officer, the functional president, would act as the nation's chief executive officer. He or she would function with all the powers of the current president but without all the time-consuming and burdensome ritualistic meetings with the Boy Scouts, Toys for Tots, Aid for AIDS Victims, and the like.

Should the judiciary retire at age seventy? By such a measure, we could provide life tenure with a termination year. This would require all the federal judiciary to either step down from the bench or elect to be a senior judge with a curtailed schedule at the lower court level. This secondary role would be subject to annual physical and mental checkups to determine fitness for office. The nation's sorry experience with the brilliant Justice Douglas's last few years should not be repeated.

These suggestions are designed to stimulate the reader. The nation recently experienced a too quiet bicentennial without national deliberation. We ought to consider ways to bring about a reformation that would change our future outlook. No other country has a mechanism for constitutional amendment that requires so high a degree of national consensus, nor does any state of the United States. Of the fifty states, twenty-one permit legislatures to submit amendments to the people by simple majorities (in three of these, the legislature must act twice in separate sessions). One state requires a two-thirds vote in its senate, but only a majority in its house. Nine states require a three-fifths vote in each house, eighteen a two-thirds vote in each house, and one a two-thirds majority of the total membership of each house. The question arises, then: should the advocates of constitutional change, in the interest of more effective government, turn their attention first to modifying the amendment process itself? To win any significant backing, this should be offered as a way to make the course easier for one or more specific popular amendments. Supporters could thereby be mobilized. I have presented some arguments for a Ninth Amendment convention. A national dialogue on our human rights could produce the consensus necessary for calling a convention. If we are to reclaim our world leadership we must stand for what we assert we believe in. Will American political leaders step forward and make such a call for a convention a part of their own agenda?

What Is the Global Context of Human Rights Today?

Humans live in such a state of uncertainty that stability can be achieved only as a state of mind. Such tranquility is not a fiction any more than is Einstein's theory of relativity, which is a state of mind. But, it is difficult to see how human rights claims can be championed, if they are regarded as fictions, however beneficial and cornucopian they may be. The historical continuum of human life shows that those societies that progress toward greater human happiness are those that ennoble the human spirit and acknowledge the dignity of their fellow man by making virtues out of fundamental human rights.

Once, "human rights" was the battle cry of the propertied bourgeoisie. Historically, it was a means for the dismantling of stratified society, to promote a more functionally differentiated form of human society. It was a proclamation of human rights as a development of social norms. Today "human rights" are necessary to develop, maintain, and restore self-esteem. We have advocated rights because of their universal validity. Therefore, it should be possible to clarify rights within the context of all cultures and traditions. We know that cultural traditions vary widely, but these traditions may eventually grow together if fundamental self-images of the human race are used to sustain the hope of human rights. If such universality of self-image were to happen, it would become possible to speak of humankind in a sense that differs from that of the natural species or that of a worldwide political and economic interdependence. Under new and unpredictable conditions, the language of the "rights of man" could recapture the resonance and fullness of meaning that possessed those who first championed rights in modernity. By sustaining the hope of human rights in the global context, modern Americans can gain ennobling meaning in their lives. The simple but profound summary of this chapter is that Americans could send a global message that would give hope to the entire world. We should hold a constitutional convention for the purpose of enumerating the political and civil rights that we consider essential for modern life in the coming century after the year 2000. It would be as an expansion of our Ninth Amendment without disparaging or denying other rights held by the people. It would be energizing.

John Stuart Mill defined the pursuit of happiness in this way:

> Those only are happy who have their minds fixed on some object other than
> their own happiness; on the happiness of others, on the improvement of mankind,
> even on some art or other pursuit, followed not as a means, but as itself an
> ideal end. Aiming thus at something else, they find happiness by the way.

It is the human condition that human happiness is balanced by suffering.
Achievement of happiness is transitory; it is the pursuit of it that is the game worth
playing. Victor Frankl, the psychiatrist, John Stuart Mill, the social philosopher,
and Ashley Montagu, the cultural anthropologist, among many other leaders, all
saw that human vision is at its best when focused on an ennobling purpose with
a faith in the future. Man's arrogant faith in his intellect has not been justified.

Human Rights Ought to Be Protected by the State

At the time of their first historical constitutional proclamation and justification, human
rights were legal entitlements that triggered intense driving motivations among humans.
We need a new transforming enlightenment. Today not all perceptions of worldly
reality and self-images are conducive to the adoption of rights as norms. Still, humans
are drifting toward another way of perceiving the world, one that enables us to
link these diverse gaps in our perceptions. We may reach agreement that the world
should be perceived as an energy field with human actions shaped according to
norms that only we as agents actually bring into play—a world that is not itself
a source of norms. Such a world would be without an anthropomorphic authority
above it as the primary source of norms. This world view/self-image, together with
its norms, would be hospitable to the notion of human rights and the idea of a
Primary Force, for many the God Force. Of course, if the norms are a covenant
arrived at among humans, there is a danger that they may be placed above question.
It would be much healthier if, as the human mind progresses, these norms can be
subject to continuous critical scrutiny. It is for that reason that this text presented
Wahl's "architectonics of the human personality." Thereby we pressed for the idea
that there is a normal mature human personality that we should all strive to be.

From these lines of thought the modern idea of an "autonomy" of reason and of a human essence—the "rational mind"—emerged.

No longer bound to the limited task of protecting life from natural adversities, human conduct could transform the basic drive of self-preservation into a rational form of conscious life. Here, rational self-preservation believes it makes the essence of man nothing other than freedom, which is an emancipation from both external influence and from previous impositions of norms. *Later the idea was broadened by maintaining that the life of human freedom is reflected in the common-order, manifested in the beauties of nature.* However, as we near the year 2000 this type of theory, like that of Locke or Rousseau, cannot be restored by calling up the past. A shift in the consciousness of our age, brought about by quantum physics and the melding with Eastern mysticism and its perception of problems, makes this impossible.

Today, our discovery of the great hormonal gland, the human brain, and our awareness of the power of irrationality, both cause us to realize the limits of reason in interpreting human conduct. These same paradigm shifts call upon our minds to have faith in tested norms to carry us through this period of uncertainty. This is the reason I called for a strong campaign to reinforce the values of the enlightenment that we find in the fiduciary agent's responsibilities of stewardship. Fidelity, loyalty, competence, duty to speak, integrity, trust, etc.,—all these norms are mutually beneficial anchors in the storm of uncertainty. These turbulent times call upon us to place our trust in some of our fellow Americans—the humans who are willing to work together under the rules of our constitutional culture and democratic capitalism. They will be the autonomous humans we can trust. By identifying them we hope to avoid being dominated by the sociopathic personalities who have no norms other than their hunger for the pornographic abuse of power to guide them. Through fundamental "natural" rights we dispel the illusion of rationality. We couple that act with the claim that humans can fulfill themselves through the imposition of their spontaneous, self-created form on the chaos found in the worlds of nature and thought. Unfortunately, today, some reduce this to an absurdity. This deliberate nihilism is a revolt against belief in reason. Worse, as such it is a derivative doctrine of human rights because it is a revolt staged by those who not only hold belief to be empty, but who also fancy themselves to be serving the cause of truth. This text has attempted to counter such a nihilistic argument and will comment further on our human need for taking rights seriously below.

The Horror of Nihilism vs. the Enlightenment of Autonomy

The horror of a kind of nihilism had a far-reaching impact on efforts of the United Nations. It buoyed the revival of the tradition of modernism to forge a new Declaration of Human Rights. It has led to the establishment within the European community of the first international institution for claiming human rights in court. *This is because nihilism in action is a direct attack upon the basic convictions that underlie human rights.* Scholars who inveigh against teaching ethics and moral conduct in our schools follow in the nihilist tradition. They justify this on the grounds that such basic convictions can only come from family training, not in the schools. They haven't met some of the horrible families this author has, both in poverty enclaves and in the enclaves of the rich and indolent as well. It has been proven by experience that schools can act as surrogate parents through ethically driven teachers acting as a kind of *loco parentis* to teach ethical conduct to the ignorant and the misinformed. Society, through the state, can take an interest in ethical norms and rights such as acknowledged fiduciary values.

At a more basic level, these theories maintain that the true origin of our current malaise is a wrong assumption. It is confused thinking when Man sets himself up as the measure of all order and as the source of binding world meaning. *An interpretation of our contemporary world demands first that we discard the notion that humans—the finite subjects—are the axis around which the world turns and evolves.* This book has been an essay to encourage the melding of the paradigms of ecological man, political man, economic man, social man, psychological man, the law's reasonable man, etc., into the holistic image of the autonomous human who is part of the natural world. The world is as Chief Seattle understood it. What Rousseau only intimated. What Kant and his successors saw more clearly: *We can understand ourselves only as part of a world, a world that includes within it the chance for freedom.* The need is to find a better way toward the unity of freedom and autonomous responsiblity. One way is found in unifying the freedom of the autonomous agent with the world. If we think of ourselves in this way, we recognize that because we are not wholly self-contained, we could not possibly generate the pathos of freedom alone. Today, the earth is temporarily overpopulated. That the dangers to self are so great is precisely why we have the need to believe in human rights.

Our modern knowledge has linked two apparently contradictory insights: *We as persons are the origin of rights claims. We are—as originally—the only being for which the earth makes possible a transitory consciousness in and through ourselves. Today, we have a good reason for holding that our conscious life is isolated in the cosmos. Moreover, we foresee an ineluctable future in which the earth is to become uninhabitable. Above all else, we are faced with a threat we alone have created, nuclear annihilation. We need and shall have a valuable human construct of existence.* We fill this need by conceiving of our world and its ultimate end within a recently developing world image. It is a construction inverse to the world-image and teleology of early modernity. First, this late-twentieth-century world view accords priority in its ontology to the accidental over the necessary. Having done so, we assert that the peripheral position of our conscious life in the Milky Way of the cosmos corresponds to its privileged, possibly lonely status. Second, this arriving world image accords priority to the transitory over the definite. As humans we then assert that our preservation also has meaning, even though lasting stability cannot be achieved. Third, this world view then permits us to say of the entire world process that humans will someday arrive at what was earlier conceived of as the "end," and that despite the threat of nuclear annihilation, we will live our lives and give them meaning. *We thus open up a limited space for a self-determined life—a life with meaning, by conscious choice. It is an intentionally tragic optimism.* Such ideas, if they were adopted seriously into our self-images, would cut off the transforming power of rampant nihilistic world views. Shorn of "illusion," these ideas about space, time, energy, and knowledge and the individual's autonomy are nonetheless meaningful.

Fortunately, a deep and powerful explanation is evolving. It is the breathtakingly, rapidly, unfolding unity of evolution—biological, cultural, and personal. The autonomous individual will be able to do more than cope with it.[1] As we are becoming, let us look to the future of the emerging possible human.

In 1977, Ilya Prigogine, a Belgian physicist, won the Nobel prize for his theory of dissipative structures. Prigogine's theory explains "irreversible processes" in nature, the movement toward higher and higher orders of life. Prigogine, whose early interest was in history and humanities, felt that science essentially ignored time. There are many aspects of time: decay, history, evolution, and new ideas. Prigogine's theory resolves the fundamental riddle of how living things have been running uphill (evolving to higher forms) in a universe that is supposed to be running down, according to the second law of thermodynamics. Remember, at the deepest level of nature, nothing is fixed. These patterns are in constant motion. Even a rock is a dance of electrons. Metroareas are the arenas for living humans involved in the pursuit of mutually beneficial happiness within the state of mind known as the human condition.

Metroareas as Open Dissipative Systems

Prigogine's term for open systems is dissipative structures. Please eliminate the emotive content of the word "dissipation" from your mind, at least for now. That is, the form or structure of open systems is shaped by a continuous dissipation (consumption) of energy. A seed, an ovum, a living creature, is a dissipative open system. Prigogine uses the example of a town, city, or metroarea as an example of such a human-made open system. The metroarea takes its energy from the surrounding area— its regional hinterland (in some cases that "area" is the entire world, for example, New York and Singapore). The region surrounding the metroarea provides power, raw materials, capital, and human labor, and the metroarea turns it into factories and adds value, returning the energy to the global environment. The continuous movement of energy through the system results in fluctuations. If the fluctuations reach a critical size they will "perturb" the system, destabilize it. This increases the number of novel interactions within it. An individual can perturb the system, as did Martin Luther King, Jr., with his dreams and marches for human rights. King's work resulted in "creative destruction," resulting in a burst of productivity that created the "new South." Autonomous humans, individual Americans, each have much power to set things in motion, to stabilize, to work toward the pursuit of happiness. It is individual action that provides the energy for the metroarea to go uphill to higher forms.

Voluntary Actions by Individuals

The staff of life and the bubbling ferment of U.S. constitutional culture are individual and group action. The most dynamic force for positive change in our culture— voluntary action—is committed to a goal for transcendental betterment of the human condition. Ordinary humans can demonstrate the power of a commitment to a clearly defined goal within a participatory society. This is possible, but at greater personal risk, even in fascistic societies. We know of the actions of such celebrities as Dostoevski, Marti, Sakharov, Garibaldi, Walesa, Tutu, and Yeltsin. Recognition for those who toil in the fields of public participation is an imperative. For example, we have accepted the idea that someone who has not succeeded on Broadway can enrich our lives in community and regional theaters. It takes arduous training and extreme specialization for such people to provide us with valuable, loving service in our metroareas. We need more adaptation of this technique for publicly recognizing people who energize us toward participation in our constitutional culture.

Jimmy Yen: Crusader for Mankind

In the chapter on energy policy and the conservation ethic, I referred to the work of Frank Laubach, who worked against illiteracy in the Philippines and East Asia. He used a messianic teaching message of "Each one teach one," by which a simple but effective reading and writing vocabulary was imparted to many. Laubach was following in the steps of a giant of mankind, Jimmy Yen, who worked for most of his life with the YMCA.[2] The Jimmy Yen story was told by John Hersey in *Reader's Digest*. It makes absolutely clear how much one man or woman can do. Although little known, Yen became one of the great forces of our century. Jimmy Yen has always believed passionately in the "strength of the common man." Immediately after his graduation from Yale in 1917 Yen was drawn into one of the most obscure and bizarre backwaters of the murderous World War I. Some Allied leaders thought that by importing Chinese coolies to build roads, railroads, and so on, Allied soldiers could be released for fighting in the trenches. Over 180,000 such peasant Chinese were imported by the British with permission of the Chinese government. It was a ragged, poverty-stricken mob who were promised daily food and about 20 cents per day in modern terms. The British deemed it necessary to demean each man by cutting off his pigtail, removing and burning his clothes, and issuing a rough cotton uniform. The men were also bathed and deloused. Worst of all, they were fingerprinted and numbers were permanently strapped to their left wrists. Thenceforth, these numbers were their names.

The only thing that thrived among the coolies was misery and homesickness. All through the Chinese corps, to their credit, there were strikes and disorder every few days over the wretched working conditions. Worse, they were often pressed into combat zone work, despite agreements with the Chinese government to the contrary. The widespread epidemic of homesickness resulted in Jimmy Yen offering to write letters in his fine Mandarin calligraphy to the worker's families. The task quickly became overwhelming. The genius of Jimmy Yen saw that out of adversity comes opportunity. He turned a catastrophe into a shining triumph for mankind. He felt that the illiterate coolies of his native China—and the downtrodden of all Third World countries—could be taught to read and write, to care for their own health, to lead useful, productive, happier lives. He set out to achieve this vision. In this mission, he felt, lay the world's best hope for peace. Ever since the Tang dynasty (618–907), China had been ruled by scholars who excelled in examinations. The Chinese language had developed forty thousand ideograms—Chinese written characters. It was firmly believed that only an excellent mind could learn to read or write. This age-old cultural bias carried over to the twentieth century. It was believed by all of China, from coolie to the mandarin leadership, that peasants were beyond education, lazy, stupid, good only for their strong backs and callused hands. The peasants themselves accepted this for many centuries. Jimmy Yen rejected it.

Pulitzer Prize–winning author John Hersey provides a complete account of Jimmy Yen's life, which is an inspiration to us all. Yen literally changed the use of the convolutions of the neo-cortex of the brains of scores, then, hundreds, then thousands, then millions of Chinese and other Asians. He did so by overcoming their lack of self-esteem and teaching them that they could read and write and learn, and use what they learned, to make their lives better. The key was a stroke of genius that comes to those who persevere against all odds. Yen developed a simple primer containing the basic Chinese ideograms of the words most frequently used in the folk tongue—the *bai-hua*. It was Jimmy Yen's *Thousand-Character Reader*. This master teacher proved himself to be also a first-rate administrator as he delegated to others the training of many who would teach others. He proved the power of self-help and self-reliance through his methods. Literally millions have learned to read by this method. They communicate news on the walls of the villages. Farming, sanitation, food preservation, and uplifting ideas have been communicated to humans who had been taught they were nothing but beasts of burden. It was a day of joy when a formerly "blinded" (because of illiteracy) peasant would graduate and receive his certificate—literate citizen of the Republic of China. Jimmy Yen, at ninety-one, continued to release the strength of the common man through the Indian Rural Reconstruction Movement. Write IRRM about Yen's programs at 1775 Broadway, New York, N.Y. 10019. To read about his example is to know how much power is within you and other volunteers who work together for a common cause.

Booker T. Whatley's Program

Ed Bean reported in a 1984 edition of the *Wall Street Journal* on the work of Dr. Booker T. Whatley, who taught social science at Tuskegee Institute for some twelve years.[3] Whatley contends that a farmer with only twenty acres can gross $100,000 per year if he or she thinks less about tractors and chemicals and more about marketing to the nearby metroareas. At the heart of Whatley's plan are ten crops, which are dependent on the climate zone, weather, consumer preferences, soil conditions, and "pick-your-own" clubs: sweet potatoes, berries, grapes, and strawberries, sweet corn, and others. Harvests are staggered so they do not compete with one another for labor. Each crop provides at least $3,000 per acre. These farms can be operated by, for example, one husband-and-wife team with three teenagers. For the system to work the farm must be no more than forty miles from a city of at least fifty thousand. The most expensive part of the farm is a drip-irrigation system. You cannot gamble with drought with this intensive farming.

The farm needs a few auxiliary enterprises and long hours of work. Dr. Whatley favors rabbits, quail, and beekeeping. Building and stocking fish ponds is something else the city folks like. Others are learning that they can make ends meet, or even do better, by developing a selective farm to serve the urbanized metroarea. A small acreage can be profitable if it is put into high-value crops such as alfalfa, sweet corn, or vegetables instead of wheat. The acreage might be used to raise Angora goats instead of cattle. Farmers in New England long ago learned the lessons of specialized farming. They farmed with an eye on the nearest urban market, tailoring their production to the needs of the ever-swelling band of specialty grocers and nouvelle-cuisine restauranteurs. To date, only 1 percent of American farmers engage in this kind of specialized "boutique" farming. It is a realistic alternative to traditional patterns of corporate agglomeration of farmland. The U.S. government may be leading the way by preparing to offer $30 million in low-interest loans to encourage farmers to grow fruit, vegetables, and even Christmas trees. The increasing population of the exurbias provide growing nearby markets, giving highly specialized farms a chance for survival if they have the skill and strict, schedule-following discipline. Whatley publishes a newsletter for $16 per year, "Small Farm Technical Newsletter," with twenty-three thousand subscribers.

Metroareas in a State of Perturbation

The elements of old ways are in contact with new ways, and new connections are being made. The development of "networks" of social entrepreneurs such as "Theobald's Action Linkage" or Atlanta's "Atlanta Networks" are positive examples. On the other hand, there are negative developments. The global invasion from rural areas and the growth of AIDS in metroareas is a perturbance that will bring vast changes in relationships. Whatever occurs, according to Prigogine's brilliant and beautiful concept, the historical continuum indicates that the various parts of metroareas will slowly and continuously reorganize into a new whole. The metroareas are a system that enables the fragmented parts (the city jurisdictions) to escape to a higher order. The more complex or coherent the structure of the metroarea, the greater the next level of complexity. Each transformation makes the next one likelier. The theory of dissipative structures says the potential to create new forms allows the shakeup of the old forms. As insects cooperate within their colonies, so also do humans within their social forms, such as metroareas. Human society is an example of spontaneous self-organization. In dense human societies such as those found in metroareas, individuals become acquainted with each other. Each soon has extremely numerous points of contact throughout the system. The greater the instability and mobility of the society, the more interactions occur. This means greater potential for new connections, new organizations, and diversification. People with common interests (that is, networks) find one another and refine their specialty by mutual stimulation and exchange of ideas. That is what I am trying to do with this book— to encourage those who find this book of interest to network.

The Possible Human

This book discussed the brain in order to confront the idea that human animals respond in both rational and irrational ways to the biospheric envelope. This book is controversial because it seeks to transform some of the paradigms of social science. However, it does so respectfully. Current social science paradigms are now holding our minds back. We need a shakeup to "perturb" the system in order to move to a higher order. The brain is an excellent example of a dissipative structure. As Bergland and others have shown, it is characterized by form, flow, and interaction with the environment in abrupt shifts. The brain has a sensitivity to being perturbed. A human's brain demands the lion's share of the body's energy: with only 2 percent of the body weight, it consumes 20 percent of the available oxygen. The theory of dissipative structures might well tie dynamic brain patterns to transitions in the mind. Such ideas appear to be a justification for permitting twice-convicted felons to volunteer for brain experiments.

Memories are dissipative structures, for they are patterns stored in the brain. Prigogine's theory helps to consider the dramatic effects seen sometimes in meditation, hypnosis, guided imagery, or the effects of prayer and the sudden relief of a lifelong phobia. An individual explores a traumatic incident by way of a highly focused inward attention—perturbs the old memory pattern—and triggers a reorganization— a new dissipative structure. This idea opens new horizons for research that could result in better mental health through pharmacology and nutrition. The research could result in more productive humans through more efficient use of energy.

Only a few hundred years ago, life was stable for the ordinary human. One knew one's place in the pattern of things. Before Jimmy Yen, this was true for the Chinese peasant only a few decades ago. Kinship was close, and rights and wrongs unquestioned. Mostly, life was a narrow, brutish fight for subsistence. Human energies were exhausted in the daily attempt to keep one's metabolism going. The Middle Ages were a settled reality. Everything fit in a scheme of things that was absolute. The entire universe revolved around God's earth, the place of his chosen creature—man. Then the Renaissance and Reformation came, and with them the revival of ancient philosophies that had been suppressed. There was an archaeology of human thought unearthed for a reawakening. Under such stimulus the human brain convoluted, and the psyche, the mind, and the soul grew. As Jean Houston, an advanced leader in research about breakthroughs for the possible human, states, unfortunately, by the nineteenth century, art and artful skill (*techne*) yielded to technique and, more recently, to technology. Skills that were once grounded in the insight that comes from a pulsing rhythm of the total body-mind-being became mechanical artifacts of a humanity increasingly fragmented and cut off from its own depth in the psyche. All over the planet a Western psychological imperialism has prevailed. Nevertheless, as is the case with dissipative structures, the transformation is taking place. Or, worse, in the interests of mechanical-technological progress, we are eroding human reality. We see that erosion being enacted and mirrored on the stage of nature by the erosion of our planetary ecosystem. The "perturbation" is ongoing. As Jean Houston relates,

> The possible human hears the call, awakening to those processes through which the brain-mind system becomes "super-conductive" and is able to enter into macro-phase functioning. There can then occur the linking of consciousness and the extraordinary statement of Being that is going on all the time. But, and there is indeed a but, you have to find this linking with intentionality and a commitment to learn from it. There are realities present here that can potentially transform the human condition.[4]

Americans Leading the Way

George Bernard Shaw once said, through the voice of Major Barbara talking to her father, the arms merchant: "You see things; and say, 'Why?' But I dream things that never were; and I say, 'Why not?' " It was a favorite quote of Bobby Kennedy.

During the twentieth century, humans have seen the great potential that is in us all through the work of Mahatma Gandhi, Winston Churchill, Albert Schweitzer, and Martin Luther King, Jr. We have seen such noble efforts cut short, as with Bobby Kennedy. We have seen much of the power of the spirit of one human fulfilled, through an Einstein, and a Jimmy Yen, peaceful crusaders for mankind. Today Jimmy and Rosalyn Carter lead us in the right direction with their noble work with Habitat for Humanity. Through the work of Millard Fuller, dramatic breakthroughs have been made in providing low-cost affordable housing for disadvantaged families. These families are able to buy these homes through the services of Habitat.

Come on all you gray panthers, and the youths who will lead us! There is more to do than watch the sunshine! Youth is not a chronological age, it is a state of mind. This book has finished its statement. It is in your hands! It can happen here! The United States of America was once the driving spirit of the world's best hope. Today, we are a mere symbol based on past achievements. This book seeks to persuade its readers that the spirit of our constitutional culture, coupled with its working partner, democratic capitalism, can be a driving force again. American metroareas and the world's metroareas can be the loci of the hope for humanity. We need to reform our attitudes for that to happen.

We face many difficult problems as we seek to reshape America. The United Way of America's Strategic Institute, working with its volunteer Environmental Scan Committee, has identified more than a hundred specific trends in society and grouped them into nine major "change-drivers" for the 1990s. Here is a taste of this analysis: The maturation of America is a population growing at a slower rate and aging. A better-educated workforce will be necessary to increase productivity. Political activism will become more pragmatic. The mass market will become more fragmented, more of a mosaic. Special interest groups will proliferate and need to be channeled into productive pursuits. Advances in information technology will enable individuals to obtain products, services, and publications at even lower cost. There will be a blurring of the boundaries that formerly defined the roles of the public sector, the private sector, and individual responsibility. Through networking we will be crossing over these former boundary separations. The globalization of the world economy will result in a relative decline in American power. We will see a vast restructuring of American business with increasing foreign ownership and management. Still, this could be misinterpreted, because America's absolute strength will probably increase, especially if we work out a common market with both Canada and Mexico, along with Central America and the Caribbean. Quality-of life issues could rapidly emerge as key areas of public concern. The American family will change into diverse family lifestyles. The family and home will grow in importance as a stabilizing sanctuary, a place for stress management with government assistance. This will all come about because of a rebirth of social activism among Americans.[5]

Will all of this happen? Only if we heed the warnings such as those set forth in this book, because such a future requires the guidance of autonomous individuals. I feel that we have often leaned on our older friend, Great Britain, for some of the strength and will that drives us. All Americans took great courage from the indomitable spirit of Winston Churchill during World War II. Today, as we have become a debtor nation, Great Britain is a creditor nation again. Many nations of the world send their best and brightest to the universities of Edinburgh, Oxford, and Cambridge, just as they do to Harvard, Cal Tech, and Stanford. Britain, not the United States, is the world leader in the dissemination of English language textbooks throughout the world. They are a nation from which we can learn.

Therefore, I close with a compilation comprising editorials by the *Economist,* a London establishment biweekly.

Whatever Happened, United States?

Americans were not born to frown. It does not suit them. The quintessentially American characteristics are cheerfulness, optimism, generosity, a general buoyancy of spirit, a belief that tomorrow will dawn a better day. So it may, but suddenly Americans seem not so sure. They learnt, more than a decade ago, of the limits to their military power, yet they still believed themselves preeminent in more pacific arts. They reckoned their economy to be incomparable; now they find it outsold by Japan, Western Europe and a string of eager newcomers. They assumed the American Century, born in 1941, would endure for a hundred years. Now, after fewer than fifty, they know it is on the wane. No wonder a frown can be detected on their faces. It is born of bafflement. . . . The frown is not universal, nothing is in America! . . . But signs of unease abound. . . . And some of these signs reflect not just bafflement, but sulkiness, defensiveness and pessimism. If these attitudes prevail, America will become a different place, one that allies and antagonists alike will find it harder to live with. Recently, we enjoyed the exhilarating success of a military adventure, Desert Storm. But its pathetic results in Kuwait and Iraq are discomforting as we await sign that our victory will have good results.

Protect and be damned. To foreigners the most alarming sign is protectionism. . . . Trade protection, however, is not the response of a self-confident person: it is a sort of considered temper tantrum, the nonviolent equivalent of smashing foreign radios on the lawn of the Capitol . . . Americans want to tackle its durable deficit with of all things, a constitutional amendment. . . . Rather than cut spending or raise taxes, they would wave a constitutional wand to banish deficits from the land. Such solutions make voodoo economics look smart. . . . The budget deficit has not been all bad for America, or for its trading partners. It helped to lift the economy out of recession in 1982, and to give America two years of cracking growth. By then it was outliving its usefulness, serving mainly to swell the trade deficit, and thus the protectionist chorus. The deficit has turned the world's richest country into its biggest debtor and put into the mouths of America's unborn not silver spoons but IOUs. The gross federal debt has more than doubled during Mr. Reagan's term, to over $2 trillion . . . Bush continues to casually increase the deficit while awaiting the miracle of growth in the tax base to turn it around. In other words, America has been living beyond its means—partly because its means have failed to expand as once they did. . . . To be sure, America is still a remarkably efficient job machine. Yet, even people at work can no longer be assumed to be prosperous, whereas those out of it can increasingly be assumed to be wretched. The pessimism, however, can be seen not just in the economic expectations of Americans, nor even in their fears about drugs, crime, and poor education. . . .

The fortieth anniversary of the Marshall Plan, perhaps the greatest example of national generosity in human history (2.5 percent of American GNP in the first year alone) passed with little notice. Americans are now more inclined to thumb their noses at internationalism. . . . This does not comport well with Japan's willingness to cooperate in international megaconstruction projects such as a new central-American cross-isthmus canal. . . .

Optimism, not necessity, has always been the mother of invention in America. This is particularly true not just for difficult problems such as crimes and drugs, but of one problem in particular: poverty. Now, after decades of experiment with more than 32 million Americans, 13.6 percent of the population (and nearly 20 percent of the children) are living below the poverty line. Optimism is no longer possible to hear. Americans shrug and say, "We have tried and failed." An under-class, isolated from mainstream America, and stubbornly resistant to incorporation within it, is now accepted by many as a fact that society can hope only to recognize, not change. . . .

Defeatism is certainly not a characteristic of Ronald Reagan nor of George Bush. But, the new mood owes much to a new and more somber assessment of the Reagan presidency among Americans at large. . . . We are now calling the 1980s, appropriately, the greed and avarice decade. Was the soaring eagle of a few years ago borne aloft on nothing more than a thermal of hot air from the White House? In any event, the presidency has few weapons more potent than hot air: what else did Teddy Roosevelt dispense from his "bloody pulpit"? The likelihood is, however, that Americans will continue to moderate their expectations and to grow a bit more cynical, a bit less boisterous. The world they ran after the Second World War was a world that could not last. Their share of gross world product was then 40 percent; today it is barely one quarter. Their share of world trade was 22 percent, today it is 9.5 percent. Americans grumble today that the burdens of world power and responsibility are unfairly distributed. They are right. America's allies must do more. Indeed, they may have to learn to live in a world without a preeminent Western leader. But the United States need have no need to sulk. On the contrary, the world today is better disposed towards democracy and capitalism than at any moment in the past forty years. It would be absurd indeed if America turned its back on that world just as it is embracing America's values.

If we are to succeed in the competitive global economy, we have much to do. A start would be radical tax reform—the adoption of the value-added tax (with border refunds for exports) and reduction of other tax rates. We should apply the doctrine of obvious change to start the next century with a celebratory spirit. A constitutional convention to reconsider the nature of our individual rights would be an intense focus of national interest.

Let's go for it! Let us make the few years leading to the new millennium a time of celebration. We can make our constitutional culture meaningful to all Americans. Democratic capitalism can work in a competitive way, making fair practices and ethical conduct its norms. We need to reenergize ourselves with chartered metropolitan reorganization. Americans, as world humans, can follow the likes of Jean Houston, Walter Adams, Norman Cousins, Marilyn Ferguson, and many others. Let us start some international cooperation projects for peace and happiness. We have leaders who are pointing the way toward a paradigm shift that could dazzle the world and lead to a true and successful pursuit of happiness.

Author's Note

Twilight's Last Gleaming is a book based on my belief in the "fire in the belly" of Americans. Most Americans really do want to make the USA a better place for tomorrow. It is my hope that this will be much more than a book to you. I have decided to ape Michael Quinn, the author of *Ishmael,* winner of the Turner Tomorrow Fellowship. He has started a network named IF to encourage others to join with him in trying to get something started. I joined. As Quinn says, that's what it's all about, isn't it?

People of the breakthrough are out there. The timeless wordplay folk story I obtained from Sharon Bennett states the problem:

> Once upon a time, there were four people. Their names were Everybody, Somebody, Nobody and Anybody. Whenever there was an important job to be done, Everybody was sure that Somebody would do it. Anybody could have done it, but Nobody did it. When Nobody did it. Everybody got angry because it was, after all, Everybody's job. Everybody thought that Somebody would do it, but Nobody realized that Nobody would do it. So consequently Everybody blamed Somebody when Nobody did what Anybody could have done in the first place.

Right now, there ain't nobody doing it. There is a failure of leadership everywhere as Americans play with their toys.

Who knows, perhaps there are enough of us to get something started here. Being there is what it's all about.

Write to: Dr. James R. Cooper
           Department of Real Estate
           CBA—Georgia State University
           P.O. Box 4020
           Atlanta, Georgia 30302-4020

Notes

Preface

1. Bolen, Jean Shinoda, *Gods in Everyman,* New York, Harper & Row, 1989, p. 44. I am indebted to Dr. Bolen for explaining the way my book presents its interdisciplinary subject matter.

Chapter 1. The American Creed

1. Ornstein, Robert, and Sobel, David, *The Healing Brain,* New York, Simon & Schuster, 1987, pp. 24, 27, and 57 are the sources for this paraphrase. Any errors or omissions are my own. I recommend this book.
2. Coles, Robert, "The Idea of Mental Health," *The American 1976,* Lexington, Mass., C. C. Heath & Co., 1976.
3. McCrum, Robert, William Cran, and Robert MacNeil, *The Story of English,* New York, Viking, 1986. Excerpts and references, p. 110.

Chapter 2. Exploring Ourselves: What Do We Believe?

1. Thompson, William Irwin, *At The Edge of History,* New York, Harper/Colophon Books, 1971, is the source for the following along with my own ideas. Any errors or omissions are my own.
2. *Bivens* v. *Six Unknown Named Agents of the Bureau of Narcotics* (U.S.), 403 U.S. 388 (1971).
3. Stone, I. F., "The Threat to the Republic," *New York Review,* May 27, 1976 (excerpts). For sources see "Foreign and Military Intelligence, Book I, Final Report," Senate Select Committee to Study Governmental Operations with Respect to Intelligence Activities, Washington D.C., U.S. G.P.O.; and "Intelligence Activities and the Rights of Americans, Book II, Final Report," Senate Select Committee to Study Governmental Operations with Respect to Intelligence Activities, Washington, D.C. G.P.O.
4. Kung, Hans, *Christianity and the World Religions,* New York, Doubleday, 1986.
5. No religious test, U.S. Constitution I-6/-/3.
6. *Swann* v. *Charlotte-Mecklenburg Board of Education,* 402 U.S. 1 (1971).
7. *Serrano* v. *Priest,* 5 Cal 3d 597, 487 P. 2d 1241 (1971).
8. *Rodriguez* v. *San Antonio School District.* See Pechman, Joseph and Okner, "Who Bears the Tax Burden," Washington, Brookings Institution, 1984.
9. Finn, Jr., Chester E., *We Must Take Charge,* New York, Free Press, 1991.

10. *Williams* v. *Florida*, 399 U.S. 78, (1970).

11. *Adams* v. *Maryland*, 347 U.S. 179 (1954).

12. *National Law Journal*, "A Bork Primer and Guide to the Confirmation Hearings," September 21, 1987, p. 1. Also *Warden* v. *Hayden*, 387 U.S. 294 (1967).

13. *Boyd* v. *U.S.*, 116 U.S. 616 (1886).

14. *U.S.* v. *Jeffers*, 342 U.S. 48 (1851), *Gouled* v. *U.S.*, 255 U.S. 298 (1921).

15. *Olmstead* v. *United States*, 277 U.S.438 (1928).

16. *Silverman* v. *United States*, 365 U.S. 505 (1961).

17. *Katz* v. *U.S.*, 389 U.S. 347 (1967).

18. *Mancusi* v. *DeForte*, 392 U.S. (1968).

19. (NYT) *Atlanta Journal Constitution*, Nov. 25, 1976.

20. *Oyama* v. *California*, 332 U.S. 663 (1948).

21. *Slaughterhouse* cases 16 Wall (83 U.S.) 36 (1873). see footnote xx. See also *U.S. Marshall Logan* v. *U.S.*, 144 U.S. 263 (1892) right to inform, *in re* v. *Butler*, 158 U.S. 532 (1895).

22. Civil Rights Act of 1866, 14 Stat 27, as amended now see 42 U.S.C. 1982.

23. *Noble State Bank* v. *Haskell*, 219 U.S. 104 (1911).

24. *New Orleans Public Service* v. *New Orleans*, 281 U.S. 682 (1930).

25. *Griswold* v. *Connecticut*, 381 U.S. 488, 491, 492 (1965).

26. *Skinner* v. *Oklahoma* ex. rel. Williamson, 316 U.S. 535 (1942).

27. *Shapiro* v. *Thompson*, 394 U.S. 618 (1969).

28. See 109 U.S. 11; 106 U.S. 629 (1883); 120 U.S. 678 (1887).

29. *U.S.* v. *Cruickshank*, 92 U.S. 542 (1876).

Chapter 3: Rights We Take Seriously

1. 6 Fed Case 546 (no. 323) (C.C.E.D PA-1823).

2. *Paul* v. *Virginia*, 8 Wall. (75 U.S.) 168 (1860); *McKane* v. *Durston*, 153 U.S. 684 (1894 and *Slaughterhouse* cases 16 Wall (83 U.S.) 36 (1873).

3. *Arizona* v. *Fulminante*, No. 898-183 6, 59 U.S.L.W. 4858 (1991).

4. *California* v. *Hodari*, D., 59 U.S.L.W. at 4869 (1991). See also Mickenberg, Ira, "Criminal Rulings Granted the State Broad New Power," *National Law Journal*, August 19, 1991, p. S10.

5. *U.S.* v. *Harris*, 106 U.S. 629 (1883). *U.S.* v. *Wheeler*, 254, U.S. 281 (1920).

6. Judiciary Act of 1789, 1 stat.73.85. On the other hand, although Congress limited the definition of judicial review (to be developed by the new United States Supreme Court), Congress did in rule 25 provide for review by the Supreme Court of apparent final judgments in state courts in the following situations: 1) where the state decisions went against the validity of a federal treaty or statute; 2) interpretations of the U.S. Constitution for the treaties and laws of the United States when the state has ruled against the aggrieved party; and 3) where some parties had claimed a right under the Constitution, a treaty or federal statute, or commission of the United States and the decisions the state court ruled against the right or privilege or exemption that had been claimed. This was the origin of the federal jurisdiction.

7. Cardozo, Benjamin N., *The Nature of the Judicial Process*, New Haven, 1921, p. 141.

8. Wards Cove, 57 U.S.L.W, at 4593.

9. 401 U.S. 424 (1971).

10. Frankfurter and Landis, *The Business of the Supreme Court*, New York, 1928, ch. 7.

11. *Slaughterhouse* cases, 16 Wall (83 U.S.) 36, 71, 77-79, (1873).

12. *Dred Scott* case, *Scott* v. *Sandford,* 19 How. (60 U.S.) 393 (1857).
13. *Insurance Co.* v. *New Orleans,* 13 Fed. Cas. 67 (C.C.D. LA 1870).
14. U.S. Constitution (1/2/3).
15. (NYT) *Atlanta Constitution,* December 9, 1976.

Chapter 4: The Supreme Court and the Federal Judiciary

1. *Abrams* v. *U.S.,* 250 U.S. 616 (1919), 40 S.Ct. 17 (1919), Holmes dissenting.
2. *Nixon* v. *United States,* 418 U.S. 683, (1974).
3. *In re Debs,* 158 U.S. 564 (1895).
4. *Adair* v. *U.S.,* 208 U.S. 161 (1908).
5. *Carter* v. *Carter Coal Co.,* 298 U.S. 238 (1938).
6. *NLRB* v. *Jones & Laughlin Steel Corp.,* 301 US. 1 (1937).
7. I am indebted to my colleague Dr. Gail Beckman for this concept.
8. In *Chicago, B&O Railroad* v. *City of Chicago,* 166 U.S. 226 (1897), which was limited to the just compensation clause of the Fifth Amendment being extended to the Fourteenth by inference.
9. *Twining* v. *New Jersey,* 211 U.S. 78, 99 (1908).

Part III: Preface

1. Sperry, Roger, "Changing Priorities," *Annual Review of Neuroscience,* 1981, vol. 4, pp. 1-15.

Chapter 5: The American Mind

1. Bergland, Richard, *The Fabric of the Mind,* New York, Viking Press, 1985, p. 27, is a source for some of the following pages along with my own ideas. Any errors or omissions are mine.
2. Holmes, Thomas H., and Richard H. Rahe, "Social Readjustment Rating Scale," *Journal of Psychosomatic Research,* Volume II, Pergamon Press, Ltd. 1967.
3. Houston, Jean, *The Possible Human, A Course in Extending Your Physical, Mental, and Creative Abilities,* Los Angeles, J. P. Tarcher, 1982. For more information contact: The Possible Society, 800 Paper Mill Rd. Newark, Del., 19711. Jean Houston is an enlightening experience. Her workshops are uplifting to the spirit. Her work is a source for some of the pages which follow along with my own ideas. Any errors or omissions are mine.

Chapter 6: The Architecture of the Brain

1. Taylor, Gordon R., *The Natural History of the Mind,* E. P. Dutton, New York, 1979, is the source of the foregoing pages along with my own ideas. Any errors or omissions are my own.
2. Restak, Richard, *The Brain,* Bantam, New York, 1984, p. 342.
3. Bergland, Richard, *The Fabric of the Mind,* New York, Viking Press, 1985, is the source for much of the foregoing pages. The book is an exuberant, path-breaking study for everyone. The other ideas expressed are my own. Any errors or omissions are mine.
4. Zimbardo, Phillip G., "From Understanding Psychological Man" (a contributor), *Psychology Today,* May 1982, pp. 58-59, is the source for the following pages along with my own ideas. Any errors or omissions are mine.

Chapter 7: The Captive Public

1. Ginsberg, Benjamin, *The Captive Public, How Mass Opinion Promotes State Power,* New York, Basic Books, 1986, is the source for the following pages along with my own ideas. However, I have freely adapted and changed materials from Dr. Ginsberg's book over the next few pages. Any mistakes and omissions are mine. I recommend this book.

2. Kuttner, Robert, "Why Americans Don't Vote," *The New Republic,* September 7, 1987, pp. 19-21, is a source for the following pages along with my own ideas. Any errors or omissions are mine.

3. Yin, Robert K., "Creeping Federalism," in Norman Glickman, ed., *The Urban Impacts of Federal Policies,* Baltimore, John Hopkins University, 1980.

4. Rubinoff, Lionel, *The Pornography of Power,* Chicago, Quadrangle, 1968, the source for the following pages along with my own ideas. Any errors and omissions are mine. I recommend this book for its valuable insights.

5. McClelland, David C., "The State of the Science of Psychology," *Psychology Today,* May 1982, p. 56.

6. Holmes, Thomas H., and Richard H. Rahe, "Social Readjustment Rating Scale," *Journal of Psychosomatic Research,* Volume 11, 1967, Pergamon Press.

Chapter 8: Maturity

1. Gazzaniga, Michael, *The Social Brain,* New York, Basic Books, 1985.

2. Frankl, Viktor, *Man's Search for Meaning,* New York, Touchstone, 3rd ed., 1984. p. 75, *et passim.*

3. Bell, David A., "The Triumph of Asian Americans," *New Republic,* July 15, 1985, pp. 24-31, is the source for the foregoing pages along with my own ideas. Any errors or omissions are mine.

4. Howard, Jeff, and Ray Hammond, "Rumors of Inferiority—The Hidden Obstacles to Black Success," *New Republic,* September 9, 1985, is the source for some of the following pages along with my own ideas. Any errors or omissions are my own.

5. Hergenthaler, R. B., "Erik Erikson's Theory of Personality," Hamline University, St. Paul, Minn. (cassette tape), is the source for the above pages along with my own ideas. Any errors or omissions are mine.

6. Wahl, Charles W., "The Architectonics of Human Happiness," Southern California Neuropsychiatric Institute, La Jolla, Ca., *Neuropsychiatric Bulletin,* Autumn 1983, is the source for the following pages along with my own ideas. Any errors or omissions are my own. It was exciting to find this article in my research.

7. Frankl, Viktor, *Man's Search for Meaning,* New York, Touchstone, 3rd ed., 1984, pp. 111-15. The following is taken from this work. Any changes or omissions are mine.

8. Huxley, Matthew, "Son of Brave New World—His Vision of the Future," an interview, *The Futurist,* December 1985.

Chapter 9: The Population Bomb

1. Rohatyn, Felix, "Confront the Mexico Problem," *Wall Street Journal,* November 26, 1986.

2. Mayur, Rashmi, and Prem Ratan Vohra, *Bombay by the Year 2000,* 22 Police Court Lane, 1st Flr., Forty Bombay, 400 001 India, 1986, and Mayur, Rashmi, "The Coming Third World Crisis—Runaway Growth of Large Cities," *The Futurist,* August 1975, pp. 168-74.

3. Cohen, Roger, "Brazil Stays Buoyant, Mexico is Dispirited—In the Face of Troubles," *Wall Street Journal,* March 24, 1987. The material on Mexico City and Calcutta is excerpted from *Time,* August 6, 1984, pp. 26-36.

4. Thurow, Roger, "African Tragedy," etc., *Wall Street Journal,* April 17, 1987.

5. Moynahan, Brian, "Marseilles at Sea," *Sunday Times London,* in *World Press Review,* April 1987, p. 56.

6. "Singapore—Lee's Creation and Legacy," *The Economist,* November 22, 1986, pp. 3-22. See also an interview of Lee Kuan Yew in the issue of June 29, 1991, p. 16.

7. Nesmith, Jeff, "Urbanization Linked to Emergence of AIDS in Africa," *Atlanta Journal-Constitution,* May 10, 1987, p. 10.

8. Brown, Lester R., et al., "State of the World Reports" 1985-1987, New York, W. W. Norton, and "Our Demographically Divided World," World Watch paper 74, by Judi L. Jacobsen, and Lester Brown, 1776 Massachusetts Ave., Washington, D.C., World Watch Institute, 20036. I am indebted to the Worldwatch Institute and its staff for much background material for this chapter on which I have freely drawn. Their publications are recommended.

9. Weinstein, Warren, "Human Rights and Developments in Africa: Dilemmas and Options," pp. 171-196, *Daedalus,* Fall 1983, issued as Volume 112, Number 4, of the Proceedings of the American Academy of Arts and Sciences.

10. See *The New Internationalist,* 1978, pp. 16-17.

11. Weinstein, Warren, "Refugees in Central Africa 1979," Paper Conference on Refugees, Department of State, Washington D.C., October 1979.

12. The Global 2000 Report to the President of the United States. Mr. James Earl Carter—Entering the 21st Century-A report prepared by the Council on Environmental Quality and the Department of State, Gerald O. Barney, study director, Summary report, vol. II, 1980).

13. Drucker, Peter F., "Where the New Markets Are," *Wall Street Journal,* April 9, 1992.

14. Wriston, Walter, "In Search of the Money Standard, We Have One," *Wall Street Journal,* November 12, 1985.

15. Kahn, Herman, *The Coming Boom—Economic, Political and Social,* New York, Simon & Shuster, 1982

16. Hall, Peter, *The World Cities,* World University Library, New York, McGraw Hill, 1980.

Chapter 10: American Chartered Metroareas

1. A source for some of the following material is Neal R. Pierce and Jerry Hagstrom, *The Book of America—Inside 50 States Today,* New York, Warner, 1984, p. 799. Other sources will be indicated along with my own ideas. Any errors and omissions are mine. This is a recommended book.

2. *Wall Street Journal,* January 15, 1985, p. 37.

3. Downs, Anthony, K. L. Bradberry, and K. A. Small, *Urban Decline and the Future of American Cities,* Washington, D.C., Brookings Institution, 1982.

4. Op. cit. footnote 1 this chapter, Pierce and Hagstrom. See the above from pp. 539-52 as a source along with my own ideas. Any errors or omissions are mine.

5. Boyer and Savegeau, *Places Rated Almanac,* New York, McGraw-Hill, 1985.

6. Rodwin, Lloyd, and Hollister, Robert, eds., *Cities of the Mind,* New York, Plenum Press, 1984.

7. Yates, Douglas, *The Ungovernable City,* Cambridge, Mass., MIT Press, 1978, p. 85.

8. *Atlanta Journal Constitution,* Homefinder, p. 3, September 26, 1987.

Chapter 11: American Metroareas—The Best Hope for Human Rights?

1. Haar, Charles M., ed., *The President's Task Force on Suburban Problems—The Final Report,* Boston, Ballinger Publishing Co., 1974.
2. Kaus, Mickey, "The Work Ethic State," *New Republic,* is my source with my own ideas. Errors and omissions are mine. See Kaus's forthcoming book for more.

Chapter 12: Metroareas and the Law

1. Op cit. footnote 6, chapter 10, pp. 239-91. I have added my own ideas. See also Frug, Gerald E., "The City as a Regal Concept," *Harvard Law Review,* 93, April 1980.
2. Chief Justice Waite announced from the bench that the Court would not hear arguments of whether equal protection was to apply to corporations, though there was much to argue about. *Santa Clara County* v. *Southern Pacific RR Co.,* 118 U.S. 394 (1986). Municipal corporations may not invoke the clause against the state. See *City of Newark* v. *New Jersey,* 262 U.S. 192 (1923); *Williams* v. *Mayor,* 289 U.S. 36 (1933).
3. Barber, Benjamin, *Strong Democracy: Participatory Politics for a New Age,* Berkeley, University of California Press, 1984.
4. *City of Lafayette* v. *Louisiana Power and Light Company,* 435 U.S. 389 (1978).
5. Mumford, Lewis, *The City in History,* New York, Harcourt, Brace and World, 1961, p. 568.
6. "The Dutch Touch," *National Geographic,* October 1986, pp. 501-526.

Chapter 13: The Spirit of Democratic Capitalism

1. Novak, Michael, *The Spirit of Democratic Capitalism,* An American Enterprise Institute, Simon and Schuster Publication, New York, 1982, is the source of much of that which immediately follows along with my own ideas. Any errors, changes, and omissions are mine.
2. Morris, Betsey, "As a Favored Pastime, Shopping Ranks High with Most Americans," *Wall Street Journal,* July 30, 1987, pp. 1 and 17.
3. Michael Harrington, in Heilbroner et al., *What is Socialism?* p. 357.
4. See *The Theory of Moral Sentiments,* IV, i, 10, and *An Inquiry into the Nature and Causes of the Wealth of Nations,* IV, ii, 9. Irving Kristol notes that, "This famous phrase appears only once in *The Wealth of Nations,* and taken in the hypothetical mood." "Adam Smith and the Spirit of Capitalism," in *The Great Ideas Today: 1976,* Chicago: Encyclopedia Britannica, 1976, p. 294.
5. See Joseph A. Schumpeter, *Capitalism, Socialism and Democracy,* 3d ed. New York, Harper & Row, 1950, especially the section entitled "The Sociology of the Intellectual," pp. 145-55
6. Op cit. footnote 5.
7. Op cit. footnote 5.
8. Op cit. footnote 1.
9. Bureau of Census, Statistical History of the United States, table D, 127-41; and Statistical Abstract: 1979, table 668.
10. Trevor-Roper, H. R., "Religion, the Reformation and Social Change," *The European Witch Craze of the 16th and 17th Centuries and Other Essays,* New York, Harper & Row, 1969, p. 21.

11. Dom Helder Camara, "A Christian Commitment is Needed for Latin American Development," *Latin America Calls,* March 1970, p. 4.

12. "Latin Power, In Venezuela, Name of Cisneros Connotes Wealth and Influence," *Wall Street Journal,* February 21, 1985.

Chapter 14: Diversity in Democratic Capitalism

1. Stigler, George J., *The Theory of Price,* rev. ed., New York, Macmillian, 1952.

2. Friedman, Milton, *Capitalism and Freedom,* Chicago, The University of Chicago Press, 1962.

3. Adams, Walter, and James W. Brock, *The Bigness Complex,* New York, Pantheon, 1986, is the source for the following pages along with my own ideas. Any errors, changes, or omissions are my own.

4. Boulding, Kenneth, "The Economics of Knowledge and the Knowledge of Economics," *American Economic Review Proceedings,* 56, May 1966, 9.

5. Haberler, Gottfried, *The Challenge to the Free Market Economy,* Washington, Free Enterprise Institute, 1976. See also Haberler, *Stagflation,* same publisher, 1985.

6. Prestowitz, Clyde V., *Trading Places: How We Allowed Japan to Take the Lead,* New York, Basic, 1988. See also "Japanese vs. Western Economics," *Technology Review,* May/June 1988, p. 27.

7. Op cit. note 5 —*Hamberg, R&D,* pp. 100-101.

8. *Wall Street Journal,* September 10, 1984.

9. The following is drawn from *McDonald* v. *Johnson & Johnson,* 537 F. Supp. 1282 (D. Minn. 1982).

10. Senate Committee on Commerce, Automotive Research and Development Hearings, 93rd Congress, 1st session 1973, esp. pp. 70 and 369.

11. Paul Blumberg, "Snarling Cars," *New Republic,* January 23, 1983, p. 12.

12. National Academy of Engineering, *The Competitive Status of the U.S. Auto Industry,* Washington, D.C., National Academy Press, 1982, pp. 20 and 70.

13. A small, lightweight car developed by General Motors was marketed in Australia in 1948 by a GM subsidiary; Ford's light car appeared the same year as the French Ford Vedette. Lawrence J. White, "The American Automobile Industry and the Small Car, 1945-1970," *Journal of Industrial Economics,* April 1972.

14. National Academy of Engineering, *Competitive Status of the U.S. Auto Industry,* Washington, D.C., National Academy Press, pp. 20 and 70.

15. National Academy of Sciences, "Report by the Committee on Motor Vehicle Emissions," February 12, 1973, reprinted in *Congressional Record,* February 28, 1973 (Senate edition), p. 5832.

16. See John Blair, *The Control of Oil,* New York, Vintage, 1976. See also Senate Committee on the Judiciary, Petroleum Industry Competition Act of 1976 Report, part 1, 94th Congress, 2nd session., 1976.

17. For additional evidence, as well as documentation supporting the thesis that the energy crises of recent years have to an important degree been orchestrated by the oil giants, see Fred J. Cook, *The Great Energy Scam,* New York, Macmillan, 1982, and Robert Sherrill, *The Oil Follies of 1970-1980,* Garden City, N.Y., Anchor, 1983. For a classic treatment, see Robert Engler, *The Politics of Oil,* Chicago, University of Chicago Press, 1961.

18. Op. cit note 3, Adams & Brock, *Bigness Complex,* p. 94.

19. For an interesting extension of this idea into modern times see Hans J. Morgenthau, *The Purpose of American Politics,* New York, Knopf, 1962, p. 286.

20. Op cit. note 3, Adams & Brock, *The Bigness Complex,* p. 96.

21. Edward S. Corwin, *Maintaining Competition,* New York, McGraw Hill, 1949, p. 3.

22. Ayn Rand, *Capitalism: The Unknown Ideal,* New York, New American Library, 1966, pp. 46, 48 (emphasis added).

23. Robert H. Bork, *The Antitrust Paradox,* New York, Basic Books, 1978.

24. Cardozo, Benjamin N., *The Nature of the Judicial Process,* New Haven, Conn., Yale University Press, 1921, p. 168.

25. For a comprehensive classification of Section 1 offenses, see Corwin D. Edwards, *Maintaining Competition,* New York, McGraw-Hill, 1949, pp. 41-42.

26. *United States* v. *Aluminum Co. of America,* 148 F. 2d 416 (1945).

27. Hamilton, Walton, and Irene Till, *Antitrust in Action,* Temporary National Economic Committee, monograph no. 16, Washington, D.C., 1940, p. 4.

28. Green, Mark J., *The Closed Enterprise System,* New York, Grossman, 1972, pp. 168-69.

29. Senate Subcommittee on Antitrust and Monopoly, Antitrust Improvements, p. 378.

30. Ross, Edward A., *Sin and Society,* Boston, Houghton-Mifflin, 1907, pp. 29-30.

31. "ITT Annual Report," 1968, p. 7.

32. Sampson, Anthony, *The Sovereign State of ITT,* New York, Stein and Day, 1973, p. 234.

33. Green, Mark, and Beverly Moore, Jr., "Winter's Discontent: Market Failure and Consumer Welfare," *Yale Law Journal,* 82, April 1973, p. 910.

34. *New York Times,* October 19, 1980. For a contrary view see Willard F. Mueller, "The Anti-Antitrust Movement," *Congressional Record,* 97th Cong., 1st sess., July 20, 1981, vol. 127, pp. S7947-52.

35. *Unites States* v. *Bethlehem Steel,* 168 F. Supp. 576 (S.D.N.Y. 1958).

36. *Wall Street Journal,* January 26, 1981.

37. Cronin, Helena, *The Ant and the Peacock,* New York, Cambridge University Press, 1992.

38. Simons, Henry C., *Economic Policy for a Free Society,* Chicago, University of Chicago Press, pp. 43-44.

39. Bruck, Connie, "The Hartz Mountain Corporate Officer's Guide to Committing Perjury, Obstructing Justice, Locking up The Market, and Paying a $20,000 Fine," *The American Lawyer,* October 1984, p. 119 *et passim.*

40. But even in this instance it appears Stern may have done well for himself. Hartz structured the settlement so that it would pay over a five-year period, making the heaviest payments in the last two years. But the company was able to accrue and take the entire amount as a tax deduction in the first year. Robins, on the other hand, had to pay taxes on the entire amount in the first year, even though it received only a fraction of it. According to one Hartz source, the tax advantage to Hartz and the inflation factor combined to make the actual after-tax impact on Hartz not $42.5 million, but closer to $12 million.

41. See note 15, Hamilton and Till, *Antitrust in Action,* p. 119.

42. Taylor, James W., and Ronald N. Paul, "The Real Meaning of Excellence," *Business,* July-September 1986.

Chapter 15: The Ethics of Pollution and the Quality of the Human Environment

1. Coates, Coates, and Heinz, "Bid the Devil Good Morning—Common Sources of Environmental Problems," *Futures Research Quarterly,* Spring 1985, p. 37. See also

"Energy: The Future has Arrived," *Future Times,* October 1979.

2. Musto, David F., "Lessons of the First Cocaine Epidemic," *Wall Street Journal,* June 11, 1986. Some of the foregoing description of the cocaine epidemic was excerpted and adapted from this article. Any errors, omissions, and additions are mine.

3. Young, Allen M., "The Rain Forest Loss Is Our Own," *Wall Street Journal,* July 11, 1985, p. 24. See also Wolfgang Schohl, "Recovery through Ecology," *World Press Review,* July 1985, p. 25

4. Rowland, Sherwood F., "Can We Close the Ozone Hole?" *Technology Review,* August/September 1987, pp. 50-59. The statement in the text was adapted from this article. Any errors, omissions, and changes are mine.

5. Raloff, J., "U.S. River Quality: Not All Signs Are Good," *Science News,* April 4, 1987, p. 214. Noel Grove, "Air—An Atmosphere of Uncertainty," *National Geographic,* April 1987. Charles E. Cobb, "The Great Lakes: Troubled Waters," *National Geographic,* July 1987.

6. Tinbergen, Jan, "RIO: Reshaping the International Order, A Report to the Club of Rome," 1976, p. 20.

7. "Conservation Power: The Payoff in Energy Efficiency," *Business Week,* September 16, 1991, pp. 86-92.

8. Hannan, Bruce, "Energy, Labor, and the Conserver Society," *Technology Review,* March/April 1977, is the source for the following along with my own ideas. Any errors, omissions, or changes are mine.

9. Pollock, Cynthia, "U.S. Trash Should Be Mined Not Buried," *Atlanta Journal Constitution,* May 17, 1987; Franchot Buhler, "Is There Gold Among the Garbage," *Sky,* April 1979, pp. 11-18; "Re-Manufacturing—A Growing Love Affair with the Scrap Heap," *Business Week,* April 29, 1985.

10. "New Environmental Control to Improve Outlook for Dumps," *Wall Street Journal,* October 2, 1987.

11. Hershkowitz, Allen, "Burning Trash: How It Could Work," *Technology Review,* July 1987, pp. 26-36. Some of this material was adapted from this article. Any errors, omissions, or changes are mine.

12. Psarras, Con, "First, Imagine Bringing Together Hundreds of Thousands of Babies," *Wall Street Journal,* no date.

13. Lubove, Seth, "Country Roads Take Me Home to the Place Where Trash Belongs," *Wall Street Journal,* April 17, 1987.

14. Hirschhorn, Joel S., "Toxic Waste and the Environmental Deficit," *Futures Research Quarterly,* Winter 1985.

15. Raloff, J., and D. E. Thomsen, "Chernobyl May Be Worst Nuclear Accident," *Science News,* May 3, 1986, p. 276. See also Christopher Flavin, "Reassessing Nuclear Power: The Fallout from Chernobyl," World Watch Paper 75, March 1987.

16. These are only estimates, because the exact arrangement and composition of the sludge is not known. No satisfactory way to remove the sludge has been developed. It cannot be redissolved in nitric acid without dissolving the tank also. Furthermore, steelwork protruding into the sludge in the tank floor will interfere with attempts to remove the sludge hydraulically or mechanically. Access to the tank is limited to a few small holes in the roof, and the sludge itself is, of course, highly radioactive. Yet the waste cannot be left indefinitely in its present form because a carbon steel tank will eventually corrode.

Chapter 16: Crime and Insecurity

1. Breining, Becci M., editorial page statement, *USA Today,* March 6, 1985.

2. Cronin and Milakovich, *U.S.* v. *Crime in the Streets,* Bloomington, Ind., Indiana University Press, 1981, is the source for the above from, pp. 163-82, along with my own ideas. Any errors or omissions are my own.

3. "Crime in America, Perceptions and Reality" (special insert), *National Law Journal,* August 7, 1989, p. S2. This survey and report will be used as a source for data in this chapter.

4. Op. cit. note 4, p. S16.

5. Op. cit., p. S4, from "Ten Crime Facts."

6. Carrow, Debora N., *Crime Victim Compensation,* Washington, D.C., United States Department of Justice, 1980, pp. 151-59.

7. Miller, Walter B., "Violence by Youth Gangs and Youth Groups as a Major Crime in Major American Cities," Senate for Criminal Justice, December 1976. See also numerous works of Marvin Wolfgang, an authority on crime.

8. Currie, Elliot, *Confronting Crime: An American Challenge,* New York, Pantheon, 1985. See also Wilson, James Q., and Richard J. Herrnstein, *Crime and Human Nature,* New York, Simon & Schuster, 1985.

9. Yochelson, Samuel, and Stanton E. Samenow, *The Criminal Personality,* Jason Aronson Inc., 1976. See also *Federal Bar Journal,* Fall 1976.

10. Bedau, Hugo A., and Chester M. Pierce, *Capital Punishment in the United States,* New York, AMS Press, 1976. See also Mack A. Moore, "Capital Punishment Justified by Cost vs. Benefit," for more material on capital punishment.

11. The Thrift gun purchasing episode is taken from *Handgun Control News,* National Coalition to Control Handguns, February 1977.

12. The above data was taken from the Federal Uniform Index of Crime Reports. See also *Atlanta Journal Constitution,* August 30, 1976. These statistics have not improved over time.

13. *Time,* April 8, 1985, p. 34.

14. Nahas, Gabriel G., "The Other Asian Success Story: Drug Control," *Wall Street Journal,* February 13, 1985, p. 30.

Chapter 17: Militarism, National Security, and a New Foreign Policy

1. U.S. Constitution, Art. I, Sec. 8, Clause 1; 1/8/15; 1/8/18 and Art. 3.

2. U.S. Constitution, 1/10/3.

3. U.S. Constitution, 1/10/3.

4. U.S. Constitution, 1/8/15.

5. "Indefensible," *The Atlantic* (special issue), June 1989.

6. Cousins, Norman, *The Pathology of Power,* New York, Norton, 1987.

7. "A New Military Budget for a New World," *The Defense Monitor,* Vol. XX, No. 2, 1991.

8. Winterbotham, F. W., *The Ultra Secret,* New York, Dell, 1974.

9. Kneale, Dennis, "It Takes a Hacker to Catch a Hacker As Well As a Thief," *Wall Street Journal,* November 3, 1987, p. 1.

10. "Toshiba vs. the U.S.," *World Press Review,* August, 1987, p. 18, from *Asahi Shimbun* (Tokyo daily newspaper).

11. *Wall Street Journal,* March 6, 1984. Generally, see James Coates and Michael Kilian, *Heavy Losses,* New York, Viking, 1985, especially pp. 247-74.

12. For a recent argument in favor of the nationalization option, see Tom Riddell, "Concentration and Inefficiency in the Defense Sector: Policy Options," *Journal of Economic Issues,* 19 (June 1985): 451.

13. A survey of these studies is tabulated in Senate Committee on Armed Services,

Competition in Contracting Act of 1983 Hearings, 98th Congress, 1st sess., 1983, pp. 264-65.

14. *Washington Watch,* March 5, 1976.

15. Slivard, Ruth Leger, *World Military and Social Expenditures,* 11th ed., Washington, D.C., World Priorities, Box 25140, D.C. 20007, 1986.

16. Krauthammer, Charles, "The Lonely Superpower," *New Republic,* July 29, 1991.

17. *China & the World,* Beijing Review-Foreign Affairs Series, Zhou Gou, ed., China International Book Trading Corp., P.O. Box 399, Beijing, China, 1985.

18. Large, Arlen, "The Spread of International Controls," *Wall Street Journal,* November 22, 1976.

19. James and Hilbert Anderson of Sea Solar Power, Inc., York, Pa., have built a working model to demonstrate how wide temperature differences between surface and deep waters in the ocean can be used to generate electricity.

20. Lenssen, Nicholas, "Turning Turbines and Profits—In the Desert," *World Watch,* September-October 1989.

21. Cleveland, Harlan, "The Future of International Governance: Managing a Madisonian World," Washington, D.C., *Futures Research Quarterly,* Summer 1986.

22. Conference Board, *The Federal Budget: Its Impact on the Economy,* New York, 1985. The Conference Board indicates in a note on page 17 that, "A substantial upgrading of weapons systems and equipment is underway—even though the Department of Defense, supported by its own inflation indexes, argues that most of the proposed large increases are merely 'inflation offsets.' The organization seems to have a healthy lack of faith in the Defense Department's credibility, which is cloaked in the secrecy of 'national security.' "

23. For a brilliant exposition on the future of our economy, the outcome of Reaganomics, and the day of reckoning that is at hand, see Peter G. Peterson, "The Morning After," *Atlantic,* October 1987, pp. 47-69.

24. "Quis Cutodiet?" *The Economist,* September 12, 1987, along with my own ideas. Any errors or omissions are my own.

Chapter 18: Private Class Actions and Other Forms of Conflict Resolution

1. Lamm, Richard D., "Colorado Lawyer," article adapted from a speech given by Lamm at the American Bar Association mid-year meeting, February 1989, *Federal Bar News & Journal,* September 1989, pp. 314-16.

2. Cappelletti, Mauro, *Access to Justice in the Welfare State,* Sijthoff, Alpha Naanden RJN, the European University Institute, 1981.

3. *Bivens* v. *Six Unknown Named Agents of the Bureau of Narcotics,* 403 U.S. 388 (1970) and *Westfall* v. *Erwin* 484 U.S. 292 (1987).

4. Caplan, A. A., prefatory note, 10 *Boston College Ind. Commercial Rev.,* 947 (1969).

5. The empirical evidence implies that in settled class actions, particularly in the securities and triple-damages antitrust contexts, the great bulk of the money received from the defendants actually is distributed to class action members, in contrast to the widely held notion that the fund is either devoured by avaricious attorneys or consumed by administrative expenses.

6. *Eisen* v. *Carlyle & Jacquelin,* 417 U.S. 156 (1974).

7. Texas Motor Freight Inc., *Rodriguez,* 431 U.S. 395 (1977).

8. *Artleson* v. *Dean Witter & Co.,* 86 F.R.D. 657, 661 (E.D.PA.1980), 541 Federal 2nd F.2D 394 (3rd cir. 1976) cert. denied, 429 U.S. 1041 (1977).

9. *Rexel* v. *Liberty Mutual Insurance Co.,* Federal 2nd 239 (3rd Cir.) cert. denied,

421 U.S., 1011 (1975). See also Miller, R., "Of Frankenstein Monsters and Shining Knights, Reality, and the 'Class Action Problem,' " *Harvard Law Review,* pp. 664-94.

10. *Eisen* v. *Carlisle & Jacquelin,* 417 U.S. 156 (1974).

11. In *Katz* v. *Carte Blanche Corp.* 416 Federal 2nd 747 (3rd Cir.) cert. denied, 419. U.S. 885 (1974). The defendant, fearing a notice of opinion class action would prejudice it with its customers, asked the court to dispense with notice and convert the action into a test case.

12. Examples are securities fraud and antitrust law, Title VII discrimination cases, etc. See also Paul M. Barrett, "Harried Judges Rely on Special Masters to Settle Tough Suits," *Wall Street Journal,* November 5, 1987, p. 1 et passim.

13. The Kansas City skywalk cases, 93 F.R.E.415, reversed 680 federal 2nd 1175 (8th Cir.) 1982, or Dalkon Shield cases (521 F.supp. 1193).

14. Wolfson, Andrew, "After 8 years a Complex Case Comes to an End," *National Law Journal,* August, 1985, p. 6. See also Andrew Blum, "It's Best to Hang Together," *National Law Journal,* September 11, 1989, pp. 1 and 54 et passim.

15. "Consumers Gain Unlikely Victory in Antitrust Action in New Mexico," *Wall Street Journal,* June 5, 1984, p. 37.

16. Sontag, Sherry, "Is a Tougher Image All Rill Can Offer?" *National Law Journal,* Ocotber 9, 1989, p. 1.

17. *Zenith Radio Corp.* v. *Hazeltine Research Inc.,* 395 U.S. 100, 30-131 (1969). The federal antitrust laws include the Sherman Act, the Clayton Act, the Federal Trade Commission Act, and the Robinson Patman Act, as well as more recent enactments such as the Parens Patriae Act, authorizing actions by attorneys general of the states, and the Hart-Rodino Antitrust Improvement Act, which was designed to clarify and extend the power of the antitrust laws to encourage a free market.

18. Kohn, Harold, "The Antitrust Class Action as a Social Instrument," 41 *Anti-Trust L.J.* 288, (1972).

19. *Reiter* v. *Sonotone Corp.,* 442 U.S. 330 (1979).

20. Pinzler, Isabelle Katz, " A Major Change in Bias Law of the Work Place," *National Law Journal,* August 21, 1989, p. S5.

21. *Carlisle* v. *LTV Electric Systems, Inc.,* 54 F.R.D.237, N.D.TEX.1972.

22. The chief advantage of solicitation over advertising is not communication of information but persuasion. It is this very persuasive force, however, which is the source of solicitation's dangers.

23. "Since 1977 Ruling, Lawyers Turn on to Television as Way to Court Business," *Atlanta Journal Constitution,* July 4, 1987, p. 25.

24. The Supreme Court has indicated in several recent decisions that First Amendment value may be given less weight where alternative means of communicating do exist. See *Pell* v. *Procuenier,* 417 U.S. 817 (1974).

25. *Lindy Bros. Builders Inc.* v. *The American Radiator and Standard Sanitary Corp.,* 487 Fed. 2nd 761 (3rd Cir.) 1973.

26. *Blum* v. *Stenson,* 465 U.S. 886 (1984). See also *Camden VI Condominium Association, Inc.* v. *Dunkle,* 946 F 2d. 768, where the 11th circuit rejected the Lindy approach and mandated use of a reasonable percentage to set attorneys fees in common fund cases.

27. Kennedy, John E., "Securities Class and Derivative Actions in the United States District for the Northern District of Texas," 14 *Houston Law Review* 769, 829 (1977). See also Benjamin S. Duval, "The Class Action as an Antitrust Enforcement Device: The Chicago Experience, 1976," *American Bar Foundation Journal* 1021, 39; "Developments—Class Actions," 89 *Harvard Law Review* 1918, 35 (1976). A commentator has stated that to the extent that there has been an increase in federal securities litigation

it is as a result of the watering down of common law fraud requirements under rule 10(b)-5 and not the evolution of the class action. See Arthur R. Miller, "Of Frankenstein Monsters and Shining Knights: Reality and 'The Class Action Problem,' " 92 *Harvard Law Review* 646-73 (1979).

28. *Richardson* v. *Ramirez,* 418 U.S. 24 (1974).

29. Supero, "Some Thoughts on Intervention Before the Courts, Agencies, and Arbitrators," 81 *Harvard Law Review,* 721 (1968).

30. "Report of Survey of Public's Attitude toward the Legal Profession," *National Law Journal,* August 1986.

31. *The United States of America* v. *Boddie* v. *Connecticut,* 441 U.S. 371 (1971).

32. *Papachristou* v. *The City of Jacksonville,* 405 U.S. 156 (1972).

33. Euler, John L., "When You're Hot, You're Hot—Alternative Dispute Resolution Hits Government," *Washington Lawyer,* July/August 1987. See text infra for more on U.S. Justice Department activities in this area.

34. Stern, C., "Alternative Dispute Settlements Procedures," 1968, *Wisconsin Law Review* 1100.

35. Ball, C., "The Plays the Thing: A Scientific Reflection on Efforts to Resolve Disputes Under the Rubric of Theater," 28 *Stanford Law Review* 81,17 (1975). See also Fuller, "Mediation—Its Forms and Functions," 44 *Southern California Law Review* 305 (1971).

36. Selinger, Carl M., "Paralegals: The British Invasion," *National Law Journal,* November 16, 1987, p. 13.

37. Cohn, C., "Some Notes on Law Change in Northern India" in Bohannan, 1981.

38. Kogan, Marcela, "The Multi-Doored Courthouse: An Answer to the Runaround?" *ALR, HALT,* January-March, 1987, pp. 18-20.

39. Euler, John L., "Alternate Dispute Resolution Hits Government," *Washington Lawyer,* July/August, 1987, p. 33.

40. Spehr, Richard A., "Court Decisions Expand (FAA) Statute's Reach," *National Law Journal,* December 2, 1991. See also *Perry* v. *Thomas,* 482 U.S. 483, (1987), *Rodrguez de Quijas* v. *Shearson/American Express, Inc.,* 490 U.S. 477 (1989), and Gilmer 111 S. Ct., 1647 (1991).

41. Furcolo, Foster, *Practical Law for the Layman,* Washington, D.C., Acropolis, 1987. The book is a useful and perceptive guide for the layman. In the words of a former dean of Yale Law School, "Furcolo has done a grand job and one badly needed."

Chapter 19: Expanding the Ninth Amendment

1. Barrett, Randy E., ed., *The Rights Retained By the People—The History and Meaning of the Ninth Amendment,* Washington, D.C., Cato Institute, 1989. The text excerpts an article by Benjamin B. Patterson, "The Forgotten Ninth Amendment," 1955. Any errors or omissions are my own.

2. Adams, Edward A., "The Law Schools," *National Law Journal,* November 23, 1987, p. 4.

3. The Fall 1983 *Daedalus,* the journal of the American Academy of Arts and Sciences, Vol. 112, No. 4, is the source for the following, along with my own ideas. Any errors and omissions are mine.

4. Coughlin, R. M., *Ideology, Public Opinion and Welfare Policy,* Washington, D.C., Brookings Institution, 1982, p. 83.

5. The Fall 1983 *Daedalus,* and Mancur, Olson, *A Less Ideological Way of Deciding How Much Should be Given to the Poor,* pp. 217-36, are the sources, as modified, of these ideas. Any errors or omissions are mine.

6. Fleming, Thomas, "Countdown to a Miracle: The Making of the Constitution," *Reader's Digest,* September 1987, pp. 132 and 179.

7. Robinson, Donald R., ed., *Reforming American Government, The Bicentennial Papers of the Committee on the Constitutional System,* Boulder, Colo., Westview Press, is the source for the following pages, except for my own ideas. Any errors or omissions are my own.

8. *Immigration and Naturalization Service* v. *Chadha,* 77 L. Ed. 2d 317 (1983).

9. Pritchett, C. Herman, *Why Risk a Convention (1980),* pp. 267-79, and Austin Ranney, *What Constitutional Changes Do Americans Want?,* pp. 280-88. See Donald R. Robinson, ed., *Reforming American Government, the Bicentennial Papers of the Committee on the Constitutional System,* Boulder, Colo., Westview Press, 1986.

10. Op. cit note 8.

11. Wilson, Woodrow, "Cabinet Government in the United States," *International Review,* August 1879, pp. 146-63.

12. Sundquist, James L., *Constitutional Reform and Effective Government,* Brookings Institution, 1986.

13. MacPherson, Harry, *A Political Education,* Boston, Little, Brown, 1972, p. 268. The measure that prompted Johnson's comment was home rule for the District of Columbia.

Epilogue

1. Ferguson, Marilyn, *The Aquarian Conspiracy,* Los Angeles, J. P. Tarcher, 1980, is the source for the following pages, adding my own ideas. Any errors or omissions are my own. Ferguson released a second edition of this book in 1987.

2. Hersey, John D., "Jimmy Yen: Crusader for Mankind," *Reader's Digest,* October 1987.

3. Bean, Ed, "Booker T. Whatley Contends His Program Will Help Small Farms Make Big Money," *Wall Street Journal,* October 4, 1984.

4. Houston, Jean, *The Possible Human,* 1415 Lenox Rd. Bloomfield Hills, MI, 48013. There are also video tapes available. Houston & Masters' work is a source of significance for social entrepreneurs.

5. United Way Strategic Institute, "Nine Forces Reshaping America," *The Futurist,* July-August 1990, pp. 9-16.

Index

Latin America, 27; monopolies in, 193-95; moral values of, 191-93
Laubach, Frank, 335
Law of Nature, 18-19; and Locke, 19
Law of the Sea Conference, 272
Leary, Timothy, 26
Lee Kuan Yew, 121
legal actions, barred, 43
legal profession, opinions regarding, 300-301
leisure, 69-70
Lemann, Robert, 166
leveraged buyouts, 12, 13
Leviathan (Hobbes), 93
Levine, Dennis, 181
Levy, Edward, 46
Levy, Moses, 51
Lewis, John L., 55, 60
Lewis, Samuel W., 269
Lexis, 238
liberal tradition, defined, 158
Lincoln, Benjamin, 320
Linder, Staffan B., 69
Lindy Bros. Builders Inc. case, 297
litigation, costs of, 39-40, 281-83
Locke, John, 14-19, 60, 93, 172, 186, 315, 317, 332; logical inconsistencies of, 18; on property, 19; on separation of powers, 19
Lombardi, Vince, 111
London Charter, 172
Lords of Discipline, The (Conroy), 259
Los Angeles Riot, 12, 89
Losing Ground (Murray), 166
Lovins, Amory B., 229
Lusinchi, Jaime, 193
Lutz, Friedrich, 200

MacArthur, Douglas, 253, 256
Macaulay, David, 77
Maccoby, Elenor, 67
Madison, James, 12, 25, 85, 175, 186, 195, 314. *See also* Constitution
magical beliefs, and maturity, 98
Malcolm X, 25
mandatory voting, 158
Mann, Thomas, 71
Manning, Bayless, 265
Man's Search for Meaning (Frankl), 99
Marbury v. *Madison,* 50, 314
Marcos, Ferdinand, 79

marketplace of ideas, 87-88
Marshall, George C., 98
Marshall, John, 25, 50, 314
Marshall, Thurgood, 25, 33, 287
Marshall Plan, 21, 264, 275, 340-41
Marti, Jose, 334
Martin, Malachi, 27, 99
Martinez, Bob, 248
Marty, François Cardinal, 263
Marx, Karl, 79
Marx, Leo, 160
Marxism, 94
Maslow, Abraham, 94, 103
Mason, George, 12, 320, 321. *See also* Bill of Rights, James Madison
Mass Psychology of Fascism (Reich), 259
mass transit, 203
Masters, Robert, 71
Mather, Cotton, 150
maturity, 98-114
Mayo Brothers, 25
Mayo Clinic, 15
McCarthy, Joseph, 259
McCarthy, Kevin, 140
McCormick, Cyrus, 25
McCormick Harvester Company, 52
McGrath, Peter, 326
McLuhan, Marshall, 26, 61
Mead, Margaret, 25
mediation, 290, 304, 306, 311
Medicare, 166
Medvedev, Zhores, 234
Meese, Edwin, III, 41; and invasion of privacy, 46
mega-engineering world projects, 263
Mellon, Andrew, 195
Meltzer, Alan, 200
men, aggressive behavior in, 67
Meninger, Carl, 196
mental health, public health attitude toward, 97
merchandising, and the political process, 85
Merhige, Robert, 215
metroareas, 12, 28; Amsterdam as model, 178; balkanizing of, 148, 158, 173; and the brain, 159; and community facilities, 147; defined, 158; and delight, 159; free-market model, 177-79; and the law, 171-80; as organism, 178; and nation states, 171; as open dissipative system, 334; and public health problems, 13;

Small Farm Technical Newsletter, 337
Small, K. A., 141
Smith, Adam, 14, 186, 188, 201, 206, 207, 318
Smith, Kate, 25
Snow, C. P., 275
Sobel, David, 13
social-auditing system, 230
Social Brain, The (Gazzaniga), 98
Social Security, 166
Social Security Act, 289
Society of Automotive Engineers, 203
sociopathic personality, 15, 242-43, 245-47, 332
solar power, 268; from ocean, 270
solar radiation, 226
Somoza family (Nicaragua), 79
South Africa, 262
Southern Poverty Law Center, 40
Sowell, Thomas, 101
specialization of scholarship, 65-66
Spengler, Oswald, 91
Sperry, Roger, 59
Spinney, Franklin C., 255
Spinoza, Baruch, 18, 62
Spirit of Democratic Capitalism, The (Novak), 184-85
Stalin, Joseph, 79, 259
Standard Oil, 260
standing, lowering barriers to, 282
Stanford Research Institute, 84
Stanford VALS typology, 84-85
Stassen, Harold E., 144
State of the World, 1990, The (World Watch Institute), 124
Steel Workers Organizing Committee, 55
Stern, Leonard, 214, 215, 216
Stevens, John Paul, 41, 287
Stimtech, 202
Stone, Dean, 300
stress, 70-72, 96; body-driven, 78-79; and cognitive psychology, 78-79
suburbs, 161; as parasite, 179; problems of, 161-62
Suliman, 16
Sundquist, James, 327
Super computer, 270
supply-side economics, 183
Supreme Court, 29, 32-34, 38, 41-43, 49, 56, 88, 287, 314; access to, 42-43; and crime, 241-42; and equal protection, 34;

and federal judiciary, 47-57; and labor-management relations, 50-57; as political rather than judicial force, 49-50; secret amendatory power of, 314-15; uniqueness of, 49
Swiss Army model, 274
Synfuels Corporation, and energy alternatives, 204
Syrus, Publius, 110
Szuch, Dean, 8

Taft, Robert, 60
Talcott, Thomas, 293
Tao of Physics, The (Capra), 64-65
Taoism, 21
taxes, 30
Taylor, Gordon, 13
Taylor, James, 218
Technology Review, 230
Tennae, Emanuel, 249
Tennessee Valley Authority, 271
Tenth Amendment, 45, 322-23
term limits, 327-28
Thanatos Syndrome, The (Percy), 114
"Theopolis America" (Mather), 150
Theory of Moral Sentiments, The (Smith), 188
Thomas, Clarence, 48, 77
Thompson, William Irwin, 26, 27
Thoreau, Henry David, 60, 160
Thousand-Character Reader (Yen), 336
Thrift, Richard, 249-50
Thurow, Lester C., 211-12
Times-Mirror, 91
Times-Mirror Center for the People and the Press, 87
Tinoco, Pedro, 192
topsoil depletion, 124
Toronto, Canada, 137-38, 153
tort law, 51
Toshiba, 257
Trading Places: How We Allowed Japan to Take the Lead (Prestowitz), 201
transcendence, 100
transportation, 150-54; decaying of, 150; and electronic license-plating, 152; and Hong Kong and Singapore, 152
Treaty of Ghent, 245
Trevor-Roper, Hugh, 190, 191
Tribe, Lawrence, 316